THE ETHICS OF MOBILITIES

The Ethics of Mobilities
Rethinking Place, Exclusion, Freedom and Environment

Edited by

SIGURD BERGMANN
Norwegian University of Science and Technology, Norway

TORE SAGER
Norwegian University of Science and Technology, Norway

ASHGATE

Published by
Ashgate Publishing Limited
Gower House
Croft Road
Aldershot
Hampshire GU11 3HR
England

Ashgate Publishing Company
Suite 420
101 Cherry Street
Burlington, VT 05401-4405
USA

www.ashgate.com

British Library Cataloguing in Publication Data
The ethics of mobilities : rethinking place, exclusion,
    freedom and environment. - (Transport and society)
    1. Migration, Internal 2. Human geography 3. Liberty
    I. Bergmann, Sigurd II. Sager, Tore
    304.8

Library of Congress Cataloging-in-Publication Data
Bergmann, Sigurd, 1956-
    The ethics of mobilities : rethinking place, exclusion, freedom and environment / by
Sigurd Bergmann and Tore Sager.
        p. cm. -- (Transport and society)
    Includes index.
    ISBN 978-0-7546-7283-8
    1. Migration, Internal. 2. Human geography. 3. Liberty. I. Sager, Tore. II. Title.

    HB1952.B47 2008
    307.2--dc22
                                        2008004795

ISBN 978 0 7546 7283 8

Mixed Sources
Product group from well-managed
forests and other controlled sources
www.fsc.org Cert no. SA-COC-1565
© 1996 Forest Stewardship Council

Printed and bound in Great Britain by
MPG Books Ltd, Bodmin, Cornwall.

Contents

List of Figures   *vii*
List of Tables   *ix*
List of Contributors   *xi*

Introduction
     In Between Standstill and Hypermobility – Introductory Remarks
     to a Broader Discourse   1
     Sigurd Bergmann and Tore Sager

PART I

1   The Beauty of Speed or the Discovery of Slowness
     – Why Do We Need to Rethink Mobility?   13
     Sigurd Bergmann

2   Mobility, Freedom and Public Space   25
     Mimi Sheller

3   Automobility and the Driving Force of Warfare:
     From Public Safety to National Security   39
     Jeremy Packer

4   Stranded Mobilities, Human Disasters: The Interaction
     of Mobility and Social Exclusion in Crisis Circumstances   65
     Margaret Grieco and Julian Hine

5   Gendered Mobility: A Case Study of Non-Western Immigrant
     Women in Norway   73
     Tanu Priya Uteng

6   Mobility as Stress Regulation: A Challenge to Dialogue in Planning?   103
     Tore Sager

7   Understanding Mobility Holistically: The Case of Hurricane Katrina   129
     Tim Cresswell

PART II

8   Existential Homelessness – Placelessness and Nostalgia
     in the Age of Mobility   143
     Juhani Pallasmaa

9   From Sacred Place to an Existential Dimension of Mobility   157
     Peter Nynäs

10   The Phenomenon of Mobility at the Frankfurt International
     Airport – Challenges from a Theological Perspective   177
     Kerstin Söderblom

11   Religion, Mobility and Conflict   195
     Elizabeth Pritchard

12   The Desire for Speed and the Rhythm of the Earth   215
     Michael Northcott

13   The Ontology of Mobility, Morality and Transport Planning   233
     Ullrich Zeitler

14   Walk the Talk – Mobility, Climate Justice and the Churches   241
     Jutta Steigerwald

15   Ecological Approaches to Mobile Machines and Environmental Ethics 255
     David Kronlid

Index   269

List of Figures

Figure 1.1	*Der Unfall*	14
Figure 1.2	*Vestbanebryggen*	15
Figure 1.3	*El Hombre en Marcha*	18
Figure 3.1	Discipline	42
Figure 3.2	Intelligent control	43
Figure 3.3	Control diagram	53
Figure 5.1	Modal distribution for immigrant men	88
Figure 5.2	Modal distribution for immigrant women	88
Figure 5.3	Car-driving license – men	89
Figure 5.4	Car-driving license – women	89
Figure 5.5	Link between enhanced mobility and better job options	90
Figure 5.6	Safety concerns in daily mobility	91
Figure 5.7	Public transport frequency during peak hours	93
Figure 5.8	Public transport frequency during evening and weekends	93
Figure 5.9	Public transport frequency during off peak hours	94
Figure 5.10	Prices of the tickets	94
Figure 5.11	Punctuality	95
Figure 5.12	Ease of travelling with children	95
Figure 5.13	Time taken to reach the destination by public transport	96
Figure 5.14	Overall view of public transport	96
Figure 7.1	View of New Orleans	133

List of Tables

Table 5.1   Comparison of daily mobility schedule between
            Norwegians and non-western immigrants   87
Table 5.2   Comparison of daily mobility schedule between
            non-western men and women   87

List of Contributors

Sigurd Bergmann holds a doctorate in systematic theology from Lund University and works as Professor in Religious Studies (Theology, Ethics and Philosophy of Religion with Theory of Science) at the Department of Archaeology and Religious Studies at the Norwegian University of Science and Technology in Trondheim. His previous studies have investigated the relationship between the image of God and the view of nature in late antiquity, the methodology of contextual theology, visual arts in the indigenous Arctic and Australia, as well as visual arts, architecture and religion. He is chair of the 'European Forum on the Study of Religion and Environment' and ongoing projects investigate the relation of space/place and religion. His main publications are *Geist, der Natur befreit* (Mainz 1995, Russian edn Arkhangelsk 1999, rev. edn *Creation Set Free*, Grand Rapids 2005), *Geist, der lebendig macht* (Frankfurt/M. 1997), *God in Context* (Aldershot 2003), *Architecture, Aesth/Ethics and Religion* (ed.) (Frankfurt/M, London 2005), *Theology in Built Environments* (ed.) (forthcoming Piscataway, New Jersey 2009), *In the Beginning is the Icon* (forthcoming London 2008) and *Så främmande det lika* ('So Strange, so Similar', on Sámi visual arts, globalisation and religion, forthcoming Trondheim 2008). Bergmann was a co-project leader of the programme 'Technical Spaces of Mobility'.

Tim Cresswell works as Professor at the Department of Geography Royal Holloway at the University of London. He is well known for his work on place and mobility. He is the author of *In Place/Out of Place: Geography, Ideology and Transgression* (Minnesota 1996), *The Tramp in America* (London 2001), *Place: A Short Introduction* (Oxford 2004) and *On the Move: Mobility in the Modern Western World* (London 2006).

Margaret Grieco holds a doctorate from the University of Oxford where she worked for many years at the Transport Studies Unit. She is Britain's first Professor of Transport and Society, and works at present at the Transport Research Institute at Napier University, Edinburgh and the Institute for African Development, Cornell University, US. Grieco has published extensively on mobility issues and has undertaken research in this area for government departments, international agencies and international research institutes. She is actively engaged in disseminating knowledge in this area through the world wide web. Her main publications are *Keeping it in the Family: Social Networks and Employment Chance* (London 1987), *Gender, Transport and Employment* ((ed.) with L. Pickup and R. Whipp) (Oxford 1989), *Worker's Dilemmas: Recruitment,*

Reliability and Repeated Exchange (London 1996), and *Transport, Demand Management and Social Inclusion: The Need for Ethnic Perspectives* (with F. Raje, J. Hine and J. Preston) (Aldershot 2004).

Julian Hine works as Professor of Transport at the University of Ulster in Northern Ireland. He has written extensively on transport policy and the links between transport provision and social exclusion, and has also undertaken research on the mobility impaired. His research interests currently include social change and transport, school transport and pedestrian behaviour. His main publications are *Integrated Futures and Transport Choices: UK Transport Policy Beyond the 1998 White Paper and Transport Acts* (Aldershot 2003), *Transport Disadvantage and Social Exclusion: Exclusion Mechanisms in Transport in Urban Scotland* (with F. Mitchell) (Aldershot 2003), and *The Role of Transport in Social Exclusion in Urban Scotland: Literature Review* (with P. Gaffron, F. Mitchell and Central Research Unit Scottish Executive) (2004).

David Kronlid holds a doctorate in ethics from the Faculty of Theology at Uppsala University. He worked as a Post-doctoral Fellow in the programme 'Technical Spaces of Mobility' at the Department of Archaeology and Religious Studies, Trondheim. Since 1998 Kronlid works as lecturer at the Centre for Environment and Development Studies at Uppsala University, and the Swedish University of Agricultural Sciences. In 2001 he was guest scholar at the Centre for Environmental Philosophy, University of North Texas. His present, cross-disciplinary research projects investigate environmental values in education for sustainable development, and climate change and justice. Kronlid's research interests are ecofeminism, environmental ethics, education for sustainable development and cross-disciplinary education and research on environment and development issues. Currently he is Associate Professor at the Department of Curriculum Studies, Uppsala University. His main publications are *Ecofeminism and Environmental Ethics: An Analysis of Ecofeminist Ethical Theory* (Uppsala 2003), and *Miljöetik i praktiken: åtta fall ur svensk miljö- och utvecklingshistoria* ('Environmental Ethics in Practice', Lund 2005).

Michael Northcott is Professor of Ethics at the University of Edinburgh. His work focuses on the interface between theological ethics and the human sciences. He is best known for his work in environmental theology and ethics and his book *The Environment and Christian Ethics* (Cambridge 1996) is in its fourth printing. He is also the author of *Life After Debt: Christianity and Global Justice* (London 1999), *An Angel Directs the Storm: Apocalyptic Religion and American Empire* (London 2005) and *A Moral Climate: The Ethics of Global Warming* (London/ New York 2007). He has written more than sixty scholarly articles on bioethics, the ethics of food, aquaculture, and genetic modification, on fair trade, globalisation, place, the sociology of religion, theological ethics, and urbanism. He is currently working on the ethics of climate change, technological ethics, and theological approaches to utopianism. He is actively engaged in speaking and writing from his research beyond the academy. In the last two years he has given public lectures at the G8 Summit Fringe in Edinburgh, the Greenbelt Festival, and the Edinburgh International Book Festival, and he writes regularly for the *Church Times*, the *Tablet*, and *Third Way*.

Peter Nynäs is an Adjunct Professor of Comparative Religion at Åbo Akademi University. He holds a doctorate of theology and works as a Lecturer in Psychology of Religion at Uppsala University. He is also a therapist and the chief editor of the academic journal *Finsk Tidskrift*. His research has mainly focused on intercultural communication and the psychology of religion. Nynäs' main publications are *'Finns det någon som känner min röst?' En religionspsykologisk studie av objektsökande tolkningsprocesser i radioandaktsreception* ('Is there anybode who recognizes my voice? Reception of religious broadcasting in radio from a perspective of psychology of religion', Nora 2007), *Kultur, människa, möte: ett humanistiskt perspektiv* ('Culture, Humanity, Encounter', Lund 2005, with R. Illman), and *Bridges of Understanding: Perspectives of Intercultural Communication* (Oslo 2006, co-edited with I. Jensen and Ø. Dahl).

Jeremy Packer is an Associate Professor of Communication at the North Carolina State University. His primary research interests are automobility, cultural governance, and the historical integration of transportation and communications technologies. He is the author of *Foucault, Cultural Studies, and Governmentality* (Washington 2003), *Mobility without Mayhem: Mass Mediating Safety and Automobility* (Duke University Press 2008), and *Secret Agents: The Many Changing Faces of a Pop-Cultural Icon* (forthcoming Frankfurt/M., New York), and he has co-edited *Thinking With James Carey: Essays on Communications, Transportation, History* (Frankfurt/M., New York 2006).

Juhani Pallasmaa is an Architect, Professor and Author in Helsinki. He has practiced architecture since the early 1960s and established *Pallasmaa Architects* in 1983. In addition to architectural design, he has been active in urban planning, product and graphic design. He has taught and lectured widely in Europe, North and South America, Africa and Asia, and published 16 books and numerous essays on the philosophies of architecture and art in 25 languages. Pallasmaa has held positions as Professor at the Helsinki University of Technology (1991–1997), Director of the Museum of Finnish Architecture (1978–1983) and Head of the Institute of Industrial Arts, Helsinki (1970–1971). He has also held visiting professorships in several universities in the US. His main publications are *The Architecture of Image: Existential Space in Cinema* (Helsinki 2001), *The Eyes of the Skin: Architecture and the Senses* (New York 2005), *Encounters: Architectural Essays* ((ed.) by P. MacKeith) (Helsinki 2005).

Elizabeth Pritchard, PhD (Harvard), is in the Department of Religion at Bowdoin College where she offers courses on Christianity, gender and religion, models of secularization and religious violence, and Marxism and progressive religious movements. Her publications include a reconstruction of the theological commitments of Theodor Adorno, a critique and reformulation of theorizations of agency in cross-cultural religious study entitled 'Agency Without Transcendence', *Culture and Religion* 7.3 (November 2006), and an analysis of the theological rhetoric of radical democratic theorists. She is currently completing a book-length manuscript entitled *Forced Religion: Liberalism and the Legacy of Locke*.

Tore Sager works as Professor in the Department of Civil and Transport Engineering at the Norwegian University of Science and Technology, Trondheim, and was the project leader of the programme 'Technical Spaces of Mobility'. His research is mostly directed at the interfaces between institutional economics, decision processes in transport, and communicative planning theory. His main publications are *Communicative Planning Theory* (Aldershot 1994) and *Democratic Planning and Social Choice Dilemmas* (Aldershot 2002). Sager is currently researching the tensions between communicative planning and neo-liberalism.

Mimi Sheller is a Senior Research Fellow at the Department of Sociology, Lancaster University, and Visiting Associate Professor in the Department of Sociology and Anthropology, Swarthmore College, PA. She is co-editor of *Mobilities*, and has published *Democracy After Slavery* (London 2000), *Consuming the Caribbean: from Arawaks to Zombies* (London 2003), *Uprootings/Regroundings: Questions of Home and Migration* (Oxford, New York 2003 (ed.) with S. Ahmed, C. Castaneda, and A.M. Forier), *Tourism Mobilities: Places to Play, Places in Play* (with J. Urry, London 2004) and *Mobile Technologies of the City* (London 2006 (ed.) with J. Urry).

Kerstin Söderblom works as a Post-doctoral Fellow at the Department of Practical Theology, at the Johann Wolfgang Goethe Universität, Frankfurt am Main, and also as Protestant pastor and adult education trainer. Her research project investigates 'Mobility, locality and migration at the Frankfurt International Airport'. Other research interests are gender studies, queer theory/queer theology, empirical theology, human rights pedagogy, intercultural pedagogy, interreligious dialogue, sport and spirituality. She has recently published *Einführung in die Empirische Theologie: Gelebte Religion erfahren* (Göttingen 2007 (ed.) with A. Dinter and G. Heimbrock).

Jutta Steigerwald works as a journalist, researcher and writer in Rome. She is active in the Italian Commission for Globalization and the Environment of the Italian Federation of Evangelical Churches (FCEI), the European Christian Environmental Network (ECEN) and The World Council of Churches' (WCC) Working Group on Climate Change. She has investigated mobility in a three years research project on 'Sustainable Mobility' in collaboration with the WCC and the Evangelical Academy in Bad Boll, Germany.

Tanu Priya Uteng works as a PhD student at the Department of Civil and Transport Engineering at the Norwegian University of Science and Technology in Trondheim. An urban planner by training, she has explored different facets of planning through various research projects and studies carried out in the field of housing, disaster management, real estate and transport planning. She has been studying mobility in the transport-planning arena through a case study of the non-western immigrants in Norway. Her present research interests include the theme of transport and social exclusion.

Ullrich Zeitler holds a doctorate in philosophy, and works as educational leader at the Diaconia College in Aarhus, Denmark. His research interests are environmental and transport ethics, and he has published *Transport Ethics* (Aarhus 1997), and *Grundlagen der Verkehrsethik* (Berlin 1999).

Introduction

In Between Standstill and Hypermobility – Introductory Remarks to a Broader Discourse

Sigurd Bergmann and Tore Sager

The imprint of increasing mobility on a globalising world is so profound that it calls for analysis far beyond the forums of established academic disciplines. Lively discussions are being held in the social sciences, humanities and cultural studies, and nascent debates are springing up in a number of different disciplines. This book offers contributions to a broader and deeper discourse with mutual enrichment between scholars from different relevant milieus.

While technology has provided the modern means for the transport of people, cargo, information, financial capital, etc., technology is also essential in the surveillance and control of mobility. The following chapters capture the recent interest in social surveillance, but broaden the theme to encompass the entire scale from freedom and escape to social exclusion and control. Half a dozen of the chapters can be ordered along this axis.

The utopias imagined in this new mobility discourse range from the 'death of distance' idea, the hypermobile society, in which most people behave as if they are footloose and fancy-free, to demands for 'de-acceleration', new modes of 'making oneself at home' (Bergmann 2008) and a flourishing world society that is characterised by ecojustice and equity with regard to climate emissions. Whether approaching the one extreme or the other, questions of ethics, identity, gender, environment and religion are sure to crop up. Attempts to come to grips with such questions constitute the second half of the book.

Technically construed artefacts of mobility cause many environmental problems, such as global warming, urban smog, suburban sprawl, and other environmental problems, and thus result in a pressing need for the planning and reconstruction of built and natural surroundings. The 'ecological crisis of reason' (Plumwood 2002) deeply and violently affects human and other life worlds as well as characterising our late modern modes of moving. These artefacts also victimise, resulting in an unacceptably high annual rate of technology-related casualties, both injuries and death. Mobility caused violence strikes human beings and animals on land, in water, and in air, as well as damages – through climate change – organisms and ecosystems in the whole biosphere. Furthermore, mobility artefacts produce asymmetries in energy use and consumption as well as in social structures of justice among different groups of citizens. Do citizens really have access to the blessings of mobility, and how are the risks of mobile (in)security distributed? Does it make sense to imagine the Earth's atmosphere as one single 'common good' and to claim the equity of all its inhabitants to 'ordinary life' climate emissions? Does global climate change force us to renegotiate most forms of technical mobility on local and global scales as 'luxury emissions' (Northcott 2007: 56) with regard to their effects on nature? How, in general, are values, attitudes and intentions inter- or disconnected with technical and cultural practices?

Although broad in scope, this book does not deal with military mobility in general. Nevertheless, one of its chapters touches on the subject in relation to terrorism. Global security and the 'War on Terror' are among the processes posing significant influence upon future mobilities, lifestyles, and social relations. Warfare-like mobility also provides many examples of 'perverted' mobility, such as piracy, bombing raids (Kaplan 2006), walking-through-walls (Weizman 2006), and turning vehicles into weapons (Packer 2006). Walking-through-walls exemplifies the military formation of swarming. It was used, for example, during the attack on the city of Nablus in April 2002. Soldiers moved within the city across hundred-meter-long 'over-ground-tunnels' carved out through a dense and contiguous urban fabric. They did not often use the streets, alleys, and courtyards; nor did they use the windows, external doors or internal stairwells, but rather moved horizontally through party walls, and vertically through holes blasted in ceilings and floors. Here, the intention is merely to point out a puzzling contrast between military and civil ways of thinking about movement in cities. The fascination with swarming shows that the military – those who force their way with bullets – want to move like a cloud, sacrificing speed for unpredictability and invisibility. The mass of civil pedestrians, on the other hand, sieving through every small opening and crevice in the urban fabric, moving through it like a cloud, seem to want to move like bullets. They wish to wrap themselves in metal and move fast along straight highways. Both strategies for mobility are destructive to cities.

Besides reflecting on patterns of movement in city space, mobility discourses have focussed on the phenomena of so-called hypermobility. Do we suffer from hypermobility as well as from a lack of reflecting on and negotiating 'the Ethics of Transport and Travel'? Does it make sense to worship 'the beauty of speed' or should we interpret technical spaces of mobility from a religious perspective, as part of an ongoing 'Crucifixion of late modernity'? How could Religious Studies and 'Theology in its spatial turn' (Bergmann 2007) lead to a turn to mobility?

Two contradictory views of technology seem to be at the heart of modernity, and they have not yet been reconciled with each other. The unlimited freedom of speed and acceleration on the one hand, contrasts with the vision of slowing down on the other, in which natural, individual, sociocultural and technical modes of moving can mutually interact. Could the 'the discovery of slowness' (Nadolny 1983) lead us and the other co-inhabitants of our common surroundings to a good, just and 'flourishing' life in truly 'ecological communities' (Cuomo 1998)?

With modernity firmly linked to rapid movement in numerous forms, it is the responsibility of social researchers to explore alternatives. Is there a 'thrill of the still' – a viable slow city strategy, for example – to counter the ideals inherent in terms like the jet set, living on the fast track, fast cars/fast food, etc.? Perhaps the values of slower modes might be expressed in phrases more memorable than energy-saving and health-improving? In a poem, August Kleinzahler (2006: 33) calls bicyclists the 'kinetic emblems of an enlightened state'. Efforts to see slow modes in a new light will have to include strategies to have these modes fully recognised as traffic. There is perhaps no better emblem of this dilemma than the feeling on the part of bicycle activists that they need to send this clear message to the public: 'We are not blocking traffic, we *are* traffic!' (Furness 2007: 299).

It might seem that philosopher and scientist Blaise Pascal (1670/2005: 38) embraces the idea of 'the thrill of the still' when asserting that 'man's unhappiness arises from one thing alone: that he cannot remain quietly in his room'. However, Pascal admits that most men do not know how to enjoy staying at home; boredom soon sets in. The French military man and writer Xavier De Maistre (1794/1908) tried to help us overcome this boredom by looking at our closest surroundings in new ways. During his 42 days arrest at Turin, he wrote a small book taking the reader on a trip around his room. He tries to convince us that this will be 'a pleasure jaunt which will cost...neither trouble nor money' (ibid. 12). The body should stay in the room, he thinks, while one can experience mobility through the imagination. Hence, de Maistre declares that: 'You cannot be other than highly satisfied with yourself if you succeed in the long run in making your soul travel alone' (ibid. 28). This is indeed a contrast to the hypermobility towards which the modern world seems to be heading.

What kind of understanding of woman and man emerges if one primarily regards human beings as mobile? How do our experiences and ideologies affect our understanding of life and nature when we are in motion? What does modes of moving do to us?

Does mobility affect us? Or is it rather lack of mobility, sometimes combined with loneliness, that gets to us? Or even the traffic itself? Sometimes it is hard to know. In his story about *The Disturber of Traffic*, Rudyard Kipling (1899) describes a lighthouse-keeper who becomes convinced that the waves in the straits he watches over are running lengthwise in sinister, parallel 'streaks' caused by passing steamers. The streaks distress him so much he eventually decides that the only way to stop them is to block the fairway, thus preventing all ships from passing his light. The story is, in effect, about a man whose thoughts are incessantly driven down narrow channels – straits indeed – from which he cannot escape. So, does mobility affect the identity and the mental state of human beings, and if yes, what should we do about it? The need for an ethical analysis of mobility, as offered in this book, is not of recent origin.

Perspectives, problems and reflections like these are formulated and intertwined in a multi-faceted way to let this book inspire, deepen and widen the interdisciplinary study of contemporary mobility. Already established academic research on mobility, such as in the fields of geography, transport engineering, and sociology, enters a dialogue with scholars in fields that have only recently observed the challenge of mobility, such as ethics, architecture, philosophy, and religious studies/theology. Through their variety and diversity of perspectives, the chapters of this book offer a substantial interdisciplinary contribution to the highly socially and environmentally relevant discussion about what technically and economically accelerating mobility does to life and how it might be transformed to sustain a more life-enhancing future.

An introductory essay by *Sigurd Bergmann* opens the reflection by emphasising the modern obsession with speed, as was expressed by the futurist painters in the 1920s, in continuity with the increasing acceleration of mobility, lifestyles and social processes as a characteristic of late modernity.

The chapters of the book are divided into two sections. While the first part reflects on themes of freedom, control and mobility's social implications, the second part focuses on spatial, environmental, gender, aesth/ethical and religious dimensions of our modes of moving. Aspects of gender and the questions of spatiality and how existing mobilities can be transformed crosscut both sections.

Freedom is at the forefront of political mobility rhetoric, but the conceptual freedom/mobility relations are not often analysed in academic writings. *Mimi Sheller*'s contribution concentrates on the links between freedom and mobility that are mediated by public space. She distinguishes different forms of both freedom and mobility, and thereby avoids the simplistic assertions that increased mobility necessarily furthers freedom, and that unrestricted mobility is always a desired public good. Sheller thinks of freedom of mobility as a spatio-temporal process of disembedding that which occurs in particular kinds of places. Her focus is on the cases in which there is a kind of freedom of mobility inherent in the space itself; town squares, local streets, public parks, and the public transport system. What troubles Sheller is that those who are able to exercise freedom of mobility regardless of others' preferences can use it to actually shape public space in ways that increase their own potential mobility and decrease the mobility of others; for example, by privatising or in other ways preventing or discouraging part of the public from using formerly free space or infrastructure.

People are regulated and treated as objects of surveillance when exercising their mobility. This is an important theme in critical literature at the intersection of information and communication technologies, mass transport, and political control. *Jeremy Packer* analyses developments in the US surveillance regime since the 9/11/2001 attacks, pointing to a shift in focus from accidents to terrorists. Vehicles can be turned into weapons. Mobility has therefore become an immanent threat, and drivers and their automobiles are cautiously approached as potential enemies and allies. Packer aims to tell us where the governance of highly mobile populations is headed. It is a source of anxiety when the rhetoric of freedom is being used to justify the war in Iraq and the global war on terrorism, while also being used to produce consumer desire for new dependencies upon mechanisms for controlling automobility.

If social and infrastructural relationships are dysfunctional under routine arrangements, then this will be clearly revealed in conditions of crisis. *Margaret Grieco* and *Julian Hine* exemplify this by looking at the disaster caused by

Hurricane Katrina in New Orleans and the havoc wrought by the earthquake in the Pakistani North West Frontier Province, Azad Jammu, and Kashmir on 8 October 2005. They apply the concept of 'stranded mobility' to shed light on social exclusion. Moreover, Grieco and Hine suggest that virtual travel would have been helpful in overcoming some of the difficulties experienced by people evacuated from New Orleans. Virtual spaces can be created in which past physical neighbours can interact and coordinate their participation in local politics and reconstruction planning.

Tanu Priya Uteng observes at the outset that mobility is not available to all alike, and that it emerges as a function of varying capabilities of the different segments of a population. Mobility deprivation can lead to exclusion from arenas of social life, which is considered a problem in societies where equitable and inclusive ideology holds a strong position. The essay is based on the belief that when social equality is the goal and spatial equality the means, equal access to transport technologies is implied. This notwithstanding, transport policies have often been gender-biased, and Priya Uteng points to ways in which the cultural struggles over gender norms influence the causes and consequences of mobility, especially with regard to non-western immigrant women in Norway. Social institutions in most of the world have traditionally been designed so that access to resources – such as time, money, skills, technology, and safety – has been highly differentiated between the genders. These traditional differences are still pronounced in education, income, and access to the labour market pertaining to men and women of the non-western communities. The result is a deficient mastering of space-time relations for the women, and this raises the question of what possible interventions can help in mobilising non-western immigrant women to becoming active members of their host society.

Mobility affects human well-being and the ways people interrelate. Therefore, mobility can facilitate or hamper public planning processes based on particular types of interrelation, such as participation and dialogue. *Tore Sager* builds on an idea that is underdeveloped in transport research, namely that travel can be motivated by stress and other unsatisfactory experiences at the origin rather than the attractiveness of the destination. The essay links to planning theory, as the problems of conflict-ridden communities will presumably be harder to deal with in a dialogical and consensus building manner the more people rely on mobility as stress regulation. Communicative planning depends on the willingness of adversaries to stay and talk instead of using their mobility to exit the place.

Tim Cresswell argues for a broader and holistic understanding of mobility, which is very much in line with the idea of this entire book. The academic disciplines analysing mobility (human geography is Cresswell's main research field) need to pay greater attention to the issues of power and politics that it provokes. Furthermore, the various disciplines should pool their intellectual resources instead of placing artificial divides between different sets of research approaches that have mobility at their centre. The aim is to connect mobilities across scales and integrate consideration of the fact of movement, the meanings attached to movement, and the experienced practice of movement. The consequences of Hurricane Katrina, which struck New Orleans on 29 August 2005, are used by Cresswell to delineate the politics of mobility. He shows how issues of mobility, income, and race are intertwined, and how they affected the evacuation of the city. Furthermore, he shows how use of the term 'refugee' to describe those fleeing the flooded city highlights the entanglement of mobility with meaning and power. In short, New Orleans is used as a metonym for an entire world on the move.

Juhani Pallasmaa approaches the theme from the perspective of an architect and emphasises the experience of homelessness. He explores the embodied mode of experiencing the world through constant motion, and discusses motorized and increasingly accelerated movement as one of the foundational phenomena of our concept and reality of modernity. The culture of slowness, roots and nostalgia are investigated as well as a homecoming that is grounded in the re-enchantment of our very existential realm.

The existential dimension of mobility is also at the core of *Peter Nynäs'* reflection from the angles of psychology of religion, emotional geography and therapy. His chapter draws our attention to religious studies, which can recognize a complex reciprocal interaction between ways of moving, the environment and human experience. Place is regarded as a tripartite synthesis of physical, mental, and social spaces operating simultaneously, as well as in an existentially evocative way that elicits an affective response and invites relationships. Nynäs accounts for the fact that place is a trajectory. The complexity of place manifests itself in and through motion, movement and mobility. It is, however, both theoretically and methodologically a challenge to account for the significant notion that place in itself is nomadic.

Frankfurt airport offers the place for an analysis from phenomenology and theology by *Kerstin Söderblom*. In this context, religion is not only a combination of biblical knowledge and traditional rituals, but rather a reservoir of symbols and metaphors that contain knowledge and attitudes about life in general. The Frankfurt International Airport represents a rich and complex built environment for the 'lived religion' of travellers, asylum seekers, personnel and social workers. It appears as a highly ambivalent place filled with advantages and disadvantages. The stress and insecurity of airport space is emphasised as well as the need for new 'passage rituals'. Identities can be invented anew in heterotopic spaces like passages and transit areas at airports.

Humanities and the social sciences have been criticised because they take for granted the fixity of their study objects, which they regard as stable and motionless. *Elizabeth Pritchard* departs from this challenge to rethink the mobility of culture and reflects on the relationship of religion, mobility and conflict in the lens of gender and comparative religion studies. The interactions between religion and mobility are complex; they range from the ability of religion to work as carrier in transnational processes, and the understanding of religion as 'the archetypal boundary crosser' to the patriarchal fears and control of women's religious mobility. Pritchard's chapter illuminates how the binary of stasis and mobility has framed and continues to frame the study of religion. It shows how this framing tacitly endorses movement and thus concomitantly obscures the ambivalence and attendant conflicts of contemporary mobility. It finally argues for a more complicated or at least ambivalent reading of mobility in order to shed light on the multifaceted constellations of contemporary mobility and religiosity. These constellations reflect my posing and tentatively responding to several questions including: Is there a correlation between mobility and increased religion or in the dominance of particular forms of religiosity? Does migration differentially affect men and women and their recourse to religion? What kinds of religious and nonreligious alliances are being set in motion?

Michael Northcott continues with reflections on speed, and discusses how our desire for speed involves displacement of the traditional conception of life as a journey of the mind and soul towards the divine. Whereas much modern travel is organised around tourism, travel in the Middle Ages was primarily ordered around pilgrimage. The contrast between the pace of medieval pilgrimage and the speed of modern tourism is significant. Walking involves slow organic movement through a landscape, such that the rhythm of movement mirrors the rhythm of the Earth and so enacts an embodied analogy of prayer and contemplation. Journeying and mobility in Jewish and Christian traditions are central metaphors of the spiritual quest and of the potential richness of life lived in dependence upon the divine Spirit rather than on the possession of many chariots, or of houses in locations distant from one another.

The concept of mobility cannot be analysed without dealing with its built-in normativity. *Ulli Zeitler*, who has earlier worked out a 'transport ethics', departs in this chapter from the moral implications of mobility and proposes an alternative ethical framework for a discourse on mobility. Against mainstream constructivist ethics (discourse ethics, utilitarianism, Kantianism and post-modern approaches to ethics) Zeitler defends ontological ethics as the relevant theoretical framework for an analysis of mobility. The main idea of ontological ethics is that morality is grounded in how things are, which means that reality has a built-in normativity. Zeitler hereby draws on the thinking of Kitaro Nishida, who is highly influenced by Zen Buddhism and German idealism, and explores his significance with regard to transport planning and our underlying views of it.

What is the purpose of mobility? In Christian churches and ecumenical processes, the challenge of mobility has in recent years become a central issue for a substantive critical discussion. Churches in Europe have so far located themselves at the front line of (new) social movements, which are critical to present modes of mobility. *Jutta Steigerwald* presents and discusses some of the central statements in this regard, which offer an astonishingly well-reflected analysis and a clear demand for transport justice and sustainable mobility.

The final chapter discusses a question that criss-crosses all the foregoing ones: What are modes of moving doing to me? *David Kronlid* emphasises the relationship between mobility and human identity, and reflects on the technogenic processes of identification. Kronlid investigates what environmental ethics can offer in the face of mobility problems. His chapter discusses a complementary approach to technology, which can shed further light on the discussion about the role of technology in environmental ethics. Reflections from environmental ethics about the moral values and ideals that are produced and sustained in different technological environments need to be developed, and these might help us understand why we keep on driving our machines of death, despite the knowledge of their catastrophic consequences that the instrumental approach to technology has provided for decades.

All together, the contributions in this book offer an exciting insight into the complexity, dynamics and political urgency of 'spaces of mobility' (Bergmann, Sager and Hoff 2008) and 'mobilities in transit'. They approach the theme with a broader interdisciplinary framework than usual. Hopefully they can take the discourse a step further through their intertwined perspectives from the different faculties of social sciences, engineering and the humanities. Spatial, ethical, and technical dimensions of mobility, so far not satisfactorily analysed, are in this collection for the first time related to established research on different mobilities in geography, economics and sociology. The book departs from the insight that human motion belongs to the existential premises of human beings in natural space as well as in the constructed space of 'postmetropolis' (Soja 2000).

Achieving a symmetry of scholarly perspectives seems necessary as society faces the highly relevant challenge of exploring and transforming modes of mobility in the late modern age. The title of the book, therefore, expresses the multi-faceted phenomenon of mobility as 'mobilities' and poses the challenge that we not only describe and explore contemporary and narrow notions of mobility but also investigate and nurture their transition to richer conceptual models and practices. It intends to encourage the reader to move on from Newtonian lifeless space to lived space, where the paths of movements are celebrated in the 'open-endedness of lines' (Ingold 2007: 170). The task to draw new lines for the transition of mobilities is a common and urgent one, shared by the book's editors, authors and readers.

References

Bergmann, S. (2007), 'Theology in its Spatial Turn: Space, Place and Built Environments Challenging and Changing the Images of God', *Religion Compass* 1 (3), 353–79.

Bergmann, S. (2008), 'Making Oneself at Home in Environments of Urban Amnesia: Religion and Theology in City Space', *International Journal for Public Theology* 2/2008, 70–97.

Bergmann, S., Sager, T. and Hoff, T. (eds) (2008), *Spaces of Mobility: The Planning, Ethics, Engineering and Religion of Human Motion* (London: Equinox).

Blackwell Synergy, <http://www.blackwell-synergy.com/doi/abs/10.1111/j.1749–8171.2007.00025.x>.

Cuomo, C.J. (1998), *Feminism and Ecological Communities: An Ethic of Flourishing* (London and New York: Routledge).

De Maistre, X. [1794] (1908), *A Journey Round My Room* (Translated by H. Attwell) (London: Sisley's).

Furness, Z. (2007), 'Critical Mass, urban space and vélomobility', *Mobilities* 2(2), 299–319.

Ingold, T. (2007), *Lines: A Brief History* (London and New York: Routledge).

Kaplan, C. (2006), 'Mobility and war: the cosmic view of US "air power"', *Environment and Planning* A 38(2), 395–407.

Kipling, R. (1899), *Many Inventions* (London: Macmillan).

Kleinzahler, A. (2006), 'Traveller's Tale: Chapter 13', *London Review of Books*, 5 October 2006.

Nadolny, S. (1983), *Die Entdeckung der Langsamkeit* (München: Piper), [*The Discovery of Slowness* (Canongate Books, 2004)].

Northcott, M.S. (2007), *A Moral Climate: The Ethics of Global Warming* (London: Darton, Longman and Todd).

Packer, J. (2006), 'Becoming bombs: mobilizing mobility in the war of terror', *Cultural Studies* 20(4), 378–99.

Pascal, B. [1670] (2005), *Pensées* (Edited and translated by R. Ariew) (Indianapolis: Hackett).

Plumwood, V. (2002), *Environmental Culture: The Ecological Crisis of Reason* (London and New York: Routledge).

Soja, E. (2000), *Postmetropolis: Critical Studies of Cities and Regions* (Oxford: Basil Blackwell).

Weizman, E. (2006), 'Walking through walls: soldiers as architects in the Israeli-Palestinian conflict', *Radical Philosophy* Issue 136, March/April.

PART I

Chapter 1

The Beauty of Speed or the Discovery of Slowness – Why Do We Need to Rethink Mobility?

Sigurd Bergmann

Speed Up or Slow Down?

> We affirm that the world's magnificence has been enriched by a new beauty: the beauty of speed,

declared Filippo Tommaso Marinetti in his famous Futurist manifest in 1909.[1] For the Futurist artists, the beauty of speed, experienced in race cars as well as in the progress of technical developments, was one of the essential signs of their time. The new experience of speed was crucial in the glorification of the future. Progress was not only a myth, but a bodily and spiritual reality. The manifest of the Futurists – who also praised the visions of a fascist world society – was not only a marginal statement by artists, but it was, as we know, a fully representative expression of the soul of the early twentieth century and its glorification of technical, social and cultural progress and acceleration.

Only a few years earlier, the introduction of railways in Great Britain and Central Europe had caused a serious debate about what the increase of speed does to our bodies, senses and souls. The experience of moving at a higher speed than in horse carriages did in fact make many people feel physically ill. Today, it might be worth remembering that the experience of speed was not a natural one in the history of humans, but demanded special training of our senses to become used to another mode of perceiving space in motion. While the average speed of boats and horse carriages was stable for a very long time, with a maximum speed of about 15 km/hour, the record speed of trains, cars, and aeroplanes has now been increased to more than 1,000 km/hour.

The vision of the freedom to engineer the future, however, had already been questioned and resisted by the beginning of the twentieth century. Among artists, the Dadaists developed the most profiled critique of modernity, which was preached by the prophets of progress. Hanna Höch's famous collage *Der Unfall* (Traffic Accident) from 1936 questions the meaningfulness of having wheels:

---

1   'Manifesto of Futurism' by F.T. Marinetti, *Le Figaro* (Paris), 20 February 1909, <http://www.futurism.org.uk/manifestos/manifesto01.htm> January 2006.

Figure 1.1   *Der Unfall*

Source: Hannah Höch (1936), collage © DACS 2007, reproduced with permssion.

The carriage after the accident has completely changed its form. We can no longer perceive the vehicle as a whole. Nothing of its systemic internal coherency is intact, only the fragments of non-connectedness are left. However, the artist weaves the wheels into a whole again, embraced in a sad act of taking care.

Every accident, today also, cries out the same question. How can an artefact fall to pieces? How can speed turn into rest? How can the freedom of moving turn into the suffering of standstill? How can mobility turn into gridlock?

My first point is that the theme of this book is not a new one at all, but that the practices and challenges of mobility and motion have represented an arena for specific kinds of conflicts for almost 150 years.

Two contradictory views of technology and its significance for modern society are at the heart of modernity's self-understanding. These have not been reconciled with each other yet. The two views can be described as the unlimited freedom of speed and acceleration on the one hand, and the vision of slowing down and

Figure 1.2 *Vestbanebryggen*

Source: Borghild Røed Lærum (1917), oil on canvas, 114 x 86 cm, © Lærum Borghild Røed. Licensed by DACS 2007, reproduced with permission.

slowness on the other, in which natural, individual, sociocultural and technical modes of moving can mutually interact. The controversy is centred on the question whether it is 'the beauty of speed' or 'the discovery of slowness' (as the title of

Sten Nadolny's famous novel phrases it)[2] that could lead us and the other co-inhabitants of our common surroundings to a good, just and flourishing life.

The Norwegian female painter Borghild Røed Lærum (b. 1877) depicts the contrast of different modes of mobility in the early industrialised harbour of Oslo. Hard work appear as rhythmic motion.

Acceleration and De-Acceleration

In his recently published and widely acknowledged study entitled 'Beschleunigung', the German sociologist Hartmut Rosa analyses how modernity is characterised not only by mobility technologies for people, goods, money and ideologies, but how acceleration represents *the* crucial element of modernisation.[3]

Not everything goes faster in modernity, as is often claimed. While some processes speed up, others are retarded and slow down. While some should move as fast as possible, others should move slowly or not at all. Rosa analyses in detail how the space-time regime in modernity has been changed by the process of acceleration, and differentiates between three modes of acceleration:

a. technologically based acceleration;
b. the acceleration of social interactions; and
c. the individual and cultural acceleration of the tempo of life.

All the three are interconnected in modernity by the power of development, while late modernity erodes them and sometimes turns them into barriers for development. The increase in speed leads in many spheres to a state of what the French media philosopher Paul Virilio has called the 'racing standstill' (rasender Stillstand).[4]

The experience becomes much more commonplace in the rich countries: Everything changes, but nothing really happens. This is true for what transport scholars call hypermobility and what some of the authors in this book describe as 'disaster', and is also true for the individual experience of many young people, who must spend much of their energy to find their place in the present and who are not offered much hope for the future.

Acceleration and the increase of speed also characterise agents on the financial markets, who need to accumulate capital quickly in order not to lose it. It also affects family relations, which change in a series of accelerating marriages and

2   Sten Nadolny (1983), *Die Entdeckung der Langsamkeit* (München: Piper) [*The Discovery of Slowness,* Canongate Books 2004].

3   Hartmut Rosa (2005), *Beschleunigung: Die Veränderung der Zeitstrukturen in der Moderne* (Frankfurt/M.: Suhrkamp).

4   Paul Virilio (1998), *Rasender Stillstand* (Frankfurt/M.: Fischer). Cf. (1999), *Fluchtgeschwindigkeit: Essay* (Frankfurt/M.: Fischer).

divorces. Acceleration is linked to technical modes of mobility, which both shrink the space-distance and widen space in a way that challenges the feeling of belonging to a place and the ability 'to make oneself at home' (German 'Beheimatung'). Furthermore, it is linked to the flows of ideas, values and cultural practices. While modernity earlier has produced the fear of being excluded (in a spatial sense), acceleration now provokes the fear of being taken down and being outdistanced (in time and speed).[5]

We can observe an exciting and challenging paradox in the diverse phenomena of modern acceleration: what was earlier experienced as the broadening of opportunities for developing business and life projects has nowadays become just the opposite. The processes of acceleration can reach their limits, and sometimes they result in explosive risks that turn the whole vehicle of modernity into an accident, which evokes Hanna Höch's collage. Hypermobility threatens social systems of planning and democracy. The increasing acceleration of financial speculation threatens the general usefulness of monetarism. Technical and social processes of acceleration become more and more insensitive and therefore destructive of ecological processes, where the speed of biological life cycles and development do not follow the principle of constant acceleration. Global climate change and energy consumption particularly reveal the completely unsustainable nature of our contemporary modes of transport. Globalisation does in fact not represent 'the end of geography' (P. Virilio), but the beginning of a new geography, where 'moving' represents a foundational category for the emergence of sacred and non-sacred spaces and places.

The modern acceleration and the acceleration of modernity itself have come to a point where acceleration threatens itself. This process violates the simple insight that every child must learn as he or she starts walking and running: If you run too fast you might fall!

This trend has led to the emergence in recent years of strong social movements critical of the acceleration of the modern world. Environmental movements argue for 'de-acceleration' (Entschleunigung); bioregionalists argue for smaller scales of transport, markets and exchanges. The World Council of Churches (WCC) and the Conference of the Christian Churches in Europe (CEC) criticise motorised mobility's environmental impact on climate change.[6] New religious movements

---

5 Might this be a reason why many drivers of private cars constantly increase their speed in spite of regulations and risks?

6 WCC (World Council of Churches), *Mobilität: Perspektiven zukunftsfähiger Mobilität* (Geneva: WCC, 1998) and *Mobile – But not Driven: Towards Equitable and Sustainable Mobility and Transport* (Geneva: WCC, 2002). For the European Churches see: http://www.ecen.org. Cf. also S. Bergmann, *Raum und Gerechtigkeit: Ethische Perspektiven eines großräumigen Umweltschutzes,* in: D. Hahlweg, D.-P. Häder, S. Bergmann, O. Seewald, J. Bauer, O. Aßmann, A. Sperling, (2002), *Großräumiger Umweltschutz,* hrsg. v. Verein für Ökologie und Umweltforschung (Umwelt: Schriftenreihe für Ökologie und Ethologie 28) (Wien: Facultas-Verlag), 33–58.

EL HOMBRE EN MARCHA

Figure 1.3   *El Hombre en Marcha*

Source: Castro Pacheco (1978), Mural, Palacio de Gobierno, Merida. Photo by the author, November 2005.

as well as established religious traditions reconstruct the practices and beliefs of pilgrimage spirituality. Walking, powered only by one's own feet, has led to the rediscovery of an intrinsic value in alternative life style projects, and is historically embedded in the European citizens' movement, where the people walk in public places in order to express their political demands for freedom, equality and solidarity.[7] Walking, however, offers a fundamental dimension of human existence and human ecology, expressed in Castro Pachera's exciting mural painting in Yucatan, which portrays the Mayan campesino's walk between the home and the 'milpa' in the bush.

My second point is that the theme of our discussions is located in a broader discourse about the acceleration of modernity. How are mobilities in transit related to the late modern dialectics of acceleration and de-acceleration? What kind of speed and acceleration benefits the good life for all? How can we negotiate about the ethical criteria for evaluating mobility systems in general and increasing or decreasing speeds in particular?

The acceleration of modernity, furthermore, is founded on a specific understanding of history that emerged in the early enlightenment. Since then, individuals and communities no longer move in a closed time and a closed space but rather re-imagine their reality as an open future in an open space. The future is no longer a given entity, but emerges as a consequence of one's actions. The meaning of life is understood as something in front of us rather than something that comes from our ancestor's past to our present.

The myth of progress and technical and social acceleration are all based on a specific modern concept of the future. Therefore, the title of this book also runs the risk of being misunderstood as a part of this concept: Do we believe in the future transition of modes of mobility? Do we want to solve the problems of contemporary mobility by designing, planning and engineering the perfect sustainable and life-enhancing mobility system of the future? Or do we simply gather in a state of critical depression, where complaining and critical analysis is the only activity left in this state of racing standstill? Or might the effort to craft a common image and analysis of the state of mobility and acceleration in itself reveal unknown potentials? Might these lie in front of us as well as in forgotten traditions behind us?

Moveo Ergo Sum – Motion and Mobility

A third aspect of the theme of this book should be continuously kept in mind. Talking about mobility is to talk about human modes of moving. The notions of mobility and motion need to be balanced in order to avoid technological or sociological reductionism. Motion represents an 'existential' state, in the sense of Heidegger's philosophy. It belongs to the essential characteristics of living beings in general, and it is therefore also a central category in biology.

---

7 Cf. Manfred Hofmann/Christina Hofmann, *Maya och mobilitet som maktmedel*, and S. Bergmann, *Auf dem Strom der Götter – Streifzüge durch die heilige Landschaft der Maya*, forthcoming.

To be in motion and to move are an essential part of being human. This insight sounds simple, but it represents one of the basic cultural elements in our civilisation, where Greek philosophy after Aristotle had built its world view on the belief of 'the unmoved mover' or 'that what moves itself' (το αυτο 'εαυτον κινου),[8] which is in fact the same Greek term we now use for 'automobility'. In late antiquity, however, Christian theologians in the fourth century revised the category of motion by changing its negative into positive connotations, where the triune God him/herself and the whole of creation were interpreted as a being-in-motion. Motion since then has represented a fundamental category in the Western understanding of reality in general.[9]

Talking about 'mobilities in transit', therefore, makes it necessary to relate the ecological, technological, and sociocultural dimensions and disciplines closely to the humanities and their capacity to interpret how perceptions, feelings, ideas and visions are affected by modes of mobility and how they themselves influence the construction and use of them. Aesthetic, ethical, spiritual and cultural aspects of the human dimension of mobility need to be included, if we want to do justice to the complexity of what it means to be in motion. For some of you, my own discipline of Religious Studies and Theology might seem to disqualify me as some kind of 'magician among engineers'.[10] For others, I hope, the discipline can function as a microcosm of the humanities and cultural studies, where different aspects of being human are explored in the frame of religion. Theology's contribution hereby is to explore what it is that functions as a 'god' in different practical and normative discourses.[11]

Mobilities in transit offer a broad field to be explored by different disciplines in all faculties, in addition to the humanities. In spite of increasing acceleration, for

---

8   Aristotle, *Metaphysics* XII, 6, 1072a; cf. XII, 7, 1072a, 23–5. Cf. S. Bergmann, *Geist, der Natur befreit: Die trinitarische Kosmologie Gregors von Nazianz im Horizont einer ökologischen Theologie der Befreiung* (Mainz: Grünewald 1995), 155f. (This section is not edited in the book's English edition, *Creation Set Free,* 2005).

9   Cf. S. Bergmann, *Creation Set Free: The Spirit as Liberator of Nature* (Sacra Doctrina 4) (Grand Rapids, Michigan: Eerdmans 2005), 115ff., and 204ff. (The English translator of the German edition has chosen to translate 'Bewegung' as 'movement'), while I here use 'movement' and 'motion' synonomously and regard 'mobility' as a sub-category of 'motion', aiming at technically constructed and socioculturally construed motion.

10   This phrase was coined in the corridors of the Faculty of Technology after it became public that my colleagues there would share the management of a high-priority university project with a religion scholar. The encouraging ironic rumour immediately grasped the central challenge: Should one relate humanities and technology to each other? Should technology really deal with human beings and what they believe in?

11   Cf. the definition of 'a god' by Luther and Paul Tillich: a god is 'what you set your heart on and repose your trust in'. Martin Luther, *Large Catechism,* First part, First command. Cf. Paul Tillich's concept that describes 'god' as 'that which is of ultimate concern to humanity'. Paul Tillich, *Systematic Theology,* three volumes in one (Chicago: The University of Chicago Press 1967 (1951, 1957, 1963)), Volume I, 220.

example in travelling through geographical or virtual space, our body becomes more and more a passive non-moving container, which is transported by artefacts or loaded up with inner feelings of being mobile in the so-called information society. Technical mobilities turn human beings into some kind of terminal creatures, who spend most of their time at rest and who need to participate in sports in order to balance their daily disproportion of motion and rest. Have we come closer to Aristotle's image of God as the immobile mover, when elites exercise their power to move money, things and people, while they themselves do not need to move at all? Others, at the bottom of this power, are victims of mobility-structured social exclusion. They cannot decide how and where to move, but are just moved around or locked out or even locked in without either the right to move or the right to stay.[12]

However, in all societies and cultures, the mode of moving has to do with human identity. Could one restate Descartes' 'I think, therefore I am' (Cogito ergo sum) as 'I move, therefore I am' (Moveo ergo sum), and 'I am how I move'?

Body language already reveals characteristic individual expressions through the way a person walks. The manner of walking can also express our emotional moods and well-being. Anthropologists have found that there is a lowest quantitative level of human activity in all cultures that is used for walking shorter and longer distances from home (the so-called Zahavi's law or Hupke's constant).[13] Does this insight generate some kind of right to move? If there is a human right to move, does this imply a right to move at any speed, or as much as possible? Obviously not, but how should transport ethics take into account the existential need for mobility?

Another aspect takes us into the reflection on the human body and the embodied mind. Human beings establish physical contact with the Earth, as we know, mainly through the eye and to a lesser extent through the other senses. Usually one does not take into account the significance of the tactile senses and what Juhani Pallasmaa has called 'the eyes of the skin'. Our feet are particularly marginalised with regard to the theories of perception. But even the sole of the foot has its own phenomenology, which interacts with our natural and built surroundings. In a sailing boat, as one example, you use the sole of your foot in order to interact with the wind, which you get through the sail rope and the rudder into your hand, and the boat's gliding on the water surface, which you get through the soles of your feet from the boat's hull. While the ocean's motion flows into your body through your feet, the motion of the wind flows through your hand, which holds the rope and the rudder. Both interact to create the bodily and technical conditions to sail the boat.

These are only a few among many examples of the human dimension of motion and mobility. To conclude, the subjective aspects of mobility and motion are still not linked in a satisfying way to the sociocultural interpretations of mobility. Our

---

12   Cf. Zygmunt Bauman, *Globalization: The Human Consequences,* New York: Columbia University Press 1998, 87.

13   Cf. Emin Tengström, *Bilismen i kris?* Stockholm: Rabén and Sjögren 1991, 66.

discussions can only contribute to visualise this lack of a truly transdisciplinary approach to mobility research. Nevertheless, my third point, therefore, takes the insight of the existential human dimension of movement and the ability to move as a starting point for a plea to develop the academic discourse on mobility in wide cooperation with different disciplines in all faculties of academia.

Such a plea is not only a demand for a transdisciplinary development of mobility studies, but points to a more complex intention, which I here only can summarise in a thesis instead of a longer argument: The study of mobility and motion challenges transdisciplinary research in general to transform itself into a new self-understanding of science; this can be characterised as a 'third space science in motion' that also does justice to the flow of cognitive processes with regard to its theme.

What I am trying to say in this thesis is that scientists cannot go on with 'business as usual', if they take the life-destructive modes of moving and accelerating seriously. On the contrary, they need to prepare themselves to change not only their interpretations of reality but also their own self-understanding as scholars in a society and a nature of flows. In this sense, mobilities in transit also demand the transition of science and its disciplines.

Transient Space

Movement and mobility always take place in space and at, or between, places. The concept of space, therefore, is a crucial and necessary element of every reflection about mobility. How do we conceive the space in which we move? Is it a mere container or a living all-embracing space? Is it an absolute entity or do we perceive it as a complex relational space?

The concepts of space and place will deeply influence the understanding of motion and mobility. And it is therefore necessary to locate the discourse on mobility in a wider discourse where concepts of space need to be revised.

The German sociologist Markus Schroer has recently shown in a detailed study that the so-called spatial turn has not taken us beyond the older problematic theories of absolute space and beyond the separation of the mental and the physical space at all.[14] Social theorists, such as Habermas, Luhmann and Simmel, still use both concepts and combine elements from both in their social theories. In communicative processes in urban and landscape planning, where transport systems are also negotiated, one usually does not conceive space and place as something that emerges from the practices, ideologies and feelings of the inhabitants and those who design, use and develop their living spaces.[15]

---

14   Markus Schroer, *Räume, Orte, Grenzen: Auf dem Wege zu einer Soziologie des Raums* (Frankfurt/M. Suhrkamp 2006). Cf. also the informative statistics from the EU Commission, which on the one hand strongly emphasises the political and social processes in the fields of 'sustainable

If we apply this to mobility, the obvious challenge is to reflect on the space that emerges through human modes of moving. Are places destroyed as a consequence of spatial mobility planning? Or do we have the tools to design mobility systems that include and promote the visions of inhabitants? What are the qualities of a place where one feels at home, and what kinds of mobility enhance these qualities? Feeling at home (Beheimatung) does not necessarily mean that one simply has to stay at home; it also must include the motion of leaving a place and returning to it.

Scholars of globalisation usually define it as time-space compression (D. Harvey) or as a process of disembedding (A. Giddens) where connections to places are dissolved. This widely accepted and often-repeated explanation, however, still operates with a static understanding of space, and does not do justice to the social processes in which people develop the places where they live. The often-declared death of the place does in fact confuse and betray our understanding of space and place. The dominance of space over place, which characterises globalisation, promotes not only the change of place but also provokes a manifold of processes of re-location. How is locality produced in the context of globalisation, and what is the function of mobility in the dialectics of disembedding and re-embedding?

A second misunderstanding that characterises various globalisation theories is the so-called shrinking of space, which is widely postulated to imply the end of geography and the end of distance. Technical forms of mobilities, such as cars, trains and planes, certainly broaden our ability to reach places far away in an easier, faster way than ever before. But the choice to travel, and the direction in which one should move, have become much more complicated. Choices about destinations are dependant on our evaluation of places and what happens there. Mobility, which produces time-space compression, therefore, does not shrink space but makes it more complex and wide. It not only disembeds us, but also ties us closer together, and strengthens the identity of places even more than before. Places do not disappear but change their quality due to the constellations and impacts of a global space of neo-colonisation.[16]

A further aspect of place and space in the context of mobility and motion is the bodily being of human life, where the body itself should be regarded as a

---

development' and 'transport', and on the other hand does not at all take into account the experiences and expressions of the citizens themselves with regard to these fundamental dimensions of being a human in Europe today: <http://epp.eurostat.cec.eu.int/portal/page?_pageid=1090,30070682,1090_33076576&_dad=portal&_schema=PORTAL>, 1 June 2006. An alternative and deeper perspective of environmental science is offered by the European Forum for the Study of Religion and the Environment, initiated by the author: <http://www.hf.ntnu.no/relnateur/>.

16   On the dialectics of 'neo-colonisation' and 'de-colonisiation' see Debora Bird Rose, *Reports from a Wild Country: Ethics for Decolonisation* (Sydney: UNSW Press 2004), and S. Bergmann, *It Can't be Locked in – Decolonising Processes in the Arts and Religion of Sápmi and Aboriginal Australia*, in: Sturla J. Stålsett et al., *Religion in a Globalized Age: Transfers and Transformations, Integration and Resistance* (Oslo: Novus 2008), 81–101.

living place. Ecological psychology, for example, can provide many stories about how artefacts affect both the environment, where they are used, and the embodied mind, which has the illusion of steering them, but is in fact more often steered itself by human-made artefacts. Usually, technological concepts, when examined by the humanities or ecological psychology, are found to be simple and reductionist. The traditional understanding of an artefact as a dead tool for the body of man denies the complexity of the interaction of the subject, its surroundings and the intrinsic value of the artefact as an actor itself. The question of what a technical artefact is and what it does to men/women and environments cannot be answered by traditional models, which do not properly consider the quality of an artefact, the bodily being of humans and the 'relationality' of space. An ecological phenomenology of nature, or as I have called it programmatically 'an aesth/ethics of space'[17] can, therefore, offer important approaches to more deeply mine the function of technical artefacts in the analysis of mobility.

One of the problems with Rosa's excellent analysis of acceleration, which I mentioned above, arises with regard to space and place. Acceleration and the modern structures of time cannot be fully understood without reflecting on the question of what acceleration does to our perception of and action in space and place. Rosa explores this aspect in his study, even if he reproduces the sociological ambivalence – analysed by Schroer – in mixing different concepts of space without a consequent application of the relational concept of space. But Rosa does not formulate at all the question of what space and place, both given natural environments and socially and technically constructed environments, do to our mode of moving. How does a place influence the form of acceleration, and how do places and artefacts interact in the complex interplay of motion that cannot be grasped by any social theory today? To say it more succinctly: How do places affect our modes of moving, and how do we perceive place and space by moving?

I am not so optimistic that I think this book will be able to create such a complex, integrated, critical, and transdisciplinary theory immediately. Such a theory should take into account the subjective, the sociocultural, the technical and the natural dimensions of human modes of moving, and it should give priority to the aesthetics and ethics of mobility, and I am grateful that so many chapters from different disciplines could be included in this publication. It would be enough, I believe, if they together could succeed in clarifying why mobilities in transit offer a crucial challenge for our future, and interconnected, research agendas.

---

17 S. Bergmann, 'Atmospheres of Synergy: Towards an Eco-Theological Aesth/ Ethics of Space', in: *Ecotheology: The Journal of Religion, Nature and the Environment* 11, 3/2006.

Chapter 2
Mobility, Freedom and Public Space

Mimi Sheller

What is the relation between mobility and freedom? It has often been assumed that mobility equals freedom, and that freedom requires mobility. Certainly constraints on mobility are experienced as a loss of freedom (think of enslavement as one extreme); and dreams of mobility are often experienced as dreams of freedom. However, I would like to complicate our understanding of the relation between these two terms by examining more closely the relationship between different forms of freedom and different forms of mobility. The question of mobility's relation to freedom is crucial to emerging debates about what constitutes a 'good' society and good governance. There seems to be a consensus that there is a crisis of public space that is related to changing patterns of mobility in terms of both the human geographical mobility that makes cities tick and the digital informational mobility that informs the media and civic life.

Especially in the United States, there has been an upwelling of debates over mobility and freedom. In the realm of physical travel we have seen recent debates over questions such as: How should the country police its borders and should illegal entry be grounds for deporting non-citizens even if it means breaking up families? Is it legal for the government to arrest suspected criminals overseas, move them to various parts of the world in so-called 'extraordinary renditions', and detain them indefinitely in secret prisons? How can dependence on the oil-based automobile transportation system be replaced by alternate modes of transport and alternate energy sources? In the realm of informational mobility we have seen Congressional, Senate and public debates in newspapers and on blogs over questions such as: How much government surveillance should be allowed of telephone and internet traffic? Should telecommunications companies be allowed to overturn the net neutrality that has allowed all customers to access communications networks at the same speed? Should cities build universal access to wireless communications networks to prevent digital social exclusion?

Alongside questions at the national scale are a set of debates at the urban and regional scale concerning the building of sustainable cities and the implementation of green urbanism (Beatley 2000), debates which are very much caught up with questions of car-use, public transit, bicycling, and changing patterns of living and working. It is charged that there is a crisis in urban public space due to what Mike Davis describes as the militarization of urban space (Davis 1992), and others describe as the creation of shopping-mall, theme-park, or analog cities (see Sorkin 1992; Boddy 1992), all of which involve the privatization of public spaces and the differentiation and surveillance of pedestrian and vehicular traffic. A focus on diverse intersecting mobilities has become increasingly central to 'reimagining the urban' (Amin and Thrift 2002) and re-designing the 'public domain' within mobile cities (Hajer and Reijndorp 2001).

Work within what I have elsewhere described as the new mobilities paradigm (Sheller and Urry 2006) has focused on issues such as mobility citizenship (see Urry 2000), mobility justice (Sheller, unpub.), uneven mobilities and the 'splintering' of urban space (Graham and Marvin 2001), and racialized or ethnic mobility injustices that impact on freedom of movement across borders and within national spaces (Hannam, Sheller and Urry 2006). These approaches concern the institutional establishment, everyday practice, and long-term protection of freedom of mobility, implying a rights-based perspective grounded in political theories of civil society and democratization of the public sphere. Hence I will first explore several ways in which we might think about mobility as a political freedom. I will draw on the work of Orlando Patterson, who describes freedom as a tri-partite chord consisting of three notes: personal, sovereignal, and civic freedoms. I will briefly define each of these, which Patterson considers core Western values, and show how each implies a different kind of freedom of mobility. Along the way, I will consider some of the ways in which these different mobility freedoms are unevenly distributed, generating different kinds of mobility injustice.

The rights-based perspective, however, does not exhaust the possibilities for how we might conceive of mobility's relation to freedom. Rather than focusing on human mobility and the rights that attach to persons and groups to enable their mobility, we might alternatively focus on the contexts and spaces that allow for or 'afford' mobility. That is, freedom of mobility might be thought of as a spatio-temporal process of disembedding that occurs in particular kinds of places. In the second half of the paper, therefore, I turn to this more abstract and spatialized sense of freedom of mobility, in which it describes a quality of particular kinds of public space, which I describe as 'mobile publics' (Sheller 2004). Here I draw on spatial theorists who have posited that increasing time-space 'distanciation' (Giddens 1990, 1991), 'liquidity' (Bauman 2000) and 'fluidity' (Urry 2000) characterize the contemporary era, as well as those who have analysed processes of urban spatial restructuring, re-scaling, and the privatization of public space.

In what ways, I ask, do such spatial mobilities relate to the forms of freedom and injustice sketched out in the preceding section? How do differing freedoms of mobility inform each other, conflict with each other, and contribute to struggles over mobility, publicity and space at a range of different scales? In the conclusion I will consider the relation between various kinds of mobility freedom and mobility injustice, and sketch some directions for future research.

Part One: Personal, Sovereignal and Civic Freedoms of Mobility

Personal freedom, according to Orlando Patterson, one of the pre-eminent sociologists of slavery, encompasses both negative and positive liberty; the sense that 'on the one hand, one is not being coerced or restrained by another person in doing something desired and, on the other hand, the conviction that one can do as one pleases within the limits of that other person's desire to do the same' (Patterson 1991: 3). When we think of personal freedom in relation to mobility we can imagine it in the ideal form as not having one's mobility constrained in any way, and being able to move about and go wherever one pleases at any time.

Now, of course, we know that there are both natural and social constraints on this kind of personal mobility freedom. Many forces constrain our personal mobility, beginning from our own physical capacities when faced with various kinds of terrain (e.g. our bodily abilities, disabilities, and needs for prosthetic or technical aids in relation to uneven surfaces, steep inclines, steps, icy or sharp surfaces). And we also know that there are many spatial and temporal constraints that keep us out of certain places (stairs, walls, gates, locks, fear of darkness, closing times, schedules, etc.). There are also social obligations (familial ties, work-related obligations, ascribed positions related to age or gender, etc.) that may prevent us from leaving certain locations, as well as mental and attitudinal constraints such as the skills and cultural outlooks that enable and encourage a disposition to be mobile.

In addition to such micro-mobilities in and around the everyday spaces that we inhabit, personal mobility freedom is often most easily imagined as the capacity to enter and exit national spaces. Article Thirteen of the Universal Declaration of Human Rights recognizes three different kinds of freedom of movement: (1) the right to leave any country (including one's own); (2) the right to return (to one's own country); and (3) the right to freedom of movement within the borders of each state (UDHR 1948). Many social scientists studying mobility are especially concerned with the extent to which there has been an increase in cross-border personal mobility for some categories of people, such as cosmopolitan 'mobility pioneers' (Kesselring and Vogl 2004; Kesselring 2006), 'mobile transnational professionals' (Nowicka 2006), tourists, business travelers, or transnational migrants. Alongside increasing frequency of air travel, extension of airline routes, expansion of airports, and infrastructural improvements to cross-border road connections, new patterns of supra-regional economic integration and labor mobility are all contributing to a trend towards greater cross-border personal mobility.

Nevertheless, gender, race, ethnicity, and nationality are some of the key axes for the uneven distribution of personal mobility. Consider for example limitations on women's personal mobility ranging from restrictive clothing, to the enforcement of *purdah* or other kind of domestic enclosure, patriarchal accompaniment rules, or simply threats of violence in public spaces. As Rosi Braidotti notes, 'Mobility is one of the aspects of freedom, and as such it is something new and exciting for women: being free to move around, to go where one wants to is a right that women have only just started to gain' (Braidotti 1994: 256). Campaigns against sexual violence such as 'Take Back the Night' were about 'the right to go where one wants to without being punished physically or psychically for being there; becoming entitled to mobility is a superb achievement for women' (ibid.). Yet we know that even in so-called free societies women cannot always move about freely, especially at night, and are often counseled to travel with companions. Other dimensions of sexual inequality may also affect women's personal freedom of mobility. Divorce and child custody laws, citizenship laws, and the greater social obligations of women to care for families may also channel or limit women's cross-national mobility in particular ways. Age, race, ethnicity, religion and nationality may likewise become factors that either enable or delimit forms of personal freedom of mobility.

Thus despite trends towards increasing personal mobility freedom in the modern West, we can say that it is still unevenly distributed, and is closely associated with forms of power that deny some groups the mobility that others exercise.

The second note in the chord of freedom, according to Patterson, is sovereignal freedom, which he defines as 'the power to act as one pleases, regardless of the wishes of others, as distinct from the personal freedom, which is the capacity to do as one pleases, *insofar as one can*…The sovereignally free person has the power to restrict the freedom of others or to empower others with the capacity to do as they please with others beneath them' (Patterson 1991: 3–4). This is less an individual freedom and more a relational freedom. This is the freedom wielded by the master over the slave, by the absolute ruler over his subjects, or in less extreme form by the husband over the wife in patriarchal societies, or by parents over children. This form of freedom, I will argue, involves issues of mobility insofar as there may be forms of sovereignal freedom that enable uneven and unequal access to mobility. It concerns a relationship with a surrounding environment, both institutional and material, that gives some people privileges over others, in particular privileges of movement, travel, and control over space. It is an exercise of power that proclaims: I am free to do this to you, and you can't stop me.

Sovereignal freedom has often been exercised as a freedom of movement which immobilizes others; in fact the sense of freedom of movement often depends on the denial of others' mobility. Hence it produces what we might refer to as mobility injustice. Here we might think of forceful restrictions on mobility such as that associated with enslavement, indenture, imprisonment or house arrest. It also encompasses taxes, tolls and charges for movement; or the requirement of particular papers, identity cards, visas or passports. But the built environment can itself enable some forms of sovereignal freedom of mobility. A presidential cavalcade can move more easily through a city when it blocks all traffic from the streets, which is just an extreme example of the sovereignal freedom exercised by all car-drivers when they take public space away from other users, preventing their use of road space in part through the threat of violent collision (Jain 2006). A business traveler can move more easily through an airport when special fast channels exist that are set apart from the gates and security checks that slow down other travelers (Wood and Graham 2006; Lassen 2006). And Cwerner has shown how the elites of Sao Paulo, Brazil, have taken to aerial travel by helicopter to bypass congested and dangerous city streets, but to do so they have seized public air space in somewhat unregulated ways and at the expense of the underprivileged horizontal city below (Cwerner 2006). These are all exercises of sovereignal freedom of mobility, in which the social and built environment empowers some to be more mobile *at the expense of others.*

In relation to this type of mobility freedom it is important to keep in mind that increased mobility is not always a desired good. If we go back to the example of slavery we are reminded that the condition of slavery begins with the coerced movement of a person who is captured and forced to travel away from their community. We could also think of more recent examples of refugees who are forced to flee their homes, poor people who are forced into the hands of human 'traffickers' in the attempt to better their living conditions, or migrants who are at the mercy of so-called coyotes and snake-heads to move them across the world in abysmal conditions often leading to death. These forced mobilities are all the outcomes of the injustices of sovereignal freedom of mobility, which not only prevents, controls, and channels the mobility of less powerful people, but also sometimes forces their mobility against their will. Against such exercises of sovereignal freedom, subordinate groups may desire to exercise a claim to settlement; in some times and places a return to stability, rootedness and claiming a home is more important than mobility as a freedom (Ahmed et al. 2003). Or the injustices of sovereignal freedom may lead to calls for a democratization of forms of mobility, such as investment in public transportation systems and the placing of limits on some forms of sovereignal mobility (e.g. exercising greater public control over the freedom of automobility).

Civic freedom, finally, according to Patterson, is 'the capacity of adult members of a community to participate in its life and governance...The existence of civic freedom implies a political community of some sort, with clearly defined rights and obligations for every citizen' (Patterson 1991: 4). Now, what is often overlooked in studies of civil society and programs for civil society enhancement is that mobility is necessary to the forming of such a political community (Sheller and Urry 2003). Citizens must be able to come together to form a public, and to come together they must be able to move about and assemble freely. They must have a public space with open access and a means to move into and through this public space, including en masse (i.e. in a march, parade, or demonstration). Public spaces are also outcomes of mobility in so far as they allow information to flow into them; they are gathering points of many messages and messengers, in which information from many points is distilled and from which it is again disseminated. Digital communication and virtual mobilities are crucial here, joining newspapers and print media as the glue that binds together publics and enables civic freedom. What we today call social movements, and more broadly publics, require both physical and informational mobility as one of their key underpinnings.

One of the key weapons against civic freedom is the limitation of mobility. When public assembly is curtailed, when communications networks are censored or blocked, when marches and demonstrations are broken up, and when political activists are put under house arrest, imprisoned, or killed, we see states acting against mobilization by controlling mobility. Many social commentators have also diagnosed the privatization of public space as a key weakening of civic freedom of mobility (Kunstler 1993; Sorkin 1992). The emergence of 'malled' shopping districts with private security guards, the huge expansion of gated communities, the spread of CCTV surveillance on the streets, and the general theme-parking and militarization of urban public space have all placed limits on civic mobility (Sorkin 1992; Davis 1990), and hence civic freedom. And as noted above, various new proposals for surveillance of internet traffic, for channeling of faster and slower forms of access, and for introducing digital censorship have all been highly contested, especially by those who wish to protect civil liberties against the growing encroachment of corporate-friendly government.

Freedom of communication is a crucial element of civic mobility, and not surprisingly many have seen great democratic promise in the emergence of the internet, the world wide web, open source software, and the development of urban public wireless networks. Information and communication systems allow for forms of virtual mobility and imaginative travel, which are as important as physical mobility (Haldrup and Larsen 2006). Electronic communication allows for social networks to be distributed over greater distances, for strong ties to be maintained across those distances, and for social capital to be built across larger geographical scales. And it is precisely such social networks and strong ties that enable and enhance greater personal mobility, and potentially instigate greater civic mobilization (as has been seen, for example, in the use of mobile telephones to coordinate mass demonstrations in several countries, including the Phillippines, Zimbabwe, and the United States).

Thus from this simple idea of a chord of freedom we have sketched out several different intersections of freedom and mobility, each of which is significant and each of which varies in different ways across different societies and across individual experiences within each society. There is no single meaning or experience of freedom, but many different combinations of the positive and negative, the fair and the unjust, the physical and the informational. And in a sense each of these freedoms of mobility also has its own forms of resistance, subversion and counter-tactics. Personal freedom of mobility centers on the scale of the body: how the body moves, where it can move, when it can move. Sovereignal freedom of mobility, in comparison, extends beyond the individual body to encompass issues of governance, legitimacy, and the exercise of power whether in a familial home, an organization, a city or a nation; thus it concerns mobilities at larger scales. And civic freedoms of mobility likewise extend beyond the individual body to the collective mobilities of multiple publics, of social movements, of bodies of citizens and far-flung networks of communication.

We can also say that these different notes of the chord are inter-related. For example, it is from the autonomous public that emerged in eighteenth-century Europe, according to Jurgen Habermas, that there also begins to emerge an expanded 'sphere of personal freedom, leisure, and freedom of movement' (Habermas 1992 [1989]: 129). The democratization of personal mobility freedom, in other words, was dependent in part on the limitation of absolute sovereignal freedom and the expansion of civic freedom. Personal mobility freedom in turn leads to new kinds of resistance against mobility injustice, such as the embrace of nomadism as a counter-tactic against sovereignal and civic forms of control over mobility, access, and collectivity (Braidotti 1994). When mobility is disrupted in one realm, it may actually be met with efforts to increase mobility in another. If border crossings are heavily protected, for example, people will resort to more circuitous and dangerous routes, by foot, by boat, or hidden in a truck. If cities are not accessible by car, people will use public transit, bikes, or foot. Exercises of civic freedom in the dynamic of social protest have sometimes taken the form of interrupting the personal mobility freedom of other citizens, for example by blockading roads or stopping traffic. Blocking personal mobility thus becomes a method for drawing attention to claimants and is especially effective if the message concerns mobility injustice. Critical Mass bike rides, for example, fill the roadways with bikes and slow traffic in order to draw attention to the usual hegemony of the automobile on public roadways.

In sum, we can envision a wide range of mobility struggles that have been ongoing over many centuries. These struggles are concerned with who has access to mobility, whose mobility is controlled by whom, and who has a say in determining mobility systems and rights. Mobility struggles also concern the relation between personal, sovereignal, and civic mobility freedoms, or the relative weighting of each in any given social setting. And we can understand mobility justice/injustice in three different senses: first, as the degree to which various personal mobility rights are evenly or unevenly distributed; second, as the degree to which sovereignal freedoms of mobility impinge upon and have detrimental affects on others; and third, as the degree to which civil societies are able to enjoy civic freedoms of mobility, or find them constrained. Freedom of mobility, in other words, is not just a personal right or capacity, but also has sovereignal dimensions that are socially relational and civic dimensions that are collective and public.

Part Two: Spatial Mobility and Free Spaces

In contrast to the emphasis on individual mobilities and collective rights in the preceding section, another way to approach the question of the relation between mobility and freedom would be to consider how spatial formations enable or constrain mobility. Freedom of mobility, in other words, might be understood as pertaining to spatial affordances embedded in socio-spatial contexts, rather than as vested in individual or group motilities ('motility' being the potential for mobility). Flamm and Kauffmann define motility as 'how an individual or group takes possession of the realm of possibilities for mobility and builds on it to develop personal projects. This potential is not necessarily transformed into travel' (Flamm and Kaufmann 2006; Kaufman et al. 2004; Kaufmann 2002). They point out that the concept of motility concentrates on 'how an actor builds his [or her] relationship with space', in contrast to the concept of 'accessibility', which relates to 'the possibilities [for mobility] afforded by a given territory'. Thus if the previous section considered mobility freedom in terms of the motility of various individuals and groups, here I want to also consider mobility freedom in relation to the accessibility of spaces and their affordance of various kinds of mobility.

What kind of space allows for, enables, or even encourages mobility? Central here would be the idea of public space – an accessible space which is open to various entrants, allows free unhindered movement through it, and connects together or bridges between various more private spaces. Public space only becomes public when people access it, but they can only do so temporarily, as it must always be accessible to others as well. It is a space on which no individual has a claim, no one can put down roots, but all can momentarily occupy. Thus it is a space that enables and encourages personal mobility freedom and civic mobility freedom, while also mediating between various agents of sovereignal mobility freedom (both governmental agencies and private enterprises) who would seek to exercise their own freedom at the expense of others.

Such public spaces have been related to the ancient Greek 'agora', the American 'town square', the European plaza, and the public spaces of contemporary urbanism such as the street, the public park, or the public transport system. There is also a more specific use of the term 'free spaces' to refer to the gathering places of civic freedom, the sites at which political gatherings and free speech can take place, especially amongst marginalized 'counter-publics' (Emirbayer and Sheller 1999; Fraser 1992). But the point I want to make is that in all of these cases there is a kind of freedom of mobility inherent in the space itself, or at least in the way it is spatially practiced. The public-ness of public space is closely related to the degree to which it allows for physical and informational mobility within and through it. Elements such as architectural framing, building use, relation to the surrounding urban fabric, design of streetscapes, and traffic management all contribute to the experience of public space in 'livable cities' (Lennard and Lennard 1987). A well-designed square or plaza comes to function as a meeting place, a point of significant conversations, and a public realm consisting of the visibility of public life, multiple perspectives, and a physical shaping of community.

Mobility is a crucial element of how such a public realm is formed. Elsewhere I have discussed Harrison White's understanding of publics as social spaces that allow for 'switching' between communicative contexts (see Sheller 2004: 48–9; White 1995: 12–14). White envisions publics as contexts for social action that allow for 'decoupling' or 'slippage' to take place, as social actors decouple from the social networks (and spatial contexts) in which they are embedded, and switch into another one. Spatial mobility is crucial to such decouplings: what allows a public to emerge is a relation between actors loosened from their immediate social networks and spaces loosened from their immediate private uses – a kind of opening up of both networks and spaces, which allows for mixing, movement, and communication. Freedom of mobility is crucially dependent on such 'in-between' public spaces.

However, we cannot simply say that the more such free spaces there are in a given socio-spatial context, the more potential freedoms of mobility there will be. A social context with reduced public spaces may also have reduced spatial mobility, which reduces opportunities for decoupling and switching between social networks and hence reduces freedom of mobility. But the correspondence between freedom of mobility and the availability of 'free' public spaces is also mediated by features of motility such as skills, know-how, and what Flamm and Kaufmann refer to as 'cognitive appropriations' involving 'the evaluation of the available options [for mobility] vis-à-vis one's projects' (Flamm and Kaufmann 2006: 169). In other words, the existence of accessible public spaces only generates mobility in so far as individuals or groups cognitively and physically appropriate that space and use it for the exercise of their personal, sovereignal, or civic freedoms of mobility. The point I want to emphasise here is that those who exercise sovereignal freedom of mobility may use it not simply to be more mobile, but to actually shape public space in ways that increase their motility and decrease the motility of others. Public space is warped to afford greater potential mobility to some groups.

As we have noted above, the exercise of sovereignal freedom of mobility may actually reduce the mobility of others, and in fact may also reduce the accessibility of public space, or even totally appropriate public space for private ends. Thus we can understand the relation between the motility of individuals and groups and the accessibility of public space as a dynamic tension full of conflict and power imbalances. The kinds of personal and collective 'projects' through which public space is appropriated include real estate development, public investment in infrastructure, urban regeneration, community development agencies, enterprise zones, and so on. Contemporary cities are constantly undergoing processes of redevelopment, which often entail what urban geographers refer to as 'respatialization' and 'rescaling'.

Recent geographies of 'state rescaling' and urban restructuring emphasise the historicity of social space, the polymorphism of geographies, the dynamic restructuring of scale, and the continuous remaking of state space and urban space (see Brenner 2004; Brenner and Theodore 2002). Urban geographers have long recognized that 'capitalist expansion has been premised upon the production and continual transformation of urban space' (Lefebvre 1991 [1974]; Harvey 1989), that industrial production has 'periodically shifted across territories and scales', and that 'places, cities, and regions are [thus] continually restructured in relation to changing spatial divisions of labor' (Brenner 2004: 118). The reconfiguration of tranportation and communication infrastructures is crucial to such capitalist restructuring. We might ask, therefore, how do changing spatializations, divisions, and mobilities of capital, labor and state regulation disassemble and reassemble the socio-spatial configurations of humans, materials, machines, architectures, etc., that we call the public space of a city? And how are these reconfigurations affecting the various freedoms of mobility discussed above?

Neil Brenner argues that 'the image of political-economic space as a complex, tangled mosaic of superimposed and interpenetrating nodes, levels, scales, and morphologies has become more appropriate than the traditional Cartesian model of homogenous, self-enclosed and contiguous blocks of territory that has long been used to describe the modern interstate system' (Brenner 2004: 66). I want to suggest that this post-Keynsian/post-Fordist shift towards more 'complex, polymorphic, and multiscalar regulatory geographies' (ibid. 67) is fundamentally related to the emergence of complex new systems of mobility and immobility and their dynamic restructuring of both space and time. Urban spatiality is produced through dynamic processes of mobilising and demobilising, assembling and disassembling, various heterogeneous elements of the social, the corporeal, the machinic, the architectural, the infrastructural, the textual and the symbolic. Not only different levels, scales and morphologies are involved here, but also different mobilities.

Urban public space is under intense pressure from competing freedoms of mobility. Personal freedom of mobility often brings new populations into urban areas, whether migrants seeking economic opportunity, businesses relocating along with their managers and workers, or new waves of homesteading gentrification. These forms of personal social and spatial mobility are closely related to the geographical restructuring of both private residential and business districts, and the reconfiguration of public governmental and civic spaces. But the sovereignal freedom of developers to buy and sell property, or of businesses to occupy commercial space and purchase and sell goods from those spaces, is often in conflict with social needs such as affordable housing, the protection of public spaces, and the guarantee of accessibility of urban areas to wider publics. The poor, the very young and the elderly especially lose some of their personal mobility freedom when they are priced out of urban centers by gentrification and must relocate to more peripheral districts which are less well serviced; and publics lose some of their civic mobility freedom when public spaces (including roadways, parks, schools, police and fire stations, playgrounds and hospitals, as well as radio spectrum, broadband networks, and public access television channels) get sold off to private operators or owners. The sovereignal freedom of mobility of a privileged elite generates re-made urban space (tied to larger scale corporate mobilities and new urban consumerism and tourism markets) which then limits the personal mobility of poorer people (tied to both migrant labor markets, public transportation and local neighborhood mobilities), unless some kind of public groups keep an eye on things and regulate the process (tied to the capacity for civic mobility and informational mobility).

Spatial restructuring disrupts the existing scale of mobility regimes. New mobility regimes tend to favor business interests, tourism, and elites under neoliberal urbanism. Neighbourhoods and accessibility of public transit routes are often disrupted by such scalar shifts.

Many social commentators have lamented the privatization of public space and the detrimental affect on civic life (Jacobs 1961; Davis 1990; Sorkin 1992; Kunstler 1993; Putnam 2000). I want to emphasize that such processes are about the contest between the different freedoms of mobility that I identified above. A 1992 collection edited by Michael Sorkin, for example, described the new city as a shopping mall and theme park. 'As phone and modem render the street irrelevant,' he suggests, 'other dimensions become preeminent. Main Street is now the space between airports, the fibre optic cables linking the fax machines of the multinational corporations' far-flung offices, and invisible worldwide skeins of economic relations. Liberated from its centers and its edges by advances in communication and mobility...the new city threatens an unimagined sameness' (Sorkin 1992: xiii). With this loosening of ties to place, Sorkin laments three features of the new city: the generic urbanism of departicularized space; the "obsession with 'security,'" with rising levels of manipulation and surveillance over its citizenry and with a proliferation of new modes of segregation' (ibid. xiii); and the gentrified ersatz 'architecture of deception' (ibid. xiv). 'What's missing in this city', Sorkin concludes, 'is not a matter of any particular building or place; it's the spaces in between, the connections that make sense of forms' (ibid. xii). It is precisely the kinds of public spaces of the town square and the plaza, as described above, which have been lost. The choreography of public mobility is lost as urban space gets re-made in response to different scalar logics than those which once informed the inclusive urban spatial order; micro-level logics of building-by-building real estate development and macro-logics of global digital connectivity circumvent and disassemble the lineaments of civic urbanism and the personal and civic freedoms of mobility that it supported and embodied. Thus new visions of livable cities and sustainable urbanism return to questions of mobility, transport infrastructure, and connectivity between various public and private space as central to the future of urbanism (e.g. Amin and Thrift 2002).

Conclusion

I hope this brief sketch of mobility and freedom offers a more nuanced approach to thinking about their relation to each other, one which does not simply assume that unrestricted mobility is always a desired public good and one which moves beyond an individualized and personalistic view of mobility freedoms. I have argued that there are personal, sovereignal and civic freedoms of mobility which each have different components, and different relations to motility. I have argued that public space supports freedom of mobility, but is also threatened by some kind of sovereignal mobilities. And I have suggested that mobile publics (publics with a high degree of motility) and the infrastructures that enable them are crucial to the maintenance of civic freedom.

I want to conclude simply by pointing toward some future avenues of research that this approach implies. First, we need to show how tourism, migration, business and residential mobility, and economic development re-shape urban public spaces. Second, we need to map the positive and negative impact of different kinds of mobilities on preserving or degrading public life. And third, we need to make policy recommendations on the preservation, control and governance of competing freedoms of mobility. With a better understanding of the different freedoms of mobility and of the relationship between motility and public space we will be better able to address questions of mobility inequality and injustice.

References

Ahmed, S., Castaneda, C., Fortier, A.-M. and Sheller, M. (eds) (2003), *Uprootings/ Regroundings: Questions of Home and Migration* (Oxford: Berg).

Amin, A. and Thrift, N. (2000), *The Democratic City* (London: Verso).

Amin, A. and Thrift, N. (2002), *Cities: Reimagining the Urban* (Cambridge: Polity).

Bauman, Z. (2000), *Liquid Modernity* (Cambridge: Polity).

Beatley, T. (2000), *Green Urbanism: Learning from European Cities* (Washington, D.C.: Island Press).

Boddy, T. (1992), 'Underground and Overhead: Building the analogous city', in M. Sorkin (ed.) *Variations on a Theme Park: The New American City and the End of Public Space* (New York: Hill and Wang).

Braidotti, R. (1994), *Nomadic Subjects: Embodiment and Sexual Difference in Contemporary Feminist Theory* (New York: Columbia University Press).

Brenner, N. (2004), *New State Spaces: Urban Governance and the Rescaling of Statehood* (Oxford and New York: Oxford University Press).

Brenner, N. and Theodore, N. (eds) (2002), *Spaces of Neoliberalism: Urban Restructuring in North America and Western Europe* (Oxford and Boston: Blackwell).

Cwerner, S. (2006), 'Vertical Flight and Urban Mobilities: The Promise and Reality of Helicopter Travel', *Mobilities* 1 (2): 191–216.

Davis, M. (1990), *City of Quartz* (London: Vintage).

Davis, M. (1992), 'Fortress Los Angeles: The militarization of urban space', in M. Sorkin (ed.) *Variations on a Theme Park: The New American City and the End of Public Space* (New York: Hill and Wang).

Emirbayer, M. and Sheller, M. (1999), 'Publics in history', *Theory and Society* 28: 145–97.

Flamm, M. and Kaufmann, V. (2006), 'Operationalising the Concept of Motility: A Qualitiative Study', *Mobilities* 1 (2): 167–90.

Fraser, N. (1992), 'Rethinking the public sphere', in Craig Calhoun (ed.) *Habermas and the Public Sphere* (Cambridge: MIT Press), pp. 109–142.

Giddens, A. (1990), *The Consequences of Modernity* (Stanford: Stanford University Press).

Giddens, A. (1991), *Modernity and Self-Identity: Self and Society in the Late Modern Age* (Stanford: Stanford University Press).

Graham, S. and Marvin, S. (2001), *Splintering Urbanism: Networked Infrastructures, technological Mobilities and the Urban Condition* (London: Routledge).

Habermas, J. (1992 [1989]), *The Structural Transformation of the Public Sphere* (trans. T. Burger) (Cambridge, MA: MIT Press).

Hajer, M. and Reijndorp, A. (2001), *In Search of a New Public Domain* (Rotterdam: Nai Publishers).

Haldrup, M. and Larsen, J. (2006), 'Following Flows: Geographies of Tourism Performances', paper presented to the 'Mobilities, Technology and Travel Workshop', Roskilde University, Roskilde, Denmark, April 2006. Accessed 5 May 2007 at http://www.ruc.dk/inst3/geo/Tpato/Articles/.

Hannam, K., Sheller, M. and Urry, J. (2006), 'Mobilities, Immobilities, and Moorings', *Mobilities* 1 (1): 1–22.

Harvey, D. (1989), *The Urban Experience* (Oxford: Basil Blackwell).

Jacobs, J. (1961), *The Death and Life of Great American Cities* (New York: Vintage).

Jain, S. (2006), 'Urban Violence: Luxury in Made Space', in M. Sheller and J. Urry (eds) *Mobile Technologies of the City* (London and New York: Routledge), pp. 61–76.

Kaufmann, V. (2002), *Re-thinking Mobility: Contemporary Sociology* (Aldershot: Ashgate).

Kaufmann, V., et al. (2004), 'Motility: Mobility as capital', *International Journal of Urban and Regional Research* 28 (1): 745–56.

Kesselring, S. (2006), 'Pioneering Mobilities: New patterns of movement and motility in a mobile world', *Environment and Planning A* 38 (2): 269–80.

Kesselring, S. and Vogl, G. (2004), 'Mobility Pioneers: Networks, scapes and flows between first and second modernity', paper presented at 'Alternative Mobility Futures Conference', Lancaster University, Lancaster, UK, 9–11 January 2004.

Kunstler, J.H. (1993), *The Geography of Nowhere: The Rise and Decline of America's Man-Made Landscape* (New York and London: Simon and Shuster).

Lassen, C. (2006), 'Aeromobility and work', *Environment and Planning A* 38 (2): 301–312.

Lefebvre, H. (1991 [1974]), *The Production of Space* (Cambridge, Mass.: Blackwell).

Lennard, H. and Lennard, S. (1987), *Livable Cities: People and Places, Social and Design Principles for the Future of the City* (Southampton, N.Y.: Gondolier Press).

Nowicka, M. (2006), 'Mobility, Space and Social Structuration in the Second Modernity and Beyond', *Mobilities* 1 (3): 411–36.

Patterson, O. (1991), *Freedom in the Making of Western Culture*, Vol. I (Cambridge, MA: Harvard University Press).

Putnam, R. (2000), *Bowling Alone: The Collapse and Revival of American Community* (New York: Simon and Shuster).

Sheller, M. (2004), 'Mobile Publics: Beyond the Network Perspective', *Environment and Planning D: Society and Space* Vol. 22: 39–52.

Sheller, M. (unpublished), 'Mobility Systems, Urban Disasters, and the Re-scaling of New Orleans', paper presented to the 'Association of American Geographer's Annual Meeting', Chicago, US, March 2006.

Sheller, M. and Urry, J. (2003), 'Mobile transformations of "public" and "private" life', *Theory, Culture and Society* Vol. 20 (3): 107–125.

Sheller, M. and Urry, J. (2006), 'The new mobilities paradigm', *Environment and Planning A* 38 (2): 207–226.

Sorkin, M. (ed.) (1992), *Variations on a Theme Park: The New American City and the End of Public Space* (New York: Hill and Wang).

Urry, J. (2000), *Sociology Beyond Societies* (London: Routledge).

White, H. (1995), 'Where do Languages Come From? I. Switching between networks, II. Times from reflexive talk', Center for the Social Sciences at Columbia University Pre-print Series (Columbia University, New York).

Wood, D.M. and Graham, S. (2006), 'Permeable Boundaries in the Software-sorted Society: Surveillance and Differentiations of Mobility', in M. Sheller and J. Urry (eds) *Mobile Technologies of the City* (New York: Routledge), pp. 177–91.

Chapter 3

Automobility and the Driving Force of Warfare: From Public Safety to National Security[1]

Jeremy Packer

The increasing mobility and destructive potential of modern terrorism has required the United States to rethink and rearrange fundamentally its systems for border and transportation security.[2] (Tom Ridge, First Director of the Department of Homeland Security)

The Department of Homeland Security is committed to further securing our nation's highways, mass transit systems, railways, waterways and pipelines, each of which is critical to ensuring the freedom of mobility and economic growth.[3] (Department of Homeland Security Press Release)

Such proclamations mark a considerable shift in the primary concern of US government agencies whose work it is to monitor, regulate, and govern transportation technologies. In short, rather than primarily focusing on avoiding accidents, the new mandate is to deter terrorists. What I want to accomplish in this essay is to explain how such a shift is being enacted through the automobile and what this may mean for future driving practices. Secondarily, this essay is an attempt to formulate a theoretical framework adequate for understanding this new formulation for the governance of automobility in the United States specifically, but with the considerable chance of such formations spreading across the globe due in no small part to the global war on terror.[4] Dangers arise when attempting to characterize the emergent, to in essence predict the future. In their essay "A History of the Future" (1970), James Carey, the founder of the American strain

---

1   Sections of this essay have previously appeared in "Becoming Bombs: Mobilizing Mobility in the War of Terror", *Cultural Studies* Vol 20, Nos 4–5, pp. 378–99.

2   http://www.dhs.gov/dhspublic/.

3   Department of Homeland Security Press Release, "Department of Homeland Security announces $179 million in grants to secure America's Ports", http://www.dhs.gov/dhspublic/display?content=3031.

4   It should be noted, that the US is also borrowing tactics already established in numerous war-zones and sites of civil strife. In that sense, the "spreading" around the globe is an already emergent fact. But, the sheer size of the automotive population in the United States, its leading role in the war on terror, and the specific historical changes taking place in the US are the focus here.

of cultural studies within the field of communications, and John Quirk argue that much critical insight can be gained through an examination of predictions about the future. As they maintain, such an undertaking does not provide guidance in accurately predicting what shall come to pass. Rather, it reveals how the blind faith in the imagined potential of technology, very often communications technology, to solve contemporaneous problems covers up the political and economic motivations behind such applications. They characterize this faith in technology to lead us into a better tomorrow the "rhetoric of a sublime future".[5]

By foregrounding Carey's insight, the following examination of past and contemporary imagined futures of the automatically driven and guided automobile provide insight into two interrelated processes. First, expectations and formulations of how to seamlessly join the driver, automobile, and driving environment expose underlying theories of governance. Such a history makes evident a shift from a disciplinary apparatus to that of something akin to control society. Second, an understanding of the imagined problems to which automobile governance might be applied makes evident a change in the political rationality of said governance. The US's response to the events of 9/11 has configured the automobile as a new site for the conduct of warfare. The political rationale for governing automobility is no longer only that of ensuring the safety of each driver as in a pastoral formulation of state-citizen responsibilities. Under the auspices of the war on terror and in the perpetual period of "the new normal"[6] all terrain is imagined as a battlefield; drivers and their automobiles are cautiously approached as potential enemies and allies. Ultimately, such an investigation of the specific technological assemblages imagineered[7] to combat such a thorny problem as suicide bombers or the increasingly popular subset, the car bomb, can potentially provide a means for making the sublime seem rather grotesque. Carey and Quirk provide appropriate context here as well. They note that in 1929 H.G. Wells imagined that the British Empire was a precursor to a World State and "the royal military equipped with the latest technology of communication and transport as the forerunners of a "world police" able to dispatch quickly to any trouble spot to quell insurrectional activity."[8] In the new formation of Empire the US military sees all communication and transport technologies as potential weapons in the global war on terror. The communications enabled, tracked, and guided automobile serves as merely one such example.

---

5   Carey and Quirk, "The History of the Future", p. 180.

6   For a characterization of how the "new normal" reconfigures politics, see Bratich (2006), "Public secrecy and immanent security: A strategic analysis".

7   Walt Disney coined this neologism to describe the work done by Disney's engineers and designers who worked to create different "worlds" within the Disney theme parks, most spectacularly in their World of Tomorrow. I borrow the term to suggest some elements of this melding of engineering and futurology.

8   Carey and Quirk, "The History of the Future", p. 184.

The imagined future of the automobile has a long history and it is dominated by one feature. Automobiles will be made to drive themselves. Drivers will be freed to conduct all forms of business and leisure from the seat of their automobile; not having to concern themselves with the tedium of paying attention to stop signs, highway exits, and the always present danger of other drivers' errors or ire. The dream of such a future has been part of the American popular imaginary for three-quarters of a century. Yet, such imagined futures have been entirely dependent upon a network of communication, control, and command technologies (C3) that could create a degree of surveillance and control over the automobile population historically only imagined in dystopic science-fiction narratives. Recent scholarship has begun to examine current technological advances in the C3-automobile couplet. Dodge and Kitchin (2006) have thoroughly examined how the automation of drivers and the driving environment have radically altered the governance of what John Urry calls "the system of automobility" (2004). They make evident how a vast array of C3 technologies work to more actively produce "safety through software" (p 10) as well as hardware (cars, roads, etc.) which ultimately create a system of "automated management". More generally, they are interested in how this complex of technologies is establishing new modes of self-disciplining and governance while altering how drivers imagine and move through space. Mimi Sheller (forthcoming) draws upon a dense complex of work (Featherstone 2004, Katz 2000, Thrift 2004) oriented by investigations into the phenomenological and embodied practices of the driver-automobile/human-technology couplet as they are reoriented due to the presence of C3 technologies in automobiles. She argues that the more profound effects upon everyday life and driving are infrastructural as the apparatus-produced agency is "increasingly impersonal, and ominously distributed amongst software, vehicles, and algorithms (25)." In this sense, Sheller pushes for a broader perspective that examines the power relations ingrained and maintained by these emergent technologies. What I want to add to this dialogue concerns the political dimensions and centrality of automobility in changing citizen-state relations and how a war-time state of exception further embroils drivers into a global network of power relations. The importance of automobility in these processes can be witnessed in how the Office of Homeland Security expects to fight national security battles in the United States and in how the US military approaches war theaters abroad. Automobility is an integral element in both. This is not the first time the automobile has figured as a key component in fighting war, nor is the rhetoric of war new to explaining how to govern automobility. Two such metaphors will now be used as a starting point for examining the shift from public safety to national security.

Discipline to Intelligent Control

For US Presidents Truman and Eisenhower the still-recent success of military and civilian operations and organization during the Second World War provided a two-prong model for attacking the perceived danger posed by the expected postwar growth in automobility. The first prong was exemplified in a photo and caption from the 1949 drivers education manual *Man and the Motorcar* (See Figure 3.1).[9] The photo features a group of soldiers marching in perfectly synchronized order, while the caption reads, "In wartime we practice self-discipline for the common good. Driving also calls for self-discipline for everyone's safety."[10]

Figure 3.1   Discipline

On the opposing page, *Man and the Motorcar* presented a second war-infused metaphor for understanding the importance of automotive safety; the atomic bomb. A photo of a mushroom cloud rising above the waves of what can only be imagined by an American audience as a far-off tropical land, featured this caption, "Today's great problem is modern man's control of power." This second metaphor was both timely,

---

9   Albert Whitney's *Man and the Motorcar* was the most popular drivers education manual in the US for many years and survived numerous updates during its numerous editions that began in 1936 and continued to be used after its final 1964 edition.
10   Ibid.

seeing as the atomic bomb was newly configuring global relations of power, and prescient given the political changes in the US that have followed the attacks of 9/11. As Whitney explained over fifty years ago, "*intelligent control*" (italics in the original) was the means for dealing with "power" whether it be "obtained from atomic fission, or from the combustion of a gasoline-air mixture."[11] This shift in emphasis from "self-discipline" to "*intelligent control*" mirrors the broad shift described as that from a disciplinary society to a control society (Deleuze 1995). Automobility provides not only a useful example for understanding how such a shift has been occurring, but it will be argued that recently formulated means for controlling automobility are experiments for the more general control of mobile populations. Strange as it may seem, the automobile's power is no longer simply metaphorically related to war. For the War on Terror and US Homeland Security, the automobile needs to be controlled precisely because it has come to be problematized as a bomb.

Figure 3.2   Intelligent control

11   Ibid. 4.

Altering driving behavior over the past one hundred-plus years through scare tactics, traffic rules, education programs, and surveillance has been a massive undertaking by a cluster of invested governing agencies. I have previously shown[12] how a series of safety crises have created different problematic mobile populations which have been the target for disciplining. Women, youth, motorcyclists, transportation laborers, and racial minorities have all been represented as automotive threats to themselves and others. As groups who historically have been lacking in political, economic, and cultural capital gained access to automobility or created different forms of automobility, their mobile behavior was popularly represented as dangerous. These "threats" were almost exclusively responded to in terms of traffic safety and police surveillance. If the danger they posed is instead understood in terms of how increased mobility disrupts social order, then safety, at least partially, needs to be understood in political terms. One question that follows is: "How has safety been used as a means for altering or maintaining asymmetric relations of power?" This is not just a question though of who gets to drive and with how much latitude as if the equation is simply automobility=freedom= equality. Automobility and the freedom it promises need also to be understood as an obligation. The systems of automobility in the United States and other highly industrialized countries very often nearly demand that one must drive a car. Thus, the disciplining of mobility organized through traffic safety is a means for keeping other interconnected economic and social systems running smoothly, including systems of social inequality.

With this said, the relationship between the state and citizen under a rubric of safety could be described as a sort of paternalism, or what Michel Foucault has described as pastoralism.[13] In this conception of automobility, each paternal subject of the state, the "safe citizen,"[14] is looked after as an individual subject worthy of care and protection as an integral part of the population as a whole, even if safety campaigns were at the same time maintaining other forms of social and political inequality. There is an assumed symbiotic relationship between the two in which what is good for the individual subject further benefits the population more generally. Health, or the maintenance and creation of the productive capacity of the body – biopower, provides a good example. The general health of the society, the "public health," depends upon the relative health of the individuals of which it is comprised. Healthier individuals for instance, minimize the spread of communicable disease, decrease the overall strain placed on the health care system, which allows for the better allocation of medical resources, which leads to healthier individuals, and so on. Traffic safety has been similarly imagined and in fact is in some governmental quarters treated as a public health issue. In order to create a safe driving environment, each individual's driving behavior is targeted for alteration both for their own benefit and the benefit of other drivers. Thus, a

---

12   See *Mobility Without Mayhem* (2007a).
13   See Foucault (1982), "The Subject and Power".
14   See Packer, J. (2003), "Disciplining Mobilty".

safe driving environment depends upon safe individual drivers, and the safer the environment, the safer each individual. Two coalescing changes in the political formulation of citizen to state are altering this formulation for the governance of automobility. The first will be characterized as a shift in how automobility, and mobility more generally, is problematized. The second alteration was initially popularized in the 1930s, but has really gained administrative force since the 1960s when technological solutions to traffic safety were beginning to be imagined as more effective than driving behavior modification.[15] Increasingly, the technological solutions as noted above are enabled by C3 networks with the military often initiating their development.

The most notable attacks against the United State's hegemony have been carried out with or on transportation technologies. The 9/11 attacks on the World Trade Center and the Pentagon are the most spectacular examples of a transportation technology being turned into a weapon – becoming a bomb – but it is only one among numerous cases in which transportation technologies have been and continue to be used as weapons against US interests, for example, Beirut 1983, Twin Towers 1994, Oklahoma City 1995, USS Cole in 2000. As Mike Davis explains in his history of the car bomb,[16] the first such attack was carried out by anarchist Mario Budo directly across from the JP Morgan Company on the corner of Broad and Wall Streets in the heart of the US financial district in New York. The blast killed 40 and wounded more than 200. Tactically it struck a metaphorical blow at the heart of US financial hegemony. The car-bomb, or what have more recently been termed Vehicle Borne Improvised Explosive Device (VBIED), has since been a weapon of choice for the IRA and liberation forces in Palestine and elsewhere. The military has spent considerable energy collecting data in order to understand the role and effectiveness of VBIEDs in combat and non-combat scenarios and the US Bureau of Alcohol, Tobacco, Firearms and Explosives has done extensive testing on their effectiveness at remote facilities in New Mexico (see Figure 3.3).[17] Such a focused effort in understanding the effects and pervasiveness of the various forms of the car bomb points out both the concern of US military and police forces regarding these threats and in a related fashion provides evidence of the incredible destructive power of the car bomb in the arsenal of the "poor man's air force".[18] One Office of Homeland Security website uses this very chart to provide the answer to the rhetorical question posted directly below that reads "What happens in Iraq

---

15   The publication of Ralph Nader's *Unsafe at Any Speed: The Designed-in Dangers of the American Automobile* in 1965, the congressional hearings that led from the publication, and the resultant creation of the National Traffic Safety Agency mark this shift.

16   Mike Davis, "The Poor Man's Airforce: A History of the Car Bomb (Part 1)" and "Return to Sender: A History of the Car Bomb (Part 2)" http://www.tomdispatch.com/index. mhtml?pid=76140, accessed on 27 March 2007.

17   Accessed   at   http://upload.wikimedia.org/wikipedia/en/0/01/Vbied-standards-chart.jpg 27 March 2007.

18   Davis, "The Poor Man's Airforce".

can't happen here?"[19] Such scare copy that connects the war in Iraq to the battle over Homeland Security is part of the logic that animates this new formulation of conducting automobile warfare everywhere. Various forms of mobility, as points of reaching the mass and as signifiers of the global reach of capital, have also been the object of attack (most notably the airplane and train). Under Section 801 of the first PATRIOT Act (Providing Appropriate Tools to Intercept and Obstruct Terrorism) attacks on mass transportation systems were newly criminalized as acts of terrorism, not simply crimes unto themselves.

Whether at border crossings, airport terminals, roadside police interrogations, ports, or security checks at government buildings, what is often referred to as "freedom of movement" has become one site where the "homeland's" security is seen to be at risk. Conceptions of who has such freedom, how, when, where, and with what velocity it can be enacted, has all changed. As the epigraph above from the Department of Homeland Security's website makes clear there is a heightened sense that modern terrorism demands a rethinking of how to govern the US transportation system. This rethinking is not purely defensive. The system is also imagined as a productive force for ensuring homeland security as a number of programs call upon the auto-mobile citizen to expand the capacities of state surveillance.

For instance the Terrorism Information and Prevention System (TIPS) calls for citizens to keep an eye out for potential terrorist activity while driving, asking them to use cell phones to alert police forces of suspicious activity. While the 300,000 transportation industry workers in the United States were called upon by the American Trucking Association and the Department of Homeland Security to take part in Highway Watch which would conscript truckers as part of a mobile surveillance system. Such governmental attempts have been used in the past to link automobility and mobile communications into a mobile surveillance system, including widespread attempts to organize Citizens Band Radio users to monitor the roadways in the 1970s.[20] But in the past automotive behavior was itself the object of surveillance. This isn't to say we are simply facing a more repressive form of power in which we are constantly being told "No. You can not enter (or leave) here." Though for many this has been the case.[21] Rather, how mobility is governed

---

19   Morgenstern, H. (2006) "Vehicle Born Improvised Explosive Device – VBIED: The Terrorist Weapon of Choice", accessed at: http://www.nationalhomelandsecurityknowledge base.com/Research/International_Articles/VBIED_Terrorist_Weapon_of_Choice.html.

20   Packer (2002), "Mobile Communications and Governing the Mobile".

21   It bears mentioning that in some cases, Guantanamo for instance, in terms that Foucault called domination rather than power in the last interview he gave before his death (*The Final Foucault*), access to mobility and the legal-juridical apparatus is completely denied. They essentially cannot act through any acceptable channels to resist, effect or reformulate their situation. In absolute terms they may, depending upon how complete their confinement, have the "power" to take their own life, thus usurping the state's sovereign potential to do the same, but for all intentions and purposes they are powerless. Deleuze suggests this return of sovereign forms may be an integral part of the changes coinciding with

has changed. It is in essence a question of "how has mobility been differently problematized?" For one, the space of governance has changed significantly. The advent of the Office of Homeland Security and the Global War on Terror, as much as the first attacks on the US mainland in nearly two centuries, have turned all of global space, all terrain, into a war zone. As such, we must ask to what degree the logic of national security now organizes policing mechanisms in the US and abroad. Further, when the secrecy of terrorists' identities creates a situation in which combatants "cannot be known," in any field of battle, this means all will be policed as if they are potentially terrorists. At the same time, all citizens are asked to join in the War on Terror as part of Homeland Security initiatives. This alteration and bifurcation in the relationship between the state and citizenry is particularly telling in terms of automobility.

One of the problematic elements of such attacks for a military operating under the Revolution in Military Affairs (RMA) and biopolitical formations of empire is that the suicide bomber makes apparent "the ontological limit of biopower in its most tragic and revolting form."[22] Where RMA military strategy minimizes its own military casualties in acknowledgement of the productive capacity of life, the suicide bomber inverts this notion to acknowledge and exploit the destructive (resistant) capacity of life. As a problematic of governance, the suicide bomber exposes the limits of disciplinarity as a means for governing at a distance; that is, organizing, regulating, and making productive the mobility of individuals and the population alike without direct or excessive governmental control.[23] If all automobiles are potential bombs, then in a time when the US government is operating under a state of perpetual warfare, governing at a distance can not merely depend upon panopticism and disciplinarity as a means for creating docile citizens. In a biopolitical order the pastoral relation of state and subject makes life the end-goal of and motor for creating a productive population and, thereby, nation.[24] When life is not equally invested as a desired ends by both state and citizen, life is not only that which must be groomed and cared for, but rather treated as a constant and immanent threat which needs diffusing or extinguishing.[25]

The governance of automobility then needs to be understood in terms of this new problematic, mobility as immanent threat. In the "new normal" of perpetual

---

the dawning of the control society. "It may be that older means of control borrowed from the old sovereign societies, will come back in to play, adapted as necessary." ("Postscript on the Control Society" in *Negotiations* by Deleuze, 1995), p. 182.

22　Hardt and Negri (2004), *Multitude*, p. 54.

23　For a historical explanation of how the articulation of transportation and communication technologies operates as the activating mechanism for such transformations, see Packer (2006), "Rethinking Dependency".

24　See Foucault (1978), *History of Sexuality*.

25　Even the notion of grooming and "caring for" gets inverted as part of the preparatory program of the suicide bomber is cutting one's hair, shaving, shining ones shoes, and generally perfecting the presentation of self for the afterlife.

war, the subject is no longer treated as a becoming accident, but a becoming bomb. For the regime of Homeland Security in the United States, it is not the safety of citizens that is at stake, but rather the stability of Empire's social order most generally, and more specifically the security of the US state form.[26] It is a war in which the state form fears all that may become problematic, become bomb. So the new mode of problematization treats all mobilities as potential bombs and thus technologies of control are being developed and applied to the automobile as a means for addressing such perceived threats.

Auto-control society

Control society is an emergent formation of power that according to Gilles Deleuze corresponds to a "particular kind of machine...cybernetic machines and computers."[27] Their modus operandi is not, as this quote might seem to imply, technologically determined. In order to understand the complexities and contours of this new formation "you must analyze the collective arrangements of which the machines are just one component."[28] Disciplinarity has in many ways structured earlier forms of automobility. Even though the space of automobility is not limited by clearly demarcated spaces of confinement, the processes of surveillance, testing, knowledge production, repetition, self-reflection, internalization of the gaze, and the partitioning and regularity of space worked in an attempt to produce docile mobile subjects. Beginning with the use of radio in the 1920s, the transistor in the 1960s, and truly gaining speed alongside the personal computer revolution of the 1980s, the use of C3 to guide and monitor automobility for safety took root.[29] This application of command and control technologies as first witnessed through the integration of two-way radio in police cruisers, allowed for the coordination of movement from a distance while increasing the range of surveillance. In this sense, the desire to control specific fleets of vehicles, like those of the police or taxis companies, has been in operation since the late 1920s. For the most part though, the application of cybernetic and computer technologies has been seen as the ultimate tool for fixing an unsafe automobility system. In this imagined future, driver error would be eliminated from the equation through the creation of fully auto-controlled automobiles. The imagined future of the automobile system answered to the dreams of a perfectly efficient and perfectly safe driving environment. Under the truth regime of Homeland Security, auto-control imagines itself as the ultimate sapper. Space is not a minefield, mobility is a mine.

---

26   See Hardt and Negri (2001), *Empire* and (2004), *Multitude* for an analysis of the emergence of Empire, the US military's centrality to its current formation and the role of biopower.

27   "Control and Becoming" in *Negotiations* (1990, 1995), p. 175.

28   Ibid.

29   See Dodge and Kitchin (2006), "Codes, Vehicles, and Governmentality" and Packer (2006), "Rethinking Dependency".

One element of the model of the control society is the management of access to space. That is, the ability to be mobile, to move from one place to another can be governed at the level of the individual. Within a disciplinary regime this access took place in terms of the precept; particular forms of mobility operated according to the rules of conduct in that space which couldn't necessarily disallow access to mobility in general or to particular spaces according to who but rather only according to how. For instance, driving might be governed according to population (only those aged 16 and older) and by the rules of conduct of the road (at certain speeds, in certain directions, in particular types of vehicles). Thus, automobility and the spaces open to it were controlled according to a set of precepts which were surveiled and in theory internalized. It was only at particular checkpoints, most notably borders, though secondarily anti-drunk driving road blocks, and in cases of witnessed rule infractions that the *who* of mobility came into being through technologies of verification,[30] most notably the drivers license, but also technologies such as proof of insurance, automobile registration and license plates. As will be noted below, these forms of verification can be made mobile and not just activated by the checkpoint. However, through the integration of various communications, insurantial, verification, and information technologies the precept/surveillance couplet can be replaced by the password.

As Deleuze argues we need to see into and before the dawning of this control society in order to prepare modes of resistance. He looks to Felix Guattari's imagined future in which all must use an electronic card to move into and out of particular spaces. This card can be made to provide access on one day, but not the next or only at specific times through particular entrances. It is not the precept, the rule for conduct that determines access, but rather the constantly modulatable password, actualized via the pass-card. If we take this future as our ground zero, we can move in time in two directions. Forward, we can imagine not simply specific sites through which one must pass, nor cards which stand in as a sign of one's identity. Rather, as recent science fiction movies *Gatacca* and *Minority Report* suggest, the body, in conjunction with biometric recognition technologies, becomes its own technology of verification.[31] But, in both of these movies there are still checkpoints or mobile surveillance forces that must surveil and search space for individuals. In simple terms it is still the space that is the site of control, not the very mobility of any given individual or population. For this second possibility to come into being, all of space would be a perpetual checkpoint. In Deleuzean terms this space would be neither striated nor smooth, but smoothly striated. Striated space is that which has been organized according to a set of rules and patterns for how the space can be used, traversed, and even imagined. Smooth space has no such rules. There would not be a grid covering space according to a set of coordinates as if

---

30   For a description of "technologies of verification", see Robertson (2006), "A Ritual of Verification?".

31   Gates (2004), "Advocating alternative futures: Screening biometrics and related technologies in science-fiction cinema".

on a map with boundaries, but rather each and every point in space would always be the center of spatial organization for the individual at that point. Forces of control would always have the potential to be focused upon on every occupied point, but ideally do so through the occupant as opposed to a spatial apparatus. Mobility would become that which is the imagined "site" of control, not space. Furthermore, the trace of movement would become the predictor for what might happen in the future. For this to happen, all mobilities would have to be fully monitored, a data base of recorded movement would need to exist, an algorithm would make predictable-sense of such movement, and all mobilities would need to be potentially remotely controlled. That is the dystopic vision of a control society future; all individuals remotely controllable. And in fact, *Minority Report* provides just such a vision when the automobile John Anderton, the movie's protagonist played by Tom Cruise, is using to escape an unjustified police arrest, is remotely controlled in an attempt to bring Anderton to the police station and "justice." The automobile, so long envisioned by Hollywood as a mode of escape, was turned into a mobile jail cell.

Historical homelands and future combat zones

It is in the past and the past future, that we can see the beginnings (for technological, military, economic, and political reasons) of this future auto-control society. The automobile in the United States currently accounts for over 90 percent of travel and, excepting for wartime rationing, its use has increased annually for over a hundred years running.[32] Even given the various nightmare scenarios regarding its ultimate demise, this astounding saturation of use continues to gain. Acknowledging the enormity and ubiquity of automobile use and its continued growth, an obvious point of investigation into the technologies and machinic arrangements of the (be)coming control society is automobility. The automobile has been a site for remote control innovations for years and it has primarily been achieved via a network of communications technologies. As noted above, it was most often done at the behest of safety and economic efficiency. What follows is a brief history of some of the developments and imagined plans for creating a fully controlled automobile/ highway system. More importantly, it is through an examination of these imagined futures that we can witness just how deeply rooted and widely spread the desire for auto-control society has been over the past century. Furthermore, contemporary imaginings regarding the automobile are taking place in two distinct arenas. First, there were a number of pre-9/11 initiatives for what have generally been called Automated Highway Systems (AHS), Intelligent Transportation Systems (ITS), or more specifically the Intelligent Vehicle Highway System (IVHS); research and development upon which began in the early 1990s via a billion US dollars

---

32   The number of miles driven per capita rose over 50 percent between 1970 and 2000. US Department of Transportation (2000), *Our Nations Highways 2000*. Accessed at: http://www.fhwa.dot.gov/ohim/onh00/onh2p1.htm.

of start-up capital from the US Congress. Second, the US military is currently developing a program they call Combat Zones That See (CTS) touted for initial use as part of the US military's operations in Baghdad. These two historically and technologically overlapping initiatives need to be thought of in tandem as a set of theaters for experimenting with implementations of control society. It is not simply that there is a desire to control automotive conduct, but increasingly under the logic of perpetual war, the more far reaching consequences are that the automobile acts as the site for experimentation on the control of all bodily mobility.

The history of the imagined future of the automobile tells us much about not simply the future, but the underlying cultural, political, and economic logics that continue to animate dreams of technological and social mastery over everyday life. Central to nearly all these envisioned futures is the fully automatic automobile or what is often called the driverless car. In these visions, driver becomes passenger in his (gender specificity used here for historical accuracy) technologically-chauffeured streamlined mobile "rocket ship." As recently as 1997, our already recent past of 2005, was predicted as the year of commercial viability of an AHS.[33] This is not too surprising. As begun at the 1939 World's Fair, predicting the driverless automobile has been an integral part of envisioning and marketing the future.

As one of the earliest, and certainly the most widely cited and recognized of these, GM's Norman Bel Geddes' designed "Highways and Horizons" (more often called "Futurama") exhibit, provided what would become a fairly common sensibility of what this future world might look like. In this vision cars were radio controlled. (A feat accomplished in 1924, in which the car was said to be driven "as if a phantom were at the wheel."[34] Somehow the frightening otherworldly nature of these technological feats would soon disappear.) The set of six enormous dioramas were viewed by Fair visitors from their moving seats which ran on a track surrounding the exhibit. Futurama envisioned a highway system that seamlessly drifted into, through, and back out of the rapidly expanding "Midwestern City of 1960." The driverless automobile and its attendant highway system was not only the engine for suburban expansion, but also an individuated coach to the furthest reaches of the US where mountains, the monotony of the plains, and vast bodies of water all would easily be surmounted in a mere twenty years in the future. Thus, the automobile would motor commerce and family adventure; free markets aligned with the freedom of movement said to be part of the natural make-up of everyday-Americans' frontier spirit. It is vitally important to note that it is a vision of the automobile as a vision of *the* future. The automobile was conceived of as the key to both understanding and implementing a supposed better life, a freer, yet controllable future.

GM would revisit the future numerous times over the next six decades most notably with their 1964 update of Futurama again at a New York World's Fair. During

---

33 "But could it do a handbrake turn?" (1997).
34 "Radio Driven Auto Runs Down Escort" (1925), p. 28.

the 1950s the future popped up all over the place for GM. In particular their Firebird series of cars (the "laboratory on wheels") with its turbine engine was presented as "an amazing experience in automatic car control." In addition to showing up at promotional events and GM's various Motorama exhibits, the car appeared in GM's 1956 women-targeted short "Design for Dreaming," in which the driver proclaims "Firebird II to control tower, we are about to take off on the highway of tomorrow", at which point the happily middle class couple drive into the future. The Firebird's electronic guidance system was said to be ready for the "electronic highway of the future" which GM, along with GE and others, flirted with throughout the decade. Given the post-war/Cold War intermingling of scientific exuberance and anxiety, GM's auto-future is no great surprise as it offers up a vision of social progress through better science and personal satisfaction through the consumption of the fruits of that science. But, at a time when the Interstate Highway System was just beginning to really take off in its already-antiquated non-electronic form, the notion that what America needed was a new system, prior to the implementation of the original, seems now more than simply a bit far-fetched. What does become clear is the longstanding desire for a truly free, yet electronically controlled freeway system. The freedom derived from the task of driving is, however, always dependent upon an obligation to an electronic system. This electronic highway would pass from designer's dream to traffic engineer's Holy Grail.

The diagram opposite comes from the US Department of Transportation's *Urban Freeway Surveillance and Control: State of the Art* (or more accurately, *art of the state*) and makes apparent the auto-centric nature of auto-control (see Figure 3.3).

This particular vision of control appeared in 1972, before a number of events radically changed the driving environment, including the OPEC oil crisis, extensive emissions controls, and safety standards that were just beginning to appear. Furthermore, the use of on-board computers, GPS systems, black boxes, and other communications devices had not yet fully arrived. In other words, much of the regulatory and technological forces currently at play simply didn't exist or had yet to be integrated into the automobile. Yet, this diagram of power points to some of the underlying methods and goals of such "surveillance and control."

The automobile quite clearly functions as the central focus of such initiatives and in essence operates as the sender, message, and receiver in a communicative network encompassing the automobile driver and "central control." Notice in the diagram the single circle titled "Vehicle presence detectors." Three important points can be gleaned from a closer analysis of this single node in the diagram. First, "presence" is primary as it is the space which is imagined to both pre-exist the vehicle and to supersede its importance. After all, it is the "freeway" being surveilled and controlled while the vehicle is treated as a potential problem, as a disrupting force in that spatial system through its potential to create inefficiencies – via breakdown, accident, or collective congestion. Second, this singular point in the diagram represents nine specific groupings of technologies including though not limited to photoelectric, infrared, sonic, radar, inductive loop, magnetic,

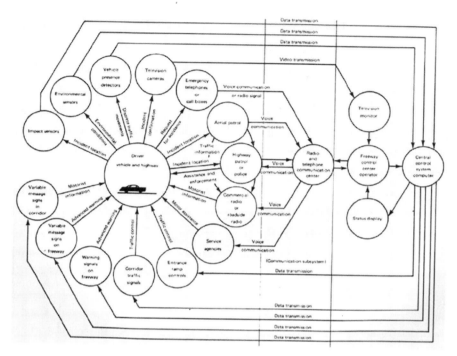

Figure 3.3   Control diagram

pneumatic, hydraulic, chemical, and smoke detectors. Thus various communicative forms are made conspicuous to the freeway monitoring systems. (Can we think of the exhaust system as a medium and CO_2 emissions as a message or sign? We must if we are to understand how these elements "speak" to each other.) The freeway is not only imagined as a track on which cars are guided and moved along, but it is turned into a surveillant recognition machine in a control network. Lastly, this recognition is just one element in what is imagined as a circulatory system akin to that in the human body in which various other systems recognize and respond to potential blockages, inadequacies of flow, the movement of contaminated elements, or even full blown rupture. The system is then what is at stake, and in many ways it is a closed system. Individual mobilities are merely an element to be managed for the relative health of the whole.

In most aspects this was still the operative logic for Automated Highway Systems (AHS) right up to 9 November 2001. Government-granted research money and the promised profits of a new market fueled extensive research, development, and public relations' hype. News stories told of a not-too distant future where highway deaths would be radically diminished by eliminating human error from the system. Furthermore, the cost benefits of developing a far more efficient automated system compared to that of building more highway lanes was said to make undeniable fiscal sense. Within the economic sector AHS was described as a boom industry worthy of capital investment and was said to be a quantum leap for efficiency and the minimization of productivity losses. On the consumer level it was sold as a means for expanding freedom and ensuring greater safety. AHS would turn the car into an efficient networked mobile office and a safe media savvy family room. These networked capabilities were not only a consumer driven "option," they were also the means by which this newly automated highway could be made to function. As in early models of highway management a command, control, and communications (C3) system was envisioned as the synaptic trigger connecting dreams with realities.

The history of the "convergence" or "synergy" of communications and automobiles goes back much further than is often imagined.[35] GPS units, satellite radio or even GM's OnStar system are merely a few of the recent combinations of communications and automotive technologies. But, as explained in regards to 1970s "art of the state," the automobile has been understood as primarily a mobile communicative actor in a larger system. Yet, the automobile wasn't exactly a networked actor, but rather a sign emitter. In the newer version of AHS/IVHS (Intelligent Vehicle Highway System) adjacent automobiles speak to each other while also speaking, more broadly, to the system. This networking capability is that which has made and will continue to make the expansion of surveillance and ultimately control possible. The system doesn't just depend on the networking capability. Rather, the networking is the system. As such, the theory for how to create a workable AHS/IVHS system has changed radically over the past 30 years. Rather than building a ground-up central control system, newer attempts have been envisioned via the networking and integration of already existent technologies which include, mobile telephony, GPS, light emitting diodes (LED), satellite radio, Black Boxes, digital video recorders, computer processors, as well as a host of internal engine, tire, weather, and performance monitors. These technologies and others have been used most extensively in private sphere fleet applications and more obviously by the military (more on this later). Integrated Communications and Navigation is the industry catch-all for such "services." "Every new wireless location tool that has appeared in the marketplace has been used in fleet tracking systems of one variety or another," claims one industry website.[36] The economic

---

35   These notions of synergy and convergence, specifically in relation to communications and automobiles, are critiqued for the simplistic notion of what comprises a technology in Hay and Packer (2004), "Crossing the Media(-n)". We argue that the automobile, GPS, or even the car radio are themselves an amalgam. The automobile in this sense is an ever changing arrangement of technologies, cultural forms, and governmental programs. It is an always in process imaginary potential that is altered through its attachment and integration with other technologies. GPS is not simply added to the automobile, it makes the automobile a new technological form.

36   Fall Creek Consultants, "Creating the Convergence", www.comm-nav/commnav. htm, visited 7 February 2005.

gains associated with employee and asset surveillance and control have pushed trucking firms and rental car companies to the forefront of such applications. The network is altered by and integrative of existent technologies and adaptable to new ones as they come on board. Of equal importance, each car is no longer imagined as a problem to be overcome (how to avoid congestion, breakdown, the accident), but rather the very means by which the system comes into being. Each automobile is a mobile intelligence collecting machine, data processing unit, and capable communicator that passes along information to other cars; all of which is then further collected, made predictive, and acted upon by a smart highway.

In control society, the stability and maintenance of a system is not necessarily what is at stake. In fact, it is precisely adaptability and mutability that signify and fuel "its" health or success. It is a constantly unfolding set of assemblages in response to changing scenarios, goals, and speeds. Yet the rhetoric used by Homeland Security's first leader, Tom Ridge, was that of systems maintenance: "The Department of Homeland Security is committed to further securing our nation's highways, mass transit systems, railways, waterways and pipelines, each of which is critical to ensuring the freedom of mobility and economic growth."[37] Through Ridge's words, rhetoric diverges from tactic, while maintaining the ironic stance on freedom of mobility. Securing here is seen as a form of stasis; in Texas they might say, "to hold down the fort." But, what happens when the state form shifts from the fortification of a position, to fortifying a means of control? How can we think of security not in terms of homeland defense, but in terms of offensive mobilizations? Can automobility become a means for an extension of control, not simply a threat to a fortified position?

If the auto-mobile individual was subject to the normalizing power of traffic safety, what animates the subject of national security? Deleuze suggests that in a society of control the individual is replaced by the dividual; a modulating subject adjustable to differing expectations for productivity, consumption, and political conduct. The vision of a control society which Deleuze describes is one that demands flexible agents, while the rhetoric of free market neo-liberal apologists equates flexibility with freedom and choice. This disconnect marks a point of seeming contradiction in discussions between the freedom-inducing potential of auto-controlled mobility and its network dependent formation. In this formulation freedom is not counterposed to power, as if power is only that which limits freedom. Rather, freedom of movement is both the problematic for control and the motor that powers its expansion, in Foucauldian terms power is always productive. It is through the mobile subject that expanded and flexible forms of productivity, consumption, and control are made possible. Yet, as the Department of Homeland Security has made so abundantly clear, mobility is also seen as a threat to the very infrastructural networks by which the mobility of US capital and military expansion/excursion are enacted. It thus should come as no surprise that the most autonomous, adaptable, and modulatable form of personal mobility,

---

37   Compare note 3.

automobile travel, is a preeminent battlefield in the war of terror domestically and abroad. It is abroad that we now turn.

In July 2003, Defense Advanced Research Projects Agency (DARPA), announced it was looking to; 1) create Combat Zones That See (CTS), and 2) recruit private industry to do the Research and Development work necessary for such creation. The Department of Defense's "high risk," "high payoff"[38] research arm wanted to "produce video understanding algorithms embedded in surveillance systems for automatically monitoring video feeds to generate for the first time, the reconnaissance, surveillance, and targeting information needed to provide close-in, continuous, always-on support for military operations in urban terrain."[39] DARPA claimed these objectives were technologically feasible[40] and, more importantly, militarily necessary where "Military Operations in Urban Terrain (MOUT) are fraught with danger".[41] What DARPA called for in essence was the full surveillance of mobility in a circumscribed zone. What would seem to be a monumental administrative and technological task was according to DARPA not simply possible, but accomplishable with fairly simple and readily available technologies, items they call COTS (Commercial Off The Shelf). CTS is an appeal to already existent private industry surveillance specialists to create an all seeing and all knowing surveillance apparatus. An apparatus that DARPA hoped would provide the exact sort of intelligence needed in the RMA-inspired (Revolution in Military Affairs) wars which are built around intelligence collection and the minimization of a loss of American lives. The specific way CTS will operate and the means by which it will do so, provides evidence for clarifying three integral logics of the terror war.

First, as numerous civil liberties watchdogs and military specialists have made clear, CTS could easily be transferred not only from a war zone to the homeland, but from urban centers to expansive spaces. As one Pentagon researcher claims, the program "seems to have more to do with domestic surveillance than a foreign battlefield and more to do with the Department of Homeland Security than the Department of Defense."[42] If we believe this sort of military intelligence regarding CTS then we must treat the war in Iraq as in part an experimental theater in which tactics for future modes of homeland governance are being invented, tested,

---

38   Defense Advanced Research Projects Agency, "Home Page," www.darpa.mil/.

39   DARPA, "Proposer Information Pamphlet (PIP): Combat Zones That See (CTS)", www.darpa.mil/ixo/solicitations/CTS/file/BAA_03-15_CTS__PIP.pdf, visited 7 February 2005.

40   "'There's almost 100 percent chance that it will work,' said Jim Lewis, who heads the Technology and Public Policy Program at the Center for Strategic and International Studies, 'because it's just connecting things that already exist.'" Noah Schachtman (2003), "Big Brother Gets a Brain", p. 2. Accessed at: www.villagevoice.com/issues/0328/schachtman.php.

41   DARPA (2003b), p. 6.

42   Schachtman (2003), p. 2.

honed, and advertised. That is, the use of such technologies and their attendant media spectacularization, make ready not only the technologies, but the American media audience which is being primed for their eventual use at home. As argued above, in this new state of war, the state of exception, all terrain has become a battlefield. The war on terror is not simply being conducted on enemies abroad, but upon citizens in the homeland. So it can be no surprise that after CTS is battle tested abroad, it very well could be implemented in the US.

Second, the operation of CTS is built upon already existent technologies and easily transferable to the US context. As with IVHS, the strength and affordability of these technologies is their networkability. Simple technologies can be made complex through their integration. CTS combines digital surveillance cameras directly linked to a processing unit, which transmit already analyzed and compressed data, thereby significantly reducing the amount of bandwidth needed if all the data captured by camera were transmitted to a central processor. Via a network of video cameras the entirety of a spatial field of governance could in theory, be completely and entirely surveilled in real time. This alone is not groundbreaking. Yet, it is partially the availability of such technologies that makes for their easy application. David Lyon (2003) makes evident that such new applications have been widespread in the US's war on terror. It is instead the recognition software under development for automobiles and movement which is new. Even this though is simply an extension of facial recognition technology. However, with facial recognition technology the "face" or identity of a conspicuous subject comes from a previously existent data base. Some process of identifying a particular individual or population as dangerous is used to create a compendium of risky identities, which facial recognition technologies comb searching for recognizable threats. With CTS however, identity is replaced by mobility; past (the accretion of one's deeds) is replaced by the future (that which might be done).

Lastly, mobility itself has now been given an identity. Not simply the individual who is mobile, but in this instance, the automobile (not necessarily the driver) is provided an "intelligence" or is made into an acting being. The activity of the being is used to predict future actions (movements and targets) of each particular vehicle. This tracking and predictive element could be viewed as an additive form of intelligence collection to be placed into the mix with other forms of dataveillance to more fully construct knowledge about the subject. Or, as I'm arguing, this mobility could be replacing the individual as the means by which dangerous identities are formulated. This production of a predictive mode of mobility assessment creates a risk identity for that mobility which in no way depends upon the individual driver. The identity of the driver is of no consequence; traditional identity categories come not to matter, only movement. As DARPA states: "Predictive modeling, plan recognition, and behavior modeling should alert operators to potential force protection risks and threat situations. Forensic information (where did a vehicle come from, how did it get here?) should be combined and contrasted with more powerful "forward-tracking" capabilities (where could the vehicle go, where is the vehicle going) to provide operators with real-time capabilities to assess potential force protection threats. MPA should assist operators in correlating and identifying links between seemingly unrelated events."[43] Recognition is dependent entirely upon pattern recognition based on movements in space and time. Through a series of ever modulating algorithms, themselves based upon the movements within the system, the imaginary future is created. In essence, the identity of a threat is the prognostication of future "force protection threats," not in terms of a terrorist, but rather "vehicles." Identities are produced through assessment algorithms of mobilities. It is not who is a threat, but what vehicular movement can be used to predict a threat. This is not to say that traditional identity categories used in profiling will disappear. But, in a state of perpetual war-mindedness, when it is unclear who may come to next threaten US hegemony, ever-modulating hybrid threat-identities are likely to be produced.

In the US Homeland, we can see some early uses of such identities as other emanations of C3 hybrids are beginning to appear in an-as-yet networked fashion. Some of these are taking place in relation to crime control, another via insurance companies' offer to decrease rates for safe drivers, at least one by Homeland Security itself, and in a related way the militarization of the driving population itself might be seen as a part of this process. One of the prime organizing forces of normalizing automobile conduct has been and continues to be the insurance industry. Two current examples will show that as they've been at the forefront of earlier safety campaigns, they are currently using risk analysis to imagine a future world in which C3 can control their own financial future and the auto-mobile future more generally. One such push by the insurance industry is the expanded use of what they call "bait cars." These are automobiles that can be fully tracked and controlled from afar by the police, which are placed in crime-susceptible areas for the sole purpose of "baiting" citizens into stealing them. As of early 2005 over 100 police departments around the US are using such bait as a means to cut down on automotive thefts. Insurance companies provide "bait cars" for police departments in many instances and the National Insurance Crime Bureau's spokesperson made clear that "everyone – me, you, even President Bush," saves money as a result of such a program. The supposed economic benefits are said to support the use of entrapment techniques and more insidiously legitimate the use of police tracking and control devices for the benefit of fighting crime. This sort of technology can already be purchased as a crime-prevention option for some cars and is part of the package of services provided by GM's OnStar system which allows for remote tracking and some elements of control, such as turning the engine on and off or locking/unlocking its doors.

Another measure in experimental use is most succinctly described by the website "Why Not", which offers up ethically challenging technology scenarios for the internet citizenry to debate and vote upon. Here is the scenario.

---

43   MPA means Motion Pattern Analysis, see DARPA (2003b), p. 13.

Create a combination of technologies (GPS, radar or sonar, automotive system monitoring, video cameras, weather devices) to monitor everything your car does and its environment. Monitor location, speed, brake application, use of turn signals, seatbelts, radio, road conditions, etc. Use this information to apportion liability in the event of an accident or as evidence in court for defense or prosecution.

Insurance companies would offer lower premiums to drivers who choose to have these technologies (collectively called "black box") installed. They would be paid for by insurance companies out of greater profits or drivers out of lower premiums. Safe drivers would choose to install the black box to be rewarded for their safe driving. Drivers with black boxes would presumably drive more safely.

Eventually, insurance companies might only insure drivers with black boxes. Then every driver would have to have one and every driver would drive more safely, saving billions in property damage, litigation and medical expenses, not to mention addressing a leading cause of death among healthy young people.[44]

The logic is that economic self-analysis, coupled with the eventual pricing out of the market of the "unsafe" (or the poor) is seen as the ultimate means by which to save lives. The insurance industry has in fact begun just such incentives based programs on a limited scale. One major concern with such technologies is their obvious potential to be integrated into a command and control scenario in which all automobiles on the road could be monitored and controlled. This neo-liberal solution to traffic safety places the onus upon the market and consumers to "freely" choose whether the system will come into being. And in case you are wondering, as of early 2007, the "yes" votes outnumber the "no" votes 4 to 1, on "whynot.net."

This "new normal" is both a historical period, hence "new," but, one that predicts its own longevity, it is now "normal." The question remains to what degree safety as the animating logic for governing automobility will indeed be replaced by concerns over national security. Regardless of the extent to which it comes to define how automobility comes to be governed and the longevity of its application, a number of key concerns need to be reiterated in terms of what the effects of such a transformation might be. Most generally safety has been used as a means for legitimating a number of restrictive measures on the mobility of subjugated populations over the past fifty-plus years in the United States. This by no means undermines the relative gains made in the survival rate of traffic accidents or the number of fatalities per 1,000,000 miles driven (the most widely used statistical measure). It does however seriously call into question the legitimacy of safety as the only means for determining policy initiatives regarding automobility. Furthermore, care has been taken to expand the debate beyond a simple binary opposition between freedom and rights vs. regulation and public good. Atomobility provides a perfect example for how freedom and regulation operate in a symbiotic relationship, not simply in opposition to each other. Of far greater importance, debate regarding safety and automobility needs

---

44   "Black Box for Cars?", *Why Not?*.

to acknowledge how different populations are adversely affected and unfairly targeted by many safety crises and subsequent crackdowns.

For instance, during the late 1960s and early 1970s hitchhiking in the US was a means for youth to organize and build community across vast spaces and in specific locales. It also aided in amassing radical protesters throughout the US during a period often glorified for just such political engagement. Lastly, it provided a form of mobility necessary, where none existed, to the everyday lives of young people making their way through a life-period generally characterized by relative economic disenfranchisement. In spite of or more likely due to these uses, police, legislators, and public interest groups joined forces to outlaw, villainize, and severely curtail hitchhiking by citing concerns for the safety of young people, young women in particular. Such an example points out the limitations of thinking about mobility purely in terms of individual rights. When particular forms of mobility are a means of constructing and maintaining community and cultural affiliation, as well as a possible means for activating political participation, the simple discourse of individual rights fails to acknowledge the complexities of culture and power. As such, it is both a violation of civil rights to unduly profile any given segment of the population for harassment, citation, and possible arrest (the three are very intricately linked as one very often leads to the other). But of equal or greater importance, this sort of profiling is an attack on the very mechanism through which these groups build, perform, and negotiate their cultural identities and their place in the larger society in which they operate. When examining the effects of post 9/11 racial profiling, we need to examine closely the economic, cultural and political effects such profiling has upon the profiled in terms of their ability to maintain the international community ties that so-often mark the space of their already liminal existence.

Before concluding a few points of clarification are in order. First, it is necessary to recognize that three very different trajectories have been discussed here. Traffic engineers have been invested in creating an AHS for decades and they've done so primarily through a systems theory approach with public safety as their guiding principal. With the advent of C3 networkability and the onset of post 9/11 US national security concerns, they have changed focus considerably toward a technologically "lighter" solution that carries more egregious social and civil liberties consequences. Two potentially overlooked aspects of networked technologies are; 1) that every actor's involvement helps spread the reach of the network, and 2) every actor's behavior is used to determine what sorts of behavior is flagged as undesirable or consider a sign of what Foucault calls "dangerousness".[45] In terms of the automobile, the first point is rather obvious. The more cars on the road equipped with a host of surveillance cameras processing data about other cars means that surveillance and dataveillance will automatically increase. The second outcome is a bit more abstract. In order for predictive modeling to work, a vast

---

45   For a fuller analysis of the relationship between algorithmic modeling, dangerousness, and Homeland Security see Packer (2007b), "Homeland Subjectivity".

amount of repeatable data patterns need to emerge. As such, "non-threatening" data patterns are as important as "threatening" data patterns – insofar as without the "non-threatening" there would be no way to measure the "threatening." Thus, regardless whether one desires to take part in what some might see as civil liberties infringements – by virtue of being networked one is not just taking advantage of the system, one is making the system work. This it seems to me is the inevitable outcome of such a future. Driving conduct will not only be surveyed and modified, but will be used to modify that of others. And this in a round-about way leads to a point regarding how we become networked. There would appear to be two models of implementation. One is linked to the rhetoric of the free market and consumer choice. Either because of the benefits of such C3 technologies or by virtue of the perceived "savings" in insurance costs, the savvy consumer will lead the way to greater safety and national security. The second model is the top-down model that invokes the dread of Big Brother, especially when one considers its military roots. Given the off the shelf and easily networked nature of all the technologies at play, it will not be particularly easy to recognize where consumer choice ends and state policing begins.

Though the history of various automobility safety crises often tells the story of oppressive restrictions and surveillance, this past may yet pale in significance to the forms of surveillance and control that seem to be arising through new communications, command, and control technologies coordinated and animated by national security concerns. The proceeding examples of just a few of the ways these technologies are currently being implemented provide insight into where the governance of highly mobile populations is headed. Particularly frightening to US drivers is the prospect that what currently passes as a counterinsurgency strategy in Iraq, could come to be used as a means for controlling the population of the "Homeland" as well. But, it is important not to miss the insight regarding how the economic logic of neo-liberal governance, coupled with risk analysis, may be equally insidious in the creation of a remote-control automobile society. Automotive design and production, the free market logic of consumer desire, and a belief in "market efficiency" all feed off the rhetoric of personal control and freedom. Yet, these purported freedoms and personal control are entirely dependent upon global positioning systems, vast networks of communications devices, an ever-widening and more integrated surveillance apparatus, and an increasingly intelligent command center. In other words, just as the rhetoric of freedom has been used in the United States, Britain, and elsewhere to justify a war in Iraq and more generally a global war against terrorism, it is also being used to produce consumer desire for new dependencies upon control mechanisms. These control mechanisms accord with what James Carey and other historians of communication long ago termed the "third communications revolution" in which knowledge production and the control and manipulation of information were to provide the next future. Though Carey wrote about the hidden perils behind such promises in 1970, his assessment seems equally as relevant today. As such, I give him the last word.

(M)odern technology invites the public to participate in a ritual of control in which fascination with technology masks the underlying factors of politics and power. But this only brings up-to-date what has always been true of the literature of the future. This literature, with its body of predictions, prescriptions, and prophecies, is a cultural strategy for moving or mobilizing or arousing people toward predefined ends by prescribed means.[46]

References

"Black Box for Cars?" (2004), *Why Not?* Available at: http://www.whynot.net/view_idea.php?id=1380, visited 2 January 2007.

Bratich, J. (2006), "Public secrecy and immanent security: A strategic analysis", *Cultural Studies* vol. 20, 4–5, pp. 493–511.

Carey, J. and J. Quirk (1970, 1989), "The History of the Future" in *Communication as Culture: Essays on Media and Society*, Unwin Press, Boston, pp. 173–200.

comm.-nav.com (2005), "Creating the Convergence" [online]. Available at: www.comm-nav/commnav.htm.

darpa.mil (2003a), "Home Page" [online]. Available at: www.darpa.mil/.

darpa.mil (2003b), "Proposer Information Pamphlet (PIP): Combat Zones That See (CTS)" [online]. Available at: www.darpa.mil/ixo/solicitations/CTS/file/BAA_03-15_CTS__PIP.pdf.

Davis, M. (2006), "The Poor Man's Airforce: A History of the Car Bomb (Part 1)" and "Return to Sender: A History of the Car Bomb (Part 2)". Available at: http://www.tomdispatch.com/index.mhtml?pid=76140, visited 27 March 2007.

Deleuze, G. (1990, 1995a), "Control and Becoming", *Negotiations: 1972–1990*, (New York: Columbia University Press), pp. 169–76.

Deleuze, G. (1990, 1995b), "Postscript on the Control Society", *Negotiations: 1972–1990*, (New York: Columbia University Press), pp. 177–82.

Design for Dreaming (1956), Producer Victor Solow, General Motors.

dhs.gov (2002), "National Strategy for Homeland Security" [online]. Available at: http://www.dhs.gov/interweb/assetlibrary/nat_strat_hls.pdf.

dhs.gov (2003), "Department of Homeland Security announces $179 million in grants to secure America's Ports" [online]. Available at: http://www.dhs.gov/dhspublic/display?content=3031.

Dodge, M. and R. Kitchin (2006), "Code, Vehicles and Governmentality: The Automatic Production of Driving Spaces", *NIRSA Working Papers Series* No 29, March 2006.

Eisler, P. (2004), "High-tech 'bait cars' catch unsuspecting auto thieves", *USA Today*, 28 November [online]. Available at: http://www.usatoday.com/tech/news/techinnovations/2004-11-28-bait-cars_x.htm.

---

46 Carey and Quirk (1970, 1989), "A History of the Future", pp. 195–6.

electronicsweekly.com (1997), "But could it do a handbrake turn?" *Electronics Weekly*, 20 August 1997 [online]. Available at: www.electronicsweekly.com/ Article8767.htm, visited 4 December 2005.

Featherstone, M. (2004), "Automobilities: An Introduction", *Theory, Culture and Society* Vol. 21, 4/5, pp. 1–24.

fhwa.dot.gov (2003), "Our Nations Highways 2000" [online]. Available at: http:// www.fhwa.dot.gov/ohim/onh00/onh2p1.htm.

fordvehicles.com (2004), "SynUS" [online]. Available at: http://www.fordvehicles. com/autoshow/concept/synus/.

Foucault, M. (1978), *History of Sexuality* (New York: Pantheon).

Foucault, M. (1982), "The Subject and Power", in P. Rabinow and H.L. Dreyfus (eds) *Michel Foucault: Beyond Structuralism and Hermeneutics* (Chicago: University of Chicago Press).

Foucault, M. (1988), "The Ethic of Care for the Self as a Practice of Freedom: An Interview with Michel Foucault on January 20, 1984", trans. J.D. Gauthier, in *The Final Foucault* (eds) J. Bernauer and D. Rasmussen (Cambridge, MA: MIT Press), pp. 1–20.

Gates, K. (2004), "Advocating alternative futures: Screening biometrics and related technologies in science-fiction cinema", Annual meeting of the International Communication Association, New Orleans, 27 May.

Gates, K. (2005), "Biometrics and Post-9/11 Technostalgia", *Social Text* Vol. 23, 2, pp. 35–54.

Gattaca (1997), Director A. Niccol.

Hardt, M. and A. Negri (2001), *Empire* (New York: Harvard University Press).

Hardt, M. and A. Negri (2004), *Multitude* (New York: Penguin Press).

Hay, J. and J. Packer (2004), "Crossing the Media(-n): Auto-mobility, the Transported Self, and Technologies of Freedom", in *MediaSpace: Scale and Culture in a Media Age* (eds) N. Couldry and A. McCarthy (New York: Routledge), pp. 209–232.

Katz, J. (2000), *How Emotions Work* (Chicago: University of Chicago Press).

Lyon, D. (2003), "Technology vs. 'Terrorism': Circuits of City Surveillance Since September 11", *International Journal of Urban and Regional Research* Vol. 27, 3, pp. 666–78.

Minority Report (2002), Director S. Spielberg.

Morgenstern, H. (2006), "Vehicle Born Improvised Explosive Device – VBIED: The Terrorist Weapon of Choice". Available at: http://www.national homelandsecurityknowledgebase.com/Research/International_Articles/ VBIED_Terrorist_Weapon_of_Choice.html, visited 27 March 2007.

Nader, R. (1965), *Unsafe at Any Speed* (New York: Grossman Publishers).

Packer, J. (2002), "Mobile Communications and Governing the Mobile: CBs and Truckers", *Communication Review* Vol. 5, 1, pp. 39–57.

Packer, J. (2003), "Disciplining Mobility", in *Foucault, Cultural Studies and Governmentality* (eds) J. Bratich, J. Packer and C. McCarthy (New York: SUNY Press), pp. 135–64.

Packer, J. (2006), "Rethinking Dependency: New Relations of Transportation and Communication", in J. Packer and C. Robertson (eds) *Thinking With James Carey: Essays on Communication Transportation History* (New York: Peter Lang), pp. 79–100.

Packer, J. (2007a), *Mobility Without Mayhem: Mass Mediating Safety and Automobility* (Durham, NC: Duke University Press).

Packer, J. (2007b), "Homeland Subjectivity: The Algorithmic Identity of Security", *Communications and Critical/Cultural Studies* Vol. 4, 2, pp. 211–15.

"Radio Driven Auto Runs Down Escort" (1925), *The New York Times*, 28 July p. 28.

Robertson, C. (2006), "A Ritual of Verification? The Nation, the State, and the US Passport", in J. Packer and C. Robertson (eds) *Thinking With James Carey: Essays on Communication Transportation History* (New York: Peter Lang) pp. 177–97.

Shachtman, J. (2003), "Big Brother Gets a Brain", *Village Voice*, 9–15 July [online]. Available at: http://www.villagevoice.com/news/0328,shachtman,45399,1. html.

Sheller, M. (Forthcoming), "Bodies, Cybercars and the Mundane Incorporation of Automated Mobilities", *Social and Cultural Geography.*

Thrift, N. (2004), "Driving in the City", *Theory, Culture and Society* Vol. 21, 4/5, pp. 41–60.

Urry, J. (2004), "The 'system' of Automobility", *Theory, Culture and Society* Vol. 21, 4/5, pp. 1–24.

Whitney, A. (1949), *Man and the Motorcar* (New Jersey Department of Law and Public Safety, New York).

Chapter 4
Stranded Mobilities, Human Disasters: The Interaction of Mobility and Social Exclusion in Crisis Circumstances

Margaret Grieco and Julian Hine

Introduction: Routine as the Mother of Crisis

Stranded mobility is a concept developed in South Africa to refer to the situation of constrained mobility and poor accessibility experienced by the black townships. This constrained mobility was the intended outcome of policies of apartheid which sought to repress the black population and privilege the white population of South Africa. South Africa, now free of these extreme formal social and political dynamics of race, now seeks to repair these conditions of stranded mobility and has entered the technical transport term 'stranded mobility' into the technical transport vocabulary. But stranded mobility is not just a feature of South Africa for it is to be found elsewhere: it is to be found on the British peripheral low income housing estates which were developed within a planning logic of low cost regular public transport to city centres and service locations but which now have highly restricted public transport as a consequence of changing economic and policy logics without any corresponding improvement in the provision of locally available facilities and services.

And stranded mobility is also to be found where extreme environmental events separate poorly resourced populations from their normal range of venues and activities. In this context, we turn to the experiences of New Orleans and Pakistan.

In the literature which has emerged in the aftermath of the New Orleans hurricane and mobility disaster, Todd Litman has done an excellent job of summarizing the vulnerability of the transit dependent residents of New Orleans:

> ...there was no effective plan to evacuate transit dependent residents. In an article titled 'Planning for the Evacuation of New Orleans' published in the *Institute of Transportation Engineers Journal* (Wolshon, 2002, p. 45) the author explains, Of the 1.4 million inhabitants in the high-threat areas, it is assumed only approximately 60 percent of the population or about 850,000 people will want, or be able, to leave the city. The reasons are numerous. Although the primary reasons are a lack of transportation (it is estimated that about 200,000 to 300,000 people do not have access to reliable personal

transportation), an unwillingness to leave homes and property (estimated to be at least 100,000 people) and a lack of outbound roadway capacity. This indicates that public officials were aware of and willing to accept significant risk to hundreds of thousands of residents unable to evacuate because they lacked transportation.

The little effort that was made to assist non-drivers was careless and incompetent. Public officials provided little guidance or assistance to people who lacked automobiles (Renne, 2005). The city established ten pickup locations where city buses were to take people to emergency shelters, but the service was unreliable. Transit dependent people were directed to the Superdome, although it had insufficient water, food, medical care and security. This lead to a medical and humanitarian crisis.

New Orleans officials were aware of the risks facing transit-dependent residents. These had been described in recent articles in *Scientific American* (Fischett, 2001) and *National Geographic* (Bourne, 2004) magazines, and from previous experience...A July 2004 simulation of a Category 3 'Hurricane Pam' on the southern Louisiana coast by the Federal Emergency Management Agency (FEMA), projected 61,290 dead and 384,257 injured or sick in a catastrophic flood of New Orleans. City and regional emergency plans describe likely problems in detail. (Louisiana, 2000; New Orleans, 2005)

Litman's summary (2006) leaves us in no doubt that the poor of New Orleans were transit dependent, that they were resident in the areas most vulnerable to flooding and that there was an official recognition of the inability and/or unwillingness of this vulnerable group to evacuate even in a declared emergency. Work using the 2000 US Census has shown the reach of poverty in New Orleans amongst the Black population, 31 percent of blacks in New Orleans were found to live in poverty.[1] In addition 21,787 black households in poverty had no car compared to 2,606 white households. That this population was primarily black has received much media attention and received explicit policy recognition of the recently re-elected New Orleans mayor to rebuild a 'chocolate city'. Why a substantial proportion of the vulnerable were thought likely to remain concerns us here: the explanation lies in the isolation of the vulnerable from access to outside resources. Not only was the whole of their physical capital located within these neighbourhoods of social and environmental vulnerability but so to was the whole of their social capital. In fact, when the disaster happened vulnerable families very often left their most physically able members behind to secure their homes and evacuated their own vulnerable members anyway that they could generating complex patterns of dispersal as a consequence of public authority action. In the aftermath of Katrina, and, more worryingly, in the age of advanced new information matching technologies, families have been split and unable to locate their full membership for some considerable time.

Later in this paper, we will turn to the role information communication technologies could have played in lessening the impact of the disaster, at this point we simply wish to indicate that routine arrangements which permitted

---

1   Poverty level is defined as those individuals living on less than $9,000 a year and families of four living on $18,000 or less.

intense urban development of the most socially vulnerable on environmentally vulnerable land created an important backdrop to the crisis. The routine social and infrastructural deprivation of a large black population was revealed by the crisis of Katrina. The lack of adequate opportunity and infrastructure which sealed this vulnerable population in on itself should have been viewed as a crisis before Katrina. The objective measurements were there to show the problem: the planning structures failed to intervene or correct the crisis potential measured under routine circumstances.

Routine neglect of the relationship between transport and social exclusion was the mother of the New Orleans crisis. If social and infrastructural relationships are dysfunctional under routine arrangements then crisis ultimately and certainly reveals the scale of the dysfunction. The evidence is clear: those without access to private means of transport died, were displaced, were impoverished and were scattered beyond their control during Katrina and its aftermath. The Louisiana Superdome and Convention Center were used a refuges of 'last resort' by those stranded in the city after the storm.

The Rapid Population Estimate Project in New Orleans has assessed the impact of Katrina in terms of residents in January 2006 after the flooding compared to population figures based on the US Census. The current population of New Orleans in October 2006 has been estimated at 187,525 although this has been disputed.

Even as New Orleans tries to develop its new evacuation plans for any future catastrophes, it has major problems. Whilst measures are being developed for keeping track of where citizens are dispersed to have been developed, arrangements as to where precisely the citizens can be evacuated to are more problematic. Louisana is a low population state and will have difficulties accommodating the displaced population within its own boundaries. It requires assistance from adjacent states and is seeking national level assistance in forming an effective plan: the immediate hinterland of New Orleans, as it is presently constituted, is not capable of absorbing crises exodus from the city. A new routine relationship between land use planning and transport is clearly needed – a relationship which extends beyond the immediate and, perhaps, even regional boundaries of a city.

Stranded Mobilities: The Public Evidence

The thrust of our discussion above is that the low income black population of New Orleans experienced stranded mobility in routine circumstances and this was exacerbated and revealed as problematic under the conditions of crisis. These low income populations had low levels of accessibility to the range of services – the high profit institutions with the ability to readily rebuild were not present in these neighbourhoods. The consequence in the present is that the impulses for restoring, renewing, renovating and reconstructing these neighbourhoods are not present: indeed, there is much concern amongst those who were displaced and those who managed to remain within the damaged areas that the reconstruction which does take place may be within a re-envisioning paradigm.[2] This re-envisioning focusing on developing a white, middle class New Orleans. The past patterns of stranded mobility and the crisis provide the platform on which such 're-envisioning' takes place: 'health and safety' concerns become the logic on which resettlement of the old black neighbourhoods by the previous black residents is held back or restricted.[3] The relocation of whole neighbourhoods intact to land above flooding level and with improved accessibilities has received little consideration.

In the case of New Orleans, urban residents experienced problems of accessibility: in the case of Pakistan, rural areas with a heavy population but poor connections to infrastructure can be viewed as experiencing stranded mobility. Remoteness can be defined as the lack of access to infrastructure which connects with facilities; it is not necessarily a register of low population densities.[4] Whereas Katrina is thought to have claimed around one thousand lives, the Pakistani earthquake claimed over eighty five thousand with over one hundred thousand injured.

The difficulties experienced in reaching the trapped, retrieving the dead and treating and transporting the injured provide an indication of the low level of facilities routinely enjoyed within the region of North West Frontier Province and Kashmir where the earthquake hit.

In Pakistan, the design of buildings (designs determined by poverty) without sufficient reinforcement for earthquake conditions accounted for many of the deaths.[5] The Engineering School of the North West Frontier Province of Pakistan estimated that 70 percent of deaths could have been avoided by improved building protocols.

After the earthquake and its devastating toll, the Aga Khan foundation has made resources available to allow redevelopment to occur within the context of earthquake preparedness technologies.[6] The funding of transport for relief operations is one aspect of this preparedness. Much redevelopment is, however, likely to take place outside of this earthquake preparedness technological framework. The poor after an earthquake are even poorer and the ability to build safer housing even weaker.

The disaster renders visible the poor routine quality of local access to healthcare within the affected region: it also reveals the levels of poverty and isolation from other social resources. Poor access in the region and the use of horse drawn transport clearly impact on the speed with which aid and resources can reach the region.

---

2   See, http://newstandardnews.net/content/index.cfm/items/2514.

3   See, http://newstandardnews.net/content/'?action=show_item&itemid=2487.

4   See, http://www.earthquakepakistan.com/road_state.pps.

5   See,   http://www.reliefweb.int/rw/RWB.NSF/db900SID/KKEE-6HWRYR?Open Document.

6   See, http://www.akdn.org/news/20051905.html.

The transport infrastructure of the affected region was very weak indeed.[7] The aid budgets needed to begin to reconstruct New Orleans and the earthquake affected region of Pakistan reveal and make public the stranded mobility experienced by these two vulnerable populations.

Prolonged Policy Failures: Extended Neglect

In both these situations of disaster we can identify patterns of extended neglect before the crisis happened. It is not that the problems of these respective settlements and settlement patterns were not understood, rather it is the case that we have developed a policy environment in which measurement routinely takes place without the necessary interventions to correct identified problems also being undertaken.

The mixture of public sector policy research and market solutions can be viewed as a backdrop to this lack of action in terms of correcting identified problems. The consequences of flooding in New Orleans and earthquakes in Pakistan were known; the occurrence of the natural disasters predictable but public policy resources for intervention and change only become available in the wake of the disasters themselves.

In both cases, even once the disasters have happened, the social and political organisation around coping with the disasters has been relatively weak. Children in Pakistan spent a winter without the most basic of transport resources – shoes; the families of New Orleans who were dispersed without adequate information tracking processes in place experienced a long and painful process in relocating one another and the speed with which the displaced have been provided for is regarded as a national disgrace within the United States.

Comprehensive after-disaster planning is not showing in either location. Within the New Orleans tragedy, trailer homes which should have been made available to residents have stood empty and sinking into the tracts of land outside the city whilst much more effort is being made to legally prosecute any persons thought to have made false claims for support. The systematic reconstruction of impacted areas on behalf and for the displaced is not visible in either location.

Virtual Neighbourhoods: Technology for Reconstruction

In the case of New Orleans, it would be possible to reconstruct virtual neighbourhoods. By virtual neighbourhoods, we mean the creation of virtual spaces in which past physical neighbours and members of neighbourhoods can interact.

---

7   See, http://web.worldbank.org/WBSITE/EXTERNAL/COUNTRIES/SOUTH ASIAEXT/0,,contentMDK:20725170~menuPK:158937~pagePK:146736~ piPK:146830~theSitePK:223547,00.html.

The use of websites, the world wide web and Internet to create interactive virtual neighbourhoods which maintained social contact by past physical neighbours in the context of restoration and planning activities is an important new social possibility. Such virtual neighbourhoods could be used to enable the social capital redevelopment necessary for a New Orleans which retains its old ethnic form and is not re-envisioned.

In line with New Orleans history in the registration of the black vote and the desegregating of schools, the electronic registration of neighbourhoods could be used to ensure that presently displaced voters continue to participate in New Orleans politics. Although, the indications are that the city is not yet ready for the return of all of its old inhabitants, electronic neighbourhoods would provide a basis for future planning which retained the social character of New Orleans prior to the disaster. An electronic Lower Ninth could participate in the reconstruction or relocation of the Lower Ninth as an entity whichever situation is the final outcome of New Orleans new planning horizons.

Virtual neighbourhoods will permit virtual travel to New Orleans for those presently located elsewhere. This simple approach does not seem to have been adopted but it is a relatively simple extension of the tracking technologies now planned for use in any future disaster. Virtual mobility may be an important element to combat physical social exclusion.

In the case of Pakistan, virtual technologies are being used to plan Aid efforts, however, these have not been brought down to the level of local participation. At the height of the disaster, cell phone use between the area and the Pakistani community of Britain were important in organizing aid. This initial use of the technology at the popular level has not been harnessed for the sustained reconstruction of the area. Setting up a high quality web site which allowed for popular international sponsorship of earthquake resistant infrastructure at the level of housing, health and local roads would be one path to change that could be taken.

Conclusion: Rethinking the Consequences of Routine Exclusion

The extent of environmental injustice under conditions of routine exclusion is laid bare by crisis. In the context of environmental crises, transport can be the key to life or death. There are very real step changes needed within the policy discussion of transport and social exclusion and such discussions are only of worth if they lead to concrete programs of action.

The importance of information communication technology in achieving the accurate charting of routine exclusion, developing protocols for maintaining order and organization within the extraordinary circumstances of crisis and disaster and for redeveloping disaster affected neighbourhoods and regions post-crisis has yet to be fully appreciated. Technology has provided a new set of tools for repair and replacement which have yet to be used to their full potential most particularly in respect of travel and transport organization.

References

Litman, T. (2006), 'Lessons From Katrina and Rita: What Major Disasters Can Teach Transportation Planners,' *Journal of Transportation Engineering* (http://scitation.aip.org/teo), Vol. 132, January 2006, pp. 11–18.

New Orleans: The Consequences of Inequities in Mobility and Accessibility: Case Study Materials

Equity discussions before Katrina: 1 – http://findarticles.com/p/articles/mi_m3724/is_2_67/ai_111269526.

Equity discussions after Katrina: 1 – http://www.democracynow.org/article.pl?sid=05/09/07/1415225.

Equity discussions after Katrina: 2 – http://www.thejournalnews.com/apps/pbcs.dll/article?AID=/20050903/NEWS02/509030322/1019/NEWS03.

Equity discussions after Katrina: 3 – http://www.ti.org/vaupdate55.html.

Equity discussions after Katrina: 4 – http://www.vtpi.org/katrina.pdf.

Chapter 5
Gendered Mobility: A Case Study of Non-Western Immigrant Women in Norway

Tanu Priya Uteng

Differentiated Gendered Mobilities

The division of activity spaces and roles within any given social fabric along gendered fault lines is a historic phenomenon. This to a certain extent could be ascribed to the different abilities assigned to the respective genders by nature itself (for example, giving birth, feeding and nurturing young lives are exclusively part of the women's responsibilities landscape). However, an inconsistency in societal development seeps in when the needs of a respective gender (which historically have been women) begin to get obfuscated, when the freedom of making choices becomes the fiefdom of men, and in most cases, the disempowered position of women comes to be taken for granted as yet another natural phenomenon. Growing up in a conservative Indian society, I was subjected to the understanding of 'fate' and 'culture' for justifying the underprivileged position of women. Though not always blatantly visible, such understandings create grave unrest that can lead to unsustainable human societies. As an outcome of realising that such faults afflict nearly every society, the western world finally picked up the issue of *unmet, unrealised and unexposed* gendered needs from the 1960s onwards, which has constituted the theme of a great deal of research undertaken in different disciplines. Further linkages in transportation research and planning have carved out a new and focused direction under the umbrella of 'gender and transport'. Attention to transport offered a way to link discussions of gender relations, transport systems, public and private spaces, accessibility, and the spatial and temporal organisation of human activity (Law 1999: 567). However, Law (1999) notes that the field is still largely defined in terms of travel behaviour and policy, as a result has stagnated to comprise a relatively limited range of themes (primarily a singular focus on women's typically shorter work trips). Could this have occurred due to a biased comprehension of mobility, of which transport is just the obvious part?

The understanding that has equally eluded transport planners and geographers for a considerable period of time is that the frame within which 'transport' is operationalised lies in the broader context of mobility. Although transport and mobility are very often used in a synonymous manner, they have distinct and different connotations. Mobility is a contextualised phenomenon whereas transport is just the revealed part of it. The concept of mobility entails a 'potential aspect', thus possessing an inherent knowledge of the potential trips that are/were *not* made due to various constraining factor(s) (social, cultural, technological, infrastructural, political and financial). From my previous analysis of mobility (Uteng 2005, 2006), and concurring with the way Law (1999: 568) envisages it, a better way to address 'gender and transport' is through reframing the issues of transport as a part of a larger project, namely, analysing the social, cultural, technological, infrastructural, political and financial geographies of mobility. This study employs an analysis of 'daily mobility', which includes issues central to gendered mobility theorisation. The concept incorporates a range of themes, including the use of (unequally distributed) resources, the experience of social interactions, and participation in a system of cultural beliefs and practices. This work offers insights into both practices and meanings of daily mobility, through a grounded study of the situation of non-western immigrant women in Norway.

A general lacunae plaguing the research agenda for 'gendered mobility' is the neglect of the relationship between immigrant women and their spatial mobilities while negotiating their daily lives. This theme, which undoubtedly has repercussions for all the other forms of mobility (social, economic, and political), has not been substantially explored.[1] Specifically, a focus on the operationalisation of gender norms among immigrants and consequently gendered mobility permits an inquiry into the theme of development, democracy, and equity. Polk (1998) states that 'Despite the complexity of reasons underlying social inequalities, if social equality is the goal and spatial equality is the means then equal access to transportation technologies can be seen as a necessity.' By enlarging the understanding of gendered mobility with reference to immigrant communities, it also becomes essential to evaluate the differential claims on genders due to cultural beliefs and norms as being equally or in some cases the most important factor dictating daily mobilities.

Further, such inquiries will also aid in a better formulation of place-making attributes as defined by the immigrant population. Tracing the shifting and contested meanings of 'good girls', 'obedient daughters', 'virtuous women', and 'respectable places' among migrants and members of their origin-site households brings into focus the ways in which the cultural struggles over gender norms influence the causes and consequences of mobility (Silvey: 145). Referring to this theme, 'moral geographies' is defined as the ways in which gendered normative ideologies operate in place making and shaping spatial mobility and spatial relations. Although clear implications of these changes for women's and men's different mobility experiences and decision-making processes have been identified in the context of gendered international immigration, a similar understanding in terms of daily mobility is still grossly under-researched. Space, whether sacred or profane, is not produced in a vacuum, but rather through a web of cross-cutting power relations that are themselves forged at multiple scales from the local to the

---

1   The analysis of the relationship between immigrant women and their mobility has been primarily conducted with reference to international immigration.

global (Massey 1994; as quoted in Secor 2002: 7). Similarly, regimes of veiling participate in the production of urban space and shape the ways in which women, both veiled and unveiled, experience mobility in the city (ibid. 8).

The next section, dealing with theoretical insights, briefly picks up the formulations of previous studies under the categories of the gendered differences in travel behaviour, the methodological flaws responsible for gender-blind transport policies, future directions that have previously been identified, and the importance of studying the non-western content of gendered mobility.

Theoretical Insights

What are the differences?

Travel behaviour research abounds with evidence illustrating the difference between women's and men's transportation demands and realities. A clear line of justifying separate treatment of women has been established owing to differentiated access and attitudes to private and public transport, differences in patterns of commuting and employment, differences in child and elder care responsibilities and finally the differences emerging from the contextualisation of traditional female roles. Although parameters like income, age, household size and structure, elder-child care responsibilities, ethnicity, employment status, degree of disability, location, class, and education can identify significant differences among the women's mobility patterns, certain key points in favour of focusing on *gendered mobility* are enumerated below:

- A number of research efforts undertaken in developed countries reported that gender-differentiated roles related to familial maintenance activities place a greater burden of time on women relative to men in fulfilling these roles. This results in significant differences in *trip purpose, trip distance, transport mode* and *other aspects of travel behaviour* (which includes *different times,* to *different locations* over *different distances*) (Erickson 1977, Andrews 1978, Hanson and Hanson 1981, Howe and O'Connor 1982, Fagnani 1983, Fox 1983, Pas 1984).
- Women *spend more time on household maintenance activities and less time on leisure* than men, with the result that women *make more frequent but short trips* (Hanson and Hanson 1981, Lu and Pas 1998, Pas 1984). Kwan (1999) restates the evidence that women have restricted space-time accessibility compared to men.
- Women's *trip scheduling and chaining also tends to be more complex* than men, especially if there are dependent children in the home, creating more spatio-temporal constraints on their activity participation (Gordon, Kumar and Richardson 1989).

- Hanson and Hanson (1981) report that women *adjust their schedules to accommodate their full-time employment* with little or no adjustments from their male partners. Women are also less able to adjust their schedules and travel patterns to accommodate alternative schedules or transportation modes (Rosenbloom and Burns 1994).
- Childcare obligations can require low-income women to *seek employment closer to home* than men (Chapple 2001).
- *Differential access* of the genders to resources, notably *time, money, skills* and *technology* lead to differences in travel and transport patterns (Law 1999, Kaufmann 2002, Turner and Grieco 1998).
- Access to automobiles appears essential for labour force participation in low-density settlements (Burns 1996, Uteng 2006). And with *restricted access to automobiles*, women's daily mobilities emerge and give rise to a differentiated labour market and personalised space-time opportunities.
- Mobility also is severely affected by labour market factors, which result in a *differentiated geography of opportunities* for men and women.
- *Security issues* affect men and women in markedly different ways. Women are more easily the targets of sexual assaults related to transport provision and delivery systems. Law's (1999: 570) literature search on the issue reveals that self-imposed precautionary measures adopted by women limit their mobility significantly.
- *The built environment*, including the organisation of land use, physical layout and design of networks (bus design, roads, paths etc.), facilities (such as bus shelters etc.) affect men and women differently (Law 1999, GLC Women's Committee 1985).

What are the methodological flaws responsible for gender-blind transport policies?

It is a well-established fact that transport sector has been gender-biased, or perhaps gender-blind is a more appropriate aphorism. This bias/blindness has been recognised as being part of a systematic methodological flaw, emerging primarily from ignoring the innate differences between the mobility patterns of men and women. Research conducted in the United Kingdom (Hamilton, Hoyle and Jenkins 1999) points out the following primary flaws plaguing the transport system:

- The scarcity of women in central positions in policy making and the planning of transport;
- The systematic failure to incorporate the voices of women users in the consultation and planning of transport systems.

Further, the growth of automobile-dependent societies points to a deliberate snubbing of the mobility needs of women. In all societies, women are primarily dependent on public transport. This has been substantially established by travel behaviour research undertaken around the world, and yet the provision of public transport is far from satisfactory in all parts of the world. And strangely enough, even developed countries are characterised by restricted and poor provision of public transport. Travel studies from the US, Scandinavia and the UK recognise that; i) automobility (car usage) is explicitly or strongly implicitly a male form of transportation, and ii) structural factors such as impediments to accessing reliable public transportation facilities and consequently low spatial mobility lead to social inequality in the disfavour of women. Despite a raft of such evidence, public transport systems continue to be built around the needs of men without adequately addressing the needs of women.

What future directions have been recognised (in past research) for further developing the agenda of gendered mobility?

The benefits of including systematic recognition and gender consultation in transport planning have long been established through research. Further linkages with social and human capital development, democracy and participation through strengthening the mobility potentials of women have also been raised both in developed and developing country scenarios. Although it is beyond the scope of this study to present an exhaustive list of the future directions recognised in the vast literature on this topic, some vital directions that have been described are (Hamilton et al. 2005: 65–72, Jauk 2005, Turner and Grieco 1998):

- Improve the provision of public transport to provide door-to-door demand-responsive services. The evolution of high-tech development management is proceeding rapidly. For it to proceed effectively, it must build in effective participation as demonstrated by the Global Knowledge 97 electronic conference hosted by the World Bank and the Canadian Government (www.globalknowledge.org). The development of electronic user groups facilitated by community communication facilities is already a possibility. Ensuring that gender is built into the electronic protocols is essential: the new social opportunity for electronic advocacy should not be wasted;
- Engage women transport users effectively in the transport policy decision-making process. Women's involvement in decision making regarding those services that affect their lives is a democratic good. At a basic level, the presence of women in the composition of user groups has to be assured. The focus on women-only user groups is derived from the evidence that when women speak within mixed groups, conversational dynamics work against them;
- Enforce more rigorous monitoring of efforts to correct gender bias;
- Devise methods to integrate transport and social policies;
- A public transport gender audit should be made part of both public sector duty and community planning strategies to enable local authorities to implement it;

- Another way advocated to address the time-poverty faced by women is through substituting real journeys by tele-journeys (Turner and Grieco 1998). But the kind of training and facilities that are required to make this a reality need to be looked into.

Why focus on the non-western experience with gendered mobilities?

Femininity, religiosity and urbanism have had a complex and invigorating relationship. They have shaped each other and have consequently evolved into different forms. Mobility is a contextual factor and the interplay of femininity, religiosity and urbanism can create very different contextualisation processes, leading to the emergence of varying mobility regimes.[2] Although migrant women are not a homogenous group, with clear differences in age, length of time in the host country, religion, ethnicity, employment, marital status and education level, there are certain commonalities between the groups. The cultural symbolism for the constrained mobility of women is one of the primary links among non-western cultures. The breaking and binding of feet of Chinese women, the enforcement of strict *purdah* on women within a variety of non-western cultures and the requirement for women to ask public authorities for permission to drive a car, all provide well known and highly transparent constraints on women's mobility.

Giddens notes that structuration maybe fundamentally a dynamic process, but it is mediated through 'social systems', the 'patterning of social relations across time-space, understood as reproduced practices' (Giddens 1984: 377). This process of mediation through 'social systems' is what sets women from ethnic immigrant minority communities apart from the native community, and thus different mobility regimes emerge.

Another aspect of structuration deals with the home/host dichotomy. This has in most cases been presented as the binary framing of immigrant women's experiences that locates gender oppression in the homeland and more independence in the host society (Andezian 1986, Hondagneu-Sotelo 1992, 1995; Lamphere 1986). As an extension of this idea, Alicea (1997: 600) notes that:

> This binary thinking mirrors earlier feminist thought that dichotomized and located women's oppression in the family and provided independence in the market place. The market/family dichotomy seems to be implicit in the home/host binary framework when scholars argue that, because it provided more paid work opportunities, the host society offered women more freedom than the home country (Lamphere 1986). Both dichotomies deny the complexity of women's experiences and cultural differences.

---

2   Sorensen (1999) uses the concept of 'mobility regimes' to highlight the historical and cultural basis of mobility. A mobility regime results from a number of factors, some of which consist of the physical shaping of cities and landscapes, the available transport systems, the relationship between mobility and *economic, social* and *cultural activities* and the meaning attributed to mobility.

Further examination by Morokvasic (1993) demonstrates the disadvantaged position that immigrant and minority women occupy in European labour markets, irrespective of if they migrated primarily for employment or to accompany their husbands. 'While migrants, both male and female, often experience a decline in their occupational status, with migration to Europe, women's position is generally worse than men's. This reflects the restructuring of female-dominated employment sectors, involved as unpaid workers in family businesses, limited employment opportunities due to their legal status as "dependants", and employers' perceptions of their skills' (Willis and Yeoh 2000: xiv). With reference to these ideas, it can be interesting to determine to what extent spatial mobility gaps create or efface labour market opportunities for immigrant women in Norway. As mobility has been linked to freedom, liberty and the ability to make choices, the analysis of its distribution among immigrant women can also provide an important postulate for the theorising of home society (equals oppression) and host society (equals freedom) dualistic arguments.

Methods

It is important that the travel behaviour research community considers techniques for collecting information from, or concerning, 'excluded' people (Clifton 2003). Though this community possesses considerable experience in data collection with an armoury of survey techniques, the issues of response rate, non-response and response bias still prevail and elude complete resolution when these techniques are applied in well-rehearsed study contexts. Lyons (2003) notes that such problems are likely to become decidedly worse when addressing the socially excluded based on the premise that people who are subject to social exclusion feel let down by society and are likely to have a low level of trust in the system. They may not be confident or competent in using the various channels of information exchange employed in mainstream surveys. Firstly, this is likely to mean that such people are not well represented or indeed represented at all in major surveys – not only are they marginalised but their behaviours become invisible to observation and understanding. Secondly, if information is to be collected from those suffering from social exclusion, then personal contact and trust between the researcher and individuals is essential. Consequently, data collection is likely to be resource intensive and may not in turn yield the numbers of respondents typically expected in surveys providing data for analysis.

In its efforts to unravel the gendered mobility bargains taking place in the non-western immigrant communities in Norway (i.e. immigrants who come from Asia, Africa, Latin America and Eastern Europe), this study faced similar constraints. Out of the 3,000 questionnaires sent out all over Norway (by post), only 215 were returned. Such a low response rate possibly accrued due to the above mentioned factors. Further, drawing on the theme of personal contact and trust, in-depth interviews were carried out with 125 non-western immigrants supported by a questionnaire format. Hence, a total of 340 respondents (174 women and 166 men) answered questions about activities, travels and attitudes related to their daily mobility. The research method used the stance of transport planning analysis through both quantitative and qualitative data sets to analyse if this particular group faces the issue of social exclusion within the realm of transportation. A gendered perspective has been put in focus through examining mobility patterns and constituent parameters such as usage of public transport, preference of mode, attitude towards a change in travel behaviour, and trends in travel behaviour. These findings are further supported by an appreciation of the structural factors linked to individual mobility (spatial structure, infrastructure, demography, technology, and cultural factors).

It is also important to highlight here that the Norwegian 'travel behaviour surveys' do not disaggregate their samples on the basis of immigration status, thus making this study the first of its kind to be undertaken in Norwegian transport research. This study should thus ideally be seen as a pilot study.

Non-Western Immigrant Women in Norway[3]

The demographic profile

The number of women with an immigrant background is increasing in Norway, both as a consequence of an immigration surplus and an excess of births. On 1 January 2001, there were 148,600 immigrant women in Norway, compared to 116,400 four years earlier. Immigrant women thereby constituted 6.5 percent of all women, up from 5.2 percent in 1997. While 84 percent had moved to Norway themselves, 16 percent were born in Norway of two foreign-born parents. A total of 99,000 women, or 66 percent of immigrant women, had a background from non-western countries comprising Asia, Africa, South America, East Europe and Turkey. While the number of immigrant women with a background from North and Central America, Oceania and Western Europe has been rather stable over the last years, there have been evident increases in the number of women from other regions.

An important feature of this group is that most immigrant women are young. Eight out of ten immigrant women are younger than 50 years of age. Amongst the non-western group, fully 91 percent of women are younger than 50. Only 11 percent of the non-western female immigrants had lived in Norway for more than 20 years, while 61 percent had short residence times (0–9 years). This figure is on the rise, given the continued influx of refugees and asylum seekers, and the increase in family reunification.

---

3   The facts and figures for this section are drawn from the following report: Byberg, I.H. (ed.) (2002), *Immigrant Women in Norway: A Summary of Findings on Demography, Education, Labour and Income* (Oslo: Central Bureau of Statistics).

Spatial profile

Over 90 percent of all immigrant women live in urban settlements. For the non-western immigrant population, the portion is even higher, amounting to 96 percent. About one-third of Norway's immigrant women live in Oslo, whereas the portion for women without immigrant background is one to ten. Oslo also sticks out because about one-fourth of the Norwegian-born immigrant women in the country also live in this area. Forty-three percent of the non-western immigrant women were residents in the capital. Oslo is followed by the urban settlements of Bergen, Bærum, Stavanger, Trondheim and Drammen (the concentration in great Oslo becomes more pronounced given the fact that Bærum and Drammen lie on the outskirts of the Oslo municipality).

Non-western immigrant women constituted 15 percent of the total female population in Oslo on 1 January 2001. Within the urban district of Oslo, there exists a clear demarcation between the living quarters of the western and non-western population. Consequently, the highest portions of non-western immigrant women are found in the eastern part of the city, comprising the districts of Gamle Oslo and Søndre Nordstrand, followed by the urban districts of Romsås, Stovner and Furuset.

Around 60 percent of the refugee women were residents in Eastern Norway, with Oslo housing the highest number of female refugees. Oslo is followed by Bergen, Trondheim, Kristiansand and Stavanger.

Family structure profile

The non-western immigrant population is characterised by a large family size. In 1997/1998, the total fertility rate was 2.4 for first generation immigrants, versus 1.8 for women without an immigrant background. For the non-western group, the total fertility rate was 2.9 children per woman. Among the immigrants, the difference between the group with the highest fertility rate (Somalia) and the group with the lowest fertility rate (Finland, Poland) is more than 3.5 children.

Education profile

More women with an immigrant background have an upper secondary education rather than a tertiary education as their highest educational attainment. This holds true for women from all world regions, with the exception of North and Central America and Oceania. In many countries, it is usually the women who never complete their education. This is also true for portions of the immigrant population in Norway. The percentage of women with an immigrant background with no completed or unknown education varies from 11 to 56 percent by country.

Labour market profile

Although a steadily increasing number of women are employed in Norway, when it comes to women with an immigrant background, especially non-western women, there are certain important hidden facts. The figures partly hide the facts that many fall outside the labour market, because they choose not to work, or because they cannot find a job, or because they neglect to register themselves as unemployed. In addition, immigrant women, much like the immigrant population at large, constitute a group that changes its composition over time, and where the young dominate (lopsided age distribution). At times something that looks like a favourable or negative change is due to a composition shift and not necessarily a new behaviour.

The immigrant population is characterised by a lower employment rate than the population at large. The biggest deviation in proportion to the population as a whole regarding employment and unemployment is found among the non-western immigrants. In 2000, the employment level among non-western men stopped 12.6 percentage points short of that for men in the whole population. Among women, these differences are even bigger. The non-western women had an employment level 17.2 percentage points below that of the Norwegian female working population. Western European immigrant women had an employment rate of 46.6 percent, a little below the level seen for women from South and Central America, who had 50.0 percent employed. Women with an African background had the lowest employment rate (33.9 percent).

Bigger employment differences exist between the sexes among non-western immigrants. The least equality, when it comes to the labour market, was found between the African and the Western European (except the Nordic) employees (a 13 percentage point difference in favour of men in both immigrant groups). The difference in labour force participation for women and men with Eastern European and Asian background was at a level in between (8.0 and 9.4 percentage points respectively). Almost no differences between the sexes regarding labour force participation were found among Nordic immigrants in the fourth quarter of 2000.

The biggest difference between the men and women's labour force participation is found among immigrants from Pakistan. In this group, the men had an employment rate 26 percentage points higher than the women, 51.5 percent versus 25.4 percent. Overall, women from Pakistan have a very low employment rate, particularly in view of the long duration of residence for most. It can also be mentioned that immigrants from Sri Lanka showed a substantial difference between the sexes of 22 percentage points regarding employment. This difference must, first and foremost, be ascribed to the exceptionally high employment rate among men, 72 percent. However, women from Sri Lanka had a high employment rate compared with other non-western groups, 49.7 percent.

Immigrant men enter the labour force more quickly than women. Non-western women need the longest time to get established in the labour market, and compared with non-western men they have a lag of three years. After seven years as residents in Norway they have reached the level the men reached after four years (about 50 percent). Western women (and men) generally settle in at a stable, high level of employment by the time they have lived for three years in the country. Non-western immigrants are over-represented in labour-intensive industries. Women with a background from non-western countries work, to a larger extent than other women, in labour intensive branches like 'Hotels and restaurants' and 'Industrial cleaning', where the portion of women with Asian background is four times as high as for women in the population as a whole. In the branch 'Industrial cleaning' we see that female African employees represent 10 percent while the corresponding representation of female employees overall is 1.1 percent.

Moreover, it can be mentioned that immigrant men seem to have an even more diverging pattern in proportion to all male employees, than immigrant women have in proportion to female employees. Non-western men are more often employed in female-dominated industries. Collectively the branches 'Hotels and restaurants', 'Health and social work' and 'Industrial cleaning' comprise over 25 percent of the occupations of male immigrant employees, and for the most part they are non-westerners.

Non-western immigrant women had a considerably higher unemployment rate than that of the population as a whole. Since the unemployment figures hide the fact that many immigrant women do not register as unemployed at all, especially for non-western women, the percentage outside the labour force is therefore actually bigger than what it first appears.

These differences are more pronounced regarding employment for refugees. Refugees have more difficulty entering the labour market than other immigrants. In all refugee groups, the rate of employment was lower for women than it was for men. While 56 percent of the female refugees from South and Central America were working, the labour force participation was down at 25 percent for African women. Eastern European and Asian women were placed in between with 42 and 34 percent of the refugees employed. The unemployment rate is markedly higher for men than for women, 9.2 and 5.6 percent respectively. At the same time, many women, both immigrants and the refugee sub-group, are never registered as unemployed at the employment offices. Fewer female refugees than male refugees are participants in labour market schemes; the portion was 5.7 percent for men and 4.4 percent for women in the fourth quarter of 2000.

Income profile

When describing the economic living conditions of non-western immigrant women, one should pay attention to the fact that many of them are part of a larger family-based economic entity, where income and expenses are shared. The household is therefore often regarded as the best analytical unit when looking at income in a context of living conditions. A consideration of household income is particularly relevant when the woman is dissociated from the labour market, something that is more often the case with non-western than western women.

In 1999 women with an immigrant background had an average total income of NOK 151,000, approximately 22 percent lower than the average income for women without immigrant background. The latter group had an average total income of NOK 193,200. Whereas women who have immigrated from Eastern Europe, Asia, Africa, South and Central America and Turkey have a total income of approximately two-thirds the average income of women without an immigrant background, women who have immigrated from other Nordic countries have a total income 6 percent higher.

Swedish women have the highest wages, Somali women the lowest. If immigrant women are compared with women without an immigrant background in the same age group, we find that women from the Nordic countries and women from the United Kingdom, Germany and the US have higher wages and salaries than women their age without an immigrant background. Among women from non-western countries, wages and salaries are the lowest, but there are differences within the group: Women from India, Poland, Sri Lanka, Bosnia-Herzegovina and the Philippines do the best. Many of these women have higher secondary or university educations, which contributes to these groups having almost as high an employment income as same-aged women without an immigrant background in some age groups. Women from Turkey, Pakistan, Yugoslavia and Somalia were the ones with the lowest income from employment.

The differences between men and women are the smallest among Finnish and Swedish immigrants, and the largest among Pakistani and Somali immigrants. Women from Pakistan and Somalia have, together with women from Turkey, Sri Lanka and Thailand, the lowest employment incomes compared with their fellow countrymen of the same age.

Women with a refugee background have a lower income than other immigrant women. Women who have come to Norway as refugees had an average total income of NOK 130,600 in 1999. For women who have come to Norway for other reasons the total income was NOK 159,500. While female refugees had a total income that was 68 percent of the average income for women without an immigrant background, the portion for other immigrant women was 83 percent. After-tax household income shows a clear division between western and non-western immigrant women. The highest household income belongs to women with a background from Western Europe and North America. The lowest belongs to women from Eastern Europe.

The Mobility of Women in Norway

The brief glimpse provided in the previous section highlights the fact that the contextual factors determining mobility regimes is substantially differentiated along gendered lines for the non-western immigrants, but quite moderate among the native Norwegian and western immigrant populations. Scandinavian nations, being among the pioneers of the women's liberation movement, have made significant achievements in providing equal opportunities to men and women. Constrained mobility can then occur out of other personal conversion factors, but definitely not due to cultural constraints on women.

However, differences still persist in certain fields. The findings presented here deal with one such difference relating to the daily mobility patterns of Norwegian men and women. These findings are drawn from the research report *National Travel Behaviour Research 2005 – Key Report*, which presents the trends that dictate the daily mobility of the Norwegian population in 2005 (Denstadli et al. 2006). The points that clearly highlight the different patterns of mobility have been culled to form the basis of comparison with the non-western immigrant population presented in the next section. The primary findings, which have a great deal of relevance to the entire gamut of discussion on the landscapes of daily mobility, are as follows:

- The car (driver or passenger) remains the predominant mode of transport for daily mobility, comprising 66 percent of the pie for all modes used. This is followed by 25 percent of the daily trips being taken by non-motorised mode (walking/cycling) and only 8 percent by public transport.
- In all age groups, men are predominantly the drivers and women the passengers. Interestingly, for rides less than 1 km, there is a shift in this pattern, where both men and women are equally likely to be the driver.
- The participation of Norwegian women in the labour market has increased from 60 percent in 1990 to 67 percent in 2000. Seventy percent of men's work journeys are taken as the driver as opposed to 60 percent of women's work journeys.
- In the 25–49 year age group, nearly 90 percent of the Norwegian population possesses a driving license. This figure holds true for both sexes.
- Women are relatively more frequent users of public transport, a fact that has remained unchanged for the last 10 years.
- Though living area and gender have been described as the factors behind the differences in transport usage, the biggest factor remains 'economic reasons'. Access to free parking and cost compensation at work were cited as the two most important factors influencing car usage.
- Automobility, the mantra of the Norwegian transportation landscape, dominates through an increasing number of and longer car trips. The Institute of Transport Economics (TØI) reported that 87 percent of the population belonged to a household with at least one car.
- The quality of public transport, which TØI measures as the distance to the bus or tram stop and departure frequency, is best for people living in Oslo. People living in Bergen, Trondheim and Stavanger have relatively good service, whereas the population living in the outskirts of the Norwegian cities, small towns and rural areas have poor service.

- As recorded in other travel behaviour research around the world, women undertake more escort trips than men. This is true for Norway as well. Sixty-seven percent of escort trips involving transportation of children were undertaken by women. And interestingly, differences between men and women are increasing. This might be explained by women's better access to a car.

The Mobility of Non-Western Immigrant Women in Norway

The findings presented here are part of an ongoing analysis. Though not exhaustive and conclusive in nature, they provide valuable insights into the realities governing the mobility of non-western immigrant women in Norway. The study of their daily mobility patterns in Norway has been divided in the following sections:

- Gendered daily mobility schedule
- Gendered access to resources
- Attitudes towards public transport
- Space as a mobility mediator

Gendered daily mobility schedule

This section analyses how and to some extent why the daily mobility patterns of the Norwegian community differs from the non-western immigrant group and further how these differences are differentiated in the immigrant community between men and women. An analysis of travel behaviour in Norway (Denstadli et al. 2006) reveals that on average, Norwegians make 3.3 trips per day of which 66 percent are taken by car (driver or passenger), 25 percent are non-motorised (walking/cycling), and only 8 percent are undertaken on public transport. The corresponding facts gathered by this study are as follows: immigrants on average make 4.1 trips per day of which 41 percent are taken by car (driver or passenger), 26 percent are non-motorised (walking/cycling), and 32 percent are on public transport.

Tables 5.1 and 5.2 present an overview of the daily mobility schedules of Norwegians compared to non-western immigrants and a comparison between non-western men and women. Non-western immigrants spend 81.6 minutes/day compared to 70 minutes/day spent by an average Norwegian on their daily mobility.

A further subdivision of the information reveals that non-western women spend 84.5 minutes/day on travel compared to 79.8 minutes/day spent by their male counterparts. These figures present a puzzling picture when analysed in light of the standard world figure of travel time budget (TTB) which is approximately 1.1 h (66 minutes) per person per day (Schafer and Victor 2000: 174). Only Norwegian travel survey data present a comparative picture of travel time budgets (70 minutes per person per day).

Table 5.1   **Comparison of daily mobility schedule between Norwegians and non-western immigrants**

	Norwegians	Non-western immigrants
Average number of trips	3.3	4.1
Minute/trip	20	19.8
Minute/day	70	81.6

Table 5.2   **Comparison of daily mobility schedule between non-western men and women**

	Non-western men	Non-western women
Average number of trips	3.9	4.3
Minute/trip	20.05	19.6
Minute/day	79.8	84.5

First proposed by Zahavi (1980, 1981), the TTB is based on the premise that on average, humans spend a fixed amount of their daily time budget on travelling. The figure of 1.1 h per person per day is remarkably stable over a wide range of income levels, geographical and cultural settings (Schafer and Victor 2000: 174). Some variations were noticed in the following cases:

- TTBs are higher in congested cities (e.g. Londoners spend 30 percent more time travelling than people in spacious Scotland (ibid. 174) and are generally highest for the largest cities (e.g. Paris);
- TTB also varies with socio-demographic groups;
- TTB per traveller is typically higher at lower incomes (Roth and Zahavi 1981).

But these variations are generally small, and the case of non-western men and women with an average TTB being 79.8 and 84.5 minutes raises several questions, some of which are:

- The immigrants under analysis belong to roughly the same income level; what then can explain the differences in the TTBs of men and women?
- Norwegian urban centres are small settlements compared to world cities, and except Oslo, the issue of traffic congestion barely arises in other parts of the country. Then why do immigrants have TTBs comparable to Paris (approximately 80 minutes)?
- Why do immigrant women have such high TTB (84.5 minutes)?

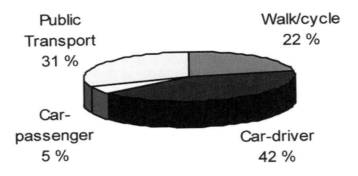

Figure 5.1   Modal distribution for immigrant men

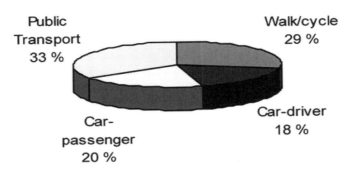

Figure 5.2   Modal distribution for immigrant women

A comprehensive and well-researched explanation to these questions is beyond the scope of this study, but it would be a worthwhile task for future research. Further, when seen in relation to the mode used (Figures 5.1 and 5.2), there is a pronounced wider spread of time-distance interplay for men as compared to women, where dependency on non-motorised modes (walking/cycling) and public transport was higher than for men. This implies that men are covering a wider geographical area for the purpose of employment and education than women, since the primary objective of trips undertaken was stated as education or work. This is also evident by a higher dependency on cars exhibited by men (47 percent) as compared to women (38 percent). Another vital aspect regarding the mode used is that a significantly lower proportion of the respondents used a combination of modes or different modes depending on seasonal variations (winter versus summer). The modal split remains practically constant irrespective of season, time of day or purpose of the trip. The availability of a car literally meant that the car would be used for all trips irrespective of the distance to be covered and the availability of public transport. Walking was selected only in the absence of any other available option and never by choice.

Gendered access to resources

Traditionally, access to resources – notably time, money, skills, technology, and safety – has been highly differentiated between the genders. With the advent of modern society and the women's liberation movement, particularly in Scandinavia, these traditional controls over resources saw a dilution, and a relatively fair distribution between the sexes developed.

However, as highlighted in the section dealing with non-western immigrant women in Norway, these traditional divisions are still overtly pronounced in the non-western community in education, access to the labour market and income between men and women. In the context of analysing differential access to resources dictating daily mobility, Law (1999: 578) notes that 'possible research questions include, for example, studies of the implications of trends in gender variations in transportation skills. As license-holding becomes more common among women, some of the gender variations in mobility now observable among older men and women may diminish, and the cultural meaning of driving as a marker of masculine power may alter.' Figures 5.3 and 5.4 reveal that compared to the 59 percent of immigrant men who have a driving license, only 42 percent of immigrant women possessed a driving license. Although these differences are

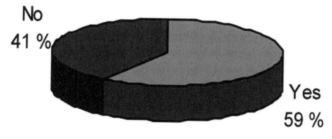

Figure 5.3   **Car-driving license – men**

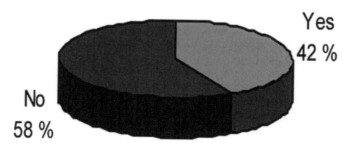

Figure 5.4   **Car-driving license – women**

high within the immigrant group, a more astonishing difference exists between the Norwegian and immigrant groups, considering that 90 percent of Norwegians (approximately the same value for both men and women) hold a driving license. The ways in which this affects one's ability to explore labour market options, learning opportunities, social networks, and leisure activities that ultimately translate into differentiated human and social capital is an extremely important piece of information to be further researched in the Norwegian context.

In an attempt to address this issue, a direct question was posed to the survey participants to see if they viewed better mobility options as an important factor in enhancing their job market position/options. In Figure 5.5, we see the distribution of responses between men and women. The values at the x-axis represent the options of (1) yes, better mobility options will make a difference in the job market, (2) maybe and (3) better mobility options will not significantly affect job market options. An interesting picture emerges out of this finding, where more men (57 percent) than women (47 percent) feel that they will have enhanced job options with better mobility potential (the percentage represents a combined figure for the option (1) yes and (2) maybe). Concurrently, more women (53 percent) than men (42 percent) saw no direct connection between enhanced mobility and labour market position. This raises the important finding that immigrant men are also being adversely affected by constrained mobility. The labour market position for both men and women is compromised by a continued dependency on automobiles and a lack of better public transport connectivity and reliability in Norway. The sample not surprisingly showed a clear divide between people who had access

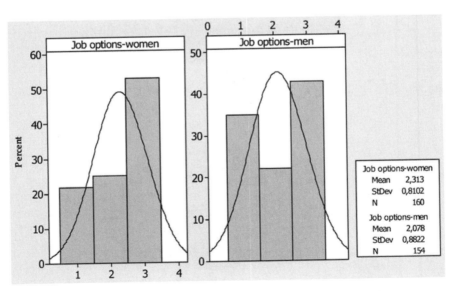

Figure 5.5   Link between enhanced mobility and better job options

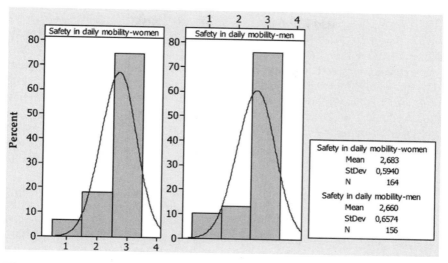

Figure 5.6   Safety concerns in daily mobility

Note: The values at x-axis represents the options of (1) Yes, I feel unsafe in my daily mobility, (2) Sometimes and in some situations and (3) No, I never/rarely feel unsafe in my daily mobility.

to a car and those who did not. The new immigrants and refugees can be singled out in this divide with poor ability to purchase a car and, more importantly, a driving license (the cost of procuring a driving license in Norway ranges from USD 3,000–4,500!). This is corroborated by findings from the Norwegian travel survey (Denstadli et al. 2006: 15), which found that 48 percent of the Norwegian population with a gross annual income lower than 50,000 NOK had access to a car, but no driving license.

Another important issue affecting the mobility patterns of women is safety. This study reveals a positive picture of Norwegian settlements (see Figure 5.6), where nearly 75 percent of the respondents (75 percent women and 76 percent men) felt safe in their daily mobility. Only 15 percent of the respondents (same figure for both men and women) felt that travelling in the late evening and at night involved some risk.

Concern for safety was most pronounced among the public transport users, who experienced feeling unsafe both on the way to and from the bus stop, at the bus stop, and in the vehicle itself. Interestingly, these responses came only from the Oslo area. Although Norway is an extremely safe society, criminal activities have been on rise in the past decade, primarily in the Oslo area. In the next section we analyse how Norwegian public transport continues to be an inadequate resource in providing a viable alternative.

Attitudes towards public transport

Although women use public transport more frequently than men in Norway, this study reveals that both immigrant men and women use public transport more than the average Norwegian population. Among men, the primary users of public transport are those without access to a car. Among women, this is divided among those without an access to a car and those who undertake trips related to shopping and social activities when the men are away at work and consequently unavailable for driving them to their various trips. These trips are mostly undertaken in the off-peak hours, and thus the issue of poor public transport availability during off-peak hours poses a problem for this group.

A direct question was put to the respondents concerning the sufficiency of public transport for their daily mobility. A surprisingly high percentage of the respondents, 69 percent of the immigrant men and 59 percent of the immigrant women, replied that they suffered from insufficient public transport to meet their daily mobility needs. A further analysis of the system's different aspects was conducted to get a better picture of the problems affecting public transport users. Respondents were asked to respond to questions on a scale from 1 to 6, where 1 and 6 represented the two poles of the continuum of extreme dissatisfaction to extreme satisfaction with the public transport system. The following attributes were analysed:

- Frequency during peak hours/evening and weekends/off peak hours (see Figures 5.7, 5.8 and 5.9),
- Ticket prices (see Figure 5.10),
- Punctuality (see Figure 5.11),
- Ease of travelling with children (see Figure 5.12),
- Time taken to reach destination (see Figure 5.13), and
- Overall view of the system (see Figure 5.14).

The satisfaction level for immigrant women was not very different from immigrant men and given the fact that both groups are equally dependent on the public transport system in Norway, the analysis was based on the reactions of the entire group. As is evident from the figures, the public transport provision leaves much to be desired in order to continue as a preferred option. The respondents identified ticket prices, frequency of service during evenings, weekends, holidays, and punctuality as the biggest problems afflicting this system. The personal interviews revealed that immigrant women in Oslo did not view their daily mobility as being compromised due to the deficiencies of the system. This was very different from the views expressed in other parts of the country, where the relatively poor public transport system afflicts the mobility of women adversely. In cases where the household has a car, the women become primarily dependent on their husbands for carrying out their daily chores. In the absence of a car, it is difficult to shop with young children, and in most cases the women had to depend on their husbands to accompanying them on shopping trips as well. The problem worsens in case of

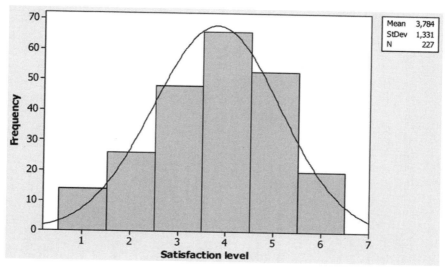

Figure 5.7   Public transport frequency during peak hours

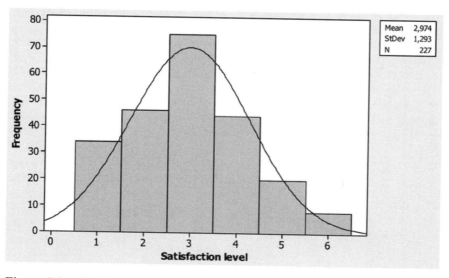

Figure 5.8   Public transport frequency during evening and weekends

single mothers where the lack of social networks and the deficient public transport system create a vicious circle of time and resource poverty.

Further, an important common theme linking Muslim immigrant women who follow the veiling traditions is their preference to be a housewife or to hold part-time

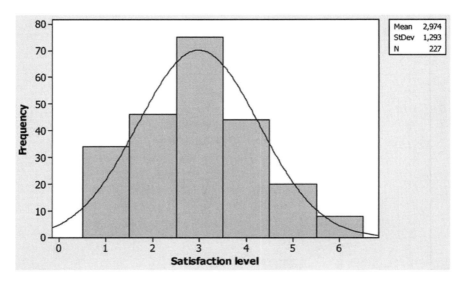

Figure 5.9   Public transport frequency during off peak hours

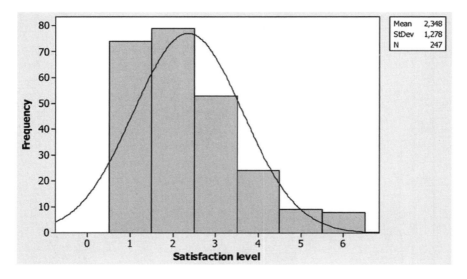

Figure 5.10   Prices of the tickets

jobs, and not even considering holding a driving license. Among all the different Muslim immigrant groups in Norway, this remains a common situation. Since the majority of existing immigrants, refugees and asylum seekers are Muslim, it is imperative that ways and means of improving the participation of these women

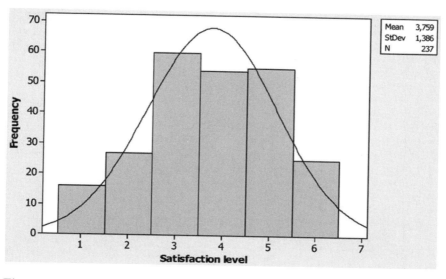

Figure 5.11   Punctuality

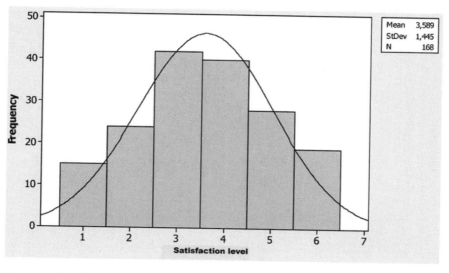

Figure 5.12   Ease of travelling with children

are developed in order to further avoid social exclusion. Refining mobility options for women who opt not to drive, to remain a housewife with a relatively large family poses complicated tasks, but this is definitely worth looking into if a more cohesive society is wanted.

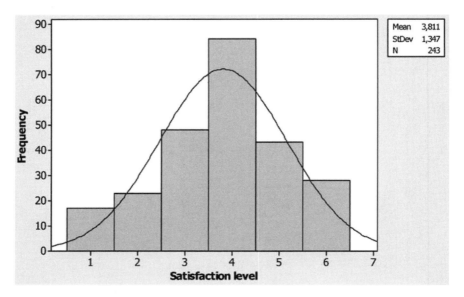

Figure 5.13   Time taken to reach the destination by public transport

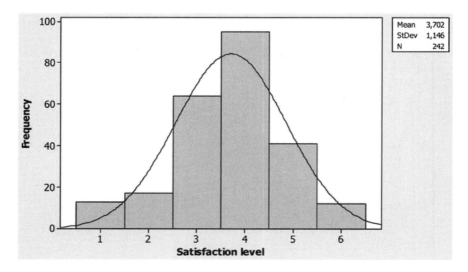

Figure 5.14   Overall view of public transport

Space as a mobility mediator

The ways in which 'space' acts as a mobility mediator is an extensive topic in itself, and is beyond the scope of this paper to cover in depth. However, it is imperative to touch upon the issue while discussing the mobility of immigrant women. An important common feature shared by Muslim immigrant women is their corporal representation (veiling tradition) as a part of their cultural domain. This infuses a space frequented by veiled women with themes that accentuate or diminish mobility. Spaces then come to be linked with identity, belongingness, culture, comfort, and convenience. Oslo provides a classic example of how the veiling tradition carves out spaces for negotiating mobility.

In Oslo, immigrants from non-western countries have clustered in and around the eastern area of the city. This area is situated on the east bank of the river Akerselva, where factories were built during early 1900s, and was primarily inhabited by factory workers and family with low incomes, many of whom were originally migrants from other provinces who had come to the capital in search of employment. Continuing this pattern, the east side of Oslo accommodated many first-generation foreign labour immigrants, primarily Pakistanis. Oslo is now nomenclatured the 'divided city' with clearly delineated wards dominated by non-western immigrants. The heart of the *Oslo østkant* (Oslo east-end) has often been considered a space of exclusion where marginalised or 'threshold people' live (Naguib 2002). But a closer look at this space reveals that this is the area where the commercial entrepreneurship of non-western immigrants is also providing opportunities for immigrant women (including those following the veiling tradition) to participate in the labour market. But then the other side of the story is that even after several years of stay in Norway, immigrant mothers have been reported to remain cut off from their children's schooling, showing little interest in being involved and not attending parent's meetings on the pretext of not knowing the language.

This highly ethnic space then creates a domain of belonging and of being different, reflecting the cultural patterns of non-western immigrants, including language, common codes of behaviour, value systems, social networks, group activities, and shared interests. To a certain degree it is possible to argue that these spaces decrease the incentive for immigrant women to interact with the Norwegian community. Barth (1982) argued for the primacy of boundaries over cultural content in multicultural societies. He explained that ethnic distinction involves mobility (social mobility in this case), by which processes of inclusion and exclusion are formed. When seen in light of spaces, I contend that these ethnic enclaves aid in reproducing ethnic distinction, which leads to both exclusion and inclusion of immigrant women in particular. These spaces both give them the opportunity to participate in their traditional culture, but shelter them from learning Norwegian, and participating in Norwegian culture and all that it entails. A space that promotes the interaction of immigrant and native women in Oslo still does not exist. Mobility in this context then becomes highly internalised, and takes place within the confines of the ethnic patterns and codes. Interpreted in terms of integration, this space can be said to be acting against integration, leading to further divisions and dissociations between the immigrant and native communities.

Conclusion

Norway, with the highest GDP per capita in the world and governance under a welfare regime, provides good examples of certain processes that can lead to differentiated mobilities. This paradoxical mobility-poverty in middle of abundance, as is evident in the case of non-western immigrants and refugees, raises an entire gamut of questions surrounding the theme of mobility. We see this process of differentiation at various levels, having significant effects on the mobility regimes of immigrant women. A very different profile at the levels of family structure, education, participation in the labour market, access to income, coupled with systematic failure in updating public transport options leads to a deficient mastering of space-time for this group. The entire idea of home/host dichotomy, which states that the home country equals oppression and the host country equals freedom for immigrant women has also been challenged by this study.

Rescher (1993: 5), while highlighting *pluralism and the pluralistic context of any society*, notes that the primary issue is of dissensus (as opposed to consensus) management. Rather than hinging on consensus building, our divided world of belief, action and value has to be mediated through negotiations and trade-offs serving the interest of all dissenting factions of the society. He further notes that (ibid. 7) that wise leaders, after all, do not ask their advisers for a collective opinion from which all elements of dissent have been eliminated: they realize that the interests of understanding are best served by a nuanced picture that portrays the state of existing information and speculation – and ignorance! – in its fully diverse complexity.[4] This study highlights a similar situation for Norwegian society, where a continued focus on auto-mobility creates processes and groups of exclusion, affecting daily mobility on a basic level, along with access to work, opportunities to undertake social activities and quality of life at the higher levels. Within the context of mobility, pluralism is expressed through free versus limited access to various opportunities, which calls for dissensus management in the Norwegian transportation arena.

Furthermore, the notion of 'ethnic spaces' inculcates a set of binary oppositions leading to both inclusion and exclusion of immigrant women. Inclusion through being neighbours to people from similar ethnic backgrounds, with similar culture, code of conduct etc. and exclusion through being alienated from mainstream Norwegian society, language, culture, politics etc. The bottom-line question then is: how do we visualise our future as a multicultural society? What possible interventions can help in mobilising both immigrant men and women to becoming active members of their host society? And finally the focus should be broadened to further explore the root causes of social exclusion, rather than an exclusive focus on the symptoms.

---

4   For further discussion, Rescher (1993: 7) suggests the deliberations in Irving L. Janis, *Victims of Groupthink* (Boston, 1978).

References

Alicea, M. (1997), 'A chambered nautilus: The contradictory nature of Puerto Rican women's role in the social construction of a transnational community,' *Gender and Society* 11(5) 597–626.

Andezian, S. (1986), 'Women's roles in organising symbolic life: Algerian female immigrants in France,' in *International Migration: The Female Experience* (eds) R.J. Simon and C.B. Brettell (Totowa, NJ: Rowman and Allanheld).

Andrews, H.F. (1978), 'Journey to work considerations in labour force participation of married women,' *Regional Studies* 12, 11–20.

Barth, F. (1982), *Ethnic Groups and Boundaries: The Social Organisation of Culture Difference* (Oslo: University paper (*Unversitetsforlaget*)).

Burns, E.K. (1996), 'Women's travel to inner city employment,' paper presented at *Women's Travel Issues Second National Conference*, Baltimore, http://www.fhwa.dot.gov/ohim/womens/wtipage.htm.

Byberg, I.H. (ed.) (2002), *Immigrant Women in Norway: A Summary of Findings on Demography, Education, Labour and Income* (Oslo: Central Bureau of Statistics).

Chapple, K. (2001), 'Time to work: Job search strategies and commute time for women on welfare in San Francisco,' *Journal of Urban Affairs* 23, 155–73.

Clifton, K.J. (2003), 'Examining travel choices of low-income populations: Issues, methods, and new approaches', paper presented at the *10th International Conference on Travel Behaviour Research*, 10–15 August, Lucerne, Switzerland.

Denstadli, J.M., Engebretsen, Ø., Hjorthol, R. and Vågane, L. (2006), *Den nasjonale reisevaneundersøkelsen 2005 – nøkkelrapport (The National Travel Behaviour Research 2005 – keyreport)* (Institute of Transport Economics, Oslo).

Erickson, J. (1977), 'An analysis of journey-to-work for women', *Social Problems* 24, 428–35.

Fagnani, J. (1983), 'Women's commuting patterns in the Paris region', *Tijdschrift voor Economische en Sociale Geografie* 74, 12–24.

Fox, M.B. (1983), 'Working women and travel: The access of women to work and community facilities', *Journal of the American Planning Association* 49, 156–70.

Giddens, A. (1984), *The Constitution of Society: Outline of the Theory of Structuration* (Berkeley: University of California Press).

GLC Women's Committee (1985), *Women on the Move: GLC Survey on Women and Transport* (London: GLC).

Gordon, P., Kumar, A. and Richardson, H. (1989), 'Gender differences in metropolitan travel behaviour', *Regional Studies* 23, 499–510.

Hamilton, K., Hoyle, R. and Jenkins, L. (1999), *The Public Transport Gender Audit: The Research Report* (London: University of East London).

Hamilton, K., Jenkins, L., Hodgson, F. and Turner, J. (2005), 'Promoting gender equality in transport', *Working Paper Series no. 34* (Equal Opportunities Commission, London).

Hanson, S. and Hanson, P. (1981), 'The impact of married women's employment on house-hold travel patterns: A Swedish example', *Transportation* 10, 165–83.

Hondagneu-Sotelo, P. (1992), 'Overcoming patriarchal constraints: The reconstruction of gender relations among Mexican immigrant men and women', *Gender and Society* 6, 393–415.

Howe, A. and O'Connor, K. (1982), 'Travel to work and labour force participation of men and women in an Australian metropolitan area', *Professional Geographer* 34, 50–64.

Jauk, D. (2005), 'Gender sensitive governance in the field of transport', paper presented in the conference stream of *Accessibility, Mobility and Connectivity: Changing frontiers of Daily Routines, at the 37th World Congress of the International Institute of Sociology*, 5–7 July, Stockholm, Sweden.

Kaufmann, V. (2002), *Re-thinking Mobility* (Aldershot: Ashgate).

Kwan, M. (1999), 'Gender and individual access to urban opportunities: A study using space-time measures', *Professional Geographer* 51(2) 210–27.

Lamphere, L. (1986), 'Working mothers and family strategies: Portuguese and Colombian women in a New England community', in *International Migration: The Female Experience* (eds) R.J. Simon and C.B. Brettell (Totowa, NJ: Rowman and Allanheld).

Law, R. (1999), 'Beyond "women and transport": Towards new geographies of gender and daily mobility', *Progress in Human Geography* 23(4) 567–88.

Lu, X. and Pas, E. (1998), 'Socio-demographics, activity participation and travel behaviour', *Transportation Research Part A* 33, 1–18.

Lyons, G. (2003), *Transport and Society, Inaugural Lecture* (Unit for Transport and Society, Bristol). See, www.transport.uwe.ac.uk/LYONS-Inaugural.pdf.

Massey, D. (1993), 'Power-geometry and a progressive sense of place', in *Mapping the Futures: Local Cultures, Global Change* (eds) J. Bird, B. Curtis, T. Putnam, G. Robertson and L. Tickner (London: Routledge) pp. 59–69.

Massey, D. (1994), *Space, Place and Gender* (Minneapolis: University of Minnesota Press).

Morokvasic, M. (1993), '"In and Out" of the Labour Market: Immigrant and Minority Women in Europe', *New Community* 19(3) 459–83.

Naguib, S. (2002), 'The northern way: Muslim communities in Norway', in *Muslim Minorities in the West, Visible and Invisible* (eds) Y.Y. Haddad and J.I. Smith (Oxford: Rowman and Littlefield) pp. 161–74.

Pas, E. (1984), 'The effect of selected socio-demographic characteristics on daily travel behaviour', *Environment and Planning A* 16, 571–81.

Polk, M. (1998), 'Gendered Mobility – a study of women's and men's relations to automobility in Sweden', *Humanekologiska Skrifter* 17 (Goteborg: Goteborg University).

Rescher, N. (1993), *Pluralism* (Oxford: Clarendon Press).

Rosenbloom, S. and Burns, E. (1994), 'Why working women drive alone: Implications for travel reduction programs', *Transportation Research Record* 1459, 39–45.

Roth, G.J. and Zahavi, Y. (1981), 'Travel time budgets in developing countries', *Transportation Research A* 15(1) 87–95.

Schafer, A. and Victor, D.G. (2000), 'The future mobility of the world population', *Transportation Research A* 34(3) 171–205.

Secor, A.J. (2002), 'The veil and urban space in Istanbul: Women's dress, mobility and Islamic knowledge', *Gender, Place and Culture* 9(1) 5–22.

Silvey, R.M. (2000), 'Stigmatized spaces: Gender and mobility under crisis in South Sulawesi, Indonesia', *Gender, Place and Culture* 7(2) 143–61.

Turner. J. and Grieco, M. (1998), 'Gender and time poverty: The neglected social policy implications of gendered time, transport and travel', paper presented at the *International Conference on Time Use*, University of Luneberg, Germany.

Uteng, T.P. (2006a), 'Mobility: Discourses from the non-western immigrant groups in Norway', *Mobilities* Vol. 1, No. 3, pp. 435–62.

Uteng, T.P. (2006b), 'Sustainable mobility: An implicit function of equity', paper presented at the *12th Annual International Sustainable Development Research Conference*, 6–8 April 2006 (Hong Kong: The Centre of Urban Planning and Environmental Management).

Willis, K. and Yeoh, B. (eds) (2000), *Gender and Migration*, International Studies in Migration Series (Cheltenham: Edward Elgar).

Zahavi, Y. (1981), *The UMOT – Urban Interactions* DOT-RSPA-DPB 10/7 (Washington D.C.: US Department of Transportation).

Zahavi, Y. and Talvitie, A. (1980), 'Regularities in travel time and money expenditures', *Transportation Research Record* 750, 13–19.

Chapter 6

Mobility as Stress Regulation: A Challenge to Dialogue in Planning?

Tore Sager

Introduction

There is a tension between the proximity required by dialogical planning and decision making and the physical distance regulation that is facilitated by great personal mobility. The tension arises from the stress experienced in the interaction, discussion and negotiation with people who are egotistical or who act on the basis of different interests or value sets on the one hand, and the use of mobility and distance adjustment as means of stress regulation on the other.

A number of ongoing trends make this tension increasingly important. Firstly, mobility is steadily rising. The average Briton travelled about five miles a day in 1950, but now travels about 30 miles (Adams 2005: 124). Schafer and Victor (2000) project that by 2050 the average world citizen will travel about the same distance as the average West European travelled in 1990. Secondly, deliberative democracy has been widely discussed recently (Bohman and Rehg 1997, Elster 1998), with the ideologically related communicative planning in the mainstream of current planning theory (Taylor 1998: 122–5). Deliberative democracy is a procedural model of politics that favours universal and unconstrained deliberation about issues of public concern, rather than the mere collection of independent opinions through voting (Weinshall 2003: 24). Thirdly, migration of millions of people across national borders is a core element of the globalisation process. Planners and decision makers are more than ever directing their attention towards the concomitant development of pluralistic and multicultural cities (Friedmann 2002, Sandercock 1998, 2003). This development augments the need for participatory planning processes, which have been mandatory in many liberal countries for some time. However, the deep differences between the values of population segments in modern multicultural cities might make involvement in dialogical planning processes more trying (Bollens 2004, Watson 2006). The following sections address three questions:

- Might stressful living conditions in local communities stimulate travel?
- Might higher mobility and more travel affect the feasibility of dialogue and discourse ethics?

- What are the implications of the answers to the previous two questions for local participatory planning?

In attempting to answer these questions, this essay contributes both to planning theory and transport research. It connects two types of phenomena; the one is dialogical processes in public planning and decision making, and the other is the increase in mobility, which increases the flows of people, goods and information. Furthermore, the essay brings together the academic fields that study these phenomena, namely, communicative planning theory and the 'new mobilities' approach to sociology. These approaches are considered important enough by prominent scholars to be launched as new paradigms in public planning and sociology, respectively (Innes 1995, Sheller and Urry 2006, Willson 2001). Very few studies discuss the effects of great personal mobility on the feasibility of planning in general and communicative planning in particular (but see Sager 2005). Likewise, transport studies do not acknowledge the stress regulating function of making short trips and longer journeys. This notable lacuna in transport research is discussed in the next section.

References to different geographical levels and various types of travel are scattered throughout the essay. The emphasis is, however, on the level of local territorial community and the trips that regulate the distance to such places.[1] Planning and dialogical processes often relate to the local level, and the entire argument in the coming sections could have been put forward without reference to entities other than local communities, municipalities, and cities (with the exception of the presentation of the psychological research on physical distance as a means for counteracting stress). The occasional references to globalisation, migration, and nomads in the following are used as exemplifications to link with topical themes.

The line of reasoning is structured in five ensuing sections. The first draws attention to the fact that travelling can be motivated by tensions at the origin; for instance, conflicts of values or interests in a local community. Tension creates stress, and the second section presents literature suggesting that altering physical distance is a well used strategy for stress regulation. To the degree that this contributes to very high mobility, dialogical planning might be unfavourably

---

1   The following definition of 'community' is used in this essay:

Community is a combination of two elements: A) A web of affect-laden relationships among a group of individuals, relationships that often crisscross and reinforce one another (rather than merely one-on-one or chainlike individual relationships); B) A measure of commitment to a set of shared values, norms, and meanings, and a shared history and identity – in short, to a particular culture. (Etzioni 2000: 188)

It is considered problematic that relationships in many territorial communities are not sufficiently laden with positive affect and do not reflect sufficient commitment. The community might then cease to be a territorial 'social entity that has the elements necessary (bonds and shared values) to contain conflict within sustainable boundaries' (ibid.).

affected, as explained in the third section. This leads to a dilemma explained in the fourth section, as consensus building dialogue is particularly called for in troubled communities likely to convert mobility into much tension-related travelling. The dilemma is that real dialogue and very high mobility might be difficult to realise simultaneously. The final section sums up and offers some concluding remarks.

Trips Motivated by Escape Rather than Attraction

This section presents the notion of origin-motivated trips, which constitutes part of the rationale for the strategy of using physical distance regulation as stress abatement. Even transport researchers objecting to the traditional view of transport as a derived demand ignore the psychological effects of travel that creates physical and thus emotional distance (Anable and Gatersleben 2005, Mokhtarian and Salomon 2001, Steg 2005). However, Ory and Mokhtarian (2005) mention 'escape' as an attractive feature of travelling. Its appeal comes from temporarily escaping obligations, routines, distress, or tensions at home or at work (ibid. 99). They found some empirical evidence for this motive for travel in their model of 'travel liking' (ibid. 121). Escape from stress contributes to the sense of freedom, which is often associated with auto-mobility (Sager 2006).

Schwanen and Mokhtarian (2005) exploit the idea of origin-motivated travel when studying the extent to which a lack of congruence between physical neighbourhood structure and preferences regarding land use near the location of one's home affects distances travelled overall and the mode. It is a task for future research to extend 'residential neighbourhood type dissonance' from a mismatch of preferences and reality related to land use characteristics to a mismatch related to social characteristics.

In principle, motives for travelling can spring from characteristics and phenomena related to the origin, the journey itself, the destination, or any mixture of the three. The sources of origin-motives (O-motives), underway-motives (U-motives), and destination-motives (D-motives) have not received even-handed treatment in transport research. Demand models depict travel as involving a disutility to be endured for the sake of arriving at a desired destination, and with the rational 'economic man' behaviour assumed in the models, this disutility should be minimised (Ortúzar and Willumsen 2001). The social benefits of mobility can be undervalued by disregarding the relief it provides from conditions at the origin, as well as ignoring the reasons why travelling can be a pleasing activity in itself. Although the local level is the focus here, it warrants mentioning that even at the international level several massive flows of people are O-motivated, such as those made up of refugees and migrating workers.

Relative prices are the pivotal independent variables in economic demand models. Analogous to this, the relative attractiveness of origin and destination determines whether or not a trip will be taken. Imagine that prospective income is the decisive variable, and that the destination offers higher income than the origin. It is quite conventional to maintain that the high income at the destination causes the journey, or that the trip is due to the low income at the origin. A biased accentuation of either O-push or D-pull seems equally fruitless for understanding travel behaviour.

The present exposition centres on trips triggered by O-motives. It might, however, be problematic to determine the relative influence of each type of motive on specific trips. The standard approach of ignoring U-motives and O-motives probably reflects the transport planning profession's forecasting ambitions. The prediction purpose gives priority to quantifiable activities and to travel resistance measured in physical or economic terms. Surely, trip generation models take origin characteristics into account, but they concentrate on easily countable variables, such as the number of inhabitants in each age cohort, their income and car ownership, and residential density or the number of housing units of different types (Ortúzar and Willumsen 2001: Ch. 4). Such O-variables do not directly motivate travel; they only indicate living conditions that might motivate trips. Standard variables might, for example, hint at the occurrence of cramped apartments with small children and thus suggest the need for parents to put some distance between themselves and domestic tensions now and then. Travel studies are not designed with such trip-generating stress regulation in mind, however. For each group in an origin zone, the emphasis is on modelling the travel consequences of its implicit preferences for activities in the various destination zones.

In the economic approach, benefits at the destination have to exceed the costs of the journey for any trip actually taken. A similar net calculation in terms of stress is pertinent in the psychological approach. The advantage of stress abatement related to origin must outweigh any additional stress due to the travelling itself. It is well known that travelling can cause stress, both when driving a private car and using public transport (Cox et al. 2006, Evans et al. 2002, Gulian et al. 1990, Koslowsky 1997, Koslowsky and Krausz 1993, Wener et al. 2003). This ambiguous association between stress and travelling does not undermine the main argument that high mobility paves the way for stress-regulating trips motivated by origin-based tensions.

The idea of journeys being engendered by O-motives is a transference to transport research of certain aspects of Charles Lindblom's 'disjointed incrementalism' model of planning and policy-making (Lindblom 1959). In that model, 'analysis and policy-making are remedial; they move *away* from ills rather than *toward* known objectives' (Hirschman and Lindblom 1962: 216). The transport analogy sees the origin as housing the ills, while travelling is the means, and destinations the ends. Remedial travel is O-motivated and aims to adjust the distance to the origin.[2] Incrementalism rejects the idea of given ends. Instead, objectives are

---

2   The means-ends scheme is hardly relevant to all types of travelling. When the movement is a core characteristic of the traveller's lifestyle, the scheme collapses. For nomadic people, the 'destinations' might be means for further travelling, just as much as travelling is a means to reach the 'destinations' (Cole 1975, Cresswell 2001, Johnson 1969).

indefinitely explored and reconsidered (ibid. 215). For O-motivated travel, this means that the destination is rather indeterminate and less important than the physical distance from the origin. Hirschman and Lindblom hold that, 'instead of comparing alternative means or policies in the light of postulated ends or objectives, alternative ends or objectives are also compared in the light of postulated means or policies and their consequences' (ibid.). This means that, in the present approach, journeys are not always the consequence of desired destinations; rather, it is the other way around. Possible destinations are compared in light of the trips called for, considering the distance they would remove the traveller from the origin. This is reinforced when ends and means are chosen simultaneously (ibid.) – meaning, here, that trip lengths do not follow from given destinations. In the incremental model, for any actor, 'analysis and policy-making are serial or successive; that is, problems are not "solved" but are repeatedly attacked' (ibid.). Analogically, O-motivated travel does not resolve the tension at the origin. But at least it gives the traveller some respite and creates an opportunity for contemplating what can be done about the conditions at the origin causing strain.[3]

The above application of disjointed incrementalism is static in the sense that there is no time dimension affecting the reasoning. However, an important difference between mainstream transport research and the 'new mobilities' paradigm is that the latter treats the traveller's means-ends scheme as dynamic (Sheller and Urry 2006). That is, in the sociology of mobility, it is of interest how destinations are transformed into new origins, and how space is turned into place (Taylor 1999), creating tensions in the process of establishing home, identity, or a sense of belonging. Moreover, how does mobility change preferences endogenously to create new destinations, and how do former origins cease to influence new movement? That is, how does path dependence influence trip generation? Can nomadism be seen as the borderline case of travelling between places that all have the character of 'origins', here calling forth associations with the – however transient – home base from which most trips start? Might the marginalisation of some nomadic cultures follow from the rapid transformation of every new destination to an origin with concomitant tensions maintaining O-motives and kindling the urge to move on (Brearley 2001)?

The approach of mainstream transport research is to start out from one basic concept, that is, 'transport'. The type of trip is then specified according to transport mode, trip purpose, what is transported, and so forth. 'Transport' covers all activity in public networks for moving people or goods, for which an origin and destination can be meaningfully identified. When O-motivated travel aiming for

---

3   Talvitie (1997) challenges the economic theory that underlies transport models by introducing psychoanalytic understandings of travel behaviour. This allows the possibility of directing attention to the escape motive, but Talvitie does not pursue this line of research. In a recent article, Talvitie (2006) suggests the reintroduction of incrementalism as a model for transport planning. He calls attention to the strategy of moving away from ills, but still does not link this insight to the possibility of O-motives shaping travel behaviour.

stress regulation is acknowledged, it might, however, serve analytical purposes to distinguish *two* basic concepts. The first, 'transport', designates movement that is instrumental in reaching a certain destination and thus a specific activity, hence, D-motivated movement. 'Wayfaring', on the other hand, designates trips and travels with a more arbitrary destination, or one to which the traveller is indifferent, and also movement caused by an intrinsic desire for travel (Ingold 2004). Wayfaring is undirected travel presupposing O-motives or U-motives. Movement and distance regulation are the immediate aims, often pursuing the objective of alleviating stress, and a destination, if there is one (or more), is largely incidental (compare Mokhtarian and Salomon 2001: 696).[4] It would nevertheless be wrong to suppose that the wayfarer wanders aimlessly over the surface of the earth, with no places of abode (Ingold 2004). Routes might be chosen because of their potential for enhancing the enjoyment of the journey. Or, when O-motives trigger a departure, a particular route might be chosen because there are places along the way that allow for stopovers in supposedly convenient distances from the origin.

Because transport research concentrates one-sidedly on the D-motivation of travellers, the rich psychological literature on personal space, relational distance and stress regulation is ignored. The next section is an attempt to link psychological contributions on 'distance' to the idea of O-motivated travel. This prepares the way for a discussion of the wayfarer setting out from troubled local, territorial communities later in the essay.

Mobility as Stress Regulation

This section situates physical distance as an element of psychological distance. It is maintained that boundary protection of a personal space, that is, the balancing of closeness/connectedness against distance/separateness, is used as stress regulation in personal relationships. Furthermore, the literature confirms that stress diminishes with increasing physical distance from traumatic, threatening or high-tension events. This suggests that high mobility, which makes physical distance regulation effective and feasible, can also be a means for stress abatement in troubled local communities.

Mobility is here seen as individuals' possibility of travelling over shorter and longer distances. Hence, mobility encompasses both revealed and potential transport of people. With increasing opportunities and means for travelling, society will sooner or later achieve a level of mobility that involves so much individual freedom of choice, so many complex combined options of activities and transport, and such intricate and shifting tactics for utility maximisation, that planners are

---

4   In principle, positive O-motives might exist. Some experiences at the origin may be so good that individuals feel they have to be shared with others, no matter whom. Also, superb ideas might have emerged that need to be diffused throughout society. Hence, there is a kind of missionary travel that is undirected and O-motivated in a positive way.

unable to adequately model when and where people will travel. Society will have then reached the state of hypermobility (Sager 2005).

Stress is pressure, tension, worry and distress resulting from problems in one's life. Still, it is not seen here as a mental and physiological reaction that should be eliminated, as some stress is hardly distinguishable from the form of arousal coming with an interesting and stimulating life. However, the level of stress can be so high, as subjectively felt by an individual, that it becomes unpleasant and debilitating. When excessive stress is felt, the individual is likely to search for strategies of avoidance, disengagement, and cognitive dissociation, in order to achieve optimal psychological distance from the source of tension (Hess 2000, 2002).

Empirical studies in psychology have found that 'distance' is related to a wide range of relational processes and outcomes, such as conflict, attachment, arousal, cognitive appraisal, relational satisfaction, and affect (Hess 2002: 663). Psychological distance is broadly defined as 'the absence of closeness, or, more specifically, as a feeling of separation from another, resulting from infrequent, weak, and/or unvaried causal interconnections' (ibid. 664). Psychological distance may be too high or too low, so closeness is a variable to be optimised rather than maximised. In planning contexts, a person might see the regulation of distance from a disagreeable relational partner as a significant mechanism by which the unpleasant but necessary relationship can be kept intact. Distancing can therefore be a maintenance process, and it can be accomplished through both cognitive and behavioural means. That is, to regulate relational distance, people may change their behaviour, or they may change the meaning assigned to the same behaviour. Adjustment of physical distance implies behavioural change; in the face of unwanted closeness it is an avoidance strategy for regulating psychological distance. It serves, for example, to prevent a tension-building interaction episode from happening. Based on a series of experiments, Hess concluded that 'avoidance is people's first choice for creating relational distance' (ibid. 676).

Kantor and Lehr (1975) documented that the tension between desire for closeness and desire for distance is an essential feature of family relationships. They recorded hundreds of events in which family members attempted to put both psychological and physical distance between themselves and relatives (ibid. 7). Physical distance expresses the extent of spatial proximity and was subsumed into psychological distance.

Stress-regulating movement takes place at many geographical levels, running the full gamut from adjusting the distance to neighbours (Crow et al. 2002) and adjusting seating distance from a disliked person in a room (micro) to emigration to a foreign country (macro). In micro settings, people generally seem to prefer greater physical distance between themselves and others in higher-tension situations (Long 1980, 1984). Children's preferred physical closeness to other persons is correlated with empathy, and proximity may be facilitated when empathy is present (Strayer and Roberts 1997). Some examples concerning the relation between stress level and physical distance from tension-building events are given below.

In some cases, there is an objective risk continuously present at a location or in a district, and this risk diminishes with increasing physical distance from that area. It seems reasonable, then, that people's stress and worries follow a similar pattern reflecting geographic proximity. In a case of serial murders at a university campus, Biernat and Herkov (1994) found that physical distance from the murder sites was associated with reduced stress symptoms. Similarly, people living close to a Russian nuclear power plant (Eraenen 1997) or near the Three Mile Island nuclear power plant (Davidson et al. 1982, Gatchel et al. 1985) showed stronger stress reactions than people living farther away.

However, in several cases, an inverted U-shaped relationship has been shown to exist between the strength of negative attitudes towards potentially dangerous facilities (such as nuclear power plants and chemical plants that are running and functioning normally) and distance of dwelling to the facility (Hüppe and Weber 1998/1999, Maderthaner et al. 1978). This means that more positive attitudes towards such facilities are registered among people living in their immediate neighbourhood. Explanations of this phenomenon are often based on cognitive dissonance theory (Festinger 1957) or other psychological processes that reduce the risk perception of the most exposed, such as the disregard of media information about environmental or industrial hazards, or an incorrect estimation of the distance between the dwelling and the dangerous facility (Hüppe and Weber 1998/1999). A caveat should be kept in mind when interpreting these kinds of studies. Although subjects living different distances from a facility may be comparable according to socio-demographic variables, those with strongly negative attitudes towards, e.g. nuclear power plants would probably avoid living in the vicinity of such a plant (ibid. 340). Hence, some people might have taken advantage of their mobility and regulated their distance to the stress-generating location prior to the interviews.

The cases below relate to situations of war and terrorism, in which the danger is over at the time of the interview, or where those interviewed were never directly at risk. Whether the interviewee lived 50 km or 500 km from the place of the incident, he or she was not *directly* affected by it. It has repeatedly been found that a greater distance from war helps children to cope when they become aware of its ugliness and cruelty (Dyregrov and Raundalen 2005, Klingman 1995, Pine et al. 2005, Schwarzwald et al. 1993). Milgram (1993) found lower stress levels with less proximity to damaged sites in a study of adult Israelis' reaction to nocturnal missile attacks during the Persian Gulf War. Riolli et al. (2002) obtained similar results when studying Albanians' reactions to the Kosovo crisis of 1999.

There have been several studies of the variation in stress level according to the distance from sites of terrorist attacks. Sprang (1999) examined mental reactions to the Oklahoma City bombing, and Blanchard et al. (2005) and Ford et al. (2003) systematised reactions to the September 11 attacks. They all found that post-traumatic stress symptoms increased with proximity to the incident.

It is argued in this section that stress experienced as a consequence of an array of tension-generating situations diminishes with a greater physical distance from the event. Thus, when the stress level becomes troublesome, people have a motive to regulate stress by adjusting their distance to stressful locations. It is not possible to infer from travel surveys to what extent this is actually done, as these surveys do not identify O-motives as reasons for making trips. The majority of daily trips are mainly D-motivated, such as journeys to work, school, and public service. Trips for shopping, visiting friends, recreation and entertainment might be prompted by a combination of D-based and O-based motives. The need for 'escape' can affect the duration of the stay away from the origin, the wayfaring character of the trip (time spent at the destination versus time spent *en route*), and the choice of destination. In any case, it seems reasonable on the basis of the present section to hypothesise that stressful living conditions, processes or events in the neighbourhood will entice people to take advantage of their mobility and thus alleviate stress by regulating the physical distance from stress-inducing circumstances.

It is uncertain, though, what the above reports on reduced stress level for different people living different distances from difficult events tell about the stress-regulating effect of taking trips out of troubled neighbourhoods. In the literature reviewed, each person reporting his or her stress symptoms stays a constant distance from the tension-producing event. In the problem situation discussed in the present essay, however, each person lives in the high-tension area, leaves temporarily and often only for hours, and then returns to face unaltered conditions. Increasing distance from the trouble spot might ameliorate stress in both cases, but not necessarily in the same way or to the same extent.

The trips generated by high-tension living conditions can be of very different types. Stress might sometimes be relieved by walking around a few blocks before returning home. Or, a couple of days away visiting relatives might create the desired distance. On other occasions, a three week holiday would reduce stress to a tolerable level. If tension tends to build up again on return, then a permanent move might be considered, although residential mobility can be trying in itself, as exchanges of social support are negatively affected (Magdol and Bessel 2003). The dissimilar trip categories bear upon the conditions for dialogical planning processes in different ways and to different degrees. As will be explained in the next section, however, the expected general tendency is that higher mobility and longer and more frequent journeys will have an adverse effect on dialogical processes in the local, territorial community to which the traveller belongs.

The Influence of High Mobility on the Feasibility of Discourse Ethics

Dialogue is a central feature of discourse ethics, and one that might come under pressure as societies grow ever more mobile. This section argues that extensive O-motivated travel can contribute to this potential problem for communicative planning by explaining why widespread and frequent travelling makes discourse ethics less workable.

Planning theory since the 1980s has given a prominent role to dialogue and communicative processes in general. Most of the contributions have been inspired by Jürgen Habermas's (1999) theory of communicative action and have been launched under the labels of communicative planning, critical pragmatism or collaborative planning (Forester 1989, Healey 1997, Innes and Booher 1999, Sager 1994). Habermas's concept of 'dialogue' occupies a central position in these planning approaches as a benchmark for evaluating processes found in practice. Dialogue ideally requires that all concerned should take part, freely and equally, in a cooperative search for truth, where nothing coerces anyone except the force of the better argument. This is 'a speech situation that satisfies improbable conditions: openness to the public, inclusiveness, equal rights to participation, immunization against external or inherent compulsion, as well as the participants' orientation toward reaching understanding (that is, the sincere expression of utterances)' (Habermas 1999: 367).

The character and function of dialogue are an integrated part of Habermas's (1990, 1993) discourse theory of democracy. Discourse ethics is a theory about the ethical implications of the presuppositions that people must make when they participate in debate. It mandates a critical interpretation and revision of private needs for the sake of reaching consensus on norms, for example, in a communicative planning process:

> The general goal of Habermas's project of discourse ethics is to develop a just method of resolving moral conflicts in a pluralistic society, in which the authority of one set of sacred texts or other authorities does not enjoy universal and politically legitimating support. (Weinshall 2003: 25)

According to Ingram (1993: 306), Habermas claims that the coordination, integration, and socialisation of persons inhabiting modern societies all depend on rational communication. This is seen as the only way to restore confidence between contending parties in the event of communication failure or disagreement. The emphasis on 'rational consensus' is retained as a regulative ideal that guides deliberation and legitimises the outcome of democratic procedures.[5] Rational communication means dialogue, so if hypermobility affects dialogue negatively, this might have profound social repercussions.

---

5 Rational consensus is explained by Habermas in an earlier work on the *Legitimation Crisis*:

> Since all those affected have, in principle, at least the chance to participate in the practical deliberation, the 'rationality' of the discursively formed will consists in the fact that the reciprocal behavioral expectations raised to normative status afford validity to a *common* interest ascertained *without deception*. The interest is common because the constraint-free consensus permits only what *all* can want; it is free of deception because even the interpretations of needs in which *each individual* must be able to recognize what he wants become the object of discursive will-formation. (Cited from Rehg 1994: 39)

Dialogical planning and decision making in the Habermasian vein is based on discourse ethics, which implies attempts at reaching consensus on norms that are in the real interests of everyone. This is an attractive but sometimes hardly realisable goal in planning processes, where deep difference is often observed between the groups involved. World-views and the very meaning of development or progress might differ, and people occasionally regard each other from within divergent rationalities (Watson 2006). The moral principle of discourse ethics – the Universalisation principle – states that:

> Every valid norm must satisfy the condition that the consequences and side effects its *general* observance can be anticipated to have for the satisfaction of the interests of *each* could be freely accepted by *all* affected (and be preferred to those of known alternative possibilities for regulation). (Habermas 1993: 32)

The Universalisation principle tells us under what conditions consensus on a norm qualifies as rational, that is, expresses an insight into the better argument (Rehg 2002: 407). Habermas argues that one must also presuppose that the following conditions are fulfilled, to give the participants reason to believe that the results of the discourse are valid:

1. Every subject with the competence to speak and act is allowed to take part in a discourse.

2 a. Everyone is allowed to question any assertion whatever;
  b. Everyone is allowed to introduce any assertion whatever into the discourse;
  c. Everyone is allowed to express his attitudes, desires, and needs.

3. No speaker may be prevented, by internal or external coercion, from exercising his rights as laid down in (1) and (2). (Habermas 1990: 89)

Discourse ethics is a vehicle for systematic reflection on the problems attending consensus in pluralistic societies. It is argued below that consensus in processes with the above characteristics will be harder to reach in conditions of very high mobility. The reasons for this are given in subsections arranged around four terms: (1) diverse preferences, (2) different life contexts foster social exclusion, (3) unpredictable consequences, and (4) loose ties with the home community. Consensus might also seem less important to the individual under hypermobility. The closing remarks of this section suggest that this is because high mobility facilitates 'voting with one's feet'.

Diverse preferences

High mobility gives the opportunity for all sorts of trips, many of them involving journeys outside the communities in which the traveller performs his or her daily activities. Visits to other communities, societies, and cultures expose the traveller to new practices, ideas, values, and lifestyles. The visited population is affected in similar ways. Whether one likes or dislikes the new influences, increased mobility is likely to change preferences and make them more unstable. This is a threat to established cultural traditions, and when traditions dissolve, it becomes less likely that all participants in a planning dialogue will endorse the same norms and physical solutions. MacIntyre (1988: 326–69) holds that until the parties in practical reasoning and dialogue have made the existential commitment to a common tradition, any conflict resolution is either accidental or manipulated, and thus irrational or impossible. Discourse ethics cannot get around the objection that rational consensus requires prior agreement on a tradition-mediated notion of the common good. Thus, by eroding tradition, hypermobility makes it harder to realise the Universalisation principle because the effects on individuals of extensive travelling weaken the foundation for solving social conflict.

In line with the above argument, increasing mobility is likely to promote cultural diversity and thus pluralistic and multicultural societies. High mobility challenges the liberal construction of the undifferentiated 'we'. This supports the assumption that high mobility makes agreement and, therefore, collective decision making more difficult. The trend towards multiculturalism has provoked serious criticism of Habermas's discourse ethics. Baumeister suggests that:

> If discursive approaches to justice are to recognise the depth and complexity of diversity, they must abandon the Habermasian search for consensus in favour of a vision of liberalism that acknowledges the plurality and incommensurability of fundamental values and which consequently accepts the pervasiveness of value conflict. (Baumeister 2003: 741)

Rational conflict resolution is possible only if the participants can take the argument to an already agreed upon notion of the good human life (Rehg 1994: 80). Habermas (1993: 91) concedes that 'the sphere of questions that can be answered rationally from the moral point of view shrinks in the course of the development toward multiculturalism', but argues that finding solutions to these few more sharply focused questions becomes all the more critical to coexistence. Moral discourse must include an empathetic sensitivity to the values and needs of other people, as well as an attention to the particularities of the concrete situation.

Diverse preferences often cause dialogical consensus building processes to be difficult and drawn out. The closer the conversations come to embodying the ideal, the more inefficient they are with respect to time (Chambers 1996: 171). Negotiation, instrumental trade-offs, and strategic bargaining are the most common alternative routes to reaching agreement and resolving disputes (ibid. 196), and they are more time efficient. The wish to save time is a strong driving force behind the ever increasing mobility. It does not seem reasonable, then, to expect that constituencies providing political backing for the funding of development towards hypermobility will vote to institutionalise discursive forums for collective will formation.

Different life contexts foster social exclusion

Under the constant influx of new ideas and preferences, life contexts formed by the pursuit of a particular set of values and a distinctive tradition of embedding them in cultural practices become vulnerable. The protection of a life context depends on the protection of the rights and norms that defend personal freedom (Baumeister 2003: 743). Habermas (2001: 767) contends that 'citizens can make an *appropriate* use of their public autonomy…only if they are sufficiently independent in virtue of an equally protected private autonomy'. Defence of freedom and protection of life context are thus closely intertwined, but while high mobility threatens the peculiarity of life contexts, it is often considered an important aspect of freedom (Sager 2006). The problem here is that particular life contexts come under extra pressure with increased mobility that leads to frequent contact between different cultures and lifestyles.

Deviating life contexts may be hard to sustain and uphold as integrated parts of a majority culture. 'And the greater this diversity is, the more abstract are the rules and principles that protect the integrity and egalitarian coexistence of subjects who are becoming increasingly unfamiliar with one another in their difference and otherness' (Habermas 1993: 90–91). To strengthen the protection of the minority's distinctive character, some distance from the predominant culture is therefore often sought, and the majority's response to this might eventually be exclusion. In fact, because of the element of bonding in communities, they all have built into them by their very nature the defect of exclusion (Etzioni 2000: 189).

However, social exclusion runs directly contrary to the principles of discourse ethics. Given that the needs of groups that are socially disadvantaged due to, e.g. ethnicity or religion are liable to differ notably from those of the principal group, and taking account of the fact that even the most benevolent majority tends to misunderstand the needs of minorities, it is vital that members of minority groups participate in public debate so as to ensure that their needs and interests are clearly articulated (Baumeister 2003: 747). With ongoing globalisation, minority groups that are vulnerable to social exclusion are often the result of inter-societal mobility.[6] The relation between daily mobility and social exclusion of immigrants with a culture that deviates from that of the host country has been studied by Rajé (2004) and Uteng (2006). Kenyon (2006) examined the relation between mobility and social exclusion in general.

---

6 In some cases, the question of exclusion relates to groups that do not share the liberal commitment to autonomy. In Habermasian (2005) dialogical theory, such groups are tolerated, but their demands cannot form part of a reciprocal discourse that pushes beyond contested interests and values in search of a common form of life (Baumeister 2003: 749). Critique of Habermas's response to the demand for recognition of difference is also voiced by Bohman (1995) and Cooke (1997).

Unpredictable consequences

The Universalisation principle of discourse theory explicitly demands that those in favour of a norm should be able to convince the others that its consequences and side effects are acceptable for all (as discussed in length by Rehg 1994). However, the higher the mobility, the more difficult it is to make predictions about travel patterns, activity structure, individual preferences, and thus collective decisions (Sager 2005). This is partly because hypermobility enables individuals to exploit their knowledge of small alterations in the supply of goods, services, and activities, as well as varying whims and tastes, and constantly change their activity patterns and trajectories of movement to maximise satisfaction of their wants. Another reason is that the widely diverging preferences likely to follow from hypermobility tend to make 'the will of the people' unstable and cyclical and thus make collective decisions arbitrary (Riker 1982, Sager 2002).

Even if all norms might not be equally affected by these implications of hypermobility, one cannot take for granted that the intended and unintended impacts of a norm can be anticipated. Hypermobility does therefore have an adverse effect on dialogical planning by dissolving knowledge about the future. Actually, Habermas insists that a broad range of personal information should corroborate practical reason when discourse ethics is to be applied: individual life histories, identities, needs, wants, and traditions (Rehg 1994: 101). Such personal profiles might be easier to elicit in a sedentary society than in a mobile society characterised by fluidity and changeableness. Without such knowledge, it would be impossible to determine whether a norm puts someone else at a relative disadvantage.

Loose ties with the home community

Very high mobility that is converted into extensive travelling seems to loosen people's ties with their home communities (Feldman 1990, Nynäs forthcoming). It might then become of less significance to the individual whether the real interests of everyone are actually satisfied when norms are deliberated. This is a way of saying that solidarity might not be appropriately valued as mobility keeps increasing. A modest claim for solidarity that must be fulfilled in processes guided by discourse ethics is that the individual submit his or her moral reflection to all those affected (Rehg 1994: 107). Stronger moral solidarity is needed, however, to support relations of mutual recognition that preserve the identity of a form of life (Cooke 1997, Fraser 2000). Furthermore,

> in seeking to convince another, a participant must be concerned that the other's conviction rests on arguments whose terms are appropriate to the other's need interpretation, i.e. arguments that do not distort the perception of the other's welfare…(H)owever, participants can neither recognize each other's needs and wants, nor argue that a norm's observance has acceptable consequences for those needs and wants, unless they

recognize values in terms of which each one's welfare becomes the concern of all, i.e. a generalizable interest calling for and structuring social cooperation. (Rehg 1994: 111)

The two elements mentioned in the citation are at the core of moral solidarity. Such empathetic concern for the individual's welfare is inseparable from justice, the normative basis of group cooperation (ibid. 111). There is a risk that more mobility weakens people's sense of belonging and their solidarity with the local home community without compensating by extending sympathy with people in larger territories. In that case, the above line of reasoning supports the claim that hypermobility does not go well with discourse ethics.

Voting with one's feet

There are two main reasons why high mobility is a challenge to dialogue. The first is the various ways in which more mobility makes consensus less likely, as argued above. The second is that mobility makes it easier to leave a territorial community temporarily or permanently when value sets diverging substantially from one's own form the basis of social organisation (Hirschman 1970, Orbell and Uno 1972). That is, mobility offers a way out of the problems to which it contributes, and the 'solution' is some kind of distance regulation.

Reaching consensus in a specific local forum might appear less important to an individual the easier it is to 'vote with one's feet'. Voting with one's feet is the archetypal mobile mode of decision making; one moves about until one finds a sufficient number of others who share one's own values and viewpoints and joins a polity of fellow partisans. This is simpler under hypermobility, and is further facilitated by looser ties with the home community.

This section has argued that consensus on norms is less likely in more mobile societies. In addition, agreement on fair substantive outcomes, e.g. public plans, is harder to reach under hypermobility. This is because a fair product relies on a fair procedure that depends on dialogue, which in turn becomes a challenge with ever increasing mobility. The main mechanism is that high mobility leads to diverging preferences and multicultural cities and societies. The same social trends do, however, also facilitate moving away from frustrating environments. This weakens the motive for revising one's preferences and reflecting critically on one's values in dialogical planning. Planning theorists' insistence on dialogue and Habermas's continued commitment to the search for consensus (Baumeister 2003: 749, Habermas 2001: 772) seem to fit better with a sedentary ideology than with the 'new mobilities' approach's idea of the fluid society and the rapidly developing technologies for communication at a distance. Nevertheless, Habermas's fear that political disputes will be reduced to a purely strategic struggle for power in the absence of a search for rational agreement is well founded (Habermas 1996). By eroding social dialogue and undermining solidarity, hypermobility would seem to make people more vulnerable to political settlements that simply favour the views of the majority. But high mobility also makes it easier to escape by wayfaring and applying the strategy of distance regulation to alleviate stress and strain caused by tensions in the home community. This ambiguity points to a dilemma spelt out in the next section.

A Planning Dilemma in Conditions of 'Splintering Urbanism'

The preceding sections have propounded that part of travelling is motivated by tensions at the origin, and that too much travelling can impede dialogue. It is left to this section to complete the argument and bring to attention the potential difficulty arising from the supposition that troubled local communities may need both dialogical consensus building processes and opportunities for stress-regulating escape.

This section argues that a dilemma emerges in conflict-ridden and fragmented urban communities – or in conditions of 'splintering urbanism', borrowing a term from Graham and Marvin (2001). While internally noncooperative communities might be most in need of dialogue and consensus building planning processes, such communities also tend to motivate much travel for stress-regulating purposes. The problem is that hypermobility undermines discourse ethics and thus dialogue.

Most nation-states are now culturally as well as religiously diverse. Deliberation in such states often involves citizens who do not share the same collective aims, moral values, or world views (Bohman 1995: 253–4, Rescher 1993). Pluralism and multiculturalism are by no means the only reasons why it can be hard to make collective decisions by dialogue in local communities. It is a general problem in communities plagued by conflicting interests that animosity can keep people away from planning processes and give them reason to utilise their mobility to create distance to local conflicts. From a social point of view this may be counterproductive, as such withdrawal tends to take place in communities much in need of inter-group dialogue to promote mutual understanding.

Assume now that it is agonizing and arduous to live in a particular territorial community. Unnerving participatory planning processes are just a symptom of the conflicting interests and values marring interrelations between the social groups. It is worth noting that there are several stress-regulating strategies besides physical distancing, and the ensuing list is not exhaustive. Each of these other strategies can also have negative consequences for public planning, as will be seen.

One strategy is to cultivate the homogeneous fragments of the multicultural mosaic. This means that each individual takes refuge in his or her own group and leaves external interaction to representatives who become responsible for creating a harmonious pattern of the many diverse pieces. The forums of dialogical planning would then be meetings of representatives, where presumably each participant would primarily be taken up with looking after the interests of the constituency in order to keep his or her back covered. Lower priority would be given to justifying their views about the best outcome by appealing to common interests or by arguing in terms of reasons that all could accept in the public debate. 'Collective decision should in some sense reflect an interpretation of the common good that could be justified by public reasons, that is, ones that are generally convincing to everyone participating in the process of deliberation' (Rehg and Bohman 1996: 81). The problem is that the various constituencies might not be convinced, as they have not attended the deliberations and have not had the opportunity to be swayed by the arguments of the other representatives.

A second strategy for relieving the stress of participatory planning is to unduly discount the future and lapse into a mode of thinking that centres on what one can have *now*. The link between waiting and expectation is broken (Gasparini 1995). The result is a culture of consumption and entertainment that places little weight on what might be achieved by patience and common effort. One shares the company of people belonging to other groups in the passive and noncommittal role of being an audience, but steps back from the more challenging task of accomplishing something together. Planning is part of a collective production process rather than consumption. It is, moreover, preparation for the future and does not pay off in the here and now. Hence, dialogical planning processes have little to offer those who adopt this second strategy.

The third strategy manipulates the time dimension to a stronger degree than the second one. The individual here opts for fully fledged time distancing. Stress in the present is kept at bay by seeking solace in 'the good old days' or in dreams of a brighter future. Nostalgia and trust in a coming redeemer both serve to lift the individual along the time axis so as to gain distance from a distressing situation. Utopias can have a similar effect (Jameson 2004), and even visions and plans might contribute to a spiritual reorientation away from present tensions. Some people might see such 'time travelling' as an easier way out of present problems than participatory attempts at planned social change.

Apart from physical distancing, the fourth and last strategy to be mentioned here is withdrawal from the public to the private sphere (Weintraub 1997), leaving the few that have not yet retreated to do their 'bowling alone' (Putnam 2000). It might seem that, on every front, 'the "public" is being privatized, the private is becoming oversized, and this undermines democratic life'. However, this is the diagnosis that Sheller and Urry (2003: 107) find is often made by others, not the one guiding their own work. They hold that the border between the public and private domains is becoming blurred, and that 'cars, information, communications, screens, are all material worlds, hybrids of private and public life' (ibid. 113). Not only citizenship and democracy, but also effective stress regulation, will depend on individuals' capacity to navigate these new mobile and hybrid worlds. Note that the analogy to physical distancing is not a one-way retreat into the private realm, but stress regulation by moving back and forth between these ever more unclear categories by ever more hybrid technologies. Involvement in planning processes exposes the individual to all the strains of arguing in public and will not seem like a good idea to anyone fighting off stress by seeking more privacy.

As demonstrated above, there are several alternatives to physical distancing as stress regulation. One might then surmise that it does not matter much if high mobility, converted into physical distance regulation, were to exacerbate the conditions for discourse ethics and thus dialogical planning. People would often use the alternative strategies for reducing stress anyway. However, the above description of the four alternative strategies purports to show that even these forms of stress regulation render social dialogue difficult in local communities that are really in need of consensus building processes. The set of stress regulating strategies discussed here therefore does not help to dissolve the dilemma addressed in this section: High tensions in a community increase the need both for dialogical consensus building and stress-regulating travel, but the lifestyle of being constantly on the move makes discourse ethics and thus communicative planning less workable. Admittedly, the practical significance of this dilemma is uncertain, as very little empirical knowledge is available about the amount of wayfaring relative to transport, on O-motivated travel in conflict-ridden local communities, and on the effect of hypermobility on dialogue in public planning processes.

Perhaps the interpretation of dialogue as implying physical co-presence and face-to-face conversation is too strict. In planning processes where great numbers of people are affected by the proposed projects, the simultaneous presence of all involved is unrealistic in any case, and especially in a citizenry with high mobility. It is obvious that everyone cannot speak to everyone in a dispute of any scope. The ideal claims of discourse ethics cannot be satisfied to the letter, as no individual would be able to argue the matter out with all other affected individuals.

A partial 'solution' might be found in the enormous growth of mobile communication technology, which blurs the distinction between presence and absence (Licoppe 2004, Sager 2006); examples are mobile phones, e-mail, peer-to-peer voice, Skype, and MSN. There is reason to put 'solution' in inverted commas, as such technologies are also part of the problem in that they are an integral part of the technical-economic developments that allow for a highly mobile society in the first place. On the other hand, mobile communication devices allegedly allow for long distance dialogue. By providing individuals with information and knowledge that they would not otherwise have access to, 'mediated quasi-interaction can stimulate deliberation just as much as, if not more than, face-to-face interaction in a shared locale' (Thompson 1995: 256, as cited in Sheller and Urry 2003: 118). Etzioni and Etzioni (1999) reach a similar conclusion regarding computer-mediated communications (CMC), finding that 'there are no conceptual reasons or technical ones, that CMC-based communities...could not become full-fledged communities'. Even so, the new technologies have not empirically been found to substitute for face-to-face contact (Licoppe and Smoreda 2005, Wellman et al. 2001).

In any case, new distance regulators are emerging that are based on the convergence of technologies for communication and transport (Sheller 2004). They have the potential for reinforcing the effect of physical distance regulation by efficiently managing personal approachability, as people simply press buttons on wireless devices. Physical distancing is generalised by technologies that make it easier to slip in and out of different public and private domains, social settings, relationships, and even identities (Kronlid forthcoming). The result is stress regulation not only by geographical movement, but through 'more complex possibilities for coupling and decoupling across time and space' (Sheller 2004: 48).

Conclusion

Public planning is a vehicle for systematic reflection on many of the problems that call for consensus building in pluralistic societies (Connolly 2005, Rescher 1993). Dialogue and discourse ethics fuel this vehicle. However, hypermobility makes it difficult to provide high quality fuel. In order to implement discourse ethics in practical dialogical processes, a break with subject-centred reason is called for. The derivation of the Universalisation principle takes the subject-centred approach to the point where it must be abandoned. Individuals only possess their autonomy by virtue of their prior mutual recognition of one another. Such solidarity involves both concern for one another's welfare as individuals and reliance on a social network within which such recognition alone makes sense (Rehg 1994: 109). However, the development towards hypermobility is to a large extent driven by the aim for individual utility maximisation and the idea of personal freedom as the ability to choose from the greatest possible set of goods and activities. Hence, the forces behind hypermobility encourage subject-centred reason. This makes for a deep-rooted dissonance between discourse ethics and hypermobility.

This essay has argued that stress regulation is an important function of mobility. When tension builds up in the neighbourhood or the local community – sometimes spilling over into emotionally challenging planning processes – people will attempt to regain peace of mind by adjusting psychological distance. The regulation of physical distance is one strategy for achieving this and thus stimulates an unknown number of wholly or partly origin-motivated trips. It is potentially problematic that dialogical planning processes based on discourse ethics make moral and behavioural claims that become harder to satisfy in highly mobile societies that increase the use of travel as stress regulation. Face-to-face dialogue implies proximity but sometimes motivates the search for distance. The aim of this essay has been to argue that this dilemma is worth studying, especially in liberal and multicultural societies with escalating mobility. Even so, the question mark in the title of the article is best retained, as little is still empirically known both about O-motivated travel and the effects of hypermobility on dialogue in public planning.

References

Adams, J. (2005), 'Hypermobility: a challenge to governance', in C. Lyall and J. Tait (eds) *New Modes of Governance: Developing an Integrated Policy Approach to Science, Technology, Risk and the Environment* (Aldershot: Ashgate) pp. 123–38.

Anable, J. and B. Gatersleben (2005), 'All work and no play? The role of instrumental and affective factors in work and leisure journeys by different travel modes', *Transportation Research A* 39(2–3) 163–81.

Baumeister, A.T. (2003), 'Habermas: discourse and cultural diversity', *Political Studies* 51(4) 740–58.

Biernat, M. and M.J. Herkov (1994), 'Reactions to violence – A campus copes with serial murder', *Journal of Social and Clinical Psychology* 13(3) 309–34.

Blanchard, E.B., D. Rowell, E. Kuhn, R. Rogers and D. Wittrock (2005), 'Posttraumatic stress and depressive symptoms in a college population one year after the September 11 attacks: The effect of proximity', *Behaviour Research and Therapy* 43(2) 143–50.

Bohman, J. (1995), 'Public reason and cultural pluralism: Political liberalism and the problem of moral conflict', *Political Theory* 23(2) 253–79.

Bohman, J. and W. Rehg (eds) (1997), *Deliberative Democracy* (Cambridge, Mass.: MIT Press).

Bollens, S. (2004), 'Urban planning and intergroup conflict: Confronting a fractured public interest', in B. Stiftel and V. Watson (eds) *Dialogues in Urban and Regional Planning* (London: Routledge) pp. 209–46.

Brearley, M. (2001), 'The persecution of gypsies in Europe', *American Behavioral Scientist* 45(4) 588–99.

Chambers, S. (1996), *Reasonable Democracy. Jürgen Habermas and the Politics of Discourse* (Ithaca: Cornell University Press).

Cole, D.P. (1975), *The Nomads of the Nomads: The Al Murrah Bedouin of the Empty Quarter* (Chicago: Aldine).

Connolly, W.E. (2005), *Pluralism* (Durham: Duke University Press).

Cooke, M. (1997), 'Authenticity and autonomy: Taylor, Habermas, and the politics of recognition', *Political Theory* 25(2) 258–88.

Cox, T., J. Houdmont and A. Griffiths (2006), 'Rail crowding, stress, health and safety in Britain', *Transportation Research A* 40(3) 244–58.

Cresswell, T. (2001), *Tramp in America* (London: Reaktion Books).

Crow, G., G. Allan and M. Summers (2002), 'Neither busybodies nor nobodies: Managing proximity and distance in neighbourly relations', *Sociology* 36(1) 127–45.

Davidson, L.M., A. Baum and D.L. Collins (1982), 'Stress and control-related problems at Three Mile Island', *Journal of Applied Social Psychology* 12(5) 349–59.

Dyregrov, A. and M. Raundalen (2005), 'Norwegian adolescents' reactions to distant warfare', *Behavioural and Cognitive Psychotherapy* 33(4) 443–57.

Elster, J. (1998), *Deliberative Democracy* (Cambridge: Cambridge University Press).

Eraenen, L. (1997), 'Finnish reactions facing the threat of nuclear accidents in Russian nuclear power plants', *Patient Education and Counseling* 30(1) 83–94.

Etzioni, A. (2000), 'Creating good communities and good societies', *Contemporary Sociology* 29(1) 188–95.

Etzioni, A. and O. Etzioni (1999), 'Face-to-face and computer-mediated communities, a comparative analysis', *Information Society* 15(4) 241–48.

Evans, G.W., R.E. Wener and D. Phillips (2002), 'The morning rush hour – Predictability and commuter stress', *Environment and Behavior* 34(4) 521–30.

Feldman, R.M. (1990), 'Settlement-identity: Psychological bonds with home places in a mobile society', *Environment and Behavior* 22(2) 183–229.

Festinger, L. (1957), *A Theory of Cognitive Dissonance* (Stanford: Stanford University Press).

Ford, C.A., J.R. Udry, K. Gleiter and K. Chantala (2003), 'Reactions of young adults to September 11, 2001', *Archives of Pediatrics and Adolescent Medicine* 157(6) 572–78.

Forester, J. (1989), *Planning in the Face of Power* (Berkeley: University of California Press).

Fraser, N. (2000), 'Rethinking recognition', *New Left Review* Issue 3 (May-June) 107–20.

Friedmann, J. (2002), *The Prospect of Cities* (Minneapolis: University of Minnesota Press).

Gasparini, G. (1995), 'On waiting', *Time and Society* 4(1) 29–45.

Gatchel, R.J., M.A. Schaeffer and A. Baum (1985), 'A psychophysiological field study of stress at Three Mile Island', *Psychophysiology* 22(2) 175–81.

Graham, S. and S. Marvin (2001), *Splintering Urbanism: Networked Infrastructures, Technological Mobilities and the Urban Condition* (London: Routledge).

Gulian, E., A.I. Glendon, G. Matthews, D.R. Davies et al. (1990), 'The stress of driving: A diary study', *Work and Stress* 4(1) 7–16.

Habermas, J. (1990), *Moral Consciousness and Communicative Action* (Cambridge, Mass.: MIT Press).

Habermas, J. (1993), *Justification and Application: Remarks on Discourse Ethics* (Cambridge, Mass.: MIT Press).

Habermas, J. (1996), 'Reply to symposium participants, Benjamin N. Cardozo School of Law', *Cardozo Law Review* 17(4–5) 1477–557.

Habermas, J. (1999), *On the Pragmatics of Communication* (ed. M. Cooke) (Cambridge: Polity Press).

Habermas, J. (2001), 'Constitutional democracy: A paradoxical union of contradictory principles?', *Political Theory* 29(6) 766–81.

Habermas, J. (2005), 'Equal treatment of cultures and the limits of postmodern liberalism', *Journal of Political Philosophy* 13(1) 1–28.

Healey, P. (1997), *Collaborative Planning: Shaping Places in Fragmented Societies* (London: Macmillan).

Hess, J.A. (2000), 'Maintaining nonvoluntary relationships with disliked partners: An investigation into the use of distancing behaviors', *Human Communication Research* 26(3) 458–88.

Hess, J.A. (2002), 'Distance regulation in personal relationships: The development of a conceptual model and a test of representational validity', *Journal of Social and Personal relationships* 19(5) 663–83.

Hirschman, A.O. (1970), *Exit, Voice, and Loyalty: Responses to Decline in Firms, Organizations, and States* (Cambridge, Mass.: Harvard University Press).

Hirschman, A.O. and C.E. Lindblom (1962), 'Economic development, research and development, policy making: Some converging views', *Behavioral Sciences* 7(2) 211–22.

Hüppe, M. and J. Weber (1998/1999), 'Effects of distance, age and sex upon attitudes toward nuclear power plants: an empirical study', *Zentralblatt für Hygiene und Umweltmedizin* 202(2–4) 331–44.

Ingold, T. (2004), *Up, Across and Along* (Unpublished paper).

Ingram, D. (1993), 'The limits and possibilities of communicative ethics for democratic theory', *Political Theory* 21(2) 294–321.

Innes, J.E. (1995), 'Planning theory's emerging paradigm: Communicative action and interactive practice', *Journal of Planning Education and Research* 14(3) 183–9.

Innes, J.E. and D.E. Booher (1999), 'Consensus building as role playing and bricolage: Toward a theory of collaborative planning', *American Planning Association Journal* 65(1) 9–26.

Jameson, F. (2004), 'The politics of utopia', *New Left Review* Issue 25 (January-February) 35–54.

Johnson, D.L. (1969), *The Nature of Nomadism – A Comparative Study of Pastoral Migration in Southwestern Asia and Northern Africa*, Research Paper No. 118 (Department of Geography, Chicago: University of Chicago).

Kantor, D. and W. Lehr (1975), *Inside the Family* (San Francisco: Jossey-Bass).

Kenyon, S. (2006), 'Reshaping patterns of mobility and exclusion? The impact of virtual mobility upon accessibility, mobility and social exclusion', in M. Sheller and J. Urry (eds) *Mobile Technologies of the City* (London: Routledge) pp. 102–20.

Klingman, A. (1995), 'Israeli children's responses to the stress of the Gulf-war', *School Psychology International* 16(3) 303–13.

Koslowsky, M. (1997), 'Commuting stress: Problems of definition and variable identification', *Applied Psychology: An International Review* 46(2) 153–73.

Koslowsky, M. and M. Krausz (1993), 'On the relationship between commuting, stress symptoms, and attitudinal measures: A LISREL application', *Journal of Applied Behavioural Science* 29(4) 485–92.

Kronlid, D. (forthcoming 2008), 'What modes of moving do to me – Reflections about technogenic processes of identification', S. Bergmann, T. Hoff and T. Sager (eds) *Spaces of Mobility* (London: Equinox).

Licoppe, C. (2004), '"Connected" presence: The emergence of a new repertoire for managing social relationships in a changing communication technoscape', *Environment and Planning D: Society and Space* 22(1) 135–56.

Licoppe, C. and Z. Smoreda (2005), 'Are social networks technologically embedded? How networks are changing today with changes in communication technology', *Social Networks* 27(4) 317–35.

Lindblom, C.E. (1959), 'The science of "muddling through"', *Public Administration Review* 19(2) 79–88.

Long, G.T. (1984), 'Psychological tension and closeness to others: Stress and interpersonal distance preference', *Journal of Psychology* 117(1) 143–46.

Long, G.T., J.W. Selby and L.G. Calhoun (1980), 'Effects of situational stress and sex on interpersonal distance preference', *Journal of Psychology* 105(2) 231–37.

MacIntyre, A. (1988), *Whose Justice? Which Rationality?* (Notre Dame: University of Notre Dame Press).

Maderthaner, R., G. Guttmann, E. Swaton and H.J. Otway (1978), 'Effect of distance upon risk perception', *Journal of Applied Psychology* 63(3) 380–82.

Magdol, L. and D.R. Bessel (2003), 'Social capital, social currency, and portable assets: The impact of residential mobility on exchanges of social support', *Personal Relationships* 10(2) 149–69.

Milgram, N.N. (1993), 'Stress and coping in Israel during the Persian-Gulf-war', *Journal of Social Issues* 49(4) 103–23.

Mokhtarian, P.L. and I. Salomon (2001), 'How derived is the demand for travel? Some conceptual and measurement considerations', *Transportation Research A* 35(8) 695–719.

Nynäs, P. (forthcoming 2008), 'Global vagabonds, place and the self – The existential dimension of mobility', S. Bergmann, T. Hoff and T. Sager (eds) *Spaces of Mobility* (London: Equinox).

Orbell, J.M. and T. Uno (1972), 'A theory of neighborhood problem solving: Political action vs. residential mobility', *American Political Science Review* 66(2) 471–89.

Ortúzar, J.de D. and L.G. Willumsen (2001), *Modelling Transport* (Third Edition) (New York: John Wiley).

Ory, D.T. and P.L. Mokhtarian (2005), 'When is getting there half the fun? Modeling the liking for travel', *Transportation Research A* 39(2–3) 97–123.

Pine, D.S., J. Costello and A. Masten (2005), 'Trauma, proximity, and developmental psychopathology: The effects of war and terrorism on children', *Neuropsychopharmacology* 30(10) 1781–92.

Rajé, F. (2004), *Transport, Demand Management and Social Inclusion: The Need for Ethnic Perspectives* (Aldershot: Ashgate).

Rehg, W. (1994), *Insight and Solidarity: The Discourse Ethics of Jürgen Habermas* (Berkeley: University of California Press).

Rehg, W. (2002), 'The critical potential of discourse ethics: Reply to Meehan and Chambers', *Human Studies* 25(3) 407–12.

Rehg, W. and J. Bohman (1996), 'Discourse and democracy: The formal and informal bases of legitimacy in Habermas' *Faktizität und Geltung*; *Journal of Political Philosophy* 4(1) 79–99.

Rescher, N. (1993), *Pluralism: Against the Demand for Consensus* (Oxford: Clarendon Press).

Riker, W.H. (1982), *Liberalism against Populism* (San Francisco: W.H. Freeman).

Riolli, L., V. Savicki and A. Cepani (2002), 'Resilience in the face of catastrophe: Optimism, personality, and coping in the Kosovo crisis', *Journal of Applied Social Psychology* 32(8) 1604–27.

Sager, T. (1994), *Communicative Planning Theory* (Aldershot: Avebury).

Sager, T. (2002), *Democratic Planning and Social Choice Dilemmas* (Aldershot: Ashgate).

Sager, T. (2005), 'Footloose and forecast-free: Hypermobility and the planning of society', *European Journal of Spatial Development*, Article no. 17, September, http://www.nordregio.se/EJSD/.

Sager, T. (2006), 'Freedom as mobility: Implications of the distinction between actual and potential travelling', *Mobilities* 1(3) 465–88.

Sandercock, L. (1998), *Towards Cosmopolis: Planning for Multicultural Cities* (Chichester: Wiley).

Sandercock, L. (2003), *Cosmopolis II: Mongrel Cities in the 21st Century* (London: Continuum).

Schafer, A. and D.G. Victor (2000), 'The future mobility of the world population', *Transportation Research A* 34(3) 171–205.

Schwanen, T. and P.L. Mokhtarian (2005), 'What if you live in the wrong neighborhood? The impact of residential neighborhood type dissonance on distance traveled', *Transportation Research D* 10(2) 127–51.

Schwarzwald, J., M. Weisenberg, M. Waysman, Z. Solomon and A. Klingman (1993), 'Stress reaction of school-age-children to the bombardment by scud missiles', *Journal of Abnormal Psychology* 102(3) 404–10.

Sheller, M. (2004), 'Mobile publics: Beyond the network perspective', *Environment and Planning D: Society and Space* 22(1) 39–52.

Sheller, M. and J. Urry (2003), 'Mobile transformations of "public" and "private" life', *Theory, Culture and Society* 20(3) 107–25.

Sheller, M. and J. Urry (2006), 'The new mobilities paradigm', *Environment and Planning A* 38(2) 207–26.

Sprang, G. (1999), 'Post-disaster stress following the Oklahoma City bombing – An examination of three community groups', *Journal of Interpersonal Violence* 14(2) 169–83.

Steg, L. (2005), 'Car use – Lust and must: Instrumental, symbolic and affective motives for car use', *Transportation Research A* 39(2–3) 147–62.

Strayer, J. and W. Roberts (1997), 'Children's personal distance and their empathy: Indices of interpersonal closeness', *International Journal of Behavioral Development* 20(3) 385–403.

Talvitie, A. (1997), 'Things planners believe in, and things they deny', *Transportation* 24(1) 1–31.

Talvitie, A. (2006), 'Experiential incrementalism: on the theory and technique to implement transport plans and policies', *Transportation* 33(1) 83–110.

Taylor, N. (1998), *Urban Planning Theory Since 1945* (London: Sage).

Taylor, P.J. (1999), 'Places, spaces and Macy's: Place-space tensions in the political geography of modernities', *Progress in Human Geography* 23(1) 7–26.

Thompson, J.B. (1995), *The Media and Modernity: A Social Theory of the Media* (Cambridge: Polity).

Uteng, T.P. (2006), 'Mobility: Discourses from the non-western immigrant groups in Norway', *Mobilities* 1(3) 437–64.

Watson, V. (2006), 'Deep difference: Diversity, planning and ethics', *Planning Theory* 5(1) 31–50.

Weinshall, M. (2003), 'Means, ends, and public ignorance in Habermas's theory of democracy', *Critical Review* 15(1–2) 23–58.

Weintraub, J. (1997), 'The theory and politics of the public/private distinction' in J. Weintraub and K. Kumar (eds) *Public and Private in Thought and Practice* (Chicago: University of Chicago Press) pp. 1–42.

Wellman, B., A.Q. Haase, J. Witte and K. Hampton (2001), 'Does the Internet increase, decrease, or supplement social capital?', *American Behavioral Scientist* 45(3) 436–55.

Wener, R.E., G.W. Evans, D. Phillips and N. Nadler (2003), 'Running for the 7:45: The effects of public transit improvements on commuter stress', *Transportation* 30(2) 203–20.

Willson, R. (2001), 'Assessing communicative rationality as a transportation planning paradigm', *Transportation* 28(1) 1–31.

Chapter 7

Understanding Mobility Holistically: The Case of Hurricane Katrina

Tim Cresswell

We are, we are told, in the middle of a "mobility turn" in the social sciences (Sheller and Urry 2006; Urry 2000). Evidence for this includes a multitude of mobility themed conferences, the new journal *Mobilities* and a significant number of books such as this one with mobilty in the title (see Kaufman 2002; Cresswell 2006). This mobility turn recognises and responds to quantitative and qualitative transformations in the empirical nature of mobility over the last few decades in addition to a what we might term "nomad thought" – theory which uses metaphors of mobility to ask new questions about the structure of society. Fixity, place, rootedness, authenticity – are all seen as of the past while flow, movement, transgression and hybridity are symptoms of the super-modern. It is tempting to think of this interest in mobility as new but, of course, it is not. Social scientists have always had things to say about people, objects and ideas on the move. Consider human geography.

In many ways the study of human mobility in geography has a history as long as the discipline itself. The migrations of humanity have always been a central concern from the ideas of origins and dispersals in early American cultural geography to the contemporary concerns with hybridity and globalisation (Sauer 1952; Massey and Jess 1995). Consider the burgeoning subdiscipline of transport geography in the 1970s and 1980s (Lowe and Moryadas 1975). Consider the models of migration patterns developed in the same period. Consider the time-geography of Hägerstrand and others at the Lund School that analyzed mobility on an everyday level (Hägerstrand and Pred 1981). Consider the idea of "journey to work" and its development by feminist geographers (Hansen 1982). Consider the debates about transnationalism, about travel writing, about exploration which all played a significant role in the new cultural geography of the nineties (Crang and Dwyer 2003; Driver 2000). Consider the more recent turn to the micro-geographies of the non-representational and the moving body (Wylie 2005). I am sure you could make similar lists for other disciplines. Sociologists, for instance, have been considering the role of mobility in modern urban life since at least the Chicago School of the early and mid-twentieth century. I think, once we have reflected on all of these, we might rightly ask what is new about the mobility turn – or as John Urry and Mimi Sheller have called it – "the new mobilities paradigm" (Sheller and Urry 2006).

I would like to point toward two ways in which I believe we have some way to go before we can put mobility centre stage. First of all we need to think about mobility holistically and second we need to pay greater attention to issues of power and politics that it provokes. When I say we need to think of mobility holistically I mean we need to stop placing artificial disciplinary and sub-disciplinary divides between different sets of research which have mobility at their centre. Returning to the various mobility agendas of human geography I would suggest that while they certainly answer questions about mobility within the remit of the particular problematics they are concerned with – be it journey to work, transport networks or dancing bodies – they also show a relative lack of concern for mobility in and of itself and a similar lack of concern for the connections between them.

When I say that there has been a lack of concern with mobility itself I mean that there has been a reluctance to move beyond the specifics of case studies to think about the nature of mobility as an achievement of people, things and knowledges and as a socially produced fact of life. In geography we have developed our notions of space or place or landscape or territory. Each of these has well developed literatures which consider them as general geographical objects of enquiry and as actors in the social, cultural and natural world. We can take a notion such as place, for instance, and use it in any number of contexts from the personal to the global. To be sure, the notion is contested and still being developed but we all know something of its history within the discipline. Can we say the same about mobility? I think not.

Perhaps this is because mobility seems a chaotic thing. Chaotic in the sense that moving things are often chaotic in the way we experience them. Stationary, sedentary life, on the other hand, is hard to see as chaos. On the other hand some might say that little that is interesting can be said about what links the movement of blood in the body and movement of jet planes around the globe. The fact of movement, our sceptics might suggest, is both obvious and uninteresting. I do not believe this and this is my second point about the various traditions that have shed light on issues of mobility. There is a need to make connections between different arenas of mobility in order to understand it more fully.

Consider three aspects of mobility: the fact of physical movement – getting from one place to another; the meanings that movement is given – discourses, narratives and stories about the fact of movement; and finally the experienced and embodied practice of movement. Different forms of mobility research are likely to explore facets of any one of these. Transport researchers, for instance, have developed ways of telling us about the fact of movement – how often it happens, at what speeds and where. They have also informed us about who moves and how identity might make a difference. They have not been so good at telling us about the meanings of mobility either at the individual level or at a societal level. Neither have they told us how it feels to move in one way rather than another. The experience of mobility has never been at the top of the agenda in transport studies. Understanding mobility holistically means paying attention to all three of these aspects.

Mobility also needs to be understood at different scales and connections need to be made between these scales. Again transport studies have been very good at explicating the processes of moving when mechanically assisted, ranging from a short drive (or ride on a bike) to a flight around the world. But smaller scale mobilities are often ignored. This is most obviously the case with walking. But consider also the movements of individual limbs, of dancing or playing at sport. I would suggest that studying mobilities across these scales shines a new light on mobility in general. When, for instance, we understand that the discovery of blood circulation by William Harvey in the seventeenth century led to city planners associating circulation with health and moral order we can better understand the urban development of cities such as Paris and Washington D.C. (Sennett 1994). When we recognise that the mobility of sperm cells has been associated with active agency in the process of reproduction and the relatively motionless egg is similarly associated with passivity we may gain new sights into the gendering of mobility at a range of different scales (Martin 1991).

Understanding mobility holistically allows us to illuminate the politics of mobility. Mobility is a resource which is differentially accessed. One person's speed is another person's slowness. Some move in such a way that others get fixed in place. Examples of this abound. Consider the school run that allows women (for the most part) to enact an efficient form of mobility so often denied them. At the same time it impacts on the ability of children to walk to school and makes the streets less safe for pedestrians. There is little that is straightforward about such an entanglement. Consider the opening up of borders in the European Union to enable the enactment of the EU mantra of free mobility. This in turn depends on the closing down of mobilities at the borders (often airports) of the new Europe. Speeds, slownesses and immobilities are all related in a way that is thoroughly infused with power.

This politics of mobility is enriched if we think about mobility in terms of material movement, meaning and practice. There is clearly a politics to material movement. Who moves furthest? who moves fastest? who moves most often? These are all important components of the politics of mobility that can be answered in part by the traditional approaches of transport studies. But this is only the beginning. There is also a politics of meaning. How is mobility discursively constituted? What narratives have been constructed about mobility? How are mobilities represented? Some of the foundational narratives of modernity have been constructed around the brute fact of moving. Mobility as liberty, mobilty as progress. We are always trying to get somewhere. No-one wants to be stuck or bogged down. These stories appear everywhere from car advertisements to political economic theory. Finally, and perhaps most importantly of all, there is a politics of mobile practice. How is mobility experienced? How comfortable is it? Is it forced or free? A line of a map linking A and B may be experienced completely differently by a man and a woman, or a businessman and a domestic servant, or a tourist and a refugee. The fact of movement, the meanings attached to it and the experienced practice are all connected. The meaning given to movement can certainly impact on the experience of its practice. Think about Mexican immigrants in the United States for instance. Compare that to a member of a multi-national corporation jetting between world cities.

To recap, I am interested in developing a more holistic approach to human mobility – one that connects mobility across scales and considers the fact of movement, the meanings attached to movement and the experienced practice of movement. Taking all these facets seriously, I argue, will help us delineate the politics of mobility. For the rest of this paper I would like to illustrate these points by thinking through the way a mobility perspective allows us to understand the recent events in New Orleans, making connections that might previously have remained unnoticed.

Hurricane

On 29 August 2005 a category four hurricane, Katrina, hit the Gulf Coast of Louisiana with 150 mile per hour winds and a huge tidal surge that broke the levees of New Orleans and flooded 80 percent of the city. Over one thousand people were killed and hundreds of thousands left homeless. New Orleans residents who could not find shelter and food with relatives and friends were evacuated to locations across the American south. The flooding had been foreseen and an evacuation of the city ordered. Along with the detritus of human life that came to the surface in the days of early September were issues of race, poverty, and mobility. After Katrina struck, media viewers like myself were inundated with images of predominantly poor black people stuck in an urban landscape that has had the majority of white people removed from it.

New Orleans is a city born out of mobility and hybridity. The city can be dated back to 1718 and was chosen as a site that could link the Mississippi to Lake Pontchartrain that was also adjacent to established Native American trading routes. It soon became an important port and the main point of entry for the trans-Atlantic slave trade. John Bachmann's aerial view of New Orleans from 1851 shows a mobility-scape (Figure 7.1). A scene of ships servicing the port and streets running off into the distance past smoking chimneys. As Mimi Sheller has pointed out it is a unique city in a North America context, "The people who have settled there include native Americans, early Spanish and French settlers, Jewish refugees, English colonists and Irish workers, enslaved Africans from Bambara, Congo and Yoruba cultural regions, and wealthy French and mulatto refugees from the Haitian revolution, as well as their creole-speaking slaves" (Sheller 2006: npn). Before the Civil War New Orleans was home to the largest free black community of the American South, many of whom were very wealthy and enjoyed more rights than free blacks in other states. In her book *Civic Wars: Democracy and Public Life in the American City During the Nineteenth Century*, Ryan describes the rapid urban growth of the city in the late nineteenth century, when tens of thousands of former slaves moved off of the plantations and into the new wage economy of the industrializing city (Ryan

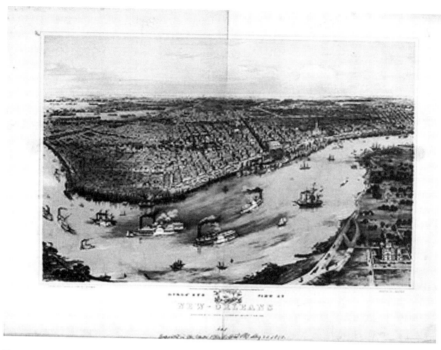

Figure 7.1   View of New Orleans

1997: 188–9). Following the Civil War New Orleans grew on the basis of the street car and the railroad which created what Ryan calls a more diffuse and boundless "heterogeneity of the city" (ibid. 203). In addition to the mobilities of people in and out of New Orleans, and the spatial impact of the street car and railroad, New Orleans was also important as a port. While originally being associated with the slave trade it is now (in 2007) the world's second busiest port (in terms of bulk cargo) and is strongly associated with the oil industry which provides the fuel for global mobility. Finally New Orleans has become a city associated with tourism. Over 14 million people visit New Orleans every year to enjoy its associations with jazz music and creole and cajun cuisine. New Orleans, then, exhibits a unique geography of mobility connecting the geography and race in unique ways. The aftermath of Hurricane Katrina needs to be understood in this context of mobilities.

The Mobility Poor

It is estimated that 85 percent of the population of New Orleans had left before the hurricane struck. This, it seems, included the vast majority of white residents. The evacuation order depended on people being able to move of their own free will – for the most part by car. Just as people were leaving en masse, bus and train services were being cancelled. A popular image circulating in the media featured around one hundred school buses parked in orderly lines and up to their roofs in water. Radio reports on the BBC featured interviews with (predominantly black) residents who stayed in the area during the hurricane. Again and again they are asked why they did not leave and the residents repeatedly informed the incredulous reporters that they could not afford to leave, did not have a car, and had nowhere to go. Automobility is, after all, central to American life and culture. To be American is to have a car. Public transport has consistently lost out in terms of subsidies and tax dollars to the automobile industry and its supporters (see Goddard 1994). The production of some kinds of mobility often effectively immobilizes others.

Before the hurricane the issue of a "low-mobility" population had come up during disaster emergency plans as reported in *The New York Times*:

> Brian Wolshon, an engineering professor at Louisiana State University who served as a consultant on the state's evacuation plan, said little attention was paid to moving out New Orleans's "low-mobility" population – the elderly, the infirm and the poor without cars or other means of fleeing the city, about 100,000 people…At disaster planning meetings, he said, "the answer was often silence."[1]

The vast majority of people immobilized in New Orleans were black. The politics of race and the politics of mobility, as so often before in American history, were joined at the hip. As a columnist for the progressive magazine, *Mother Jones*, put it:

> What many of those people shared that night was this: they didn't own a vehicle. They had no car, no truck, no SUV to point north or west, away from the storm and the flood waters. They had no "extra set of keys" to tuck into their "Disaster Supply Kit," as recommended by the New Orleans Emergency Preparedness Guide. They had no gas tank to keep half-full at all times, a key evacuation preparation step suggested by the Department of Homeland Security.[2]

There have been attempts to deracialize the crisis by dislocating issues of mobility from issues of race. Consider a news piece written for the *Hawaii Reporter* by Randal O'Toole of the American Dream Coalition – a right-wing/libertarian organization that opposes the development of light rail initiatives and supports "automobility". In response to Hurricane Katrina, O'Toole writes:

> What made New Orleans more vulnerable to catastrophe than most US cities is its low rate of auto ownership. According to the 2000 Census, nearly a third of New Orleans households do not own an automobile. This compares to less than 10 percent

---

1   *The New York Times* (http://www.nytimes.com/2005/09/02/national/national-special/02repsonse.html?th=&emc=th&pagewanted=all) accessed 5 October 2005.

2   Alison Stein Welner, "No Exit" 13 September 2005, *Mother Jones* (www.mother jones.com/news/update/2005/09/no_car_emergency.html) accessed 5 October 2005.

nationwide. There are significant differences by race: 35 percent of black households but only 15 percent of white households do not own an auto. But in the end, it was auto ownership, not race, that made the difference between safety and disaster.[3]

According to the US Census Bureau over 77,000 households in New Orleans had no form of private transportation, leaving around 200,000 people without an immediate way out of the city when Katrina struck. The New Orleans city government knew this was the case. A year earlier the mayor, Ray Nagin, had explained that he could not order an evacuation of the city when threatened by a hurricane because he had no way to evacuate people who did not have access to cars. This is despite the sentence in the New Orleans Emergency Preparedness Guide that reads: "Local transportation will be mobilized to assist persons who lack transportation" (Wellner 2005). Evacuation plans, in New Orleans and elsewhere, simply assume that American citizens are car owners – that their mobility is automobility. The *Mother Jones* article reports Havidan Rodriquez, the director of the Disaster Research Center at the University of Delaware, as stating that car ownership data is simply not taken into account when considering evacuation plans. And yet it is precisely those people without cars who need to be at the center of emergency evacuation planning. To Rodriguez the most poignant image of the disaster in New Orleans was the widely circulated photograph of a hundred school buses with only their rooftops showing above the water. While the image was used to illustrate the depth of the flood waters, it represented a missed opportunity to Rodriguez. They could, after all, have been used for an evacuation. Evacuation plans included an assumed model of mobility based on privatized automobility, when instead they should have worked on a model of mobility as a public need.

The argument that those who suffered most from the effects of Hurricane Katrina were those without cars is often contrasted to the argument that there is a racial politics to the disaster. Mobility, in this formulation, is emptied of social content. Separating mobility from race (and class and age in particular) is simply nonsensical. While speaking to members of the Bus Riders' Union in Los Angeles – a radical group who advocate increased expenditure for low pollution buses rather than expensive light rail systems – it was frequently observed how transport planners sought to dissociate transit from race. The Bus Riders' Union response was that they could not be so easily dissociated. In the United States the politics of race and the politics of mobility (particularly public transit provision) have moved side by side through the civil rights movement. Think of Jim Crow. Think of Rosa Parks. The population of New Orleans that was left behind were indeed the transit dependent but they were overwhelmingly black. In the New Orleans metropolitan area only five percent of non-Hispanic white people did not have access to an automobile. For the black population the figure was 27 percent (Beruba and Raphael 2005). The elderly and the very young were similarly transit

3   Randal O'Toole, Hawaii Reporter (www.hawaiireporter.com/story.aspx?0c98e6ee-047f-41cd-9f86-3e450a4391bf) accessed 5 October 2005.

dependent. Some of the worst scenes from New Orleans were of elderly hospital patients abandoned as the waters rose. Many died. To say that the human disaster that followed Hurricane Katrina was not about race or age or class, but, instead, about car ownership is to divert attention to how mobility is social through and through. Mobility is about more than transport.

Tourists/Refugees/Evacuees

The issue of the "mobility poor" was not the only way in which the politics of mobility came to the surface in the early days of September. They also arose in the accounts of some British tourists who had joined New Orleans residents in the Superdome as the floodwaters rose. The Superdome had been designated as a safe space for those many people who could not simply leave the city. Much of the media coverage following the hurricane focussed on the dome as a Dante-like dystopia of death, rape and filth. Numerous accounts tell of the US military taking tourists out under cover of night to make sure they were safe and able to return home. Clearly the designation "tourist" merits special treatment. Every other person in the Superdome surely needed the same kind of help and also needed to be "safe". Tourists, however, were separated out and taken over the road to what had previously been a luxury hotel before being flown to their home countries.

New Orleans is an important tourist destination. Its famous "French Quarter" provides an atmospheric backdrop to jazz and blues music and free-flowing alcohol. The tourist industry brought $4.9 billion to the city in 2004 and was the city's second largest employer.[4] In many ways, the city was dependent on mobility for its prosperity. It is perhaps unsurprising, therefore, that the biggest single investment in the urban public transport infrastructure in the years leading up to August 2005 was $160 million on a tourist-oriented streetcar line and a planned $120 million on another line. In May 2004, US Secretary for Transportation, Norman Mineta, visited New Orleans to congratulate them on the opening of the Canal Street streetcar line; he applauded the public-private finance initiative that had brought the streetcar into being. The conversion of a bus line into a streetcar, he said "will improve the environment, encourage economic development, and expand tourism."[5] He continued by stating that "Besides the advantages of moving people and attracting tourists, the streetcars behind me are important to building the economy of New Orleans, which will be dependent upon this city's ability to move people and goods, safely and efficiently…The work that you do, every day, keeps New Orleans moving." Mineta could hardly have been more mistaken. While the streetcars certainly provide an attraction for tourists, and are convenient

---

4   CNN "Mayor moves to heal New Orleans' lifeblood industry" (www.cnn.com/2005/US/10/07/neworleans.casinos/) accessed 5 October 2005.

5   This and further quotes are taken from US Department of Transportation (www.dot.gov/affairs.minetasp051804.htm) accessed 5 October 2005.

for those who live along it, they were woefully inadequate when it came to moving people safely when safety was at a premium. It was tourists and their mobility that benefited most from the new streetcar lines. As Mineta joyfully recounted: "the rebounding economy means that Americans are traveling again for both work and pleasure at record numbers, and New Orleans is one of the destinations to which they're headed." As Zygmunt Bauman has reminded us, the figure of the tourist can "travel at will, get much fun from their travel...are cajoled or bribed to travel and welcomed with smiles and open arms when they do" (Bauman 1988, 89). Indeed, streetcars are made for them and, when disaster strikes, they can be rescued and flown home while the metaphorical vagabonds, many of whom work in the tourist industry, remain where they are, unable to escape.

Tourists were not the only mobile figures to become an issue following Katrina. In the days and weeks following Hurricane Katrina, stories began to emerge about the categorization of people who were displaced by the hurricane and the floods that followed it. These displaced people were increasingly upset about being referred to as refugees. Black New Orleans citizens displaced by the storm were featured on BBC news stating that they were not refugees. Soon it became a political issue, as Rev. Jesse Jackson claimed: "It is racist to call American citizens refugees."[6] The word refugee, it seems, was quickly associated with notions of race (the majority were black) and foreignness. Refugees were effectively second-class citizens – not quite American. Soon President Bush had joined the debate declaring: "The people we are talking about are not refugees...They are Americans and they need the help and love and compassion of our fellow citizens." Over the next few days, various media outlets in the United States stopped talking about refugees and started to refer to displaced people or evacuees. *The Washington Post* and *The Boston Globe* both banned the use of the word refugee, while the *Associated Press* and *The New York Times* continued to use it when it seemed appropriate. The *Associated Press* executive editor stated, "Several hundred thousand people have been uprooted from their homes and communities and forced to seek refuge in more than 30 different states across America. Until such time as they are able to take up new lives in their new communities or return to their former homes, they will be refugees." William Safire, *The New York Times* columnist, insisted that a refugee is simply someone looking for refuge and can be from any race or nation. Mike Pesca, a reporter for National Public Radio, went further in defense of the term refugee, focusing on a claim by the black activist, Al Sharpton, that the use of the term strips people of their dignity. "They are not refugees wandering somewhere looking for charity," he said. "They are victims of neglect and a situation they should have never been in the first place."[7] While Sharpton made the claim that these people were not

---

6   This and following quotations are from *Associated Press* online (www.wwltv.com/stories/ww;090605refugees_.306635fl.html) accessed 5 October 2005.

7   This and the following quotations are from Mike Pesca, "Are Katrina's Victims 'Refugees' or 'Evacuees'" National Public Radio (www.npr.org/templates/story/strory.php?storyId=4833613) accessed 5 October 2005.

refugees because their plight was the product of politics, Pesca writes that perhaps the term refugee is appropriate for exactly that reason.

> They're refugees because circumstance is turning them into refugees. I was at one of the evacuation points the other day. Thousands of people were standing in mud…If you watched this situation on television, you might not realize how dirty and foul-smelling these people were. There was a reluctance on the part of the rescuers to touch the people. There was a total unwillingness to walk among them.

Later in the article, Pesca makes the point that the contrast between armed men in fatigues on one side of a barricade and bedraggled survivors on the other brought to mind scenes from "Haiti or Kosovo…The people who heeded warnings and had the wherewithal to leave town before Katrina hit were evacuees. These beleaguered people who had lost everything were something else."

The use of a term such as refugee highlights the entanglement of mobility with meaning and power. A whole host of mobile characters have inhabited the pages of social and cultural theorists of late. Nomads, travelers, tourists, vagabonds, and exiles have all been used to illustrate contemporary concerns with a world in motion. While each tells us something about mobility, each also tells us something about the social baggage that accompanies those on the move. The word refugee is no exception. There is no inherent reason why Jackson, Sharpton, and others should deem the use of this particular term racist. What their criticism highlights, however, is how the history of the term has loaded it with connotations of subversive and threatening mobility. The word crisis often accompanies the word refugee, as do the words foreign and immigrant. A term first used to describe wealthy Protestants who had been forced to leave France has become a term of abuse. In Britain and the United States, refugees have been seen as people seeking to take advantage of the state's generosity. They are people who do not belong to a host nation and are therefore not entitled to the rights of citizenship. They are people without place who need to be regulated. While it is strictly true that a refugee must be "outside the country of his nationality" (according to the Geneva Convention), this ignores the wider use of the term to apply to anyone who has been displaced and is seeking refuge. Indeed, it is often the case that those who need the most help are those who cannot move. An event such as a hurricane, as we have seen, effectively immobilizes the most vulnerable (Tuitt 1996). Nevertheless the term refugee has become wrapped up in notions of being out of place, of being foreign and suspect. The term is, as Jackson and Sharpton indicate, heavily racialized because of a long history of negative representations of refugees as other, as being from somewhere else, as threateningly mobile.

Conclusion

There are any number of ways that the analysis of mobility could shine light on the aftermath of Hurricane Katrina. We might look at the "fact of movement" – who moved? who stayed? where did people move to? Traditional transport studies could tell us all of this. What could the "mobility turn" add? One answer is an holistic analysis of the politics of mobility. As well as these questions we might ask about the meanings given to mobility here. Labels such as "mobility poor", "refugee" and "tourist" all connect the fact of movement into narratives about mobility which, in turn, make it possible to move in a particular way – as a tourist or as a refugee for instance.

Hurricane Katrina and its aftermath have highlighted the politics of mobility. The material infrastructure of mobility opportunities has been shown to serve some more than others. The term mobility poor has become a part of the media lexicon. A diverse array of mobile practices – driving, using public transport, going on holiday – have been shown to be related to each other in a myriad of ways. The meanings of mobility associated with tourists, drivers, refugees, and evacuees have been a matter of public debate. But New Orleans, in this instance, is but a metonym for an entire world on the move. In this world it is important to understand that mobility is more than about just getting from A to B. It is about the contested world of meaning and power. It is about mobilities rubbing up against each other and causing friction. It is about a new hierarchy based on the ways we move and the meanings these movements have been given.

References

Bauman, Z. (1998), *Globalization: The Human Consequences* (New York: Columbia University Press).

Berube, A. and Raphael, S. (2005), "Access to Cars in New Orleans" Brookings Institute (www.brookings.edu/metro/20050915_katrinacarstables.pdf) accessed 5 October 2005.

Crang, P. and Dwyer, C. (eds) (2004), *Transnational Spaces* (London: Routledge).

Cresswell, T. (2006), *On the Move: Mobility in the Modern Western World* (London: Routledge).

Driver, F. (2000), *Geography Militant: Cultures of Exploration and Empire* (Oxford: Blackwell).

Goddard, S. (1994), *Getting There: The Epic Struggle Between Road and Rail in the American Century* (Chicago: University of Chicago Press).

Hägerstrand, T. and Pred, A. (1981), *Space and Time in Geography: Essays Dedicated to Torsten Hägerstrand* (Lund: CWK Gleerup).

Haggett, P. (1965), *Locational Analysis in Human Geography* (London: Edward Arnold).

Hanson, S. (1982), "The Determinants of Daily Travel Activity Patterns: Relative Location and Socio Demographic Factors", *Urban Geography* Vol. 3: 179–202.

Kaufmann, V. (2002), *Re-thinking Mobility: Contemporary Sociology* (Aldershot: Ashgate).

Lowe, J. and Moryadas, S. (1975), *The Geography of Movement* (Boston: Houghton Mifflin).

Martin, E. (1991), "The Egg and the Sperm: How Science Has Constructed a Romance Based on Steroetypical Male-Female Sex Roles", *Signs: Journal of Women in Culture and Society* 16: 458–501.

Massey, D.B. and Jess, P.M. (1995), "A Place in the World? Places, Cultures and Globalization, Shape of the World", *Explorations in Human Geography*, 4 (Oxford, England and New York: Oxford University Press).

Ryan, M. (1997), *Civic Wars: Democracy and Public Life in the American City During the Nineteenth Century* (Berkeley: University of California Press).

Sauer, C.O. (1952), "Agricultural Origins and Dispersals, Bowman Memorial Lectures" Ser. 2 (New York: American Geographical Society).

Sennett, R. (1994), *Flesh and Stone: The Body and the City in Western Civilization*, First edn (New York: W.W. Norton).

Sheller, M. (2006), "Mobility systems, urban disasters, and the rescaling of New Orleans", Paper Presented to the Association of American Geographer's Annual Meeting Chicago, March 2006.

Sheller, M. and Urry, J. (2006), "The New Mobilities Paradigm", in J. Urry and M. Sheller (eds) "Mobilities and Materialities", special issue of *Environment and Planning A* 38/2 (2006): 207–226.

Tuitt, P. (1996), *False Images: Law's Construction of the Refugee* (London: Pluto).

Urry, J. (2000), *Sociology Beyond Societies: Mobilities for the 21st Century* (London: Routledge).

Wolff, J. (1992), "On the Road Again: Metaphors of Travel in Cultural Criticism", *Cultural Studies* 6: 224–39.

Wylie, J. (2005), "A Single Day's Walking: Narrating Self and Landscape on the South West Coast Path", *Transactions of the Institute of British Geographers* 30/2: 234–47.

PART II

Chapter 8

Existential Homelessness – Placelessness and Nostalgia in the Age of Mobility

Juhani Pallasmaa

[T]he more one travels, the more complex one's sense of nostalgia becomes.

Joseph Brodsky[1]

Things fall apart: the centre cannot hold...

W.B.Yeates[2]

Mobility is, of course, a huge subject matter, extending from the movement cycles and patterns of the primordial human settlements of the world, and the great expeditions and the European re-discovery of the world, to our characteristic bi-pedal motion and horizontal gaze, and the mobility implied by countless human modes of livelihood and production. The theme also contains matters such as our embodied mode of experiencing the world through constant motion, the fundamental human right of mobility as specified in the Declaration of Human Rights, and the significance of mobility for human interaction on a cross-cultural as well as on intimate and social levels. The significance of human mobility also evokes essential ecological and ethical questions; we may soon be reaching the very limits of unlimited and irresponsible mobility. We must also include the conditions that limit mobility which result from cultural conditions, gender, forced restrictions, economy, or physical disabilities.

I will, however, focus on the dimensions of mobility that are closest to my personal interests as an architect, cultural observer and frequent traveller: the notion and consequences of geographic mobility and, particularly, of motorised and increasingly accelerated movement that is one of the foundational phenomena of our concept and reality of modernity. I am intentionally going to valorize a very narrow strip of the spectrum of human mobility, in full awareness of the vastness of issues that I am thus excluding from my study.

---

1 Joseph Brodsky, *On Grief and Reason* (New York: Farrar, Straus and Giroux, 1997), 35.

2 As quoted in Hans Sedlmayr, *Art in Crisis: The Lost Centre* (London: Hollis and Carter, 1957), III.

New Nomadism

Somewhere in literature I have encountered the notion of an "urban nomad". This notion refers to the increasing frequency of changing one's domicile (the average period of living in one location in the US is barely over four years, I recall), or, perhaps, more specifically to a contemporary metropolitan nomadism, a novel life style without a home altogether, without a fixed point of reference and return. The mobility of life today, however, extends far beyond urban nomadism; it is turning increasingly into an existential nomadism, an experience of life itself in constant transition without roots and domicile. The human capacities of dreaming and imagination offer us a means of immaterial transit, but today's technologies, from machines that provide physical mobility, to electronic transit and fictitious and virtual mobility, overrun the capacities of our imaginations. We can say that reality replaces imagination, and that facts surpass fiction. However, Jorge Luis Borges makes a significant remark on the interplay of the real and the imaginary: "Reality is not always probable, or likely. But if you are writing a story, you have to make it as plausible as you can, because otherwise the reader's imagination will reject it."[3]

Biological life is bound to space and place, and so is human culture. Territoriality is a significant force in all animal life. We humans are fundamentally biological, cultural and historical beings, and the development towards increasing mobility, detachment and speed must have dramatic consequences for our consciousness, our sense of belonging and responsibility, and our ethical responses. And for human imagination itself, I believe.

In his seminal book *Place and Placelessness* (1976) Edward Relph introduces the notion of "existential outsideness": "Existential outsideness involves a self-conscious and reflective uninvolvement, an alienation from people and places, a homelessness, a sense of the unreality of the world, and of not belonging."[4] Relph explains his concept further by quoting Max Scheler: "To find one's place in the world, the world must be a cosmos. In a chaos there is no place."[5] In my view, there can hardly be any sense of self in chaos, either. The world and the self define each other mutually in accordance with Merleau-Ponty's notion of chiasmatic intertwining.

Scheler's argument evokes the question: What kind of a concept of cosmos are we projecting today in order to structure our brave new world? Haven't we lost our sense of cosmos and centre entirely?

I wish to use the anthropological example of the nomadic Rendile tribe living in Kenya to point out the significance of the image of cosmos as an organising image of human life. The Rendile people are constantly on the move. Every morning the women of the tribe disassemble the huts constructed of arcing wooden frames and

---

3   Norman Thomas di Giovanni, Daniel Halpern, Frank MacShane (eds), *Borges on Writing* (Hopewell, New Jersey: The Eco Press, 1994), 45.
4   Edward Relph, *Place and Placelessness* (London: Pion Limited, 1986), 51.
5   Relph, ibid. 43.

leather surfaces, and load them on camels to move on to the next destination on their endless journey. In the evening the women unload the huts and reconstruct them in the configuration of a circle that has a wider open space towards the rising sun in the east. The chief's hut is always erected on the opposite side of the circle with its door facing the rising sun. These traditional nomads carry the structure of their cosmos in their memory and they reconstruct the image of their world, their *Imago Mundi*, the temporal cycle of the day, as well as their social order, every single day. They make concrete their space and time as well as their social hierarchy through the very structure of their settlement. Cosmological narratives, rites and rituals of other cultures serve the very same purpose. The Dogon people, for instance, living in Mali, south of the Sahara, re-enact their complex cosmology every single day in each one of their daily chores. Permanence and change are bound in a closed and meaningful circuit.

Mobility and Modernity

Cosmopolitanism, travel, and increasing detachment from cultural as well as social ties were seen early on as desirable qualities of modern life. The modern hero was the flaneur, globetrotter, and explorer. With the recent explosive expansion of globalised economies and businesses, world-wide trends and fashions, and constant acceleration of change, culture is becoming increasingly independent from locality and historicity, and turning into an endless and restless flux; materials and products, people and capital, ideas and desires all orbiting the globe at an ever-increasing pace.

The digital universe is the newest expansion of this flux. The amount of placeless digital information is already truly dizzying: today there are one billion PC Internet users, 600 billion Internet pages, 2 billion Google searches per month, and 1 million e-mails sent every second.[6] In addition to the fact that material goods and people are today detached from their origins, information, knowledge and entertainment are also increasingly displaced. This implies the loss of origins, or the truth of origin. The ideal of mobility is accompanied by the seductive appeal of speed and immateriality. "All that is solid melts into air", as Karl Marx predicted as early as 1856.[7] and this evaporation and disappearance is certainly

---

6   Lecture by Anssi Vanjoki, executive Vice President of the Nokia Group, at a seminar on technology and culture, Espoo, 12 May 2006.

7   "All fixed, fast-frozen relations, with their train of ancient and venerable prejudices and opinions, are swept away, all new formed ones become antiquated before they can ossify. All that is solid melts into air, all that is holy is profaned, and men at last are forced to face…the real conditions of their lives and their relations with their fellow men", Karl Marx, "Speech at the Anniversary of the *Peoples Paper*, 1856". As quoted in Marshall Berman, *All That Is Solid Melts Into Air: The Experience of Modernity* (New York: Verso, 1990), 21.

true today. We are lost in a simultaneous and placeless world of endless mobility. Characteristically, the beginning sentence of any mobile telephone conversation today is: "Where are you?" "Here no longer exists; everything is now", as Paul Virilio argues.[8]

"To be modern is to find ourselves in an environment that promises us adventure, power, joy, growth, transformation of ourselves and the world – and, at the same time, that threatens to destroy everything we have, everything we know, everything we are. [...] As a result of all this, we find ourselves today in the midst of a modern age that has lost touch with the roots of its modernity", writes Marshall Berman in his book that quotes the prophecy of Karl Marx as its very title.[9]

Berman points out the catastrophic consequences of the very dynamism of modernity: "The [...] dynamism of the modern economy, and of the culture that grows from this economy, annihilates everything that it creates – physical environments, social institutions, metaphysical ideas, artistic visions, moral values – in order to create more, to go on endlessly creating the world anew. This drive draws all modern men and women into its orbit..."[10]

In 1862 Fyodor Dostoevsky made a thought-provoking remark on our modern desire to create and construct, on the one hand, and our incapability to dwell, on the other: "Man loves to create and build roads, that is beyond dispute. But [...] may it not be that [...] he is instinctively afraid of attaining his goal and completing the edifice he is constructing? How do you know, perhaps he only likes that edifice from a distance and not at close range, perhaps he only likes to build it, and does not want to live in it."[11] Marx was, in fact, commenting on the Crystal Palace, built in 1851 in London, one of the true marvels of human construction. Our incapability to dwell was, of course, one of Martin Heidegger's themes a full century later. Aren't we even today obsessively making and building a new world and, at the same time, detaching ourselves from an erotic intimacy with the world, from the "flesh of world", to use the poetic notion of Maurice Merleau-Ponty?[12]

---

8   Paul Virilio, *The Information Bomb* (London, New York: Verso, 2000), 125.

9   Berman, ibid. 15 and 17.

10   Berman, ibid. 288.

11   As quoted in Berman, ibid. 242.

12   Merleau-Ponty describes the notion of the flesh in his essay "The Intertwining – The Chiasm", *The Visible and the Invisible* (ed.) Claude Lefort (Northwestern University Press, Evanston, 1969): "My body is made of the same flesh as the world [...] and moreover [...] this flesh of my body is shared by the world [...]" (248), and; "The flesh (of the world or my own) is [...] a texture that returns to itself and conforms to itself" (146). The notion of "the flesh" derives form Merleau-Ponty's dialectical principle of the intertwining of the world and the self. He also speaks of the "ontology of the flesh" as the ultimate conclusion of his initial phenomenology of perception. This ontology implies that meaning is both within and without, subjective and objective, spiritual and material. See Richard Kearney, "Maurice Merleau-Ponty", *Modern Movements in European Philosophy* (Manchester and New York: Manchester University Press, 1994), 73–90.

Aren't we more interested in efficiency and production than our own existence itself? Aren't we more interested in having than being, as Erich Fromm suggested? Are we losing our capacity to dwell, to inhabit the world poetically, as Heidegger suggested?

The modernist poet Octavio Paz points out the tragic loss of roots in modernity as a consequence of its mere speed: "[Modernity is] cut off from the past and continuously hurtling forward at such a dizzy pace that it cannot take root, that it merely survives from one day to the next: it is unable to return to its beginnings and thus recover its powers of renewal."[13] The poet's remarks suggest that in our obsession with progress we could well be regressing and going qualitatively backwards. This paradox of apparent material progress and spiritual impoverishment has, indeed, been pointed out by numerous thinkers.

In the beginning of the modern era, Baudelaire depicted a modern hero in his essay "Painters of Modern Life", who should "set up his house in the heart of the multitude amid the ebb and flow of motion, in the midst of the fugitive and the infinite in the midst of the metropolitan crowd. [...] This love of universal life [must] enter into the crowd as though it were an immense reservoir of electrical energy [...] Or we might compare him to a kaleidoscope gifted with consciousness."[14] Doesn't this weird image of infiniteness, cosmopolitan collectivity and kaleidoscopic consciousness resemble our current reality as represented by the ever-expanding labyrinth of the digital Web?

The Significance of Roots

Allow me to quote an entirely opposite view on the crucial importance of cultural and mental roots. This view is expressed by Simone Weil in her book *L'enracinement, The Need for Roots*, which has a poetic title in its Swedish translation, *Att slå rot*: "To be rooted is perhaps the most important and least appreciated need of the human soul. It is one of the hardest to define. A person has roots by virtue of his real, active and natural participation in the life of the community, which preserves in living shape certain particular expectations for the future [...] Every human being needs to have multiple roots. It is necessary for him to draw well-nigh the whole of his moral, intellectual, and spiritual life by way of the environment of which he forms a part".[15]

The protagonist of *Homo Faber*, written by Max Frisch (an architect by training) exemplifies the modern mobile and emancipated hero. He is a UNESCO expert who constantly travels the world on his expert missions. His apparent freedom brought about by mobility and detachment from place, finally turns into an unbearable tragedy; the protagonist ends up making love to his own daughter

---

13   Octavio Paz, as quoted in Berman, op. cit., 35.
14   Charles Baudelaire, as quoted in Berman, op. cit., 145.
15   Simone Weil, *The Need for Roots* (Boston: Beacon Press, 1995).

whom he cannot identify because of his loss of roots and the memory and moral criteria brought about by human placedness. This is the delusion of space and time; as the criteria of "where" and "when", place and time, lose their meanings, the existential situation loses its gravity, its sense of the real and authority, as well as its very ethical ground.

The ceaseless exploration of the secrets of the world has the tendency of eliminating the mythical, magical and enticing dimensions of reality; the realm of myth and belief turns into scientific knowledge and rationality, magic turns into utility, and symbols into everyday reality. The primordial world of dream, imagery and mental projection is emptied of meaning. This is the ground for the existential poverty and boredom of our scientific world. The Moon used to be symbolised by silver and it was itself the symbol of romantic love, not to speak of being the projection of countless aspects of "the other". Man's first journey to the Moon devaluated this celestial body to a mere dead mass of matter and dust. The advancement of our mobility and rationalisation turned the credo of the Futurists, "Down with the Moon", into an experiential reality.

The victories of progress also, sadly, imply the loss of the utopian dimension; there is no utopia on this Earth any longer, only progress and its reversal, dystopia.

The Collapse of Time

Philosophers of postmodernity, such as David Harvey, Fredric Jameson and Daniel Bell,[16] have identified distinct changes that have taken place in our perception and understanding of space and time. "Space has become the primary aesthetic problem of mid-twentieth century culture as the problem of time (in Bergson, Proust and Joyce) was the primary aesthetic problem of the first decades of this century", Fredric Jameson writes.[17] These writers have, for instance, pointed out a curious reversal, or exchange of the two fundamental physical dimensions: the spatialisation of time. In my view, the other reversal has also taken place: the temporalisation of space. These reversals are exemplified by the fact that we commonly measure space through units of time and vice versa. The postmodern era of speed and mobility has also brought about a curious new phenomenon; the collapse or implosion of the time horizon onto the flat screen of the present. Today we can appropriately speak of a simultaneity of the world; everything is simultaneously present to our consciousness. David Harvey writes in 1989 about "time-space compression" and argues: "I want to suggest that we have been experiencing, these last two decades, an intense phase of time-space compression

---

16   See for instance, David Harvey, *The Condition of Postmodernity* (Cambridge, Mass., Oxford, England: Blackwell Publishers, 1992); Fredric Jameson, "Postmodernism, or the Cultural Logic of Late Capitalism", *New Left Review* 146, 53–92; Daniel Bell, *The Cultural Contradictions of Capitalism* (New York: Basic Books, 1978).

17   Fredric Jameson, as quoted in Harvey, op. cit., 201.

that has had a disorienting and disruptive impact upon political-economic practice, the balance of class power, as well as upon cultural and social life."[18] This process of compression has certainly dramatically continued and accelerated during the two decades since Harvey made his argument.

Mobility has other mental consequences, too; it has the tendency to cancel the vertical dimension in our experience of the world. Until a century ago, the vertical tension between Heaven and Hell, the above and the below, divinities and mortals, dominated the human experiential world. Today's world of quasi-rationality, physical mobility and digital nets is a world of mere horizontality. We do not look up into the sky any longer, our gaze is fixed on the horizon; we do not look at our ultimate future in the heavens but beyond the horizon. The mythical and cosmic dimensions are lost. Gaston Bachelard points out that even dwelling has lost its vertical dimension and has turned into horizontality. He quotes Joë Bousque, the French poet, who writes of a "one-storied man who has his cellar in his attick".[19] We have our Heaven in Hell, and vice versa; this loss of the "second dimension", or "the other" of our lives had already been suggested by Herbert Marcuse in his *One-Dimensional Man* (1964).[20]

Another evident consequence of mobility and speed is the shrinking of the world. In fact, the instantaneity of the world eliminates the geographic reality of the world altogether; the world turns into a collection of images, travel posters and TV programs. In his book *A Landscape of Events*, Paul Virilio, the philosopher of speed, mentions Donald Trump's "supersonic golf tournament". The performance took place on three different continents on one and the same day: apparently organized on 3 August 1996, the sixty participants were able to putt successively in Marrakesh (Africa), Shannon (Europe), and Atlantic City (United States). Thanks to the chartering of a special Concorde, three continents were reduced to the size of a golf course and the confines of the Earth to those of a golf green.[21]

In this process of time-space compression, time has lost its experiential depth, its plasticity, as it were. This collapse is brought about by an incredible acceleration of time in the contemporary world. Speed is the most seminal product of the current phase of industrial culture; the industrial world is not primarily producing products and services, but it is accelerating consumption and oblivion. This development has given rise to a "philosophy of speed", as exemplified by the writings of Paul Virilio;[22] Virilio calls his science of speed "dromology". The aesthetics of speed,

---

18   Harvey, op. cit., 284.

19   As quoted in Gaston Bachelard, *The Poetics of Space* (Boston: Beacon Press, 1969), 26.

20   Herbert Marcuse, *One-Dimensional Man: Studies in the Ideology of Advanced Industrial Society* (Boston: Beacon Press, 1991).

21   Paul Virilio, *A Landscape of Events* (Cambridge, Mass., London, England: The MIT Press, 2000), 10.

22   For instance, Paul Virilio, *Katoamisen estetiikka* [Ésthétique de la disparaition] (Tampere, Gaudeamus Kirja, 1994).

however, had been already introduced by the first decades of last century. "The world's magnificence has been enriched by a new beauty; the beauty of speed", F.T. Marinetti declared in a futurist Manifesto almost a century ago.[23]

An Architecture of Death

A fascination with speed and the unavoidable collisions of matter and thought, as well as rejection of causality, are clearly the essence of deconstructivist thinking. It is also characteristic of current avant-garde architecture to question traditional humanist architectural values and ethics.

Coop Himmelblau, one of the leading avant-garde architectural offices of the past two decades, declares an "architecture of desolation", an architectural aesthetics of speed, compression, fragmentation and death: "The aesthetics of the architecture of death in white sheets. Death in tiled hospital rooms. The architecture of sudden death on the pavement. Death from a rib cage pierced by a steering shaft. The path of the bullet through a dealer's head on 42nd Street. The aesthetics of the architecture of the surgeon's razor-sharp scalpel. The aesthetics of peep-show sex in washable plastic boxes. Of the broken tongues and the dried-up eyes."[24]

This culturally aggressive nihilism, or cultural terrorism inspired by technological determinism and speed, has its predecessors in the Futurist Movement almost a century ago: "Take up your pickaxes, your axes and hammers, and wreck, wreck the venerable cities, pitilessly! Come on! Set fire to the library shelves! Turn aside the canals to flood the museums!",[25] commands the Futurist Painters' Manifesto from 1910. "We look for the creation of a nonhuman type in whom moral suffering, goodness of heart, affection, and love, those corrosive poisons of vital energy, interrupters of powerful bodily electricity, will be abolished",[26] F.T. Marinetti prophesied a year earlier. This is, indeed, a reality today in the world of entertainment, and, increasingly, in real life. Aestheticisation and the ritualisation of cruelty, madness and the death of empathy are clearly emerging in real life too.

The Culture of Slowness

The dizzying acceleration of experiential time and the accompanying sense of disaster during the past few decades is rather easy to recognise in comparison with the slow and patient time projected by the great Russian, German and French

---

23   As quoted in Thom Mayne, "Statement", Peter Pran (ed.), Ligang Qui (China, DUTPress, 2006), 4.

24   Coop Himmelblau, "Die Fascination der Stadt", as quoted in Anthony Vidler, *The Architectural Uncanny* (Cambridge, Mass., London, England: The MIT Press, 1999), 76.

25   As quoted in Berman, op. cit., 25.

26   Ibid.

classical novels of the nineteenth century. It suffices here to mention the languid description of the protagonist Hans Castorp's seven-year stay in the Berghof Sanatorium in Thomas Mann's novel *The Magic Mountain*, or the three thousand and five hundred pages of Marcel Proust's *In Search of Lost Time*.

Italo Calvino comments interestingly on this acceleration of time over the past century: "Long novels written today are perhaps a contradiction: the dimension of time has been shattered, we cannot live or think except in fragments of time each of which goes off along its trajectory and immediately disappears. We can re-discover the continuity of time only in the novels of that period when time no longer seemed stopped and did not yet seem to have exploded".[27]

It is quite astonishing to find the lament of Abbé Lamennais about the disappearance of time, written in 1819: "Man does not read any longer. There is no time for it. The spirit is called upon from all directions simultaneously; it has to be addressed quickly or else it disappears. But there are things, which cannot be said or comprehended quickly, and exactly these are most important for man. This rushing of movement, which does not allow man to concentrate on anything, finally shatters the entire human reason."[28] I give this piece of literary evidence, dating back two centuries, as evidence that this problem has its roots deep in the history of modern culture. Our loss of time and place is the consequence of a historical process.

Marcel Proust makes an interesting comment on the alteration of our consciousness of time since the Roman era: "Since railways came into existence, the necessity of not missing trains has taught us to take account of minutes, whereas among the ancient Romans, who not only had a more cursory acquaintance with astronomy but led less hurried lives, the notion of not only of minutes but even of fixed hours barely existed."[29]

The postmodern philosophers point out a distinct "depthlessness" as a characteristic of today's art, and we cannot but agree with Charles Newman's sad description of the American novel today: "The fact of the matter is that a sense of diminishing control, loss of individual autonomy and generalized helplessness has never been so instantaneously recognizable in our literature – the flattest possible characters in the flattest possible landscapes rendered in the flattest possible diction. The presumption seems to be that America is a vast fibrous desert in which a few laconic needs nevertheless manage to sprout in the cracks."[30] In my view, the same flatness and lack of epic depth characterises the mainstreams of other art forms as well, including architecture.

---

27 Italo Calvino, *If on a Winter's Night a Traveller* (San Diego, New York, London: Harcourt, Brace and Company, 1981), 8.

28 As quoted in René Huyghe, *Dialogue avec le visible: Connaissance de la peinture* (Paris: Flammarion, 1955), page unidentified.

29 Marcel Proust, *In Search of Lost Time*, volume 4: Sodom and Gomorrah, 258.

30 As quoted in Harvey, op. cit., 58.

I wish to point out a fundamental change that has recently occurred in minute and commonplace detail; the difference in the reading of time by means of a traditional watch and a digital watch (my quote derives from a book entitled *Conversations About the End of Time* published at the turn of the Millennium): "When you look at a watch dial for the time that is situated within the circle of time, you immediately recall what you have done in the course of the day, where you were this morning, what time it was when you bumped into your friend, you remember when dusk is going to fall, and you see the time that's left before bedtime, when you'll go to bed sure in the knowledge of another day well spent, and with the certainty also that on the following day time will resume its daily course around your watch. If all you've got is a little rectangle, you have to live life as a series of moments, and you lose all true measure of time."[31] This is the fundamental experiential difference between analogue and digital measuring. What is lost with the digital watch is the cyclical nature of natural time.

What is even more essentially lost in the digital world is our natural sensory memory. Milan Kundera makes a remark to that effect: "The degree of slowness is directly proportional to the intensity of memory; the degree of speed is directly proportional to the intensity of forgetting."[32] This text of mine intends to point out the virtues and benefits of slowness, or the "chemistry of time",[33] to use a notion of Proust, and the "poetic chemistry" of Bachelard.[34]

We have all the reason to be frightened by the disappearance and abstraction of time and the curiously related phenomenon: the expansion of boredom. I am not going to address this subject matter, however, beyond simply referring to a recent book on the philosophy of boredom by the Norwegian philosopher Lars Svendsen.[35] It seems to me that a distinct slowness reveals the depth and detail of life, whereas speed and mobility wipe those dimensions away, causing a sense of intolerable flatness, sameness and boredom. Besides, speed and transition eliminate the erotic dimension of the world. Just think of the absolutely least erotic places on earth – international airports.[36] For me, the ultimate criteria of architectural quality is whether you can imagine falling in love in the space in question – can anyone of you imagine yourself falling in love at an airport?

---

31 Catherine David, Frédérick Lenoir and Jean-Philippe de Tournac (eds), *Conversations about the End of Time* (London: Penguin books, 2000), 139.

32 Milan Kundera, *Slowness* (New York: Harper Collins Publishers, 1966), 39.

33 Proust, op. cit., volume 6: *Time Regained*, 331.

34 Gaston Bachelard, *Water and Dreams: An Essay on the Imagination of Matter* (Dallas, Texas: The Pegasus Foundation, 1983), 46.

35 Lars Fr. H. Svendsen, *Ikävystymisen filosofia* [The Philosophy of Boredom] (Helsinki: Kustannusosakeyhtiö Tammi, 2005).

36 Nevertheless, Alberto Pérez-Gómez's book *Polyphilo or the Dark Forest Revisited: An Erotic Epiphany of Architecture* (Cambridge, Mass., London, England: The MIT Press, 1992) is a novel of erotic events taking place at airports; the book is a re-staging of Francesco Colonna's mystical novel *Hypnerotomachia Poliphili*, published in Venice in 1499.

I would like to suggest that we have lost our capacity to dwell in time, or inhabit time. We have been pushed outside of the space of time. Time has turned into a vacuum in opposition to the "tactile sense of [time]"[37] in Proust's writings, for instance. We live increasingly outside of the continuum of time, the Bergsonian duration;[38] we dwell solely in space. It is tragic, indeed, that in the era of four-dimensional, or multi-dimensional, space in our scientific and operational thinking, we are experientially thrown back to Euclidian space, restricted to its three spatial dimensions. We have every reason even to be worried about the disappearance of the third dimension, the depth of space. The substance of time seems to exist nowadays only as archaeological remains in the literary, artistic and architectural works of past eras. Similarly, the original silence of the world exists only in fragments, but as Max Picard, the philosopher of silence, suggests, we are frightened by all fragments.[39] We are equally frightened by fragments of silence, time and solitude.

Living in Digital Space

The simultaneous placelessness and timelessness of modern existential space, and the consequent detachment from a haptic realism and intimacy has been violently reinforced by the digital reality. The computer and the digital universe are frequently greeted with unconditional enthusiasm. I do not wish to promote a Luddite attitude towards the advancement of technology, but I want to consider the potential negative consequences of these entirely unforeseen dimensions of reality in relation to our bio-cultural essence, our profound historicity as well as our fundamental sensory mode of existence. Our bodily, sensory and mental constitution is clearly tuned to the characteristics of our natural habitat, not to a digital unreality.

The fabricated space of the digital age can be subdivided into three categories: cyberspace, hyperspace and exospace. *Cyberspace* is defined as the digitally supported information space of the Internet, *hyperspace* as the computer-induced perception of virtual space in real time, whereas *exospace* is a digitally supported imagery of extraterrestial spatial conditions.[40]

"Technology today is more precise and more powerful than the human body. [...] We're no longer limited in space to the biosphere [...] We're heading for extraterrestial space, but our body is only designed for this biosphere", Stelios

---

37   Jean-Claude Carriére, "Answering the Sphinx", *Conversations on Time*, op. cit., 95.

38   Henrik Bergson, *Matter and Memory* (New York: Zone Books, 1991).

39   Max Picard, *The World of Silence* (Washington, D.C., Gateway Editions, 1988), 212.

40   Gül Kaçmaz, *Architectural Space in the Digital Age: Cyberspace, Hyperspace and Exospace Through Science Fiction Films* (Istanbul: Istanbul Technical University, Institute of Science and Technology, 2004).

Accadiou argues.[41] I would like to also add that our sensory systems are tuned for a world of material and gravitational realism. I would venture to argue that the experiences of beauty that our senses enjoy derive from the natural materiality, rhythm and causation of the natural world. I do not argue that the experience of beauty could not be expanded beyond the "natural", I simply believe that our sense of beauty has its bio-cultural origins. Joseph Brodsky, the poet, argues emphatically: "Believe it or not, the purpose of evolution is beauty."[42]

In her doctoral dissertation *Architectural Space in the Digital Age* Gül Kaçmaz concludes wisely that, "Cyberspace, hyperspace and exospace all have spatial qualities; they are forms of space, but none of them can be considered as architectural space. Features of architectural space contradict these spaces. Digitally supported spaces are like the opposite of architectural space: they have features that are the reverse of architectural space. They are actually 'the other' for architectural space."[43] Architectural space is real, it has materiality, it is continuous and static, and architectural space is extroverted, she argues.

Nostalgia for the Absent Home

As Joseph Brodsky argues in the introduction of my essay, mobility complicates our sense of nostalgia. The word "nostalgia" was introduced in 1678 by a Swiss medical student, Johannes Hofer, who described an illness that was characterised by symptoms such as insomnia, anorexia, palpitations, stupor, fever, and especially persistent thinking of home. Hofer and later physicians of the seventeenth and eighteenth centuries believed that this disease, the longing for home, or homesickness, could result in death if the patient could not be returned home.[44]

One of the most touching expressions of nostalgia, the reverse side of mobility, in our time is Andrey Tarkovsky's film *Nostalghia* (1983), in which the protagonist, the Russian poet Andrei Gorchakov, finally dies of a heart attack and his strange friend, the mad mathematician Domenico, commits suicide by self-immolation. Both men are estranged, the first from the reality of place and the second from the reality of sane judgement.

Nostalghia is a film about longing, the sorrow for an absent home: "I wanted to make a film about Russian nostalgia – about that state of mind peculiar to our nation which affects Russians who are far from their native land [...] In Italy I made a film that was profoundly Russian in every way: morally, politically, emotionally."[45] The film achieves its unique intensity because it expresses Tarkovsky's own

---

41   As quoted in Kaçmaz, op. cit., 51.
42   Joseph Brodsky, *On Grief and Reason*, op. cit., 207.
43   Kaçmaz, op. cit., 103.
44   Relph, op. cit., 41.
45   Andrey Tarkovsky, *Sculpting in Time – Reflections on the Cinema* (London: The Bodley Head, 1986), 110.

yearning and nostalgia for home: "The protagonist virtually becomes my alter ego, embodying all my emotions, psychology and nature. He is a mirror image of me. I have never made a film which mirrors my own states of mind with so much violence, and liberates my inner world in such depth. When I saw the finished product I felt uneasy, as when one sees oneself in a mirror."[46] The very personal nature of the sentiments expressed in the film is a clue to their exceptionally painful tenderness. "It would never have occurred to me when I started shooting, that my own, all too specific, nostalgia was soon to take possession of my soul forever."[47] In his diary, Tarkovsky echoes Gorchakov's pain and alienation: "I am so homesick, so homesick."[48]

Tarkovsky and the protagonist of his film suffer from the same longing for home that countless Russian writers, musicians, and artists have endured and documented both in their correspondence and their artistic works.[49] More than a century before Tarkovsky, Fyodor Dostoevsky, who had escaped the wrath of his creditors by fleeing to Milan with his wife in 1868, had reported similar sentiments in a letter: "My heart is very heavy; I am homesick and I am uncertain of my situation; my debts [...] make me awfully depressed. In addition I have distanced myself from Russian life to the degree that I find it difficult to write anything at all since I miss fresh Russian impressions. Just think: in six months I have not seen a single Russian newspaper."[50] Dostoevsky wanted to return to Russia regardless of the threat of being deported to Siberia.

In an interview, Tarkovsky defined this Russian illness further: "It is not only a feeling of homesickness. It is an illness because it robs mental strength, it takes away the ability to work and even the desire to live. It is like a handicap, the absence of something, a part of oneself. I am certain that it is a real illness of the Russian character."[51] Ultimately, he defines this nostalgia as the loss of faith and hope. The tragic homesickness of the protagonist is echoed in a story in the film. Eugenia, the poet's guide, recalls reading a newspaper article about a Calabrian domestic worker, serving a family in northern Italy, who burns down the house of her employer because of her desperate homesickness for her native Calabria. The incident also introduces the final theme of the film, the violence of fire.

All of Tarkovsky's films are about the perpetual search for home, the lost home of childhood. The tension between the notions of "house" and "home" is a central

---

46   Tony Mitchell, "Andrey Tarkovsky and *Nostalghia*", *Film Criticism* 8, no. 3 (1984), 5.

47   Tarkovsky, op. cit., 216.

48   Andrey Tarkovsky, *Martyrologia: Päiväkirjat 1970–81* [Martyrology: Diaries 1970–1981] (Joensuu: Kustannus Oy Mabuse, 1989), 342.

49   Some of the leading masterpieces of Russian literature were written abroad; for instance, Dostoyevsky wrote *The Idiot* and Nikolai Gogol wrote *Dead Souls* in Italy.

50   Anders Olofsson, "Nostalghia", *Tanken på en hemkomst* (ed.) Magnus Bergh and Birgitta Munkhammar (Stockholm: Alfa Beta Bokförlag, 1986), 150.

51   Olofsson, ibid. 152.

motif in Andrey Tarkovsky's life's work as well as in the poems of his father. In the Communist state, home also implied being under control – home came to mean a concentration camp. That is why home turned into a mystical dream in their artistic work.

The conflict and dialectics between the notions of "architecture" and "home" should also be a central concern for architects. The separation of notions of house and home is at the root of modernity. The dialectics of alienation and belonging, and the difficulty, or impossibility of homecoming, are central themes of modern existence. Homecoming is necessarily grounded in remembrance, and implies the conservatism of returning, whereas the essence of modernity implies forgetting and a brave journey without return towards an emancipated future. Consequently, the modern position denies the conventional dimensions of dwelling; the notions of home and homelessness, specificity and generality, fuse tragically with each other in the modern project. The ideal of the perfectly functional house, the modern "machine for dwelling"[52] aims at eliminating discomfort and friction, but the realisation of the self within the world implies a confrontation. As a consequence, the dialectics of intimacy and distance, invitation and rejection, are necessarily characteristic of architectural works capable of evoking an existentially meaningful experience.

Aldo van Eyck, one of the modern master architects who questioned the very essence of modernity, sought to re-root architecture in its authentic anthropological soil: "Architecture needs no more, nor should it ever do less, than assist man's homecoming".[53] The alienation and detachment caused by modern projects call for the acknowledgement of our very historicity and our essential need for a spiritual homecoming. This homecoming can only be grounded in the re-enchantment, re-mythification and re-eroticisation of our very existential realm.

Antoine de Saint-Exupéry, one of the early avian heroes of modern mobility, gives a surprisingly sensual and poetic account of his sense of homecoming: "I was the child of that house, filled with the memory of its smells, filled with the coolness of its hallways, filled with the voices that had given it life. There was even the song of the frogs in the pools; they came to be with me here."[54]

Philosophy is really homesickness, an urge to be at home everywhere. Where, then are we going? Always to our home.

Novalis[55]

---

52   Le Corbusier, *Towards a New Architecture* (London and Bradford: Percy, Lund, Humphries and Co., 1959).
53   *Aldo van Eyck*, Herman Hertzberger, Addie van Roijen-Wortmann, Francis Strauven (eds) (Amsterdam: Stichting Wonen, 1982), 65.
54   Antoine de Saint-Exupéry, *Wind, Sand and Stars* (London: Penguin Books, 1991), 39.
55   Novalis, *Fragments*, as quoted in Berman, op. cit., 329.

Chapter 9

From Sacred Place to an Existential Dimension of Mobility

Peter Nynäs

We migrate from one place to another in search of a better life, for clean water and food. We escape because it is dangerous to stay where we are. We are not allowed to settle down, and are forced to move on. We are expatriated for the benefit of various organisations. We travel for temporary enjoyment, to refresh the body and the soul. Mobility cannot be generalised, or as Siikala (2001a: 40) writes: "[T]he movement of a nomad is not the same as that of a migrant."

Still, mobility is probably one of the more profound features of human life, and whether we are forced to move or we move just for the fun of it, mobility affects us as human beings. From a perspective of religious studies, studies of sacred places provide some good examples of this. Pilgrimage, to visit a sacred site like Mecca or Santiago de Compostela, is often characterised by a sweeping or profound experience of inner transformation (see Gothóni 1993). This may also shed light on why religious buildings are among the most popular tourist sites for people in common, even for those of us who are not devout pilgrims. In this article I will, however, turn away from religious phenomena like these. Instead I will shed light on a transformative dimension common to more ordinary experiences of place and mobility, which resembles that of religion.

There is a significant emotional geography connected to the landscapes we move through. Place and mobility sensitise our inner selves and ways of being in the world. I consider this an existential dimension, but this concept is, of course, of an evasive character. In order to explore it, I will elaborate some examples that focus on the emotions and qualities involved in experiences of place and mobility. This implies an emphasis on the recent spatial turn with an explicit interest in its psychological implications. Should we reconceptualise sacred place in terms of an existential dimension of mobility?

Sacred Place and the Spatial Turn

A concern with place has been a part of religious studies from the beginning. From a very brief overview, we can conclude that this has mainly been related to a basic distinction between the holy and the profane, even though there have been different theoretical and conceptual emphases of a psychological, phenomenological or sociological nature.

In the beginning of the twentieth century, the concern with place involved an interest in people's experience of sacred places (James 1902; Otto (1950 [1917]), with an emphasis on experiences of the wholly other (ganz andere) and the numinous. However, it was with Eliade (1957) that the sacred place became the subject of theoretical inquiry. Eliade brought to the discussion a process of sanctification, i.e. how the sacred arises in the world in "hierophanies" as sacred places, imbued with religious meanings. Thus, the emphasis was on the sacred place as a centre (axis mundi), set apart from ordinary and profane space, enabling communication between different domains. In addition to the idea that the primary characteristic of religion is its division of the world into two domains (sacred and profane), Durkheim (1912) underscores that sacred reality is a projection of a social reality. The intensification of feelings that goes with experiences of sacredness is related to social reality, whether or not it is symbolised by a building, an image or a totem.

With modernity, secularisation and a growing awareness of diversity followed a need to re-evaluate the assumed distinction between sacred and profane. According to Knott (2005a: 110), Smith (1987) has "dislodged theory on sacred space from its previous base in a phenomenological conception of the sacred and re-engaged it with social and cultural constructionist approaches". A recent article by Kong and Kiong (2000) exemplifies this shift. They emphasise the need to acknowledge how sacred places are negotiated or reinvented because of contextual changes. Modernity does not simply lead to the downfall of religious beliefs and practices but also allows for a continuation of religion. This means that traditional rituals are being modified, reinterpreted and invented to fit with modernity. Further, modernity also develops its own "sacred" conditions that have nothing to do with religion in the conventional understanding of the word. In their study of how religion is modified and negotiated as modern living makes new demands on society and individuals, Kong and Kiong (2000) point out these processes are embedded in the relationship between social processes on the one hand, and spatial conceptions, forms and structures on the other. Therefore, as Kong (2005: 246–7) argues in a separate study, "[t]he geographer of religion is therefore required to go beyond a focus on religious landscapes of churches, temples, mosques, synagogues and so forth, as has hitherto been the primary focus."

This theoretical perspective represented here by Kong and Kiong is, however, situated within a theoretical development that has taken place in the understanding of place and space, especially within human and cultural geography. The so-called spatial turn focuses on how socially constructed and negotiated cultures, identities, and meanings, both produce and are produced by place and space. Henri Lefebvre's book *The Production of Space* from 1974 (Lefebvre 1991) has been important in this shift towards thinking in terms of place. In this book, Lefebvre rejects the idea that space would be a box without content. In general, the spatial turn implies a re-conceptualisation of space, which emphasises space as a tripartite synthesis of physical, mental, and social spaces operating simultaneously (Lefebvre 1991). In a similar manner, the complexity of place can be recognised in terms of; (1) the physical-geographical dimension, (2) the sensory-emotional dimension, and

(3) the socio-cultural dimension (Karjalainen 1997: 41). An observance of this complexity is also important for the study of religion (see Knott 2005b; Knott 2005c; McAlister 2005).

The spatial turn brings about an understanding of place and space as e.g. symbolically condensed. This resembles earlier studies of symbolism and religious space to some extent (Tillich 1966; Dillistone 1966). Kong and Kiong (2000) refer, among others, to Soja's (1985; 1989) understanding of how capitalist urban space "reverberates complex meanings and symbols whose essence it helps construct" (see Wilson 1993: 75) and, also to Cosgrove and Jackson (1987: 96), who argue that symbolic landscapes "produce and sustain social meaning". Ward (2000: 59) exemplifies the concrete nature of this:

> The staging of public spectacle (festivals for this and that, open-air concerts in central parks etc.), the exaltation of kitsch, the glorification of the superficial, the enormous investment in sports and leisure centres, the new commodification of the city's past (manufacturing a nostalgia that substitutes for continuity and tradition), the inflationary suggestions of the state-of-the-art future, its "under-construction" technicolour present (China towns, heritage centres, gay villages, theme bars etc.) – these are the characteristics of the new city myth, the postmodern city-myth which has come to replace modernity's city-myth so powerfully evoked in *Metropolis*.

Generally, we have two intertwined processes at hand here. First, we can recognise that late modern processes relocate and reshape sacred spatiality. Danièle Hervieu-Léger (2000: 176) writes: "What clearly emerges here is the ambivalent character of religion in modernity, in which the traditional religions can hold their own by tentatively exploiting the symbolic resources at their disposal in order to reconstruct a continuing line of belief for which the common experience of individual believers provides no support." Second, we can recognise the symbolic complexity of the spatiality outside traditional sacred places. The profane can no longer be defined as non-sacred and the distinction between the sacred and profane is blurred. The citation from Ward (2000) clearly shows the relevance of thinking of place in terms of e.g. the imaginary, desire and fantasies. As Baudrillard (1995, cited in Ward 2000: 52), concludes: Disneyland is "presented as imaginary in order to make us believe that the rest is real". The spatial turn questions distinctions like these. Religion can also be located in secular places (see Knott 2005b).

As a means to understand this new condition from a perspective of sociology of religion, Hervieu-Léger emphasises the *act of believing* in addition to beliefs and convictions as such. We need to incorporate in our understanding of religion the practices, languages, gestures and spontaneous automatism in which these beliefs themselves are seated: "To believe is belief in motion, belief as it is lived." Her observation is relevant for our understanding of sacred places. Knott (2005a: 113) writes: "space [...] is thoroughly enmeshed in embodiment and everyday practice". Additionally, in the exploration of place and in particular sacred place in the context of modernity, Sheldrake (2001) underscores the fact that the experiential or spiritual dimension related to sacredness needs to be considered a manifestation of practice. Practice is here understood in a broad way as the practice of everyday living. He exemplifies the relevance of this by underscoring that "the city [...] represents and creates a climate of values that defines how humans understand themselves and gather together" (Sheldrake 2001: 145).

The particular aim of this article is to shed light on the existential dimension of place and mobility, i.e. to apply a psychological perspective. The recognition of the condensed symbolic complexity of space also demands a shift from an understanding of symbolic place as illustrative to an understanding of how place interprets, elicits an affective response, and invites relationships (see Seasoltz 2005: 65). In line with the spatial turn, a new interest also in emotion is evident (Bondi, Davidson and Smith 2005: 1). This is not opposed to the former interest in social processes and practices. Emotional geography attempts "to understand emotion – experientially and conceptually – in terms of its socio-*spatial* mediation and articulation rather than as entirely interiorised subjective mental states" (Bondi, Davidson and Smith 2005: 3).

My aim to shed light on an existential dimension of place and mobility is framed by the spatial turn and the emotional geography in particular. In order to address this dimension I will explore some examples related to individual experiences of spatiality and mobility. My main concern is how spatiality and mobility sensitise and move the human self. They evoke affective responses, invite various forms of relatedness, and shape the subjective being and becoming. Inspired by phenomenological thinking (see e.g. Husserl 1958), we can take these phenomena as exemplifying an essential structure (Casey 2000: 22). Still, my interpretation and understanding of these examples is influenced by psychology (mainly object relations theory), and further by architectural theory and human geography.

In Search of a Presence

I will turn to a case history from my therapeutic practice. The woman who told me this was about 40 years old, and was experiencing a difficult crisis due the divorce she was going through. In the decade previous to her divorce, she had been mostly working at home caring for the children and the household. Therefore, when her husband wanted to divorce her she experienced this as a betrayal and abandonment. Furthermore, the situation demanded that she find a job and provide for the children, something that would be difficult. She did not have a good education and had very little work experience. In short, the divorce confronted her with a number of challenges related to her emotional, social, and economic capabilities. However, from my point of view her crisis also seemed to trigger an underlying depressive borderline character. Her experience of reality was partly distorted by strong aggressive and sexual fantasies of a psychotic and disorganised character. These fantasies communicated her sense of having no value in her self and her longing for someone who would care for all her needs.

In response to the overwhelming demands she faced, the woman decided to commit suicide. Late in the night she left her children at home and went down to the sea. This was a place she had often liked to visit. It was a scenic place but also a place were things melted together, as she put it. The horizon disappeared and the difference between land and sea was dispersed by the waves. She liked the place especially when the weather was bad, grey and stormy. Her favourite spot was a cliff, on a tongue of land partly surrounded by the sea and the waves. In the way that she described the landscape, it struck me that it was a symbolic and idealised externalisation of the emotional geography of her inner self and its borderline character, an external manifestation of a low structured landscape of chaotic, eruptive and invasive affects. Such was the place she had chosen to be her grave. Put another way, the drama she enacted in relation to the particular place was an attempt to reach her inner and most early experience of a caring body, unfortunately associated with or available to her only within a field of chaos, affective turmoil and aggression (see Bollas 1996).

When she came to the shore that night her eyes happened to fall on a metal plate fastened to one of the cliffs. The metal plate had engraving and the text was from the Bible, verses 9–10 from Psalms 139: "*If I rise on the wings of the dawn, if I settle on the far side of the sea, even there your hand will guide me, your right hand will hold me fast.*" Next to the metal plate was a small box, like a mailbox, where she found slips of paper with all the verses from this psalm:

Where can I go from your Spirit?
Where can I flee from your presence?
If I go up to the heavens, you are there;
 if I make my bed in the depths, [a] you are there.
If I rise on the wings of the dawn,
I settle on the far side of the sea,
 even there your hand will guide me,
 your right hand will hold me fast.
If I say, "Surely the darkness will hide me
and the light become night around me,"
 even the darkness will not be dark to you;
the night will shine like the day,
 for darkness is as light to you.

After the woman had read the text, she sat down, waited for a time, and went back home. She gained confidence and trust in not being alone or abandoned in the abyss of her inner turmoil. The nightly journey became a journey of inner transformation, a beginning of a long struggle to manage her life. For my specific purpose in this article it is not necessary or even possible to dismantle the complex relationships between the inner chaos of the woman, her relationship to the landscape and the biblical text, but I will make some observations of importance.

This short case history highlights the profound significance and complexity we may find in the relationship between the human self and place. It sheds light on mobility as a vehicle for inner change and development. Reflecting on the woman's story, it might be wrong to assume that her inner purpose was to end her life the night when she left her home. On the contrary, we can assume that she had experienced a dead end on her life path and hence felt a strong urge to change her life, to find a new direction. The change she experienced was not primarily caused by the text or its contents. The text – experienced as a voice directed to her personally – was a vehicle for the structuring presence she was looking for and trying to integrate with the help of the landscape she intended to surrender to.

Weiss (1999: 33) suggests that early body images can be re-enacted in a moment "as when we return to a childhood 'haunt' and find ourselves haunted by an earlier body image that was able to negotiate the childhood space with peace". In the case of the woman, the haunting inner body image of self and other was perhaps not good enough for negotiating peace, but maybe good enough for re-enacting a sense of presence. The harsh spatiality of the landscape was an essential part of the drama the woman had to reinforce and enact in order to enter a journey towards inner consolidation. Her struggle over life and death with the landscape was first and foremost a struggle over the potential presence she needed to discover in her inner landscape.

A Reach for Being and Becoming

This introductory example from the beginning of a therapeutic process highlights a dimension of place and mobility, which I have conceptualised in terms of an existential dimension. By this I primarily mean that some places sensitise the self. Hence we attach importance to them and seek them out in times of crises. A central feature is further that we interact with the place as if it was a person of great importance in our lives. This is not an unusual way to relate to places. On the contrary it is quite ordinary. Human relatedness and object seeking are not directed towards human beings alone but also towards the non-human environment: "[F]ar from being of little or no account to human personality development, [the non-human environment] constitutes one of the most basically important ingredients of human psychological existence" (Searles 1960: 5f, 23). Thus, needs for inner development require mobility and movement.

In my example above there was an inner transformative potential attributed to or experienced in relation to place or spatiality. This transformative aspect can be more obvious and condensed in relation to sacred places or against the backdrop of an acute personal or social crisis. However, if we take a closer look at more ordinary narratives of experiences of the environment we can often find similar significant features. The following example illustrates a specific location, which is a shelter associated with life and growth. Wright (1996: 71) recalls his early wanderings in the woods in the following way:

...as a child, I spent a lot of time wandering about on my own. In some ways, the world was not dangerous as now, and my mother gave me considerable freedom to wander as I pleased. So, for me, the fields, the woods, the trees, perhaps even the sky were like an extension of home. They were part of my territory – a kind of outreach of it – but one in which I could feel alive and nourished, rather than oppressed and hemmed in.

In this outreach – open but still safe – Wright was during his childhood able to relate to himself in a life-sustaining way in contrast to experiences of being oppressed. Later on in his life – as an adult – his memory of the place seemed to function in a similar way. The memory offered him virtual access to a spatial relatedness of both refuge and vitality. The wandering in the woods and in the fields had been internalised as a set of mental images. Jones (2005: 215) writes that "[g]eographies of memories and memories of geographies are complex and emotional, not least because some, perhaps the most powerful, will be the geographies of our childhood". Many people carry similar memories and attach similar emotional contrasts to a personal geography. Such virtual or mental outreaches are valued and can be used for both inner consolidation and escapism.

In the following example, another aspect of the existential dimension becomes evident. A Finnish writer describes her relatedness to nature in this way:

> The lake was about to wake up. It was all empty, just mist on the surface of water, and it waited for me to put into words the message of its silence. Of course I have to use what is around me, everything growing, withering, blowing, shining...All this takes place inside us as well. Nature does not need my interpretations. I need nature.

In this example, nature is more than a place of refuge and vitality. Through its ability to reflect on the inner self, place also gives shape and colour to human existence, and the sense of being. Pallasmaa (1996: 27) writes from a perspective of architectural studies that "*[t]he world and the self inform and redefine each other constantly*". He accounts for a relationship between place and the human self in which the two constitute each other in a reciprocal way. Casey (2001: 406) argues in a similar way: "In effect, there is *no place without self; and no self without place*". This reciprocity is not only of a social character. It is also of an existential character involving a profound emotional aspect. Places may be vehicles of both being and becoming. Entering a place may be a movement into a self-structuring process.

Place and Language

The example above brings one more aspect to the matter at hand. The Finnish poet experiences her own words as inferior to nature's interpretations. Spatial relatedness also becomes part of a process of articulation. This is relevant. It indicates that spatiality and our movements in landscape resemble the work of language. Like the complexity of language (see Taylor 1985), space gives form and shapes to our being in the world. We do not only interpret and give individually or socially constructed shape to place. There is a significant reciprocity in the correspondence between the human self and place. Places also interpret us. They express and articulate us and are thus constitutive of who we are and become.

This aspect introduces the question "Can nature speak to us?" Smith (2005) explores this question from a hermeneutic point of view and clearly recognises the difficulties involved. Gadamer's hermeneutics gives the impression that "expression and interpretation are wholly dependent on *people putting things into words*, into a human language" (Smith 2005: 225), which constitutes a hermeneutic gulf between culture and nature. In this sense, interpretation is a movement into culture and historicity and a movement away from nature. However, Smith questions the accuracy of this gap and states that we must remove the anthropocentrism present in modernist discussions of the nature of language and the languages of nature. Smith argues that despite Gadamer's emphasis on "openness" and "sensitivity", Gadamer still underplays the role of feeling in understanding. He writes (Smith 2005: 226): "Establishing an affective relation through sensual experience is as much a part of understanding as anything delimited linguistically, and is not something extra to, but a part of, understanding." This, Smith concludes, means that we recognise the interpretative role not only of culture and abstract reason, but also of our experiences of nature and of embodied feelings. The structure of experience that Gadamer defines as the background against which and within which interpretation takes place, must refer to both historically effective consciousness and affective natural history (Smith 2005: 227).

We can also recognise the language of spatiality from another perspective, which also brings us back to mobility in its virtual forms. In many movies, environment and place are an essential part of the story, a language through which essential things are communicated. In his study on architectural images in films, Pallasmaa uses the concept "existential space" to highlight the profound significance of spaces and places we enter (Pallasmaa 2001). Pallasmaa is an architect and his ideas are of course grounded in a more general inquiry into man and the (built) environment (see Pallasmaa 2005, e.g. 69f), but referring to the director Tarkovsky (1986: 150), Pallasmaa (2001: 9) exemplifies the existential dimension of space with the poetic dimension of films and images. According to Pallasmaa, these poetic images are condensations of numerous experiences and invigorate our imagination by opening streams of association and affect. They sensitise the boundary between the world and our selves.

The movie *Brokeback Mountain* offers an interesting example on the theme of language and landscape. It is based on a short story about an intimate relationship between two cowboys, written by E. Annie Proulx, adapted for the screen by Larry McMurtry and Diana Ossana, and directed by Ang Lee. This movie also touches on the necessity of movements and spatiality as a vehicle of inner development and profound transformative articulation. In a very obvious way, the film constructs movements between contrasting places: the world of closed and claustrophobic interiors and the open world of the mountains and forests. In particular, the ongoing chat between the two sheep-herding men, Jack and Ennis, in the camp up on the mountain is striking. A theme they have in common is a sense of paternal oppression and exclusion, which encloses a sense of marginalisation, something that is also verbally manifested. Their way of speaking is to a large extent characterised by insecurity, their inability to express themselves, and a difficulty putting their lives into words. All this, however, grows into a shared sense of dialogue.

- – Man, that's more words than you've spoken in the past two weeks.
- – Hell, that's the most I've spoken in a year.

In this film, the lifelong inner struggle to transform a sense of fundamental loneliness into a sense of related and shared solitude is captured through movements and spatial constructions. This is often possible to experience in a very sensible way through a movement of the camera, and subsequent shifts of visual perspectives, which also engages the audience. Siikala (2001b: 2) writes: "Closeness in space is linked with closeness in mind or memory." Moments of conflicting experiences of isolation and presence visually open up a birds-eye's view of life of the scenic mountain landscape. The audience can continuously follow and feel this underlying movement in the film, where the presence of the other is integrated in an open landscape. The director Ang Lee states: *"That's what gives this movie its existential feel, because the whole drama takes place in that void...in that negative space, in longing"* (Monk 2005).

It needs to be underscored that this is not a negative space in the sense of being an empty or dead space. It is a potential or transitional space, using the words of Winnicott (1971). Our relatedness to external landscapes is characterised by the human capacity to nurture and develop within relatedness, by a fundamental relatedness between self and other that is constituted by play, fantasy, creativity and growth. Thus, experiences like the ones referred to above are common and easy to recognise. Even though the narratives and contexts might constitute very different stories, the profound reciprocity they involve is somewhat archetypical. As the director Ang Lee (Monk 2005) put it, we all have a *Brokeback Mountain* in our heart.

Place and movements are existential trajectories of being and becoming. I use the word trajectory in order to express the fact that it is not only our inner world and self that is reflected or externalised in spatial experiences. Externalisations of our inner world are seldom only a static projection or an image painted onto our surroundings. They are not mere illusions or unreality. They constitute what is real. They give space to a dynamic way of relating, an intrinsically human effort to reach out, to encounter, to move and to be moved. There would not be a space for us without such externalisations. Nor would we be anything without spaces to reach out in and be interpreted by. The act of interpretation is also an act of trust in the other, and thus an act of giving one's self to the other.

Places of Disruption

In the vital reciprocity between place and the self, enacted within different forms of mobility, imagination plays an essential role. I have already recognised the negative space as a transitional space. In this intermediate space between fantasy, reality and the interpreting subject, human creativity becomes possible and communication meaningful. We are alive as human beings in this transitional space (Ogden 1985). However, as I have already indicated with reference to Ward and Baudrillard, the borderline between the real and the unreal is worth challenging. From the construction of a place as fictive follows that the everyday world we live in is different from this unreality and only real. This depicts the social and moral landscape in a particular way and involves the distribution of particular practices.

The vital reciprocity between fantasy and reality in transitional space is a difficult balance to maintain. "[I]magination can lead us astray – into [...] the unreal, and the grotesque; and it can tempt us into first picturing, then (too often) acting out evil" (Tuan 1998: xv). This statement by Tuan exemplifies a possible disruption of transitional (or potential) space discussed by Ogden (1985). A disruption of this balance may take the form of imbalance, the "dialectic of reality and fantasy collapses in the direction of fantasy" (Ogden 1985: 133). This means that fantasy invades potential space in a way that negates the involved reciprocity, and with that the potential creativity. In his interesting analysis, Pile (2005) has brought to the fore the dream-like and ghost-like experiences of city life. He writes: "Wishes, moreover, are intimately connected to anxieties, inhibitions and the like: with dreams, there are also nightmares. Once we think about cities, though, we must take into account the sheer variety of desires and anxieties that might motivate space-work" (Pile 2005: 49).

Thus far I have exemplified the profound nurturing and sustaining influence place and mobility might have on people, but I would also like to point out other examples. In these examples we do not necessary encounter only a self-sustaining dimension. We can see how place is existentially disruptive in relation to the self. An extreme example of profound experiences related to pilgrimage is known as the Jerusalem syndrome (Leppäkari 2005). An identifiable number of people who visit Jerusalem more or less as religious tourists experience strong emotions. Their arrival in the city forces them to act in an unexpected way, and perhaps perceive themselves as prophets. The latter can be said to suffer from a temporary psychosis structured by religious models. An individual history of psychopathology does not explain this temporary psychosis, as a previous history of mental instability cannot always be found. Instead, it indicates that the city of Jerusalem may have an existential effect on people. It is evocative of affective structures that manifest themselves in transformed patterns of acting, thinking and relating in the temporary enactment of a religious role model.

This disruptive reciprocity between place and mobility on the one hand, and the human self, on the other, is not typical of religion only. "La sindrome de Stendhal" is a phenomenon quite similar to the Jerusalem syndrome, but it is of a non-religious character. Some visitors to Florence have had to be hospitalised in psychiatric clinics due to the intense and overwhelming aesthetic experience of the city (Magherini and Zanobini 1987). According to Kjellqvist (2004: 127), this syndrome sheds light on how an aesthetic experience related to a specific place can recall a strong inner sense of longing and want. This inner sense of lacking and longing can be disruptive. With desire for presence follows anxiety of loss.

A disruptive space-work might be a characteristic not only to extreme experiences like these, but to the modern condition in general. Siikala (2001b) refers in an introductory article to an anthology on mobility to the classic study *Industrial Revolution* by Carl Bücher (1901). Bücher (1901: 349) had by that time observed that modern migration, in contrast to earlier forms of migration, was a matter of private concern. Referring to this, Siikala (2001b: 2) concludes that "the modern one [migration/moving] is individually based and thus *without organisation*". Further, he (Siikala 2001b: 3) argues that this results in a problem because "the overall social integration requires the point of origin – be it imaginary or real – to be remembered". This can also be observed on an individual level related to how places are existentially evocative in a more disruptive way in global work-related mobility. Lack of socio-spatial organisation corresponds with inner disorganisation.

Global work-related mobility is a condensed form of mobility typical of modern times. This long-distance international work mobility is typical of the "knowledge industry", i.e. organisations in the global knowledge- and network-based economy (Castells 1996: 77). Here, we encounter the kind of mobility between places that Bauman (1999: 89) refers to in his reflection on the human consequences of globalisation. He distinguishes between the inhabitants of the first and the second world. The first, he writes, travel at will and experience a great deal of fun from their travel, while the second often travel illegally, and if they are unlucky are arrested or deported. Despite the fact that the first group travel out of free will, the travel is not always as glamorous as this brief description lets us believe. The important "feel" of a place and the attachment to place, take a long time to acquire. They need to be integrated in both the body and the subconscious (Tuan 2003: 183ff). Having one foot in local cultures and the other in the global economy can be characterised as a stressing "time-space intensification" (Riain 2000: 179).

These observations were central in my own research on work-related mobility (Nynäs 2007). Global vagabonds are in the long run prone to detach from the landscapes they move through and the process of detachment is also emotionally turbulent. The initial pink period dominated by the longing for a paradise is soon followed by contrasting experiences of "godforsaken places" or a "hell on earth" generally experienced in terms of chaos, fears and a lack of meaning. In contrast to tourists moved from place to place by the attraction they experience, and in contrast to how we usually depict global jet sets, this group of global vagabonds are forced to move on by their perceptions that their surroundings are inhospitable or hostile. However, in the long run, these vagabonds tend to leave their desire for a paradise behind them together with the contrasting experiences of godforsaken hells. Instead they enter a "life of grey corridors", as one engineer put it. At the bottom of this experience of place is the corresponding experience of a sense of losing one self. The lack of spatiality prevalent in global work-related mobility disrupts the fundamental sense of a self in a profound way.

Emotional Landscapes and Morality

Tuan (2003: 158) also points out that the nomads of modern society share the common human need to attach to a homeland. They have a craving for a permanent place to which they can project their minds, vividly externalised in paradise images, but they adapt to various circumstances out of necessity. On the one hand, this calls for a need to reconstruct a sense of home among e.g. co-workers, and with the help of particular places the people start to visit habitually. On the other hand, this fundamental threat to the inner sense of self is also acted upon or defended against with various forms of aggression. The latter aspect is here of particular importance as it indicates a connection between a sense of being a self and a sense of being a moral subject, and finally a sense of place. It also indicates that the emotional inner landscape is transported into the external socio-spatial landscape.

In my research (Nynäs 2007), experiences of a place as hostile and chaotic also involved dissolution of acquired norms and corresponding behaviour of a more suspicious and violent character. This was vividly expressed by one of the vagabonds, an experienced engineer: "*Look at us old men here. We are lechers, alcoholics, divorced, ageing vagabonds, but the truth is that we built this factory and it will be a flagship of our company. These project jobs are like this: When the boss commands the team to go to the destination place, all Ten Commandments have already been broken.*" From this follows an important question of general concern. Are places constructed in a process of time-space intensification typical of modernity places, which also eliminate the moral subject?

The process of detachment reflected in my study is similar to a process of displacement, that is, a forced loss of spatial relatedness. Displacement of people is known to have psychological effects. Displacement erodes the traditional psychological support system. As the following quotation points out, this involves also a sense of losing one's moral subjectivity: "*In this place you just get into bad shape and what little sense of responsibility and energy that you have left is ruined. Even though you do not drink alcohol, the common depression and the circumstances kill your capacity for thinking.*" Feelings of insecurity, fear, and loss of identity might engulf the minds of people displaced, and manifest themselves in various forms of violence (Kakar 1995). Sack (2001) points out an intrinsic relationship between place, reality, and morality. He argues that some places increase and enrich reality and others may diminish our awareness of reality and thus our moral sensitivity. A moral place is thus a place that helps us see through to the real, he argues. In other words, a moral place is a place that does not lead us astray with the help of a disrupted balance between reality and fantasy.

This part of my reflection has not only shed light on the fact that the human self is dependent on spatial relatedness and that a loss of such attachment has a profound and negative influence. I have also indicated that an intrinsic relationship exists between spatial relatedness and a sense of being a moral subject. This implies that analyses of emotional landscapes are significant to the understanding of moral landscapes. Being a moral subject in relation to something is related to a sense or self and a sense of relatedness. Before experiencing a moral dilemma or the moral aspect of an action, the world has appeared to the subject as moral in some sense.[1] Due to the modern worldview, we have misinterpreted ethics and morals as rational constructs and neglected how a fundamental and ambivalent relatedness constitutes ourselves as moral. Bauman (2002) argues that our first sense of being a self is through relatedness and therefore also deeply rooted in trust. We, ourselves, are thus continuously constituted in our morality. Morality is more or less the recognition of our vulnerability in our dependence on others and vice versa. This sense of relatedness is not the same as acting according to certain norms or values. Underneath articulated norms and values dwells a moral subject constituted by its ability to recognise relatedness. When practitioners recognise both that "*regular rules do not apply in this place*" and that the place deprives them of their sense of responsibility, it can be understood as a deteriorating sense of being a moral subject. One practitioner quoted a senior project manager: "*Everything is allowed in love and war, and in building power plants.*" The difficulty of dwelling in the real exemplified in citations like these is not typical of this kind of international mobility only. Oakes (2005: 53) highlights a somewhat similar problem when he reflects on the need for reflexivity in the encounter between tourists and place. This disruption takes another form, however.

Generally, place and mobility evoke a general human dilemma of ambiguity due to their capacity to sensitise the self: "On the one hand, we need to maintain a sense of the internal equilibrium between mental forces [...] On the other, we need to be integrated into the social world, in which we must respect the separateness [subjectivity] of other minds, while being able to build flexible bridges across that separateness, to create close emotional and working relationships." (Fonagy et al. 2004: 19ff) This dilemma is manifest in the difficulty of maintaining unbalance between fantasy, reality, and the interpreting subject evoked in international work-related mobility. The unbalance equates to an escape from place and the self, an escape from the real, and finally an escape from moral subjectivity in interpersonal relatedness.

---

1   Raimond Gaita made me observe this fact in a lecture he held at Åbo Akademi University, Finland, 13 October 2003.

Place and the Human Self

My reflections above are of an interpretative character, and my aim to bring to the fore a deep-seated existential dimension can be considered an effort to interpret the deep structure of how mobility affects us. My methodology is influenced by deep hermeneutics (see Latomaa 2005). However, this raises a theoretical concern. Aside from my interpretations and observations, are there reasons to assume a profound correspondence between the human self and place? Does psychology support such assumptions?

The modernist understanding of the human self has been unable to account for a relation between self and place, due to its strong focus on consciousness (Casey 2001: 405). In contrast to this, there is today a growing interest in human intersubjectivity, which offers theoretical tools to grasp the transformative relatedness between man and place. Among several contributors from the perspective of psychology (Trevarthen 1998; Meltzoff 1985; 1990; Beebe et al. 2005), Daniel Stern's understanding of the human self is most useful. The self is put at the centre of his thinking as an intersubjective matrix (Brinich and Shelley 2002: 40f). Stern (1991) considers the self to be a main organising principle in human life. Furthermore, he considers the self to dwell in continuous restructuring throughout life due to its intersubjective nature. Thus, the central character of the human self is one growing and evolving, than that of a fixed stable being.

According to Stern (1991: 39ff), a sense of self develops during infancy through different processes of relatedness between self and other. The earliest development is characterised by cumulative integration and organisation when different perceptions are linked to each other in the continuous interaction between the self and the environment. Later, this evolves into a sense of being separate from the environment. Senses of contiguity, continuity and coherence experienced in relatedness to the other become a barrier against the threat of fragmentation, depersonalisation and disintegration. When relatedness is recognised and realised as a potential this is followed by a sense of subjectivity on behalf of both self and other, based on sharing affects, attention, intention, and of course its contrast. Finally, verbal relatedness evolves and symbolic relatedness is developed e.g. as language, transforming intersubjectivity between self and other into a less direct and more impersonal mode.

Stern's theoretical perspective is important in several ways. The first implication is that place and environment are one of the fundamental building blocks of the human self. A subjective sense of self is not formed within interpersonal relations, but also out of one's awareness of one's body in time and space (Beattie 2005: 22). Early experiences of sensory contiguity define a surface, a sense of place, upon which later experience is created and organised (Ogden 2004: 31ff). The organising, structuring and meaning-creating capacity of the human mind (i.e. later developmental achievements) originates in early self-environment relatedness. This spatial relatedness has an ontogeneric character: the sense of both the self and the other – and reality in general – are rooted in spatiality. Different dimensions of the sense of being a self are therefore related to, or dependent on spatiality.

Generally, from a perspective of object relations theory, this implies that place sensitises an archaic and significant relationship between self and other. It evokes the memory of a primary object. This primary object is not just a subconscious memory of significant persons in early development. Rather, it originates from the early sensory relatedness between the body and its environment and the inherent ontogeneric potential in this. This memory of transformative sensory relatedness is vital in human life and is symbolically enacted throughout life (Bollas 1987).

From a perspective of early infant development (and more recent object relations theory) we can account for a relationship between place and the human self in which the two continuously constitute each other in a profound reciprocity: "In effect, there is *no place without self; and no self without place*" as Casey (2001: 406) argues. However, there is one more important implication we can draw from this psychological perspective. To some extent it is wrong to locate the ontogeneric and transformative potential in spatial relatedness only. The cumulative organisation and integration during the earliest development is connected to a continuous interaction between the self and the environment, whereas not only recognition of patterns (i.e. spatiality) but also their continuous changing and evolving character is a central feature. Rosenfeld (1992: 85) states: "Awareness is change, not perception of stimuli". This indicates that movement and mobility is of a more profound character than space and place.

Some Final Remarks

The examples above are very different from each other, but they have some central features in common. They all highlight an existential dimension of place, i.e. how spatial relatedness is existentially evocative. These examples shed light on how places become locations of experiences – or profound centres of human existence – including perceiving, doing, thinking, and feeling in a certain way (Walter 1980–1981: 162; Relph 1976: 141). They also point out the need to acknowledge the experiential and subjective dimension of place (Relph 1996: 907). Places are shaped by memories, expectations and by stories of real and imagined events. Places are of significance to people and infused with feelings and meanings, which include perceiving, doing, thinking, and feeling in a certain way. Further, places are rooted in visceral feelings. They are known not only through the eyes and mind but also through the more direct modes of experience, which resist objectification (Tuan 2003).

Bergmann has brought our understanding of this complexity one step further. From a perspective of human ecology he points out that a "spiritual perspective retains a significance for our understanding of secular architecture" (Bergmann 2005: 46, 55). In a similar manner I have tried to bring my reflections beyond a mere recognition of the complexity of place. In the examples that I have described above I have paid attention to a significant sense of presence. Furthermore, places are not only distinguished from each other by how they meet human desire(s) related to a sense of presence, but also by their capacity to develop and transform this desire. Places give shape and form to human beings – they interpret us – and, thus, also constitute us as moral subjects. We might say that places talk to us. Inherent as a potential in spatial experiences is an existential correspondence with the human self, which is of a transformative character.

In general, these observations correspond with Pallasmaa's definition of the general task of architecture in that the role or function of place is "to reconstruct the experience of an undifferentiated interior world, in which we are not mere spectators, but to which we inseparably belong" (Pallasmaa 1996: 16, 22). Further, even though the experiences are not religious in a strict sense, the two aspects pointed out above also resemble some central elements in the individual religious experience. This can be described as an experience of breaking constraints and borders and allowing for participation in something different, through which the subject becomes a part of a dialogue with – or an intervention by – the other (see Wikström 1999: 89). Still, the experiences neither have an explicit sense of holiness or the sacred, nor is the crossing of borders a breaking of the constraints of this world.

Wright's definition of spirituality contributes with a more psychological emphasis. He writes: "[S]piritual is anything that contributes to keeping our humanity alive. It is anything that helps us to stay in touch with the life of the self and anything that enriches that life. It is also anything that safeguards the self against the dangers of dissolution or petrification, of being transformed into the Other's object or thing" (Wright 2005: 50). Both sides are present in spatial relatedness; hopes and fears, desires and anxieties. The correspondence between the human self and place is not necessarily developing. It might also be disruptive, and a threat to our sense of being a self and a moral and emotional agent. Places also touch on general fears of being trapped in repetition in a way that is deeply antagonistic to the necessity for inner change and development (Callard 2003).

Finally, Siikala (2001a: 41) writes: "Different kinds of activities can go on somewhere else [...] The encompassing nature of nomadic place always makes it difficult to comprehend for the cadastral mappers as well as ethnographers who tend to see their objects in delimited places. The place of the society is where 'it is going on'." From a sociological perspective, Urry (2000) makes a similar emphasis on the relevance of mobility and argues for a "sociology of mobility". In the introduction I referred to pilgrimage as an example of existential mobility. In the examples above, motion, movement, and mobility have been significant features of the existential space-work that I have observed.

Religious studies recognise a complex reciprocal interaction between ways of moving, the environment and human experience: "ritual-like behavior demonstrates the importance of the body and its way of moving in space and time. The body acts within an environment that appears to require it to respond in certain ways" (Bell 1997: 139). In addition to the important recognition that place is a tripartite synthesis of physical, mental, and social spaces operating simultaneously in an existentially evocative way that elicits an affective response and invites relationships, we need to account for the fact that place is a trajectory. The complexity of place manifests itself in and through motion, movement and mobility. It is, however, both theoretically and methodologically a challenge to account for the significant notion that place in itself is nomadic.

References

Bauman, Z. (1999), *Globalization: The Human Consequences* (Cambridge: Polity Press).

Bauman, Z. (2002), *Postmodern Ethics* (Oxfordshire: Blackwell Publishers Ltd).

Beattie, M.T. (2005), "Consciousness and the Personality Disorders: Developmental and Clinical Perspectives", in Masterson, J.F. (ed.) *The Personality Disorders Through the Lens of Attachment Theory and the Neurobiologic Development of the Self: A Clinical Integration* (Phoenix: Zeig, Thucker and Theisen Inc.).

Beebe, B. et al. (2005), *Forms of Intersubjectivity in Infant Research and Adult Treatment* (New York: Other Press).

Bell, C. (1997), *Ritual: Perspectives and Dimensions* (New York: Oxford University Press).

Bergmann, S. (2005), "Space and Spirit: Towards a theology of inhabitation", in Bergmann, S. (ed.) *Architecture, Aesth/Ethics and Religion* (Frankfurt am Main: IKO – Verlag für Interkulturelle Kommunikation).

Bollas, C. (1987), *The Shadow of the Object: Psychoanalysis of the Unthought Known* (London: Free Association Books).

Bollas, C. (1996), "Borderline Desire", *International Forum for Psychoanalysis* vol. 5:1, 5–10.

Bondi, L., Davidson, J. and Smith, M. (2005), "Introduction: Geography's 'Emotional Turn'", in Davidson, J., Bondi, L. and Smith, M. *Emotional Geographies* (Hampshire: Ashgate).

Brinich, P. and Shelley, C. (2002), *The Self and Personality Structure* (Philadelphia: Open University Press).

Callard, F. (2003), "The taming of psychoanalysis in geography", *Social and Cultural Geography* 4, 295–312.

Casey, E.S. (2000), *Imagining: A Phenomenological Study*, 2nd Edn (Bloomington: Indiana University Press).

Casey, E.S. (2001), "Body, Self, and Landscape", in Adams, P.C., Hoelscher, S. and Till, K.E. (eds) *Textures of Place: Exploring Humanist Geography* (Minneapolis: University of Minnesota Press).

Castells, M. (1996), *The Information Age: Economy, Society and Culture. Vol. 1: The Rise of the Network Society* (Oxford: Blackwell).

Cosgrove, D. and Jackson, P. (1987), "New directions in cultural geography", in *Area* 19, 2, 95–101.

Dillistone, F.W. (1966), "The function of symbols in religious experience", in Dillistone, F.W. (ed.) *Myth and Symbol* (London: S.P.C.K.), 1–14.

Durkheim, É. (1965/1912), *The Elementary Forms of the Religious Life* (New York: The Free Press).

Eliade, M. (1957), *The Sacred and the Profane* (San Diego, New York and London: Harcourt Brace Jovanovich) (1959 edition).

Fonagy, P. et al. (2004), *Affect Regulation, Mentalization and the Development of the Self* (London: Karnac).

Gothóni, R. (1993), "Pilgrimage = Transformation Journey", in Ahlbäck, T. (ed.) *The Problem of Ritual* (Åbo: The Donner Institute for Research in Religious and Cultural History).

Husserl, E. (1958) *Ideas* (New York: Macmillan).

James, W. (1902), *The Varieties of Religious Experience: A Study in Human Nature* (New York: University Books) (1963 edition).

Jones, O. (2005), "An Ecology of Emotion, Memory, Self and Landscape", in Davidson, J., Bondi, L. and Smith, M. *Emotional Geographies* (Hampshire: Ashgate).

Kakar, S. (1995), *The Colors of Violence* (New Delhi: Viking).

Karjalainen, P.T. (1997), "Maailman paikoista paikan maailmoihin – kokemisen geografiaa", *Tiedepolitiikka* 4, 41–6.

Kjellqvist, E.-B. (2004), *De får vingar: anden och psykoanalysen – en civilisations-kritik* (Stockholm: Carlsson).

Knott, K. (2005a), "Space", *Revista de Estudos da Religião* 4/2005, 108–114.

Knott, K. (2005b), *The Location of Religion: A Spatial Analysis* (London and Oakville, CA: Equinox).

Knott, K. (2005c), "Spatial Theory and Method for the Study of Religion", *Temenos* 41:2, 153–84.

Kong, L. (2005), "Religious Processions: Urban Politics and Poetics", *Temenos* 41:2, 225–49.

Kong, L. and Kiong, T. (2000), "Religion and modernity: Ritual transformations and the reconstruction of space and time", *Social and Cultural Geography* vol. 1:1, 29–44.

Latomaa, T. (2005), "Ymmärtävä psykologia: psykologia rekonstruktiivisena tieteenä", in: Perttula, J. and Latomaa, T. (eds) *Kokemuksen tutkimus. Merkitys – tulkinta – ymmärtäminen* (Helsinki: Dialogia).

Lefebvre, H. (1991), *The Production of Space* (Cambridge, MA: Blackwell).

Leppäkari, M. (2005), "Berusad av Jerusalem: Jerusalemsyndromet i religionsvetenskaplig belysning", *Nordisk Judaistik* 25/2.

Magherini, G. and Zanobini, A. (1987), "Eventi e piscopatologia: il perturbante turistico: nota preliminare", *Rassegna Studi pischiatrici* 74, 1–14.

McAlister, E. (2005), "Globalization and the Religious Production of Space", *Journal for the Scientific Study of Religion* vol. 44:3, 249–55.

Meltzoff, A.N. (1985), "The roots of social and cognitive development: Models of man's original nature", in Field, T. and Fox, N. (eds) *Social Perception in Infants* (Norwood: Ablex).

Meltzoff, A.N. (1990), "Foundations for Developing a Concept of Self: The Role of Imitation in Relating Self to Other and the Value of Social Mirroring, Social Modeling, and Self Practice in Infancy", in Cicchetti, D. and Beeghley, M. (eds) *The Self in Transition: Infancy to Childhood* (Chicago: Chicago UP).

Monk, K. (2005), "Heartbreak range, interview with Ang Lee" in *The Ottawa Citizen*, 29 November 2005.

Nynäs, P. (2008), "Global vagabonds, place and the self – the existential dimension of mobility", in S. Bergmann, T. Hoff and T. Sager (eds) *Spaces of Mobility: Essays on the Planning, Ethics, Engineering and Religion of Human Motion* (London: Equinox).

Oakes, T. (2005), "Tourism and the modern subject", in Cartier, C. and Lew, A.A. (eds) *Seductions of Place: Geographical Perspectives on Globalization and Touristed Landscapes* (London: Routledge).

Ogden, T.H. (1985), "On Potential Space", *International Journal of Psychoanalysis* vol. 66.

Otto, R. (1950), *The Idea of the Holy* (2nd edn, translated by J.W. Harvey, first published in 1917) (London: Oxford University Press).

Pallasmaa, J. (1996), *The Eyes of the Skin: Architecture and the Senses* (London: Academy Editions).

Pallasmaa, J. (2001), *The Architecture of Image: Existential Space in Cinema* (Hämeenlinna: Building Information Ltd) (Helsinki: Rakennustieto).

Pallasmaa, J. (2005), *Encounters, Juhani Pallasmaa: Architectural Essays* (Helsinki: Rakennustieto) (ed. by Peter MacKeith).

Pile, S. (2005), *Real Cities: Modernity, Space and the Phantasmagorias of City Life* (London: Sage Publications).

Relph, E. (1976), *Place and Placelessness* (London: Pion).

Relph, E. (1996), "Place", in Douglas, I., Hugget, R. and Robinson, M. (eds) *Companion Encyclopaedia of Geography: The Environment and Humankind* (London: Routledge).

Riain, S.Ó. (2000), "Net-work for a Living: Irish Software Developers in the Global Workplace", in Burawoy, M. et al. (eds) *Global Ethnography: Forces, Connections and Imaginations in a Postmodern World* (Los Angeles: University of California Press).

Rosenfeld, I. (1992), *The Strange, Familiar and Forgotten* (New York: Knopf).

Sack, R.D. (2001), "Place, Power, and the Good", in Adams, P.C., Hoelscher, S. and Till, K.E. (eds) *Textures of Place: Exploring Humanist Geography* (Minneapolis: University of Minnesota Press).

Searles, H.F. (1960), *The Nonhuman Environment: In Normal Development and in Schizophrenia* (Madison: International Universities press, Inc.).

Seasoltz, R.K. (2005), *A Sense of the Sacred: Theological Foundations of Christian Architecture and Art* (London: Continuum).

Sheldrake, P. (2001), *Spaces for the Sacred* (London: SCM – Canterbury Press Ltd).

Siikala, J. (2001a), "Tilling the Soil and Sailing the Sea: Cadastral Maps and Anthropological Interpretation", in Siikala, J. (ed.) *Departures: How Societies Distribute their People* (Helsinki: The Finnish Anthropological Society).

Siikala, J. (2001b), "Introduction", in Siikala, J. (ed.) *Departures: How Societies Distribute their People* (Helsinki: The Finnish Anthropological Society).

Smith, J.Z. (1987), *To Take Place: Toward a Theory of Ritual* (Chicago: Chicago University Press).

Smith, M. (2005), "On Being Moved by Nature: Geography, Emotion and Environmental Ethics", in Davidson, J., Bondi, L. and Smith, M. (eds) *Emotional Geographies* (Hampshire: Ashgate).

Stern, D. (1991), *Spädbarnets interpersonella liv ur psykoanalytiskt och utvecklings-psykologiskt perspektiv* (Stockholm: Natur och Kultur).

Taylor, C. (1985), *Human Agency and Language: Philosophical Papers I* (Cambridge: Cambridge UP).

Tillich, P. (1966), "The religious symbol", in Dillistone, F.W. (ed.) *Myth and Symbol* (London: S.P.C.K.), 15–34.

Trevarthen, C. (1998), "The Concept and Foundations of Infant Intersubjectivity", in Bråten, S. (ed.) *Intersubjective Communication and Emotion in Early Ontogeny* (Cambridge: Cambridge UP).

Tuan, Y.-F. (1998), *Escapism* (London: The John Hopkins University Press).

Tuan, Y.-F. (2003), *Space and Place: The Perspective of Experience* (Minneapolis: University of Minnesota Press).

Urry, J. (2000), *Sociology Beyond Societies: Mobilities for the Twenty-first Century* (London: Routledge).

Walter, E.W. (1980–1981), "The place of experience", in *The Philosophical Forum* 12, pp. 159–81.

Ward, G. (2000), *Cities of God* (London: Routledge).

Weiss, G. (1999), *Body Images: Embodiment as Intercorporality* (London: Routledge).

Wilson, D. (1993), "Connecting social process and space in the geography of religion", *Area* 25, 1, 75–6.

Wright, K. (2005), "Have 'objects' got faces?" in Field, N. (ed.) *Ten Lectures on Psychotherapy and Spirituality* (London: Karnac).

Wright, K. (1996), "Looking after the Self", in Richards, *The Person Who is Me: Contemporary Perspectives on the True and False Self* (London: Karnac Books).

Chapter 10

The Phenomenon of Mobility
at the Frankfurt International Airport –
Challenges from a Theological Perspective

Kerstin Söderblom

Point of Departure

There is no such thing in Germany as a specific theology of mobility or a theology of globalised spaces. However, researchers are in the process of developing ethical positions on globalisation and mobility. Additionally, there are phenomenological approaches to different life worlds beyond institutional church activities, and there has been research on the relationship between secular and sacred times and spaces, and how religious expressions and traces are not only woven into sacred spheres but also into our daily lives. At the Faculty of Practical Theology at the University of Frankfurt, where I work, empirical research is conducted based on a phenomenological methodology, introduced by Husserl, Merleau Ponty and Waldenfels.[1]

This approach to research requires an open mind, and a curiosity towards daily life phenomena in the mode of Husserl's epoché. The use of this research approach involves perceiving and documenting phenomena, situations, atmospheres, and even the smallest incidents with all the senses, in field diaries and sketchbooks. Presuppositions, assumptions and previous experiences are bracketed during the process of participant observation and during interviews while in the field, in areas such as the Frankfurt International Airport. These data have to be consciously written down, but are included in the reconstruction and interpretation of the research only later in the process of analysis.

In our context, religion is not only seen as a combination of biblical knowledge, dogmatic teachings and traditional rituals formulated by church institutions and theological authorities, but rather as a reservoir of symbols and metaphors that contain knowledge and attitudes about life in general. As the cultural anthropologist Clifford Geertz has put it: Religions carry a model character for culture in a dual

---

1 Regarding the phenomenological approach to Empirical Theology in Frankfurt see Dinter, Astrid/Heimbrock, Hans-Günter/Söderblom, Kerstin (ed.), *Einführung in die Empirische Theologie. Gelebte Religion erforschen*, Göttingen 2007.

manner. They function as a *model of* something and as a *model for* something.[2] They thus reflect reality symbolically in order to understand it better, and to offer sense and meaning to it. Furthermore, religions provide directives and criteria for attitudes and behaviour. Hence, religions express life in context and shape it at the same time. Religion is about interruptions of daily routines, little surprises and incidents of 'small and medium transcendences' as Thomas Luckmann has called it, and as often occur at airports. In that sense I see that religions function in ways similar to the arts and architecture, which also open up and provoke views and perspectives into deeper dimensions of our lives – into the reality of transcendence, emotions, dreams, images and memories. These dimensions are never neutral but are outspokenly subjective, and carry normative implications.

The Finnish architect Juhani Pallasmaa has formulated a view of multi-sensory architecture that embraces empathy, social vision and commitment.[3] This view highlights the 'cultural turn' of the last two decades in Practical Theology. But we need the means and tools to reconstruct life world phenomena and expressions in order to recognise and reconstruct religious traces and their significance for people. In Frankfurt we do this by relating empirical data to adequate theoretical concepts in various interrelated steps. We work from a theological perspective, while maintaining a phenomenological approach and attitude towards reality.

I conducted two one-month field studies in 2005 and 2006 at my research area, the Frankfurt International Airport, as a participant observer. In the first round I moved around and observed the airport in a very unfocussed and open way. In the second round I studied and observed the work of the airport chaplains and other church employees as they counselled and supported passengers, airport personnel, and asylum seekers at the airport. Furthermore, I interviewed passengers, various airport personnel, two airport chaplains, and social workers working at the refugee camp at the airport. This paper confronts and discusses the results of my analysis of this empirical data, using theoretical concepts that are relevant to my research question of how people move around and experience the Frankfurt International Airport from their own perspectives, and how they perceive themselves, other people and the world at the airport. Mobility was one of the key phenomena that was touched on regularly in interviews and during my participant observations at the airport.

---

2   See Geertz, Clifford, 'Religion als kulturelles System', in *Dichte Beschreibung. Beiträge zum Verstehen kultureller Systeme*, Frankfurt/Main 1987, 52.

3   See Pallasmaa, Juhani, *Touching the World. Auf der Suche nach einer Theorie der Architektur*, Hamburg 2005; Pallasmaa, Juhani, *The Eyes of the Skin: Architecture and the Senses*, London 2005; Pallasmaa, Juhani, 'Six themes for the next millennium – Architecture for improving humanity', in *The Architectural Review* (July 1994), http://findarticles.com/ p/articles/mi_m3575/is_n1169_v196/ai_15718505.

Phenomenological Perceptions of Mobility at an Airport

The Frankfurt International Airport can function as a strong symbol for mobility, and the advantages of modern transport bridging long distances, cultures and nations – and even different continents. The airport can almost be seen as a key entrance gate for those who have succeeded in mastering globalised markets, world travels, and the international flow of money. The more negative aspects of this world economic competition can also be found and observed at airports. Control points, borders and security surveillance reflect the complex problem of access to the glittering and wealthy side of globalisation. At the same time these aspects of the airport underscore the problems of modern 'capitalist colonisation', of culture clash and increasing migration. It is therefore helpful to have a closer and critical look at airports as an equivocal symbol of mobility and control. In this case, the focus will be on the Frankfurt International Airport.

A sense of freedom

Frankfurt International Airport. Monday morning 9:05. Departure Hall B of Terminal 1 looks pretty crowded. I sit in my favourite café, called 'Connections', where I can oversee the crowds going to and coming from the check-in desks, getting rid of luggage, receiving boarding cards and proceeding to the boarding card control. I sense a hectic feeling, stress, busyness and frenetic movement from people who are pulling and carrying luggage from one departure hall to another, from one check-in-line to another. The announcements from the information desk echo through the halls and corridors and it never seems to be quiet. The information screens change constantly: The plane from Rio de Janeiro just landed, the plane to Oslo took off five minutes ago, and the plane to Tokyo is ready for boarding…the information is constantly updated and floating over the screens.

Five people with jet set equipment – two ladies wearing greyish costumes, three men wearing dark suits and ties – approach the boarding card control area. They seem to be relaxed, seem to know the procedure and the place. They talk casually and do not seem to look around at all. The control procedures seem as if they are executed automatically. That's at least how I perceive it. But I also observe tourist groups, families and couples in sweat pants and jogging shoes, casual wear, or trekking outfits; some come with kids, most of them have lots of suitcases or backpacks and often look confused. They try to find their way, talk to their companions, laugh, discuss and argue…some rather calmly, some more loudly and aggressively regardless of the people around. The airport seems to be strange and unfamiliar to them, and orientation is anything but easy. I see sun hats, beach towels and smell sun cream. Immediately, images of blue water, sun and long white beaches arise in front of my inner eye. I sense holidays, the joy of spare time and fun, and I envy the group that seems to travel south. In spite of their difficulties with orientation, they radiate excitement because of their anticipated adventure and break from daily life. Longings, hopes and dreams can be sensed, almost be touched. The huge lighted commercial advertisements behind glass and steel frames about exotic places to visit underline the free floating promise: Precisely here is the start of your adventure holiday, and the airport will lead you straight to freedom and experiences beyond any imagination – in fact, the airport represents and even incorporates this space of freedom already. The huge glass and steel front windows, with their view of the runways where the airplanes take off and land, strengthen the sense of liberty and a life beyond daily misery. The airport is literally about leaving earthly matters behind, about getting away from trouble and problems. Small and medium transcendences are in the air and, in fact, are ready to take off, too.

Control and limitations

I observe how undefined masses miraculously seem to move in certain given directions. Information personal, pictograms and signs, screens and control points channel the crowds. The seemingly open hallways are actually controlled and limited. And video cameras are installed everywhere to observe the scene. Narrow tunnels and pipelines that follow broad hallways show what the airport actually is all about. It is a transit place that people have to pass through in a specific and pre-ordained order, in order to be identified, security checked and affirmed as ticket holders for a certain flight. Therefore airports employ very efficient and functional architecture and places in order to channel and filter people to their gates according to their flights. The broadness of an airport, which is often overwhelming at first glance, is shrinking by step by step – from checkpoint to checkpoint – accompanied by strict rules and tough restrictions. Various doors are forbidden for entry. Thus, space at an airport is divided into accessible and inaccessible parts, according to an individual's status. Visible places cover the invisible, lighted places throw shadows over dark and hidden areas, wide halls help with forgetting about the narrow tunnels, control points and locked doors and places.

People who work at the airport have special permits and entrance codes; people who travel have passports, tickets and visas, whereas visitors have none of it and must stand outside the transit area. As an observer I am not entitled to enter anywhere beyond the visitor's area. But as a participant observer and researcher I went through a long and time-consuming procedure to get special permission to receive an airport pass to be allowed to enter the transit area. It showed me, through personal experience, just how sensitive security matters are, and how difficult it is to cross certain lines at the airport, especially after the events of September 11, 2001. Airport space is restricted, enclosed and heavily guarded. It is similar to a high security prison or a refugee camp, without the people knowing it. But it can be perceived. When I wanted to take a picture into one of the tunnel pathways from the boarding control area to the security control area, two officers immediately approached me and warned me not to do so, or my camera would be confiscated. I did not see where they were coming from, but they were right there – observing everything. At the other end of the tunnel, after having passed another security check, one can breathe normally again and relax in the wider and more open waiting halls. There, people are invited to spend time and money at the duty-free shops, bars and restaurants – but even here only in restricted time and space zones that are defined by airport schedules and procedures. Even the waiting chairs and low waiting tables force the people to sit uncomfortably, one by one. Lying down and sleeping is not desired, and almost impossible on these chairs. The functional inner architecture and artefacts create a certain 'behaviour setting'[4] that forces people to behave in a certain way, beyond individual movements. You must not lie down, linger or laze around. Airports are not 'places to hang around', like train stations or parks. That is the clear message. Artificial light, air conditioning, and materials like hard plastic and steel produce a rather artificial, antiseptic and sterile atmosphere. This feeling also influences the behaviour of the people who try to adapt to the atmosphere of the place, and simultaneously also shape it through their behaviour.

But the place also reflects routine, stability and calmness. Everything seems to be under control. Nobody has to worry about security matters. That is the one big message that has to be transmitted to people in order not to disturb the realm of hope, dreams and transcendence created by the airport atmosphere. Space not only reflects emotions of hopes, dreams, fears and stress, but it is also supposed to produce it. Thus, it is a productive factor.

Spatial ambivalences

For those who work at the airport, place and space are familiar and transparent. Workers are constantly shifting between the public and the limited-access spheres. Space is conquered by daily routines, which radiate security, oversight and authority.

For those who do not know the place, an airport evokes insecurity, confusion, and even fear.

For those who get to the airport as asylum seekers, the barriers and borders of the airport are almost invincible and impossible to overcome. They are sorted out immediately and sent to an asylum camp within the airport system. The only 'free spaces' at the asylum camp in the middle of nowhere are the TV and eating room, and the Christian and Muslim prayer room. And even these are observed by video cameras. But in these spots, people have at least some space and time for themselves. The bright and lighted space with ceilings like glass domes – like at the Frankfurt Airport in Terminal 2 – are sharply contrasted by enclosed and heavily guarded places like the asylum camp, the control areas and the transfer tunnels and pipelines.

---

4   Greverus, Ina-Maria, 'Zur kulturanthropologischen Relevanz des Behavior-Setting Konzepts', in: Kaminski, Gerhard (Hg), *Ordnung und Variabilität im Alltagsgeschehen*, Göttingen – Toronto – Zürich 1985, 179–89.

While the latter at least lead to somewhere where freedom supposedly begins, the asylum camp for most of the asylum seekers is a 'dead end'. Segregation and restrictions are the main characteristics of these equivocal places at the airport. Thus, airports are highly symbolic places of mobility and the ability to bridge long distances, but at the same time they are places where mobility is heavily restricted.[5]

Theoretical Concepts of Space

In order to understand and evaluate the spatial ambivalence of an airport in terms of enabling or denying mobility, it is important to understand some theoretical concepts of space, which specifically relate to airports. These concepts can serve as an analytical background folio to explain phenomena of mobility and stability, openness and limitations at airports. In this context, I will employ the concept of 'non-places' by Marc Augé, the concept of 'heterotopia' by Michel Foucault, and later the concept of 'passageways' by Victor Turner.

Non-places

According to Marc Augé, an airport is a 'non-place' that has no specific history, no identity and no relationship to its surroundings and people.[6] He also regards gas stations, shopping malls, train stations, motels, highways and all the various means of transportation and transit areas as non-places. He points out that people have to identify themselves before and/or after they use non-places through the use of passports, credit cards, driving licenses, and so on, but afterwards, people can hide and disappear into an anonymous space where one can actually reinvent one's self if desired, and one only has to reappear after leaving those non-places. His analysis is helpful in understanding the specific dynamics of mobility in transport systems and areas, where people leave their private homes, their places of relaxation, work, meetings and leisure time, and where they are 'on the road' with all its specific conditions. It is a status of 'in between', where nothing is fixed and stable and where time and place are fluid and hybrid and seem to follow their own rules. Local stability, orientation and historical identity-building do not seem to exist.

But various scholars criticise this concept because they point out that airports and other transit places have just as much of a history and a specific identity as any other place, even if it is very specific one, a 'transit history and identity'.

---

5   Regarding various problems of mobility see Thomsen, Thyra Uth/Drewes Nielsen, Lise/Gudmundsson, Henrik (ed.), *Social Perspectives on Mobility*, Hampshire, Ashgate 2005.

6   See Augé, Marc, *Orte und Nicht-Orte. Vorüberlegungen zu einer Ethnologie der Einsamkeit*, Frankfurt/Main 1994.

Many people who work at airports are proud of this. Some even call the airport their second home and their colleagues their second – or even their one and only – family. Even after decades of working at an airport, many employees are still fascinated by the place as an international meeting point, which opens new horizons and creates different world views and opinions. A considerable number do their errands at airports, go to the hairdresser and to the airport supermarket, use the pharmacy and the fitness centre for airport personnel and drink a coffee with colleagues after work at the airport. According to my research, these people often identify quite emotionally with the airport, and see it as an international, multi-cultural and multi-religious melting pot where people from all nationalities and backgrounds can be met and talked to. And they appreciate it. On the other hand, there are a considerable number of employees at the airport who leave the airport after work as quickly as possible in order to flee the noise, the hectic feeling and the stress. But generally, they also have a very personal and specific relationship to the airport; they can tell stories and recall special incidents, and often relate their personal history to developments at the airport. Jetsetters, frequent flyers and the thousands of people who work at airports have their own ways of 'place making' and even 'intermediate home building' by using small rituals or private belongings to 'occupy' the space.

Some scholars have pointed out that Augé has not so much focused on the people who use transit areas, but more on the places itself. However, in spite of these critiques, the concepts can be helpful in characterising transit areas and places, and in decoding specific atmospheres and spatial 'specialties' at transit places such as airports.

Heterotopias

Michel Foucault has described the concept of heterotopias to highlight specific spaces and places that are somewhat different.[7] These special places are either protected, restricted, or out of sight or reach. In these places, time seems to slow down or disappears completely, while the life surrounding them stays just the same. They can be seen as anti-spaces, where time, movement and action seem to follow different rules. These places function as a negative foil to 'other' places and spaces. In that sense heterotopias can be seen as a different approach to transit places, in contrast to Marc Augé's concept of non-places. But Foucault's reflections are not limited to transit places. Hospitals, centres for the elderly, graveyards, prisons, asylum camps and transit places such as airports can all be regarded as heterotopias. But gardens and sacred places can also be seen as heterotopias, where rules, movements and activities are different from elsewhere. These places do, in fact, have a history and a space identity in relation to their social and cultural surroundings and to people. In that sense they do not count as non-places, even if the concepts share similarities.

---

7   See Foucault, Michel, *Die Heterotypien. Der utopische Körper*, Frankfurt/Main 2005.

Space is enclosed, controlled, limited, fenced, protected or guarded. But according to Foucault, these enclosed spaces can also be seen as frames that enable 'free space' for different encounters, role play, performances, experiments and experiences that would not happen without specific space and time limitations. Heterotopias produce hybrid spheres of an in-between, where the unexpected 'other' can happen in many different ways. This sphere is best described by Victor Turner, who calls it the 'liminal' or 'liminoid' phase of passageways, which I will introduce in a subsequent part of this paper.

According to Foucault's concept, heterotopias are mostly used as a means to analyse the power and control structures that shape and regulate spaces. The concept also underscores the effect these places can have on the individuals who live or move around in them, or on those who are forced to stay in them, as in prisons and psychiatric hospitals. In that way the concept can be helpful in understanding the atmosphere and condition people find themselves in when they are in airports. Control and restrictions cause stress and fear. But this 'different' space also radiates 'free space' – hope and the sense of leaving the routines of daily life behind.

But, again, it is important to clarify that an airport is not the most typical of all heterotopias, even though it can be seen as one. The controlled, limited and totally guarded space in opposition to the outer world is a fact, just as much as the authority of security personal, police and even the military who establish and regulate the dynamics of an airport, with the result of making it a high security area. This is in contrast to the view that an airport is an open gate to the world, a reference point for myths and (adventure) stories, and a landscape of hopes and dreams. At non-places, just as much as at heterotopic places, mobility is regulated and controlled and limited to those who use transit areas as get-away from home and work to 'other' places. Hence, mobility is connected to money, tickets, and passports, and to the ability to use planes for private or business reasons.

Passageways or the process of transit

Victor Turner has observed and reconstructed passage rituals in many different indigenous tribes.[8] He identified three steps common to all rituals:

1. Separation;
2. Passage;
3. Reconnection.

He eventually transformed these three steps into three phases of passages in different cultural settings in the western industrialized world. Transit passages are just one of many examples of the passage movements that can be structured and reconstructed after Turner's approach.

---

8   See Turner, Victor, *Das Ritual. Struktur und Antistruktur*, Frankfurt/Main, New York, Paris 2000.

1. Separation   At an airport, the first phase of separation is passing through the various control points such as check in, the check of a boarding card, and security control. During this phase, the person leaves home and his or her private life on the outside of the transit area. The person has to prove his or her identity to come this far, but after the control point he or she enters a different landscape and setting with a different atmosphere, rules and language codes. The separation is completed, and the person is left alone in the middle of the (transit) passage.

2. Passage   Turner's second phase, the passage, is the phase when rapturous and intense experiences can be had. Certain rules of the daily world are suspended. Status, possessions and private identities do not count for much, creating a somewhat free-floating time and space, which Turner calls liminoid (fluid, hybrid). This situation can only occur because the space is framed, controlled, and clearly distinguished from other places. In that sense this state of passage fits well with the descriptions of heterotopias and to a certain extent even with the notion of non-places. It is an 'in-between time' and 'in-between space'. In fact, it is a phase *outside* of time and space within another time and space frame, which seems to be free and anarchical, but which is actually completely controlled and regulated. The atmosphere and emotions can be existentially touching and moving. This is often precisely the case in the transit areas of an airport, as I have pointed out earlier. During this phase, many hints of religious feelings can be found, even if the individuals involved do not recognise them as such. Existential feelings such as fear and hope, experiences of transcendence, limitations and interruptions of daily life are clear elements of religious experiences that can – but do not have to – be interpreted and explained in this way. This phase is different from 'life outside'. It marks a phase that is important in almost all expressions of mobility. It is the phase of 'being on the way'. This 'in-between' phase between departure and arrival is the crucial phase where things happen or do not happen, and where atmosphere, mood and the space-time frame somehow all seem to 'tick' differently. Theologically, this phase is very interesting because it is characterised by the same structure as can be found in religious rituals or experiences of transcendence. Here, more research should be undertaken in order to understand the phenomenon better and to be able to compare religious rituals with transit rituals.

3. Reconnection   After the airplane lands, passport control and baggage claim symbolise the third phase, the re-entering of the old-new, which stands for the re-connection to one's own life. Identity, status, personal goals and schedules are set in place again now, whereas before they were stored in a 'time-out sphere'. Individuals regain their own lives, but nevertheless their lives are different. New time and space experiences have been had and will still be noticeable in jetlag, culture and language lags. The passageway can serve as an anti-structure or a backdrop to experiences that can be profiled or understood better because of the 'other' place; a different place where time and space seemed to have been free floating. For some it was a time of rest with reading, observing, eating or just being in waiting halls. For others it was time of stress, restlessness or even fear until the flight was over. Others have used the transit time to invent themselves anew while talking to people they did not know before and will never meet again afterwards. They invent stories about themselves and change their biographies without any harm. It all stays in the anonymous sphere of transit.

Whatever it is, it is an 'in-between' which can be undefined and fluid because of strict outer rules and limitations. It can be seen as interruption of the 'normal', of daily routines, which are often expressed in religious terms.[9] Religious language and symbols offer at least the possibility of helping express feelings and emotions, dreams and hopes, questions and fears. It can be an experience of opening spaces for new experiences. Theology can offer passage rituals to accompany such liminoid phases, whether they are happening at an airport or at any other space and time where mobility and migration force people to move through insecure phases of an 'in-between'. Theology can also help to provide calmness in a hectic hyper-mobile world and to become aware of the need and the possibility to set up little oases and islands in the floating stream of mobility. Theology can help to find rhythms and reserved spaces for meditation, prayer or rest. Architecture can help to set up and design existential places in a human and respectful way, so that they help people cope with constant mobility. At an airport, these places can be recreation areas, such as playgrounds for children, garden arrangements inside airports, meditation fountains or rooms, such as prayer rooms or rooms of silence or spaces for meditation or music. Thus, theology and religious elements can help set up rhythms, specific time periods and space demarcations for recreation. They can facilitate a process of grounding and meeting other people and/or with God in a protected place. An architecture that respects life in all its forms is necessary, not only as a visible but as a hospitable and comfortable place, as has been highlighted by Juhani Pallasmaa and by Sigurd Bergmann.[10]

People at Airports

I agree with philosophers such as Michel De Certeau[11] and Otto Friedrich Bollnow,[12] who state that it is not only important to reflect upon places as places, but to understand the dynamics and the relationship between people and places. The central question is how this relationship shapes atmosphere, and the effect that places have on people and vice versa.

---

9   See Luther, Henning, *Religion im Alltag. Bausteine zu einer praktischen Theologie des Subjekts*, Stuttgart 1992.

10   Bergmann, Sigurd, 'Space and Spirit. Towards a Theology of Inhabitation', in: S. Bergmann (ed.) *Architecture, Aesth/Ethics and Religion*, Frankfurt/Main, London 2006, 45–103.

11   See Bollnow, Otto Friedrich, Mensch und Raum, Stuttgart 1990.

12   De Certeau, Michel, Kunst des Handelns, Berlin 1988.

How can people at airports cope with places that reflect a high level of mobility, a hectic feeling, stress, disorientation, and which at the same time radiate a heavy burden of hopes and dreams? These are questions that a life-world-oriented and topographically interested theology must address.

Concepts such as 'non-place' and 'heterotopia' show that a transit space such as an airport shapes the people moving through it. Power, authorisation, money and control allow movement, regulate or stop it. Specific configurations of time and space, broadness and limitations, transcendence and control influence behaviour, movements, and a sense of well-being or stress. An airport promises mobility, free access to transport and world-wide freedom. Reality however is more about earthly matters of control, behaviour and borders. Mobility at the airport is always related to space, status, finances and the right papers to be able to pass control points and borders.

Personal stories about airports

However, the airport is also connected to various myths, memories and personal stories about incidents and happenings that occur there. The stories can be happy or exciting, sad or frightening. Almost everybody who has ever flown in a plane can tell a story about airport experiences. Here is a place where there are hellos or farewells, tragic separations and hopeful re-unifications; families, friends, partners and colleagues meet and part, move on or arrive, fear the flight or look forward to it. In short, the airport is a whole arena of stories, feelings and emotions that vibrate through the halls, tunnels and waiting areas. These stories are created by the people who move through these places, but at the same time the places shape the people in them, and reflect their emotions. Many people use waiting time to breathe the fascinating atmosphere and to watch people. Countless women told me in interviews that they feel safer at airports than at bus or train stations. They do not fear rape or violence, because the airport is secured and guarded 24 hours a day.

Other people try to cope with fear and stress by creating certain rituals such as praying, meditating, and asking for a blessing, or buying goods in duty free shops as a distraction or an act of relaxation. Some wear a talisman, others bring along guardian angels, symbolic jewellery or teddy bears, or other symbols of protection, identity and well-being. With a little bit of time and patience, all can be observed and perceived at airports. Others write about the experience in diaries or novels. Movies such as *The Terminal* by Steven Spielberg, starring Tom Hanks, are testimony to this truth.

Place-making rituals

Frequent flyers often perform 'place-making rituals'[13] by setting up their computers in airport lounges or cafés. Some use transit hotels as interim homes that they immediately personalise by putting up personal belongings, checking wireless LAN connections, going to the fitness studio, and meeting colleagues at airport or hotel bars. The whole jet set equipment is a part of their ground equipment that they use to travel the globalised market world from one meeting to another. Of course, they are highly privileged. It is still just a minority that can afford this high mobility level, and who have passport, credit card and a business company at hand which pays for their travel, or at least helps with the infrastructure and support system.

Multi-Sided Ethical Challenges at an Airport

The problems of access and exclusion

The problems of access prevail at an airport, even though air traffic has become more democratic in recent decades. Valid passports, money, tickets and visas are still a huge obstacle for people from developing countries and refugees. Hence, airports are still a symbol of a globalised transport system for a privileged international class of people who can afford to fly and who use air travel on a regular basis as a normal mean of transport, much like others use the bus or train.

Furthermore, mobility is shaped by means of transport, and of places and spaces that channel, regulate and sometimes stop movement and mobility. These spaces reflect certain atmospheres, the light and smell, the air and temperature that enable or foreclose the possibility of mobility and therefore have to be analysed by interdisciplinary studies where architectural, religious, ethical, functional and technical perspectives are included.

Ecological challenges

Ecological problems from pollution and the destruction of forests and fields as a result of airport expansions cause huge problems, which are far from being solved. Airports have to be monitored closely in terms of their contribution to air, soil and water pollution. Strict controls have to be enacted, and airport businesses have to invest in research into alternative energy, ecological airport systems, and into a reduction of the use of kerosene and fuel dependency. Forests and ecological landscapes have to be protected or re-established elsewhere if they get destroyed during airport expansions. An ecologically conscious airport management has to

---

13   See Vonderau, Asta, *Geografie sozialer Beziehungen. Ortserfahrungen in der mobilen Welt*, (Berliner Ethnografische Studien 4), Münster 2003.

be established and monitored by experts in the field. A critical eco-theology can help set up criteria for protecting nature and (social) landscapes as people's life world and God's creation.

Migration and asylum problems

Where there is mobility there are also migration, refugees and asylum seekers, which cause many problems. Some flee from civil war areas; others have to flee because of their involvement in political, religious or cultural fields that are opposed to a government or the military. Others have to flee because of being a woman in a patriarchal context and a world full of violence against women, or because of their sexual orientation, their religion or because of poverty and/or natural catastrophes.

Many of them end up in asylum camps right at the airport, where they have to wait and are sometimes never released from the camp, but are sent back to where they came from. It is a situation of enclosure without any sense of hope or transcendence as is usually promised by airports. Hence, mobility and the will to move and migrate far too often get stopped by laws and authorities who use heterotopic places and the phenomenon of no-man's land – like the transit part of an airport – to rid themselves of unwanted refugees or immigrants without really giving them a chance. The atmosphere of fear, distress, and desperation can be sensed just as much as the hopes and dreams. Theological work needs to be conducted in the middle of transit areas to accompany and support people during the large and small transits and life passages that can be traced so clearly at the crossroads of an international airport. Airport chaplains and social workers offer counselling at airports and support people their endeavour to receive asylum status with legal and financial help. But most of the time there are simply not enough people to help.

Provisional Results

Mobility at airports is equivocal

Advantages   The potential offered by airports is clearly hopeful and enriching, particularly if more people are able to travel long distances by car, bus, train or even airplane. Travel opens new horizons and supports international learning experiences. The exchange of cultures, life styles, religious and philosophical ideas and convictions is fruitful and can be exciting. The process of mobility is connected to uncountable dreams and hopes for adventure, changes to a better life, experience of the exotic and a break from daily routines. Road movies, countless travel books, diaries and adventure tales, myths and sagas bear witness to humankind's fascination with travel and the notion of transcendence, which is connected to mobility. These are also some of the reasons that led the first travel pioneers and pilgrims to leave their homes. They travelled to often unknown lands and places, hoping to find new insights, inspiration or even a new place to call their home. Literature, arts, cultural and religious studies can capture these notions and give them a voice and creative images and forms. Airports are a very specific symbol for the ability to be mobile, to bridge long distances and to leave daily routines behind. But they only offer this promise to people who have money, papers and permission to fly. In this respect, airports are also a symbol of control and exclusion.

Disadvantages   Mobility has many downsides as well. Many people are forced to be mobile, whether they want to be or not. Work conditions, life contexts and lifestyles are more and more dependent on globalised companies, international money and culture flow; only the fittest and those most capable of adapting to the high speed and hyper mobility of modern business live can survive in the system. In fact, only a minority of individuals really has free access to transportation means, and the associated advantages conferred by mobility and globalisation. In spite of the democratisation of air travel, the majority is still not able to pay the price, or are physically and/or psychologically not able to move at the speed that is expected of them. They are excluded and left behind within the global 'motion game'. A critical theology has to develop ethical standards to ensure guidelines and codes of conduct that restrict the power of multinational companies. It also has to monitor international asylum policies and the concrete procedures at asylum camps so that human dignity and human right standards are protected and adhered to. Therefore, social workers, lawyers and church personnel have to be well trained and have to be present to support migrants, refugees and asylum seekers at international airports and other areas, as is already done – to a certain extent – in Frankfurt and elsewhere.

Mobility causes stress and insecurity

As can be easily observed at airports, hypermobility leads to stress, insecurity, fear, loss of identity, and the inability to adapt to quick changes of time and space for many people. The soul and the body system are often left behind somewhere over oceans and mountains that airplanes pass almost unnoticed. Jet lag, culture lag, and health lag are just some of the symptoms that a globalised society has to cope with – next to the financial and economic dependencies on big international business companies and banks. Theology, psychology and architecture are challenged to monitor these developments. They should offer counter strategies to support and accompany people on the move with passage rituals, short-term 'transit counselling', and places and space of rest and recovery.

Mobility requires passage rituals

Transit places should include 'safe spaces' where rituals can be consciously enacted so that travels and high mobility can be handled in a safe, healthy manner. Waiting time and waiting space should be designed by architects who are interested in human and empathic architecture, so that airports can include islands of 'safe spaces' that facilitate relaxation, meditation and recovery. Prayer rooms at some airports serve that function. Prayers, singing, meditating, lighting a candle or talking with church workers can create informal passage rituals that help to calm people and reduce stress and fear.

An area such as a garden installation or a meditation space with music showers or a silent room can serve that purpose, too. Furthermore, sleeping and resting areas should be available not only for first class tourists and travellers in certain lounges. Playgrounds, transit hotels, facilities for children, the elderly and handicapped, cinemas and sport facilities should be more integrated into transit spaces. In designs for airport cities ('Aerotopias') – such as the design for an extended airport in Frankfurt – these elements have already been embraced, but very often are not realised because of money and space problems. However, these areas of 'open space and time' should be given high priority, because they can offer a balance for at least a part of the anonymous movement through the airport's maze-like tunnels and cavernous waiting halls, where many people lose their sense of direction and orientation. Theology, architecture and the arts could cooperate more to achieve these goals.

Mobility can encourage place making and interim home building

Identities can be invented anew in heterotopic spaces such as airport passages and transit areas. Daily life, social relationships and status symbols are far away. One is 'off guard', and free to 'play' and experiment with life. Stories can be told, imagination realised and people are free to try things that they might not normally. The no-man's land stories that are associated with airports certainly provide an insight into the mood, atmosphere and the effect that these liminoid areas have on people. Place making rituals and the manner in which people place personal artefacts offer potentially interesting fields of study to better understand identity construction in the context of mobility.

An attentive theology can perceive these processes. It can reconstruct the significance of these rituals for identity building and self confidence, and can supply a language, images and symbols. In that sense theology functions as a model *of* life, according to Clifford Geertz's view.

Mobility is a talisman of the globalisation, migration and refugee problems that have to be solved collectively

The airport is a multi-dimensional crossroad of migration and a strong symbol of mobility that clearly illustrates the refugee questions that need to be solved. Mobility implies a possibility and a right to move freely, and the liberty to go and work wherever people want. But that is not always the case. Refugee questions and asylum policies lead to asylum camps that essentially function as prisons.

These camps are shoved into the no man's land areas at airports or pushed to the margins of society in order not to disturb the rest of society. Ethical standards need to be applied by theologians, lawyers, social worker and others to monitor asylum politics and questions of human dignity and human rights of asylum seekers. According to Clifford Geertz, theology can function here as a model *for* life.

Mobility can lead to transcendence – or dead ends

As I have shown, the shining surfaces and the lightness of the glass and steel used at airports allow views to the runways, providing a promise – the promise of adventure and the fulfilment of dreams. The experience of taking off can be had in a dual manner, the literal and the symbolic, through moments and places of transcendence. These are important points of departure for a theology that is interested in daily life transcendences instead of only focusing on 'high church expressions' of religion.

But it also shows the equivocal nature of transit places. They are restricted and controlled and can quickly lead to dead ends, such as the denial of entrance to a country, the denial of a visa or even the denial of access to an asylum camp. Here the notion of wideness, light and euphoric feelings are shattered and destroyed by narrow walls, fences and tough scrutiny. Theology, social sciences and laws have to cooperate to be present, and to support and counsel refugees and people who are stranded at airports.

Elements for a 'Topographic Theology'

Passage rituals

A theology open to cultural expressions of life – such as mobility – can be a tool to balance travel's hectic pace, and its stress. It can create 'safe spaces' and times where it is possible to slow down and interrupt the flow of travel. With stop-and-go rituals people can be accompanied for a while on their way and thereby be strengthened and encouraged. Theology has to be open and curious about life world phenomena. Techniques employed by social sciences, such as interviews and participant observation, can help researchers perceive life in all its ambiguity, and also theology has to relate to this ambiguity. Coming to and going with people on the road can make a difference. Protected spaces such as a prayer room, with its offer of short-notice counselling and in-between prayers in difficult situations of crisis and grief can help make theological perspectives more visible and present in secular places such as airports. Theology therefore has to develop rituals for daily transits, for passages where people have to cope with distance, culture shock and mobility that sometimes are just overwhelming. Theology can offer language, images and symbols to interpret passages, to give people the tools to express them in order to handle them.

Expression of and reflection on existential feelings

Airport places embody and embrace experiences of all kinds of existential feelings. Theology can reflect them and give them a place to resound and to be taken seriously. Theology consists of time and space itself, not only word and message. Thus, a theology that takes part in daily lives, and is incorporated into life phenomena can turn the protestant 'audio world' into a visual and topographic world, where mobility in all its ambiguities is embodied, experienced and lived through.

Space of rest and quietness

Theology can offer space of peace and quiet for rest, meditation and prayer. Together with artists and architects, theologians can create oases and islands of rest in busy surroundings. They can create passage rituals for people on their way to ensure a successful and safe journey, while slowing down the speed of mobility at the same time. Theology can offer daily prayers, services, counselling and special services for people in need – such as the sick, the elderly and the handicapped, people in a crisis, asylum seekers, or even those with stolen or lost luggage or passports. Theology can function in these kinds of situations, not only with words but with 'safe spaces'. Hence, a topographic theology addresses mobility and all its consequences, and offers support 'on the way' – outside of church walls, but inside of specific places and certain space-time constellations.

Chapter 11
Religion, Mobility and Conflict

Elizabeth Pritchard

In 2004 Stephen Greenblatt noted that apart from "significant and well-circumscribed exceptions," the Humanities and Social Sciences have inherited "a strong assumption of rootedness as the norm of human culture...Many of the established conceptual tools for cultural analysis take for granted the fixity of the objects of study or at least assume that in their original or natural state, before contamination, the proper objects of study are stable and motionless."[1] This assumption certainly guided the founding of the discipline of comparative religion, despite its being afforded by data collected by mobile colonial administrators and missionaries. The discipline of comparative religion rendered the "world religions" as discrete bounded entities centred on texts, the marginal outliers of which were branded, disparagingly, as "syncretistic." Of course, such an assumption serves well the discipline of knowledge gathering. How might one execute due diligence on a moving target? And if it is all flux, if one cannot step into the same river twice, then our descriptions are neither adequate nor authoritative. Academic credibility would seem to be dependent upon the stability of objects and intact boundaries. But Greenblatt spies a more nefarious history behind the academic assumption of rootedness. He argues that the bureaucratization of modern universities "conjoined with a nasty intensification of ethnocentrism, racism and nationalism produced the temporary illusion of sedentary, indigenous literary cultures...The reality, for most of the past as once again for the present, is more about nomads than natives."[2] Consequently, Greenblatt urges scholars to embrace mobility as "the constitutive condition of culture and not its disruption." Indeed, he proposes that we refer to this new cross-disciplinary enterprise as "mobility studies."[3]

Greenblatt's proposal makes abundant good sense. Take my field, religion. Although the word "religion" comes from the Latin "religare" which means "to restrain, tie back or to bind," even the briefest consideration of history reveals that religious convictions and practices have been carried over extensive territory, not altogether different than the parachuting seeds of dandelions. Consider, for instance, the linkages between the Phoenician goddess Astarte, the Greek Aphrodite, the Roman Venus and the Egyptian Isis – linkages established by maritime trade on the Mediterranean.

---

1   Stephen Greenblatt, "Cultural Mobility," http://www.fas.harvard.edu/curriculum-review/essays, 2004.
2   Greenblatt, ibid.
3   Greenblatt, ibid.

But note the normative valence of Greenblatt's evocation of mobility. Static and bounded cultures are not just illusions; they are evidence of "nasty" politics. Hence, enjoining mobility represents not just sound scholarship but progressive politics. What Greenblatt seems not to have noticed is that this binary of stasis and mobility has its own history in the academy. For the map of discrete literary cultures was crisscrossed by evolutionary trajectories in which all of humankind ranged on a single scale from primitive to civilized, in which Enlightenment cosmopolitanism was celebrated over ties to the local and parochial, and in which stateless, universal Christianity triumphed over Jewish theocracy. Even if one studies bounded objects, knowledge of such objects is begotten by evocations of mobility as well as actual travel. Mobility is the prerogative of the critical observer keen to distance himself from his own origins and objects of study, to compare seemingly remote and unrelated objects, to question authority, to transgress boundaries. The contrast is striking: academic flights, both real and imagined, and tradition-bound persons awaiting the interpreters who will finally tell them the scripts they have unknowingly embodied. Hegel observed of Africa that it "is no historical part of the world; it has no movement or development to exhibit. Historical movements in it – that is in its northern part – belong to the Asiatic or European part."[4] Jonathan Z. Smith argues that it is a peculiar feature of the modern West that it identifies itself as *the* diasporic culture as opposed to the stasis of archaic cultures. Smith writes: "The West is active, it makes history, it is visible, it is human. The non-western world is static, it undergoes history, it is invisible, it is non-human."[5] Denied to the cultures under scrutiny, mobility is the prerogative of the academic alone.

Of course, Greenblatt is challenging precisely this assumption that the objects of study are static. But without attention to the persistence of the accompanying valorization of the mobile, critical, progressive West, Greenblatt's call for "mobility studies" is in danger of obscuring the power dynamics that make experiences of mobility drastically different. Not all mobilities are the same; not all mobilities are enabling. If we default to a normalization, prioritization or insidious valorization of mobility, we are bound to produce a class of persons who are regarded as "backward and unenlightened" if they appear to resist mobility. Accordingly, conflict situations will be read as yet more episodes of conservatives or fundamentalists reluctantly dragging their heels in a fast moving, globalizing world.

---

4   G.W.F. Hegel, *Lectures on the Philosophy of History*, trans. Leo Rauch (Indianapolis: Hackett, 1988), 92.

5   Smith 1993, 295. Jean Baudrillard recalls that during the Cold War, which is when the project of US development of the Third World began, the "congealed" state was the recurrent metaphor of the "East," and "fluidity" that of the "West" (Baudrillard 1990, 100). Peter Gay insists that the Enlightenment entailed a profound shift from a near universal fear of change to a fear of stagnation (Gay 1966, II:3).

The study of the interconnections of mobility, geography and religion is an exciting development and is rapidly gaining momentum.[6] I wish to appeal to my fellow scholars, however, that we be more circumspect about the valence of "mobility." In what follows, I first illuminate how the binary of stasis and mobility has framed and continues to frame the study of religion. I show how this framing tacitly endorses movement and thus concomitantly obscures the ambivalence and attendant conflicts of contemporary mobility. I then argue for a more complicated or at least ambivalent reading of mobility in order to shed light on the multifaceted constellations of contemporary mobility and religiosity. These constellations reflect my posing and tentatively responding to several questions including: Is there a correlation between mobility and increased religion or in the dominance of particular forms of religiosity? Does migration differentially affect men and women and their recourse to religion? What kinds of religious and nonreligious alliances are being set in motion?

The assumption that true religion is essentially mobile has a troubling history in the study of religion. Movement or expansion is explicitly espoused as the mark of genuine religion to the extent that persons come to realize that religion is essentially about belief and not about the body.[7] It is then claimed that this insight is specific to (or most developed in) Christianity, as the religion that trumps all parochial loyalties – loyalties that reflect stasis, closure and rigidity. As one of the founders of the field of comparative religion, F. Max Müller, wrote in 1870:

> It is Christianity alone which, as the religion of humanity, as the religion of no caste, of no chosen people, has taught us to respect the history of humanity, as a whole, to discover the traces of a divine wisdom and love in the government of all the races of mankind and to recognize, if possible even in the lowest and crudest forms of religious belief, not the work of demonical agencies, but something that indicates a divine guidance, something that makes us perceive, with St. Peter, "that God is no respecter of persons, but that in every nation he that feareth Him and worketh righteousness is accepted with Him." In no religion was there a soil so well prepared for the cultivation of Comparative Theology as in our own…If we have once learned to see in the exclusive religion of the Jews a preparation of what was to be the all-embracing religion of humanity, we shall

---

6   See, for instance, Elizabeth McAlister, "Globalization and the Religious Production of Space," *Journal for the Scientific Study of Religion* 44.3 (2005: 249–55), for a thoughtful summary of the work to date and questions for future research.

7   In his *A Letter Concerning Toleration* (of 1689), John Locke writes, "[T]rue and saving Religion consists in the inward perswasion of the Mind…And such is the nature of the Understanding, that it cannot be compell'd to the belief of anything by outward force…It is only Light and Evidence that can work a change in Mens Opinions." See his *Letter Concerning Toleration* (Illinois: Hackett, 1983), 27. He adds, "No body is born a member of any Church; otherwise the Religion of Parents would descend unto Children, by the same right of Inheritance as their Temporal Estates…No Man is by nature bound unto any particular Church or Sect…No Member of a Religious Society can be tied with any other Bonds but what proceed from the certain expectation of eternal Life," (ibid. 28).

feel much less difficulty in recognizing in the mazes of the other religions a hidden purpose; a wandering in the desert; it may be, but a preparation also for the land of promise.[8]

For a number of Christian writers, the mistake of Judaism was its attempt to institute a theocracy, whereas the true God cannot be constrained by such boundaries.[9] As Calvin remarked, "It is Judaic folly to look for the kingdom of Christ among the things that make up this world."[10] The true God is transcendent, otherworldly, asking only for our unfailing belief and obedience to the moral law. Here Müller echoes the Protestant Enlightenment view that Christianity is the truly universal religion precisely because it does not respect ties of family, tribe or nation.

A similar appeal has been recently reintroduced by Slavoj Zizek who declares that it is the particular genius of Christianity (and Buddhism "in its own way"), to rupture the obligations of Jewish "national substance" and Pagan hierarchical order. Zizek cites Jesus' declaration that anyone who is to follow him must hate his "father and his mother, his wife and children, his brothers and sister," arguing that "family relations stand here metaphorically for the entire sociosymbolic network, for any particular ethnic 'substance' that determines our place in the global Order of Things." Zizek, claiming to heed Paul, bids his reader to "unplug" from the organic community into which we are born.[11] According to this logic, the true religion subverts the parochialism of tribe and nation. The conviction that true religion entails a potential break with kin and community, of which Christianity and Buddhism "in its own way" are exemplary, is often coupled with the claim that Judaism, as well as Hinduism and Confucianism, are appropriately termed

---

8   F. Max Müller, *Lectures on the Science of Religion* (New York: Scribner, Armstrong and Co., 1874), 22. Müller, like Zizek after him, admits that this description applies also to Buddhism "perhaps."

9   "Judaism is not really a religion at all but merely a union of a number of people who, since they belonged to a particular stock, formed themselves into a commonwealth under pursely political laws, and not into a church," Immanuel Kant, *Religion Within the Limits of Reason Alone*, trans. by Theodore M. Greene and Hoyt H. Hudson (New York: Harper and Row, 1960 [1793]) 116.

10   Calvin, "On Civil Government" (*Institutes* Book IV, chap. 20), in *Luther and Calvin on Secular Authority*, 48.

11   Zizek, *The Fragile Absolute: Or Why is the Christian Legacy Worth Fighting For* (London: Verso, 2000) 120–21. Zizek has been criticized for reproducing an "imperial/colonial model of religion." See William David Hart, "Slavoj Zizek and the Imperial/Colonial Model of Religion," in *Nepantla: Views from South* 3.3 (2002): 553–78. Zizek's response is that he has never denied his Eurocentrism and his privileging the Judeo-Christian tradition. Zizek is convinced there are emancipatory impulses, visions and histories to retrieve from these resources. Hence he demands to be shown exactly where his descriptions of Christianity go wrong; he dismisses those who, in his view, would simply scold him for being Eurocentric. See his reply to Hart, "I Plead Guilty – But Where is the Judgment," *Nepantla: Views from South* 3.3 (2002): 579–83.

"cultures" or "nations" in so far as one is born a member of these collectives rather than choosing association as an adult.[12] Recent comments by Francis Cardinal George suggest, however, that the picture is changing and that the distinguishing mark of the religious, i.e. that it ruptures all national and familial boundaries, is spreading like a virus. He writes: "In the next millennium, as the nation-state is relativized into societal arrangements still to be invented, it will be increasingly evident that the major faiths are carriers of culture and that it is more sectarian to be French, American, or Russian than to be Christian or Muslim, Hindu or Buddhist."[13] Those religions that embrace mobility, that serve as "carriers," are touted as progressive alternatives to purportedly fading nation states.

Although recent scholarship on religion and mobility, specifically transnationalism, does not at all evidence a bias for Christianity as the consummate expansive, boundary-negating religion, these studies, nonetheless evidence a tacit valorization of mobility as the constitutive or perspicacious feature of religion. Peggy Levitt, who has done significant and revealing research on the role of religion in transnational networks remarks, "God needs no passport…Religion is the archetypal boundary crosser. It's the vehicle that carries people between different sociocultural worlds – it transports them between one nation and another and helps them make the cultural transition to a globalized world."[14] For Levitt, religion is not a shackle but a vehicle; it does not hold people back but carries them forward to a seemingly brighter future: the globalized world. Levitt carefully examines the material and social aspects of transnational religious networks. Nevertheless, with these above remarks, Levitt augments a longstanding tendency to see religion as primarily theological and spiritual, and thus as fluid or mobile (because the spiritual is not materially confined and because transcendence means "to climb across"). This assumption drives her research insofar as she sees religion as essentially enabling or facilitating migration. Although this can certainly be the case in certain instances, it is certainly not the case in others. Moreover, by declaring that religion is essentially compatible with easy (no passport needed)

---

12   Jacqueline Stevens, *Reproducing the State* (Princeton: Princeton University Press, 1999) 242–4. Related to this point is Mohandas Gandhi's declaration, "Religion is not like a house or a cloak, which can be changed at will. It is more an integral part of one's self than one's own body," Gauri Viswanathan, *Outside the Fold: Conversion, Modernity and Belief* (Princeton: Princeton University Press, 1998) 231. This remark came in opposition to Bhimrao Ramji Ambedkar, leader of dalit efforts for a separate electorate movement in post-independence India. Weeks before he was to die in 1956, Ambedkar led one of the largest mass conversions (to Buddhism) in modern history. He had declared that whereas he had no choice in being born a Hindu, he was resolved not to die as one.

13   Francis Cardinal George quoted in Jose Casanova, "Religion, the New Millennium, and Globalization," *Sociology of Religion* 62.4 (2001): 434.

14   Peggy Levitt quoted in Bob Brustman, "Have Religion, Will Travel," *Harvard Divinity Today* 2.1 (Spring 2006) 9. Levitt has just published *God Needs No Passport: Immigrants and the Changing American Religious Landscape* (New York: New Press, Distributed by W.W. Norton and Company, 2007).

boundary crossing, one tacitly endorses secularism whereby true religion is primarily about belief, is unencumbered with property, and readily bows, or is indifferent, to nation-state boundaries. I do not believe that one can tacitly endorse secularism and do justice to the multiple configurations of religion and contemporary migration.

In his 2006 book, *Crossing and Dwelling*, Thomas Tweed offers a new theory of religion. He writes, "*Religions are confluences of organic-cultural flows that intensify joy and confront suffering by drawing on human and suprahuman forces to make homes and cross boundaries.*"[15] According to Tweed's s definition, religion is somehow both the very flow of people and the conductor of those moving people. This bit of confusion aside, Tweed's analyses of migrating, pilgrimage-making, rolling, and motorcycle-riding religious bodies is a refreshing and resounding rebuttal of the Enlightenment assumption that true religion is about the salvation of the soul and not about the body or its extension in "property." Tweed insightfully reminds us that religions are *spatial* practices, but his study is no mere emphasis on ritual. His study extends to the ways religious persons comport themselves, inhabit homes, circuit through community networks, build shrines which evoke homelands, and bus people from distant communities. One might suppose that the more people and goods enter into circulation in this globalized world, the less sacrality, the less religion, there would be. One might suppose, building on the meaning of religion "to bind," that the more people move away from their roots, the less religious they would become. As Emile Durkheim explained, to make something sacred is to "withdraw it from circulation."[16] With modernity comes increased mobility, comes, supposedly, secularization. Tweed's study quickly shows the naiveté of that assumption. Indeed, one has to admire the alacrity with which religious communities exploit mobile technologies in order to retain a hold on their moving targets. VCRs bring television broadcasts of the Hindu epics into homes around the globe; people tuning into the Ramayana feel a sense of unity with family and friends back in India, lighting candles, saluting deities, performing puja.[17] God TV is in Africa, Asia and Europe; it is on its way to the US. It is available in prisons in South Africa. It can be accessed via cable by 21 million homes in India. It has a 24 hour prayer line. Nigerian-led Christian churches in Amsterdam worship in parking lots. Haitian practitioners of Vodoun avail themselves of cassette tapes. Churches like the US megachurch Radiant feature podcast technology boasting: "22 acres. 52,000 square feet. 6000 people. Fits in your shirt pocket. Radiant podcast."[18] The church houses a Starbucks coffee shop in the lobby as well as a

---

15   Thomas Tweed, *Crossing and Dwelling: A Theory of Religion* (Cambridge: Harvard University Press, 2006) 54; italics in original.

16   *The Elementary Forms of Religious Life*, trans. Karen E. Fields (New York: The Free Press, 1995) 133.

17   Steven Vertovec, *The Hindu Diaspora: Comparative Patterns* (London: Routledge, 2000) 155.

18   www.RadiantChurch.com, accessed 6 June 2006.

separate drive-through window for coffee. Similar churches make use of 24-hour web casts and daily e-messaging. Of course, mobile technologies facilitate both the preservation and reconfiguration of religion. Steve Vertovec mentions the case of a young Trinidadian Muslim woman using the internet "to try to sort out in her own mind which aspects of her practice were orthodox and which were local."[19] Indeed, increased mobility most likely impacts the dominant religious idioms and theologies on offer. Katy Gardner claims, for instance, that "the culture of migration is interwoven with the culture of miracles."[20]

Nonetheless Tweed, like Greenblatt, presumes that the academy has long presupposed the fixity of location. Speaking of various schools of theorists, he writes, "I reject a presupposition they all share...that the theorist and theorized are static. To highlight the shifting position of the theorist, while also acknowledging the movements and relations I found among transnational migrants in Miami, I endorse James Clifford's suggestion that we turn to the metaphor of travel" (8). Tweed opts for the metaphor of travel precisely to avoid "essentializing religious traditions as static, isolated, and immutable substances," (60) and to convey the relationality and distance, the "in-between-ness" of the ethnographer who shuttles between insiderhood and outsiderhood. On this latter point, he applauds and amplifies Robert Orsi's denunciation of religious scholarship that "seals the borders of our own worlds of meaning" and creates a comfortable distance between us and "the others."[21] Orsi invites scholars to suspend their ethical judgments, to move "back and forth between two alternative ways of organizing and experiencing reality," to stay in this space in between two worlds (no man's land?) and "refuse the closure" of boundaries (223). But can such an approach to studying religion do justice to those religious cultures whose spatial practices include tirelessly monitoring boundaries? Can this approach help us understand the contemporary configurations of religion and migration? To the extent scholars of religion are convinced that scholarship on other cultures is best done by tacking back and forth in an imaginary liminal space that is both in and out, I am convinced those same scholars may not be doing justice to the various constellations of mobility and religion.

To be fair, Tweed refers to the significant difference between his mobility and that of the exiles he studies. He also notes that religious spatial practices include boundary-making and thus the delineation of *us* and *them* (111).[22] Tweed notes

---

19   Vertovec, "Religion and Diaspora," 26.

20   K. Gardner, *Global Migrants, Local Lives: Travel and Transformation in Rural Bangladesh* (Oxford: Clarendon Press, 1995), 262.

21   Robert Orsi, "Snakes Alive: Resituating the Moral in the Study of Religion" in *In Face of the Facts: Moral Inquiry in American Scholarship* (eds) Richard Wightman Fox and Robert B. Westbrook (Cambridge: Cambridge University Press [and Woodrow Wilson Center Press]) 219; see also 203, 211.

22   Thomas Tweed, "On Moving Across: Translocative Religion and the Interpreter's Position," *Journal of the American Academy of Religion* 70.2 (June 2002): 270–71.

that he reproduces dissenting voices in his text – including one that speaks of an insuperable boundary between Catholicism and Santeria. Nonetheless, these references are very brief and the decided emphasis is on flowing, moving, crossing – terms which obscure encumbrances, obstacles, barriers, and dislocations. Tweed is aware that metaphors "illumine some features of the terrain and obscure others" (46). I wish to highlight what can be obscured by a theory of religion that defines it as flow. Let me put the matter a different way. Religion is often included in a list of identity markers. Hence, we might gainfully portray race, class, ethnicity, sex/gender, age as spatial practices. But surely it would be misleading to insist upon the fluidity of these lived realities or to lose sight of the privilege of declaring them so. To put the matter still another way: what is illuminated when we frame the religious regulation of gender as the production of "stranded mobilities?"[23]

A theory of religion whereby it essentially constitutes or conveys modern waves of moving people echoes the long-standing and problematic valorization of movement, fluidity, and open-endedness as the quintessential mark of the authentically religious. Of course, these theorizations of religion as inherently mobile are themselves symptomatic of the ongoing impact of a world in flux. Nonetheless, if religion is theorized as a flow of bodies or as facilitating that flow, then scholarship informed by such a theory will obscure the diversity of migration experiences and the conflicts produced by the speed and intensity of contemporary movements. The danger is that this theory of religion will lend unwitting endorsement to simplistic analyses of contemporary conflict. Such analyses attribute conflict to those religious bodies/cultures that fail to see that religion is essentially fluid and is thus inimical to the conflicts associated with rigid boundaries of identity (something that this theory explicitly repudiates on the part of the scholar). One frequently meets with comments such as, "Thus it is more than a little ironic that the term *shari'ah*, which has the idea of fluidity and mobility as part of its very structure, should have become the symbol of rigid and unchanging laws to the Bali bombers."[24] Religious conflict is attributed to religious groups that have not yet fully secularized, that is, those religious communities that focus on boundary maintenance. In a recent article on "Religions in Global Civil Society" George Thomas chastises religious persons who have not yet "deterritorialized" their religion, as evidenced, for instance, in their prohibiting proselytizing and conversion.[25] Yet to reduce religious conflict to blindness to religion's essential and congenial fluidity or to stubborn attachment to place or identity simplifies the relationship between mobility and religious conflict. Moreover, it obscures the fact that contemporary mobilities create and exacerbate vulnerabilities and attendant conflicts.

---

23   The phrase "stranded mobilities" is taken from Margaret Grieco and Julian Hine's chapter in this book, "Stranded Mobilities, Human Disasters".

24   Phar Kim Beng, "The Bali bombers' real crime," *Asia Times*, 7 June 2003, www. atimes.com, accessed 6 March 2007.

25   Thomas, "Religions in Global Civil Society," *Sociology of Religion* 62.4 (Winter 2001): 526ff.

Rather than indicting "maximalist" or "primitive" or "fundamentalist" religiosities, we might better study the effects of modern mobility.[26] Is it just coincidence, after all, that so many recent acts of violence involve vehicles? Recall the fiery planes of 9/11, the smashed trains in Madrid and London, the poison gas in the Tokyo subway station, the bus-stop honor killing of Hatin Surucu, a Turkish immigrant in Germany, the taxicab abductions of brides in Kyrgyzstan, the 1997 car kidnapping of Nadia from Oslo, Norway to Morocco, because she was "becoming Norwegian."[27] One might conclude from these examples that religious "fundamentalists" are looking to take revenge on a mobile globe that is threatening their way of life. These are the communities that do not get on board their religion, so to speak, and surf into the transnational civic community.

Arjun Appadurai has suggested that contemporary migrations beget feelings of vulnerability that are then expressed as potentially conflictual religiosities in the transnational civic society. He writes, "Deterritorialization, whether of Hindus, Sikhs, Palestinians or Ukrainians, is now at the core of a variety of global fundamentalisms."[28] In other words, it is not that such persons have not yet been converted to the pleasures of boundarylessness and refusals of closure, but that the pressures and anxieties of migration prompt insecure religiosities. Similarly, Gerrie ter Haar points out:

> It is not religion, but migration, regional and international, that is the truly controversial issue of politics worldwide…Migration and the presence of migrant communities, whether in Africa, Europe or anywhere else, is symbolized by religious difference, conceived as a form of "otherness." This can be politically exploited to create in- and out-groups; or, in other words, to introduce a politics of identity. In none of these cases should religion be mistaken for the real issue. The real issue is the pressure to share resources with others.[29]

Surely, in this context of vulnerability inducing or compounding movement, it is smug romanticism to preach the progressive possibilities of deterritorialized, unplugged, disembedded or diasporic religion. Nor can it be a solution to remind the antagonists that "real religion" entails transcending the body when vulnerable

---

26   The phrase "maximalist religion" was coined by Bruce Lincoln; see his *Holy Terrors: Thinking About Religion After September 11* (Chicago: University of Chicago Press, 2003).

27   Saphinez-Amal Naguib, "The Northern Way: Muslim Communities in Norway," in *Muslim Minorities in West: Visible and Invisible*, edited by Yvonne Yazbeck Haddad and Jane I. Smith (Walnut Creek, CA: AltaMira, 2002), 170.

28   Appadurai, "Disjuncture and Difference in the Global Cultural Economy," in M. Featherstone (ed.) *Global Culture: Nationalism, Globalization and Modernity* (London: Sage, 1990) 301, quoted in Vertovec, 144.

29   Gerrie ter Haaar, "Religion: Source of Conflict or Resource for Peace?" in Gerrie ter Haar and James J. Busuttil (eds), *Bridge or Barrier: Religion, Violence and Visions for Peace* (Leiden: Brill, 2005) 15.

bodies are competing for scarce resources. Instead, we must face head-on the complex and contradictory realities of both contemporary migration and religiosity. As Katy Gardner has written:

> How can we reconcile the prosperity and economic growth which migration graphically engenders, with the exploitation (both between places, and between groups of people) with which it is also associated?…[M]igration is inherently contradictory. As we shall see, it brings economic, social and geographical mobility, yet in other ways heightens social and economic dependence; it binds families together, while also pulling them, apart; it is a central source of advancement, and a symbol of power, yet also resisted through stress upon local sources of power and religious revivalism.[30]

It will hardly do to attempt to restrict migratory flows. Indeed, the fact that people are on the move is not a peculiar feature of modernity. Nonetheless, there are distinctive features of contemporary mobility. These distinctive features, moreover, appear to have predictable effects on religiosity.

Modern mobility is more intense. From the time of agricultural societies until the present, migratory flows have decreased in extensity but increased in intensity, velocity and frequency. The contemporary flows of people are primarily from undeveloped or less developed regions (the periphery) to the developed regions of the US, Canada and Europe. Nonetheless, as one source states, "There is now almost no state or part of the world that is not importing or exporting labor."[31] Most contemporary migrations are driven by economic necessity. Migrants are seeking relatively more secure lives. They are looking for jobs. They are looking for safety and shelter. Indeed, a significant number are refugees fleeing civil wars – sometimes with religious causes. One source predicts "at some point in the near future the number of asylum seekers will exceed the number of voluntary migrants presenting themselves at the borders of OECD countries."[32] These moving bodies are not yet afforded the same layers of protection as the flow of capital and goods between developed states. "Although the treatment of refugees and asylum seekers has been increasingly regulated by international treaty and agreement, no codified international regime or body of law has emerged to regulate the movement of labour [read: bodies] that bears any comparison with those regulating trade and

---

30   Katy Gardner, *Global Migrations, Local Lives* (Oxford: Clarendon, 1995) 3. See the recent *New York Times* article describing the rising rates of college educated migrants moving from one rich country to another. Jason DeParle, "Border Crossings; Rising Breed of Migrant Worker: Skilled, Salaried and Welcome," *The New York Times*, 20 August 2007, www.nytimes.com, accessed 12 September 2007.

31   David Held, Anthony McGrew, et al. *Global Transformation: Politics, Economics and Culture* (Stanford; Stanford University Press, 1999) 297.

32   Held et al., 302. OECD stands for "Organization for Economic Cooperation and Development."

capital movements."[33] Add to these migratory pressures, daily commutes on public transportation or lengthy and burdensome walks as well as increased working time and one feels justified in observing that many of today's moving bodies experience a decrease in leisure time and an increase in perceived vulnerability.

What effect might all this have on religiosity? Pippa Norris and Ronald Inglehart argue that people with "existential security," that is "the feeling that survival is secure enough that it can be taken for granted," are becoming less and less religious. Whereas people who have experienced risks in their formative years or continue to experience risks to themselves, their families and their communities will tend to be more religious.[34] They further argue that because the fertility rates are so high in poorer and traditional societies and among their mobile members (two and three times replacement levels) and so low in rich nations (below replacement levels), "rich nations are becoming more secular, but the world as a whole is becoming more religious."[35] So what accounts for the persistence of religion in the prosperous United States? Norris and Inglehart provide two reasons: the influx of religious immigrants with higher birth rates and the existential insecurity of life in an America with a very thin welfare net, or perhaps euphemistically, with its "entrepreneurial culture of personal responsibility."[36] Rates of religiosity remain relatively high in the US because religious immigrants have more children and the natives are nervous.

But can one extend Norris and Inglehart's argument in order to say more about migrants and religiosity, apart from religious immigrants having higher birth rates? If one were to do this, the argument would go something like this: If the majority of moving people are moving in order to gain security, and if the process of moving and settling is itself full of risks, and if, over time, the move does not afford *existential* security, the level of religiosity of such groups would be stable if not increased (and perhaps transformed). Conversely, if migration brought prosperity and security, materially and existentially, formal religiosity would decline (and perhaps birth rates as well). Recent data appears to bear out this extension of Norris and Inglehart's analysis.

Cities such as Rio de Janeiro, Lima, São Paulo and Santiago have experienced exponential growth as well as church expansion. The Nigerian city of Lagos contained a quarter of a million people in 1950. It is projected to be bursting with 25 million people by 2015. Although the city is divided among Christians and Muslims, it has recently hosted some of the world's largest evangelical revivals. In one night alone in 2000, some 1.6 million people took up the German Pentecostal preacher Richard Bonnke's offer to: "Come and receive your miracle."[37] In January

---

33   Held et al., 314.

34   Pippa Norris and Ronald Inglehart, *Sacred and Secular: Religion and Politics Worldwide* (Cambridge: Cambridge University Press, 2004) 5.

35   Norris and Inglehart, 23.

36   Norris and Inglehart, 108.

37   Philip Jenkins, *The Next Christendom* (Oxford, 2002) 74.

2005, Bonnke was hosted by 2 million Christians and Muslims in Jos (central state in Nigeria) interested in his message of reconciliation. Bonnke insists that the "[B]lood of Jesus is the best medicine for the healing of a sick land." Christians and Muslims in this area have been mutually displaced by ongoing hostilities that have claimed over 84,000 lives since 2001.[38]

In London, half of all churchgoers are from Africa or the Caribbean. Kingsway International Christian Centre was founded in 1992 by Pastor Matthew Ashimolowo who hails from Nigeria. It is the largest church created in Britain since 1861. It seats 5,000 people at its main facility, "The Miracle Centre," which is double the capacity of Westminster Abbey or St. Paul's Cathedral. Ashimolowo has urged that the Anglican Church die gracefully and hand over its buildings to newer groups such as his own.[39] Apparently, the increasingly secular English are reluctant to do this. After thirty years of resistance, the empty Mount Zion Methodist Church in Clitheroe, England (which had been a factory for forty years) will finally become a mosque. Clitheroe, like many other English towns, reflects the changing demography effected by immigration from former British colonies.[40]

Again, it is important to keep in mind that Norris and Inglehart focus on "existential" insecurity. Thus whereas immigrants might do well enough economically relative to native neighboring populations, they may still retain or heighten their religiosity in contexts in which they perceive latent or experience outright hostility on the part of the receiving nation. As Grace Davies remarks, "There exists in fact an odd irony in the self-perception of Europeans. At one and the same time, they perceive themselves as increasingly secular and draw the boundaries of their continent – known sometimes as 'fortress Europe' – along Christian lines…Muslim states will find it harder [than Orthodox nations] (if not impossible) [to join the European Union], despite the existence of significant Muslim communities within most, if not all, West European nations."[41] This observation most certainly accounts for the thirty years it took for the Muslims of Clitheroe to lay claim to a defunct Methodist church.

Recent data suggests that some immigrants to America are experiencing increasing prosperity and existential security – albeit decreased leisure time – and that these immigrants' formal participation in religion is decreasing. One US priest working with migrants from the Dominican Republic muses, "Those who do well seem to need God less."[42] Peggy Levitt's report on immigrants from Miraflores, Dominican Republic shows that priests and people have much more contact in

---

38   Obed Minchakpu, "Healing a Sick Land," at www.christianitytoday.com/ct/2005/004/4.23.html, accessed 26 May 2006.

39   Philip Jenkins, 98–9.

40   Jane Perlez, "Old Church Becomes Mosque in Uneasy Britain," *The New York Times*, 2 April 2007, www.nytimes.com, accessed 7 April 2007.

41   Davies, "Global Civil Religion: A European Perspective," 467–8.

42   Quoted in Peggy Levitt, *The Transnational Villagers* (Berkeley: University of Berkeley Press, 2001) 174. Levitt's report is echoed by a recent report released by *The New York Times*;

the home country; everyone in the US is so very scheduled, including the priest, that no one has time for casual mealtimes. Whereas some priests complain that immigrants do not need them, it appears that Irish immigration made multitaskers of US priests. The difference is attributable to the significant amount of illegal immigration (and thus heightened vulnerability) among the Irish and the lack of it among the Dominicans.[43]

Studies of Canadian and American regional migration indicate that this type of migration does not appear to produce a net decrease in religiosity. More important factors than mobility for determining religiosity are the level of religiosity at the destination (which, if higher, can increase the religiosity of the migrant) and one's religious identity. In the latter instance, being a Roman Catholic or Conservative Protestant overrides the negative effects of age, region and residential mobility.[44] In the US, American citizens are moving from, for instance, California, to Texas, Florida, Arizona, North Carolina and Nevada.[45] Most of America's 100 fastest-growing counties, spread across 30 states, are known as "exurbs." The term covers those areas that are too far from the city to be "suburbs" and too bustling to be considered "rural." They are communities of subdivisions filled with middle-class families who are likely to move again and again, putting down no real roots.[46] Many of these one hundred counties have a large and growing evangelical Christian megachurch. One of these churches, Radiant in Surprise, Arizona, was started in September 1997 with 147 people; it currently has 6,000 and is the 18th fastest growing church in the United States. It is the fastest growing Assemblies of God church in the US.

---

see Laurie Goodstein, "For Some Hispanics, Coming to America Also Means Abandoning Religion," *The New York Times*, 15 April 2007, www.nytimes.com, accessed 18 April 2007.

43   See her "Redefining the Boundaries of Belonging: The Institutional Character of Transnational Religious Life," *Sociology of Religion* 65.1 (2004):1–18.

44   Roger W. Stump, "Regional Migration and Religious Commitment in the United States," *Journal for the Scientific Study of Religion* 23.3 (1984): 292–303. Reginald W. Bibby, "Going, Going, Gone: The Impact of Geographical Mobility on Religious Involvement," *Review of Religious Research* 38.4 (1997): 289–307. See also Frank van Tubergen, "Religious Affiliation and Attendance Among Immigrants in Eight Western Countries: Individual and Contextual Effects," *Journal for the Scientific Study of Religion* 45.1 (2006): 1–22.

45   "It is estimated that, as of the 1990s, approximately one in two Canadians and Americans change their residences within a five year period," from Bibby, 290. Texas had a net gain of 51,067 new residents in 2005; California lost 239,417 Americans in 2004–2005 but gained 232,700 international newcomers. See Mark Babineck, "People Flocking to Texas from the Rest of America," *Houston Chronicle*, 8 January 2006, at www.HoustonChronicle.com, accessed 10 January 2006.

46   Jonathan Mahler, "The Soul of a New Exurb," *The New York Times Magazine*, 27 March 2005, 33; Mahler mentions towns such as Lebanon, Ohio; Fridley, Minnesota; Crabapple, Georgia; and Surprise, Arizona. See also Jason P. Schachter, Rachel S. Franklin and Marc J. Perry, "Migration and Geographic Mobility in Metropolitan and Nonmetropolitan America: 1995–2000", *US Census Bureau*, August 2003, 3.

Clearly not all immigrants experience exacerbated vulnerability. But of those who do, religion can provide a generally approved system for generating and expanding social capital, whether to compensate for low levels of physical and human capital or to facilitate in the acquisition of these latter two. Becoming part of a community of people with shared beliefs and practices provides emotional support, especially in an unfamiliar and possibly hostile context. But a religious community can also be a gateway to employment, food, shelter, and social services, as well as a means for developing leadership and organizational skills. Religion may also facilitate connections to the wider receiving society if it is an approved category of identity. As one scholar notes:

> Immigrants are religious – by all accounts more religious than they were before they left home – because religion is one of the important identity markers that helps them preserve individual self-awareness and cohesion in a group...In the United States, religion is the social category with clearest meaning and acceptance in the host society, so the emphasis on religious affiliation and identity is one of the strategies that allow the immigrant to maintain self-identity while simultaneously acquiring community acceptance.[47]

US appreciation of religion as a social category of identity and positive character is both informal and formal: the government has required immigrants from the Dominican Republic to supply baptismal certificates in addition to birth certificates![48] Although Christian identity is usually an asset for US immigrants, it does not necessarily usher in their assimilation to the wider society. Other factors, such as the historic relationship between the church and colonial regimes in the sending country, or conservative gender codes, appear to affect rates of assimilation.[49]

I have suggested that the increasing intensity, velocity and frequency of global mobilities play a role in sustaining and possibly increasing religiosity. Many studies report that religion provides emotional and material resources for facilitating the transitions induced by migration. Religion provides a serviceable identity for negotiating reception in the new territory or for maintaining ties to the "homeland." Religion can also provide justifications for low aspirations, continuous struggle

---

47   Raymond B. Williams, *Religions of Immigrants from India and Pakistan: New Threads in the American Tapestry* (Cambridge: Cambridge University Press, 1988) 29.

48   Levitt, Transnational Villagers, 176.

49   See Ana-Maria Diaz Stevens, "Colonization and Immigration in the Process of Latino Identification," in *Religion and Immigration: Christian, Jewish and Muslim Experiences in the United States*, edited by Yvonne Yazbeck Haddad, Jane I. Smith, and John L. Esposito (Walnut Creek: Alta Mira Press, 2003). See HaeRan Shin, "Korean Immigrant Women to Los Angeles: Religious Space, Transformative Space?," in *Women, Religion, and Space*, Karen M. Morin and Jeanne Kay Guelke (eds) (Syracuse: Syracuse University Press, 2007) 127–47.

and deprivation.[50] Thus, in many different ways religion can be used to preempt or mitigate conflict whether between family members, community members or immigrants and natives.

Religion, however, can also be symptomatic of and exacerbate anxieties and conflicts brought on by a world on the move. Such conflicts are particularly visible around issues of gender. Mark Juergensmeyer attributes the rise of religious violence to men's frustration with their marginality and threatened masculinity in the light of women's changing status – a change that entails women's increasing spatial, social and economic mobility. Juergensmeyer points to militarism, marginality and masculinism as contributing causes to the rise in religious violence. I suggest the addition of a fourth "M:" mobility.[51] Less violent expressions of religiosity may take the form of efforts to police boundaries of gender, bodies and states (or perhaps texts as in literalist readings). For instance, Roger Friedland declares "Religious nationalisms are boundary politics." Friedland sees parallel figurations between the anxiety over national borders (and their penetration by polluting foreign currencies and consumer items) and anxiety over controlling the boundaries and movements of women's bodies – a preoccupation of religious fundamentalisms.[52] The flow of goods and circulation of women raises the specter of promiscuity, which, in turn, threatens the continuity of well-defined identities and collectivities. Friedland's analogy is supported by additional research by Pippa Norris and Ronald Inglehart. They argue that the so-called "clash of civilizations" between the secularizing nations of the West and the sacralizing nations of the Global South and Middle East consists not in contradictory positions on democratic values and institutions (as is the argument of Samuel Huntington), but rather on gender equality and sexual liberalization (including homosexuality, abortion and divorce).[53]

---

50 Shin, "Korean Immigrant Women to Los Angeles: Religious Space, Transformative Space?"

51 See Juergensmeyer, *Terror in the Mind of God: The Global Rise of Religious Violence*, 3rd edn (Berkeley: University of California Press, 2003), chapter 10.

52 Roger Friedland, "Money, Sex, and God: The Erotic Logic of Religious Nationalism," *Sociological Theory* 20.3 (November 2002): 409, 411, 401, 395. Friedland reminds his readers that Yitzhak Rabin's assassin, Yigal Amir, feared Rabin's removal of Jewish settlers in Hebron. Amir felt justified in killing Rabin based on his reading of Numbers 25 in which YhWh punishes the Israelites with a plague as a result of their having sex with Moabite women and being lured to their god, Ba'al. An Israelite named Pinchas slays an Israelite man and Moabite women who publicly display their affection. This is against Torah; nonetheless, the plague is lifted and YhWh declares that he will make of Pinchas' line a perpetual priesthood.

53 Pippa Norris and Ronald Inglehart, *Sacred and Secular: Religion and Politics Worldwide* (Cambridge: Cambridge University Press, 2004), chapter 6. Norris and Inglehart do not include African nations in their survey. In light of the conflicts of the Anglican Church, it seems reasonable to extend their thesis to this region. Contemporary religious responses to prostitution and sex-trafficking are often based on human rights discourse. They merit further study. Sometimes mobile religiosity and promiscuity go hand-in-hand. In the

Recall that Nigeria has experienced a significant amount of regional migration. In northern Nigeria at least 12 of its 36 states have imposed strict *Shari'a* (Muslim religious law) over the entire state. This has entailed curbs on women's mobility and harsh punishment for their violation. In 2005, the adoption of *Shari'a* rule in Kano led to the establishment of a single sex bus system throughout the city. Villagers in Sylhet, Bangladesh, made recourse to *purdah* in order to lend wives left behind by husbands who migrated to London for jobs, an appearance of control and status, offsetting their chance of penetration and possession by ghosts.[54] Women left behind by migrating men, may enjoy an enhancement of status through their husband's financial remittances but also are subject to more restrictions on their movements as unattached and thus vulnerable, and even dangerous, women.

If successful migrating women are accompanied by men whose employment is insecure, low status or in feminized fields, such men may actually utilize (and even create) religious leadership roles to compensate for this loss of status. For instance, Kerala Orthodox Christian husbands who move with their wives, who are recruited to work as nurses, make recourse to several strategies. They split congregations (so there are more leadership opportunities for men); they take on most of the communal cooking; and they explicitly discourage their daughters from caroling with them despite the girls expressed desire and discipline and their sons' apparent lack of both of these characteristics. One man states: "Nurses over here make good bucks and the men go for a clerical job – whatever – and the women make more money…In the house the husband does not have his proper status. In the society, you are an Indian – what status do you have? For men – where are they are going to show their macho nature? That's why they play in the church."[55] Ai Ra Kim and HaeRan Shin report a similar pattern among Korean Christian male immigrants in the nonprofessional sector.[56]

Immigration may bring empowerment to women, especially for women newly entering the work force or educational institutions. As one Dominican migrant woman to the US reports: "One sees things, one works, one manages one's own money and isn't dependent on anyone…The woman that migrates develops in many ways. She has to learn how to live alone, to do everything, and not to

---

middle of her description of a grand pilgrimage to Sodo, Haiti, site of a Marian apparition, Elizabeth McAlister mentions, "Young sons may go out into the night in search of the many bouzen (prostitutes) who come into the town especially for the feast." McAlister, "The Madonna of 115th Street Revisited: Voudou and Haitian Catholicism in the Age of Transnationalism," in Warner, *Gatherings in Diaspora*, 136.

54   Gardner, *Global Migrants, Local Lives*, esp. chapter 7.

55   George, "Caroling," 274.

56   Ai Ra Kim, *Women Struggling for a New Life: The Role of Religion in the Cultural Passage From Korea to America* (Albany: State University of New York Press, 1996) 67. HaeRan Shin, "Korean Immigrant Women to Los Angeles: Religious Space, Transformative Space?," in *Women, Religion, and Space*, edited by Karen M. Morin and Jeanne Kay Guelke (Syracuse: Syracuse University Press, 2007) 142.

ask for anything."[57] Migration may also afford women new opportunities for religious and community leadership. Studies show that a major trend of immigrant religious communities, especially in the US but also in some European countries, whether they are Indian Orthodox Christians or Buddhists or Muslims is to adopt a congregational structure.[58] (This, of course, does not apply to Catholics.) Moreover, these congregations, catering to a transient or settling population, generally become multi-purpose community centers. Consequently, the denser structure of these religious institutions offers a number of status-enhancing roles to women.[59] Women prepare beloved native foods, serve as religious educators of children, manage and perform music, and supervise family life. They may also launch women's ministries or groups. These roles grant women visibility and leadership skills; in a number of instances, women serve on decision-making boards. It would be a grave mistake to dismiss the significance of these activities as "women's work." To do so is to reinscribe the tendency to devalue women's role in reproducing the nation. This work becomes especially important, and perhaps finally recognizable for the public, political work it is, in the immigrant context. In this context, religion is often the key to cultural reproduction and women have the primary role in this process as "ethno-religious educators."[60] In some instances, they are able to parlay religious charitable work into active citizenship in national and transnational publics. This was the case with the Pakistani women's movement in Manchester, England, Al Masoom, which began with fundraising for a children's cancer hospital in Pakistan and moved on to marching for human rights in Kashmir and Bosnia and delivering medical aid, food and clothing to Bosnian

---

57   Gloria, 48, return migrant (Boston to Milaflores, Dominican Republic), quoted in Peggy Levitt, *The Transnational Villagers* (Berkeley: University of California Press, 2001) 102. Levitt describes how these returning migrants bring word and experience of these new gender relationships and thus influence some local women's and men's expectations; nonetheless, she cautions against overestimating the local impact of the "social remittances" of more egalitarian gender relationships.

58   Helen Rose Ebaugh and Janet Saltzman Chafetz, *Religion and The New Immigrants* (Walnut Creek, CA: AltaMira, 2000) 362. See also Rogaia Mustafa Abusharaf, "Structural Adaptations in an Immigrant Muslim Congregation in New York" in *Gatherings in Diaspora: Religious Communities and the New Immigration*, edited by R. Stephen Warner and Judith G. Wittner (Philadelphia: Temple University Press, 1998) 254.

59   Ebaugh and Chafetz, ibid. See also Sheba George, "Caroling with the Keralites: The Negotiation of Gendered Space in an Indian Immigrant Church" in *Gatherings in Diaspora: Religious Communities and the New Immigration*, R. Stephen Warner and Judith G. Wittner (eds) (Philadelphia: Temple University Press, 1998) 267 for confirmation of women's generally increased participation in US immigrant religious communities.

60   See also Merryle McDonald, "Rituals of Motherhood Among Gujurati Women in East London," in R. Burghart (ed.) *Hinduism in Great Britain* (London: Tavistock, 1987) 50–66 and Aparna Rayaprol, *Negotiating Identities: Women in the Indian Diaspora* (Delhi: Oxford University Press, 1997).

refugees – all in the name of the international Islamic *ummah*.[61] So, too, in the first part of the twentieth century immigrant Korean women formed relief societies in their churches; their activities included marching, boycotting, writing letters to US political leaders, and raising $20,000 for the cause of Korean independence from Japan, all the while cooking, cleaning and carrying children.[62]

Women's religious mobility is not, however, always welcomed by men. In the 1920s the male members of the Greek Orthodox church in Houston, Texas made the women who wished to form a "Church Women's Club" swear in front of the statue of the Virgin Mary to "disband immediately and never again instigate such a subversive movement." Yet such an organization got underway in the 1940s and women now serve in all sorts of lay leadership roles including the Board of Trustees, practices that are not mirrored in contemporary Greece.[63]

In light of these different outcomes, it is clear that mobility and religiosity interact in varied and complex ways. I would suggest, however, that the data reveals some patterns to this interaction. If *both* men and women benefit from the educational and employment opportunities in the receiving country, it appears that there will be less recourse to religion in order to provide traditional forms of gender discipline. Such seems to be the case among, as noted earlier, secure Hispanic immigrants to America. It is also evident among Kosovo Albanians in London; though there is still pressure for Albanian women to marry Albanian men and for Albanian men to obtain wives from home – thought to be pure.[64] If, however, mobility is asymmetrical (between men and women or across different ethnic or religious groups or natives and immigrants), segregates men and women, or entails a decline in status for both men and women, recourse to religious forms of boundary maintenance, gender discipline and even violence may ensue.

But the patterns are, of course, subject to the continuous modifications and repositionings that mobility brings. Indeed, when bodies of different religiosities and nationalities collide, unexpected cooperation rather than conflict sometime ensues! One thinks, for instance, of the development of the African Religious Health Assets Programme based in Cape Town which more effectively serves the healthcare needs of migrant populations by drawing on the effective hybridization of indigenous African traditions and Charismatic (Pentecostal) and Evangelical

61   Pnina Werbner, "The Place Which is Diaspora: Citizenship, Religion and Gender in the Making of Chaordic Transnationalism," *Journal of Ethnic and Migration Studies* 28.1 (January 2002): 119–33.

62   Ai Ra Kim, *Women Struggling for a New Life: The Role of Religion in the Cultural Passage From Korea to America* (Albany: State University of New York Press, 1996) 34–5.

63   Ebaugh and Chafetz, 366.

64   Deniuse Kostovicova and Albert Prestreshi, "Education, Gender and Religion: Identity Transformations Among Kosovo Albanians in London," *Journal of Ethnic and Migration Studies* 29.6 (November 2003): 1079–1096.

Christianity.[65] Who would have thought such hybridization possible or productive for bodily health? In another example, the Nigerian police's anti-trafficking task force has collaborated with the Illinois-based Christian group "Lost Coin." Lost Coin counsels West African women sex slaves trafficked to Greece who fear escaping their horrendous lives for fear of consequently activating Voodoo or juju curses on their families; their message is that "the one almighty God who is above all can undo the voodoo."[66] Finally, evangelical Christians wish to proselytize in Muslim areas – a demand that will probably prompt them to reexamine gender relations in their churches.[67]

Mobility suggests change, dynamism, life. Immobility suggests decay, stasis, death. It is no wonder that one would wish to align one's scholarly endeavors with the former rather than the latter. Nonetheless, we must be careful that our scholarship is not compromised by a secret or not so secret homage to the unbearable lightness of movement. We should not lose sight of the terrors, vulnerabilities, and conflicts contemporary mobility brings. Mobility is profoundly ambivalent; it brings prosperity and dislocation. It sends children to school and their parents away. If we keep this in mind, instead of valorizing fluid religion, we will better account for the complex and conflictual constellations of religion, mobility (and gender).

It has been an enduring presumption of modern Western societies that the truly awful conflicts are religious and that they are best solved by religion transforming itself into mere belief, freeing itself from the inertia of money, land and family. Or, if it cannot do this, to at least confine itself to the private sphere in order that a "public sphere" might emerge. The public is purportedly free and open, where no one is excluded, where all voices may have their say, where bodies can come into close proximity without regulation or injury. This is the dream of secularism (and *laicité*) which imagines that its "public" is not composed of disciplined bodies and its own spatial practices of exclusion.[68] But that is a topic for another paper.

---

65 In 1999, the Democratic Republic of Congo turned over responsibility for the healthcare of 12 million people to a faith-based health organization, under a contract administered by Interchurch Medical Agency in cooperation with the Protestant Church of the Congo. In Kenya, religious organizations own 34 percent of the hospitals; in Zambia the figure is 53 percent. In Nigeria, the Christian Health Association of Nigeria (CHAN) includes more than 300 health institutions and 3,000 outreach facilities, serving at least 40 percent of the country population. See James R. Cochrane, "Religion in the Health of Migrant Communities: Asset or Deficit?" *Journal of Ethnic and Migration Studies* 32.4 (May 2006): 18.

66 *Associated Press*, *Guelph Mercury*, Ontario, Canada, 28 May 2005. Apparently only invocations of the "even greater might of God" can undo voodoo's "heavy power over these women."

67 Thomas, 530.

68 See, for instance, Banu Gökariksel, "A Feminist Geography of Veiling: Gender, Class, and Religion in the Making of Modern Subjects and Public Spaces in Istanbul," in *Women, Religion, and Space*, 61–80.

Chapter 12

The Desire for Speed
and the Rhythm of the Earth

Michael Northcott

The availability of speed in modernity produces a desire for speed as the technological marker of an exalted way of life. The resultant compression of time and space reproduces and magnifies disruptions and injustices in human and human-nature relations. The desire for speed also involves displacement of the traditional conception of life as a journey of the mind and soul towards the divine. Whereas much modern travel is organized around tourism travel in the Middle Ages was primarily ordered around pilgrimage. The contrast between the pace of medieval pilgrimage and the speed of modern tourism is significant. Walking involves slow organic movement through a landscape such that the rhythm of movement mirrors the rhythm of the earth and so enacts an embodied analogy of prayer and contemplation. Journeying and mobility in Jewish and Christian traditions are central metaphors of the spiritual quest and of the potential richness of life lived in dependence upon the divine Spirit rather than on the possession of many chariots, or of houses in locations distant from one another.

> Whan that Aprill, with his shoures soote
> The droghte of March hath perced to the roote
> And bathed every veyne in swich licour
> Of which vertu engendred is the flour
> Thanne longen folk to goon on pilgrimages
>
> Geoffrey Chaucer[1]

> For the last twenty years neither matter nor space nor time has been what it was from time immemorial.
>
> Paul Valery[2]

---

1 Geoffrey Chaucer, *The Canterbury Tales: General Prologue* in *The Works of Geoffrey Chaucer* (ed.) F.N. Robinson (London: Oxford University Press, 1957), 17.

2 Paul Valery, 'La conquete de ubiquite', cited in Walter Benjamin, 'Art in the Age of Mechanical Reproduction' in *Illuminations* (ed.) Hannah Arendt, trans. Harry Zohn (New York: Schocken Books, 1969), 32–47.

Ownership of private cars has long been the defining feature of the consumer society since Henry Ford invented his Model T which sold 15 million units and was designed to bring to the masses the technology of the horseless carriage which previously had only been available in the smaller production runs of Benz, Peugeot and Rolls Royce of much more luxurious and expensive vehicles. The proliferation of private car ownership on every continent has however not been accompanied by a genuine leveling in human access to mechanical mobility. There are presently 300 million private cars on the roads but 75 percent of these are in developed countries. Deaths from road accidents are also unequally shared between developed and developing. Of the 50 million people who are annually injured in road accidents, and the estimated 1.2 million road deaths, 85 percent of these are in developing countries.[3]

The unequal distribution of access to road transport, and the even more unequal distribution of traffic accidents, are both powerful examples of the way in which, as Ivan Illich and Paul Virilio suggest, speed creates a hierarchy which privileges an elite who enjoy the power it confers at the expense of others who live life in the 'slow lane'.[4] Speed depends upon the harnessing of biological power concentrated by an extractive economy which draws resources from a range of spaces including those regions where coal and oil are extracted, often with deleterious consequences for local inhabitants.[5] Speed involves the servitude of others who labour to construct railroads and highways, and to manufacture, maintain and repair the technological devices which confer speed and the infrastructure they require. Speed also requires sacrifices in the wellbeing of those – human and nonhuman beings – whose places are deracinated and polluted by the pathways of speed devices.

Concentrated material power is morally ambiguous because its production necessitates the imposition of a range of ecological and human harms which include growth in extreme weather events associated with human induced climate change as well as more localized harms. Those regions and communities of being, human and nonhuman, where these harms are visited are often remote from the corporations and bureaucrats who impose them and so the true costs of speed are politically obscure.[6] And because of the global scale of the decision-making chains involved the ecological footprints of the technologies of speed are imposed without proper moral and political deliberation on indigenous peoples

---

3   Abudlbari Bener, 'The neglected epidemic: road accident statistics in a developing country', *Journal of Injury Control and Safety Promotion* 12 (2005), 45–57.

4   Ivan Illich, *Energy and Equity* (New York: Harper and Row, 1974) and Paul Virilio, *Speed and Politics* (New York: Semiotext, 1986).

5   On the deleterious economic, ecological and social effects of oil on producer countries see Christian Aid, *Fuelling Poverty: Oil, War and Corruption* (London: Christian Aid, 2003).

6   On the ecological implications of remoteness see Val Plumwood, *Environmental Culture: The Ecological Crisis of Reason* (London: Routledge, 2002), 71–80.

who are thus rendered even more powerless.[7] In Columbia and the Niger Delta indigenous groups vigorously protest the ecological and social problems that oil extraction visits on their lands and communities. This resistance to the extractive economy of energy is a significant exemplar of what Martinez-Allier calls the 'environmentalism of the poor'.[8]

The ecological ill effects and social injustices associated with the manufacture of speed – wildernesses despoiled and ecosystems threatened by oil wells and highways, the location of lower income housing adjacent to motorways or heavily trafficked urban roads, the disproportionate number of children from poorer households killed or injured on such roads – are then connected with the material base of speed as concentrated fossil fuel power. And these injustices are not confined to present generations.[9] Future generations will be significantly disadvantaged by the dramatic and irreversible changes to the climate system created by the continuing growth in the use of fossil fuels required by the growing speed of movement of persons and goods in the global industrial economy. If present levels of greenhouse gas emission growth are sustained the Intergovernmental Panel on Climate Change predict a temperature rise of up to 6 degrees centigrade by the end of the present century, a rise which will make large parts of the planet uninhabitable.[10] Transport is responsible for one third of carbon emissions, and 60 percent of oil consumption. Energy use in the sector will contribute 50 percent to the projected annual growth in greenhouse gas consumption in the next 30 years.[11] Aircraft emissions alone on present rates of growth in air travel will reach 1 billion tonnes of carbon by 2050, which is one seventh of present total world production of carbon.[12] The total emissions of transportation devices rises even further if a full accounting is performed of the energy used in their manufacture and the infrastructure they require for their propulsion, parking and maintenance.

The disordering of human as well as ecological relations by the compression of time and space which modern speed produces is indicated by the intentional lack of speed with which the nation state responds to certain humanly caused disasters,

---

7   On the moral ambiguities of economic compulsion see Albion Barrera, *Economic Compulsion and Christian Ethics* (Cambridge: Cambridge University Press, 2005).

8   Joan Martinez-Alier, *The Environmentalism of the Poor: A Report for UNRISD for the WSSD* (August 2002) at http://www.webct.ed.ac.uk:443/SCRIPT/DV0158_4/scripts/serve_home.

9   Wolfgang Sachs, *Planet Dialectics: Explorations in Environment and Development* (London: Zed Books, 1999), 191.

10   Intergovernmental Panel on Climate Change, Working Group 1, 'Climate Change 2007: The Physical Basis: Technical Summary' Fourth Assessment Report (penultimate draft), p. 6.

11   International Energy Authority, 'Transport Technologies and Policies for Energy Security and CO_2 Reductions', IEA, Washington D.C. (2003), http://www.iea.org/textbase/papers/2003/transport_techfair.pdf.

12   Dave Reay, *Climate Change Begins At Home: Life on the Two-Way Street of Global Warming* (London: Macmillan, 2005), 47.

such as the Chernobyl nuclear accident, or the failure of the complex levee system of New Orleans during the sustained landfall of Hurricane Katrina in 2005. It was not until the Swedish authorities noted the radioactivity of rain over Sweden a week after the nuclear explosion at the Chernobyl nuclear reactor in Ukraine that the Soviet authorities began to even contemplate evacuating the human population proximate to the burning and irradiated power station. Similarly it was not until the bloated bodies of black and poor Americans were filmed floating in the floodwaters of New Orleans that the Federal Government ordered troops and supplies to be flown into the stricken city: by contrast in 1906 at the time of the great San Francisco earthquake the House of Congress met through the night and ordered immediate relief supplies and military assistance to be sent to the stricken city by rail. As Matthew Tiessen suggests, where the nation state would rather ignore the accidents technology makes possible, or where responding to such accidents threatens vested interests, then there is no desire for speed. Hence the time-space compression which speed makes possible 'exists only within a space wherein that speed is desired and applied to accommodate particular interests'.[13] Whereas the resources of the Federal Government had made possible the invasion and 'conquest' of Iraq at unprecedented speed in 2003, that same commitment of resources necessitated the withdrawal of resources elsewhere from disaster prevention – fortifying the levees which were known to be inadequate would have saved New Orleans from the Katrina disaster, and from disaster relief – there were so few reservists in the Southern States at the time Katrina hit because most of them were serving in Afghanistan and Iraq.[14] Again the inverse relations of the power of speed and the practice of justice are revealed in these acknowledged interconnections.

There is another aspect to the spiritual pathology of concentrated power of the kind speed machines make available that is connected to their phenomenological effect on human consciousness of relation to the earth. The speed machine – whether a high speed train, plane or car – confers on the driver or passenger a sense of mastery of the landscape, or in the case of a plane, of the spherical globe as its curved horizons rapidly shrink through the speed of the modern jet. In moving at great speed through or over a landscape the human being loses bodily and sensual connection with the organic rhythms of life on earth. This loss is important in the construction of the modern imaginary of conquest over, and independence from, the forces of nature. John Urry suggests that the car in particular is a crucial site of the specific pattern of domination over nature, which Martin Heidegger described as a vital component of the modern technological condition.[15] The one who is master of devices which confer power and speed is likely to set reliance upon the

---

13   Matthew Tiessen, 'Speed, Desire and Inaction in New Orleans: Like a Stick in the Spokes', *Space and Culture* 9 (February 2006), 35–7.

14   Tiessen, 'Speed, Desire and Inaction', 36.

15   John Urry, 'Automobility, Car Culture and Weightless Travel: A discussion paper', Department of Sociology, Lancaster University (1999) at http://www.comp.lancs.ac.uk/sociology/papers/Urry-Automobility.pdf.

sense of mastery such machines confer over trust in the life sustaining properties of the more than human world.

This is powerfully illustrated in a recent Volkswagen advertisement which shows a man and a boy riding in a new Passat. The driver uses an array of remote controlled and electronic devices to manipulate the condition of the car. The car opens automatically when the driver approaches it; with a push of a button a sunshade glides up behind the back seat where the boy is sitting, and when the journey is over a remote control opens the boot. The boy is shown wondering at these seemingly magical happenings. Throughout, the music from the Harry Potter films is playing in the background and the implication is elaborated when the boy leaves the car and goes through the house into his bedroom: he points to the window blind and says 'open' and of course the blind does not move. The implication is already clear before the punch line is delivered: the Passat is a car which gives the user such extraordinary control over the car's environment that its users 'could get used to it'. As the advert makes clear the sense of mastery over the glass and metal bubble of the car is not limited to the car itself. The driver and the passenger are trained by their use of the car to expect this kind of control in other environments.

Given that the excessive use of fossil fuel in the production of speed is responsible for the production of around half of the greenhouse gases which are responsible for changing the climate, this training is highly problematic. Far from manifesting the human mastery of natural forces, the attempt of modern humans to live as if they have conquered nature results in them being conquered by nature. And there is an ethical as well as an ecological aspect to this ironic outcome.[16] Detachment from and technological control over the environment produces a qualitative change in the ethical and social character of modern life. Traditional pedagogy involves disciplined, skillful and embodied engagement with the natural world.[17] But modern humans are trained by their ritual engagements with servo-mechanical and electronic devices no longer to subject their desires to the external referents of the other than human world. The paradoxical result is that humans are overcome by nature: with fewer opportunities for the training of their desires and instincts in disciplined and embodied skills, humans are increasingly mastered by instinct such that, as C.S. Lewis puts it, 'man's conquest of nature turns out, in the moment of its consummation, to be nature's conquest of man'.[18]

Writing in the midst of the Second World War Lewis reads the rise of totalitarianism as closely connected with the disordering of ethical and political life which is on this account a central feature of the technological condition. Analogously Paul Virilio argues that there is a close connection between speed and the disordering violence of war. He reads the movement of Western history from

---

16   C.S. Lewis, *The Abolition of Man* (London: Fount, 1978).

17   See further Albert Borgmann, *Technology and the Character of Contemporary Life* (Chicago: Chicago University Press, 1984).

18   Lewis, *Abolition of Man*, 41.

feudalism to capitalism as having been directed by the growing mechanical power of military technology, and the increasing speed of armies and the machines of war.[19] He also suggests that an obsession with immediate and quantifiable results measured by mechanical time is in part responsible for war itself. He observes that the First World War was triggered not so much by the assassination of Archduke Ferdinand as by the fact that the Serbs were given only 48 hours to explain what had happened. Similarly the invasion of Iraq in 2003 was in part precipitated by the unwillingness of President George W. Bush and Prime Minister Tony Blair to await the outcomes of the necessarily lengthy investigations of United Nations weapons inspectors. To search a vast country for the remaining 4 percent of potential WMD materials that earlier reports had indicated might still remain in Iraq would have taken more time than Bush and Blair were prepared to countenance. On this account instantaneity, the time space compression involved in what Virilio calls 'real time', is now the principal cause of global war:

> The twin phenomena of immediacy and of instantaneity are presently one of the most pressing problems confronting political and military strategists alike. Real time now prevails above both real space and the geosphere. The primacy of real time, of immediacy, over and above space and surface is a *fait accompli* and has inaugural value (ushers a new epoch), something nicely conjured up in a (French) advertisement praising cellular phones with the words: 'Planet Earth has never been this small.' This is a very dramatic moment in our relation with the world and for our vision of the world.[20]

Instantaneity also breeds accidents. Accidents and speed are so closely related that it is impossible to speak of those who die on the roads as having died 'accidentally' for road deaths are a direct consequence of the extensive use of hard metal machines as transportation devices at speeds which, on impact, are detrimental to soft-bodied mammals. This is a manifestation of a larger problem with the speed of modern life which has precipitated such a large array of humanly caused accidents that death and suffering from such accidents exceeded death and suffering from natural disasters in the present decade according to the large re-insurance company Swiss-Re.[21] In this sense climate change may also be considered an inevitable accident, and part of a larger inevitability of ecological collapse necessitated by the speed of the capitalistic transformation of the earth.

The modern obsession with mechanically derived speed is such that it eviscerates moral deliberation over its ecological or human costs. Speed produces an altered state of consciousness, 'a delirium broken only by the crash' (Baldwin,

---

19   Paul Virilio, *Speed and Politics: An Essay on Dromology*, trans. Mark Polizotti (New York: Semiotext, 1986).

20   Paul Virilio, 'Speed and Information: Cyberspace Alarm!', Ctheory.net (August 1995) at http://www.ctheory.net/articles.aspx?id=72.

21   Paul Virilio, 'The Museum of Accidents', *International Journal of Baudrillard Studies* 3 (July 2006) at http://www.ubishops.ca/baudrillardstudies/vol3_2/virilio.htm.

2002). As Milan Kundera puts it 'speed is the form of ecstasy the technological revolution has bestowed on man.'[22] This form of ecstasy generates detachment from the violent effects of the ownership and use of devices which confer speed on the millions who have been killed and seriously injured by them, and from their systemic effects on the ecology of the earth. Something more than distancing is involved here. Speed involves a kind of moral perversion which is indicated in the extent to which danger to life and limb from fast cars forms part of the appeal of cars and other such devices to some of those who use them. In an ethnographic study of Norwegian young people Pauline Garvey found that they regularly used fast or even intentionally dangerous driving as a device for the expression of angry emotions or to provoke pedestrians and other road users:

> You are so angry you can't think clearly so you just think, OK let's try it, God damn you. So it can be dangerous, but that is what is good about me because when I am driving I block everything out. I think I know a lot – or I remember talking to others, who say when they need a break they take the car for a ride, it just helps I don't know why.[23]

The same paper records observations of young people using cars to indulge in more extreme and criminal kinds of behaviour such as driving cars on the wrong side of the road towards oncoming vehicles, driving at pedestrians, or at excessive speed. In Britain the phenomenon of 'joy-riding' or 'twocking' – Taking Without Owner's Knowledge – causes extensive use of police time and is responsible for many accidents, deaths and serious injuries each year. A small number of young people see taking, driving and even crashing cars at high speeds as a kind of sport, and certain housing areas are regularly terrorized by individuals who use cars to indulge in such behaviours.[24]

The cultural adulation of fast cars and speed does not just infect a small minority of criminal teenagers. Such criminal uses of cars are related to a more generalized cultural obsession with speed associated with the adulation of large and extremely fast cars, and other devices – high speed trains, planes and ships. This adulation takes symbolic form in car advertisements which portray lone vehicles moving rapidly through wilderness or empty city streets, unrestrained by traffic jams or other physical or statutory constraints. Millions of people in Britain regularly drive at speeds far in excess of legal speed limits, and protest at the use by the police of speed cameras and other devices intended to reduce speeding on public

---

22   Milan Kundera, 'Slowness' cited in Sandy Baldwin, 'On Speed and Ecstasy: Paul Virilio's "Aesthetics of Disappearance" and the Rhetoric of Media', *Configurations* 10 (2002), 129–48.

23   Informant quoted in Pauline Garvey, 'Driving, Drinking and Daring in Norway' in Daniel Miller (ed.) *Car Cultures* (Oxford: Berg, 2001), 133–52.

24   Eileen Spencer, 'Car Crime and Young People on a Sunderland Housing Estate', Police Research Group: Crime Prevention Unit Series, Paper No. 40 (London: Home Office Police Department, 1992) at http://www.homeoffice.gov.uk/rds/prgpdfs/fcpu40.pdf.

roads. The car and the speed it is capable of gives the owner a sense of control over the physical environment, and a quality of freedom, of which the speed camera is seen as an undue curtailment, even although death and injury on the road, and damaging greenhouse gas emissions, are associated with excessive speed.[25]

The desire for speed is pathological in part because it curtails moral deliberation on the effects of speed. The evident lack of deliberation over the immoral consequences of speed is part of a larger 'loss of orientation' which both physical and virtual speed visit on the individual, and this loss of an orienting sense of place has moral consequences. As Virilio suggests, 'to exist is to exist *in situ*, here and now, *hic et nunc*' (Virilio, 1995). The ability to experience the moral claims of others, and the restraint such claims properly represent to the expression of individual desire, arises in part from the location of individuals in communities of place such as are constituted by families and place-based communities. The erosion of a sense of being in place is consequently intertwined with a lack of moral deliberation over the sacrifices of human, as well as planetary, wellbeing, that excessive speed involves. In this climate the victims of speed become statistical persons, or statistical beings in the case of 'road kill', in the larger utilitarian calculus of the corporation and the nation state. An analogous moral loss occurs for citizens whose communities are disturbed and deracinated by new roads and the speeding cars that use them.[26]

The moral as well as spatial disorientation produced by technologies of speed is central to the reasons why many Amish communities still refuse to own cars. Amish culture is delineated against 'moral worldliness', which for the Amish in the modern world indicates the complex kinds of control of natural and social power that technological devices such as cars and tractors confer on the individuals who own them.[27] Against worldliness the Amish practise a collective form of ascetic holiness which involves revolutionary subordination of each to the other. Cars and like technologies threaten this subordination because the power they confer on an individual distances him from the collective deliberation of the community and hence subverts the communal ethic. Cars represent a threat to the spatial as well as relational characteristics of Amish communities since 'ownership would intensify the pace and complexity of Amish living'.[28] By increasing speed and distance traveled Amish who owned cars would break down the close-knit communities that are the foundation of Amish culture. The distinctive moral economy of Amish

---

25   On the emotional phenomenology of car driving see further Mimi Sheller, 'Automotive Emotions: Feeling the Car', *Theory, Culture and Society* 21 (2004), 221–42.

26   Oliver O'Donovan, 'The Loss of a Sense of Place' in Oliver O'Donovan and Joan Lockwood O'Donovan, *Bonds of Imperfection: Christian Politics Past and Present* (Grand Rapids, MI: Eerdmans, 2004), 306.

27   Romand Coles, 'The Wild Patience of John Howard Yoder: "Outsiders and the Otherness of the Church"', *Modern Theology* 18 (July 2002), 306–331.

28   Donald B. Kraybill, *The Riddle of Amish Culture* (Baltimore: John Hopkins University Press, 1989), 165–8.

communities therefore involves the eschewal of the speed and complexity which characterize the modern technologies of cars, computers, tractors and televisions. Against these they set the communal values of family, church and community, and the virtues of faithfulness, self-denial, humility and meekness.[29] Bans on car and tractor ownership reflect restraints on the expression of individual desire which education into such shared virtues is said to require. Wendell Berry observes that the refusal of the Amish to seek the controlling 'efficiency' of mechanical speed in their farming methods, as in their communities, has made them better stewards of the soil than industrial farmers, and ironically has seen Amish farms thrive while many of their machine-dependent neighbours have gone into bankruptcy.[30] By remaining rooted in place, and refusing speed and excessive mobility, the Amish have not only turned out to be among America's most successful farmers: they have also created a physical landscape which is ecologically and *spatially* oriented by their relational and spiritual practices.

The word orientation originates from the practice of building Christian churches that are oriented towards the East. Orientation means literally to be turned toward the orient and the orientation of the church building toward the East is an aid to the worshipper who through this physical analogy is said to be enabled to orient her life toward those moral and spiritual ends which were commended by the Incarnate Son of God who walked in what Jews and Christians call the Holy Land. The other form of spiritual orientation towards the Holy Land, and in particular Jerusalem, which has definitively marked Christian sacred geography and mobility is the practice of pilgrimage. I suggest in the second half of this paper that the phenomenology of pilgrimage provides a valuable frame for critiquing and resisting the modern pathology of speed, with its deleterious effects on the physical climate, on the human psyche and on patterns of association and settlement, but without requiring a return to the kind of extreme sedentariness associated with the Amish.

The market for cars, planes and trains in the twentieth century was driven by a number of factors other than simply the desire for speed of movement as an end in itself. One crucial driver was the potential these devices offered for householders in urban and rural settings to visit other locations either on weekend trips or for extended holidays. The growth of tourism is such that in many cities and coastal areas it is one of the largest economic sectors, and tourism remains a prime function of the technologies of speed and hence a prime driver of the annual growth in greenhouse gas emissions. China is the latest region of the world to become a net exporter of tourists. The desire to visit exotic places at some distance from the work place and home is not new to modernity. As Theilmann suggests pilgrimage provides a significant pre-modern analogy to the mobility of travel associated with

---

29   Donald Kraybill, 'Introduction: The Struggle to be Separate' in Donald Kraybill and Marc A. Olshan (eds), *The Amish Struggle With Modernity* (New Haven, CT: University Press of New England, 1994), 7.

30   Wendell Berry, *The Unsettling of America: Culture and Agriculture* (San Francisco: Sierra Club Books, 1996), 176.

modern mass tourism, and while not all pilgrims were, like Chaucer's Wife of Bath, journeying to see the sights and to get away from home, most nonetheless attended to sights along the way.[31] But unlike tourism pilgrimage represented a form of travel that was not fossil fuel but *time* dependent since it was traditionally conducted at walking pace, and, in the case of more distant pilgrimages with the aid of sail power.

Christian pilgrimage was the principal reason for travel by pre-modern Europeans who did not by dint of itinerancy of profession have reason to travel beyond the environs of home and workplace. It had precursors in Jewish and Egyptian cultures, and in particular the veneration of places associated with sacred journeys such as the Exodus journey from Egypt through Sinai, and places of burial of venerated figures such as patriarchs and saints.[32] The first Christian pilgrimages were to Jerusalem to which, as Saint Jerome observed 'every man of Gaul hastens hither', while the Briton 'no sooner makes progress in religion than he leaves the setting sun in quest of a spot of which he knows only through Scripture and common report.'[33] Rome also became a place of pilgrimage because of its association with the Apostles Peter and Paul. Subsequently pilgrimages to a range of other shrines developed, among the most popular of which were those of St Thomas a Becket at Canterbury and St James at Santiago de Compostella.

The conceptual root of pilgrimage is the idea of the Christian as traveler and of the spiritual life as a journey or quest for holiness.[34] The travels of Abraham and the Israelites in the wilderness, the classical account of the travels of Ulysses, and the itinerant nature of the lives of Christ and St Paul, are all important precursors of the idea of pilgrimage in early Christian thought. The Gospels record Christ valorizing his own mobility as an aspect of the way of the cross when he says 'foxes have holes and birds of the air have nests; but the Son of man has nowhere to lay his head' (Luke 9. 58). The writer to the Hebrews similarly speaks of the followers of Christ as those who in this world 'have no lasting city' and 'seek the city which is to come' which is the heavenly one (Hebrews 13. 14). Augustine in *De Civitate Dei* similarly speaks of the City of God as the Church in pilgrimage on earth.

It was in the Middle Ages that pilgrimage acquired widespread appeal. Many thousands in the fourteenth century regularly traveled to shrines and holy places far distant from their places of abode on a quest for transforming experiences of the holy at sacred sites and through the penitential rigors of the road. As Eamon

---

31   John M. Theilmann, 'Medieval Pilgrims and the Origins of Tourism', *Journal of Popular Culture* 20 (Spring 1987), 94.

32   See further David Frankfurter, 'Introduction' in Frankfurter (ed.), *Pilgrimage and Holy Space in Late Antique Egypt* (Leiden: Brill, 1998), and R.A. Markus, 'How on earth could places become holy? Origins of the Christian Idea of Holy Places', *Journal of Early Christian Studies* 2 (1994), 257–71.

33   Letters of Saint Jerome, 46. 10, at http://www.newadvent.org/fathers/3001046.htm.

34   John C. Olin, 'The Idea of Pilgrimage in the Experience of Ignatius of Loyola', *Church History* 48 (December 1979), 387–97.

Duffy observes pilgrimage required the pilgrim to leave the 'concentric worlds of household, parish or gild' where she laboured and worshipped on a journey to a sacred site or shrine far distant and such leavings 'provided a temporary release from the constrictions and norms of ordinary living, an opportunity to review one's life'.[35] The long journey with its trials and pains was also a penitential practice, a *via crucis*, which offered a redemption and a liberty of its own, while the end of the journey – worship at the sacred shrine and its holy images and objects – offered the pilgrim a new perspective which might transform and redirect his life on his return home, setting work, home and worship in a larger and more meaningful symbolic and spiritual context.[36] For some this new perspective concerned the restoration of the inner life, while others sought physical restoration as the Holy Land and other shrines became associated with a range of curative properties and claimed miracles recorded by their guardians.[37] In an influential study the Turners suggest that the ultimate goal of the journey was to enable the pilgrim to identify in a new way with the founder of their faith:

> For them the founder becomes a savior, one who saves them from themselves, 'themselves' both as socially defined and personally experienced. The pilgrim 'puts on Christ Jesus' as a paradigmatic mask, or persona, and thus for a while *becomes* the redemptive tradition.[38]

The Turners suggest that the form of *communitas* that pilgrims experienced on the road and at the shrine was central to the liminal quality of the experience of pilgrimage.[39] Through *communitas* individuals on pilgrimage are liberated from the mundane hierarchies they endure in secular life and connected with a deeper sense of the holy.[40] Chaucer's descriptions in *Canterbury Tales* of pilgrims on the way to Thomas a Becket's shrine lends weight to this account. Chaucer describes a remarkably disparate group of people who nonetheless form a company and exchange stories along the way. A crucial element of pilgrimage which helped produce this kind of social solidarity on the way was the sharing in the sometimes

---

35   Eamon Duffy, *The Stripping of the Altars: Traditional Religion in England c. 1400–c. 1580* (New Haven, CT: Yale University Press, 1992), 191.

36   Victor Turner and Edith Turner, *Image and Pilgrimage in Christian Culture: Anthropological Perspectives* (Oxford: Basil Blackwell, 1978), 6–8. Duffy, *Stripping of the Altars*, 191.

37   Blake Leyerle identifies a heightened role of healing in records of pilgrimages to the Holy Land between the fourth and fifth centuries: Blake Leyerle, 'Landscape as Cartography in Early Christian Pilgrimage Narratives', *Journal of the American Academy of Religion* 64 (Spring 1996), 119–43.

38   Turner and Turner, Image and Pilgrimage, 11.

39   Turner and Turner, Image and Pilgrimage, 1 and 33–4.

40   Urry's concept of 'meetingness' bears strong analogies with the Turner's account of communitas: Urry, 'Social networks, travel and talk', 162.

painful ordeal of the long days of walking in pre-modern foot-ware on unpaved paths, in inclement weather.[41]

The Turners' anti-structural account of the function of displacement in pilgrimage has been highly influential in pilgrimage studies and also in the ethnography of modern mobility and mass tourism. James Clifford suggests that displacement, being 'en route', provides a powerful trope for interpreting the ways in which mobility and flux shape the multivalent character and multicultural nature of modern cities and of modern identities and modes of dwelling.[42] But the Turners' account of the *communitas* of pilgrimage has also been contested in subsequent studies, which have indicated that sacred sites and not the journey are at the heart of the pilgrimage phenomenon. This focus on the site of pilgrimage is ironically connected with the time pressures under which modern anthropologists work. Instead of spending weeks or even months on the way with pilgrims, they tend to focus their ethnographic descriptions on behaviours at the sacred sites themselves. This is the case for example with Sallnow's essay on Andean pilgrimage as with other papers in Eade and Sallnow's *Contesting the Sacred*.[43] The fieldwork schedule results in lack of attention to the extended period of time, and slow pace of movement through the landscape that *walking* on the pilgrim way traditionally required. And it is this slow pace which is the strongest point of contrast between traditional pilgrimage and modern mass tourism which in other respects manifests some of the same functions as pilgrimage – escape from the mundane, simplicity of clothing, enjoyment of a different locality, the *communitas* of other holiday-makers. The Turners provide a substantial excerpt from a description of pilgrimage to Guadalupe in Mexico, published by the basilica in Guadalupe, which reveals the spiritual significance of walking:

> Year after year, from 1890 onwards, the Guadalupan devotees of Queretaro have made the pilgrimage on foot from their city to the sanctuary of Tepeyac. In eight days they traverse the rough road 260 kilometres in length – the old royal road, broad and austere – which joins Querétaro to the metropolis. Eight days during which the weariness of the body is submitted to hard, voluntary discipline, loosening the bonds of matter to liberate the spirit. The rhythm of the march is set by collective prayers chanted in the plains under the mid-day sun, in the cool dawns when leaving towns, in the evenings at the end of a day's journey. It is a march of religious folly in which the Indian – who comes on it propelled by his strong will against his better nature – is freed from his bonds, while the rich man punishes his own softness by the austerity of prayer and walking.[44]

---

41   Analogously in modernity John Urry suggests that mobility is an important source of social networks beyond the local: see Urry, 'Social networks, travel and talk'.

42   James Clifford, *Routes: Travel and Translation in the Late Twentieth Century* (Cambridge, MA: Harvard University Press, 1997).

43   M.J. Sallnow, 'Communitas Reconsidered: The Sociology of Andean Pilgrimage', *Man*, New Series 16 (July 1981), 163–82 and John Eade and Michael Sallnow (eds) *Contesting the Sacred: The Anthropology of Christian Pilgrimage* (London: Routledge, 1991).

44   La Voz Guadalupana (July 1940) in Turner and Turner, *Image and Pilgrimage*, 95.

But though they cite this description at length the Turners, like many other ethnographers, attend in their commentary only to the behaviour of the pilgrims at journey's end, and not at all to the manner of their processional walking on the way.

If modern anthropological studies of pilgrimage have been over-focused on sacred sites, pilgrims' own records of their journeys, like literary and mythic narratives of heroic quests, put more emphasis on the journey, seeing the journey as a paradigm of life itself. The centrality of the trope of journeying in traditional as well as contemporary literatures indicates that, as Richard Niebuhr suggests, the desire to travel and to be in motion represents 'a deep characteristic of human nature', and the kinds of motion involved in this desire are psychological and spiritual as well as physical.[45] Similarly Oliver O'Donovan suggests that mobility is central to human identity and to being in place for humans are not stationary like trees.[46]

Literary accounts of heroic journeys that encapsulate the archetypal desire to travel are, like traditional pilgrimage, set apart from the rapid mechanical journeys of the modern tourist in their description of the formative role of chance and circumstance that the hero encounters on the way. At the outset of the journey the hero often has little idea of the end in view and even less confidence in his capacity to reach it. Hence the learning opportunities which occur on the journey are crucial to the acquisition of the virtues and skills which the hero needs in order to attain the goal.[47] J.R.R. Tolkien's *The Lord of the Rings* powerfully evokes the way in which the hero starts out as a kind of antihero, hobbits being at first sight too quirky, short and physically weak to perform the valiant task set before them by Gandalf. Along the way Frodo, the hobbit chosen for the quest, is constantly open to self-doubt about his ability to succeed, and it is only by being open to the gifts and interventions of friends, strangers, elves, ents and even enemies that the hobbit who becomes a hero is eventually able to complete the quest to cast the ring into the lake of fire, and so save Middle Earth from the militaristic and technological darkness of Mordor. Whereas mythic shamanic tales describe the hero as gradually acquiring mastery and new powers through the journey which enable him to fulfill his quest, at no point on his quest does Frodo become a master of the ring or even master of the journey. On the contrary he relies on Gollum to guide him for much of the way and by the end Frodo has so fallen for the dangerous attraction of the ring that he only succeeds in destroying the ring through the intervention of his traveling companion Gollum who in one last desperate attempt to wrest the ring from Frodo falls into the lake of fire with the ring in his clutches and so destroys it, and with it the rising and destructive power of Mordor.

---

45   Richard Niebuhr, unpublished lecture, as cited in Corelyn F. Senn, 'Journeying as Religious Education: The Shaman, the Hero, the Pilgrim and the Labyrinth Walker', *Religious Education*, 97 (Spring 2002), 124.

46   O'Donovan, 'The Loss of a Sense of Place', 306.

47   Senn, 'Journeying as Religious Education', 129–30.

With this crucial twist in the tale Tolkien has evoked an essential feature of the Christian conception of life as journey or pilgrimage which is that of learned dependence. Far from achieving mastery and autonomy the Christian pilgrim goes the way of the cross and therefore seeks to remain humble and open to the gifts and trials which each turn in the road, each step along the way may bring. Mastery and control are not the ends in view but instead encounter and submission to the Master, and a related preparedness to endure the rigors and rewards of life on the road. As Christ himself puts it 'if any man would come after me, let him deny himself and take up his cross and follow me.' (Mark 8. 34). Stanley Hauerwas suggests that Christ's whole life is narrated in the Gospel of Mark as the expression of 'noncoercive power': Christ does not compel but call others to follow him 'and he does not try to control their responses'.[48] Neither does he try to control the events which lead to his eventual crucifixion, nor even the future destiny of those who followed him and who would become the founders of the Church. This element of living life 'out of control', in dependence on a higher power, is the hallmark of Hauerwas' distinctive critique of the moral pathology of contemporary culture, and it is precisely this quality which sets the traditional walking pilgrimage apart from the pace and control of modern tourism and from the mastery of time and motion that the devices of speed confer.

Hauerwas's ethic of dependence is also delineated in contradistinction to the emphasis in modern consequentialist and deontological ethics on the autonomy of the self as a reasoning moral agent. The underlying assumption in both these modern styles of moral reasoning is that the individual reasoner is sufficiently in control of events, and of her own intentions, as to be able to rely on her own autonomous judgment. This critique of the modern conception of the unsituated, and hence disoriented, autonomous reasoner involves the Aristotelian recognition of the significance of external referents in the formation of the self in those habits and practices which Aristotle identifies as the virtues to which we have already alluded.

In the practice of pilgrimage as walking external referents play a crucial role in the formation of the pilgrim. The companions on the way, the length of the road, the vagaries of climate, all involve openness to the influence of externalities on the body and mind. In this intentional and embodied openness to the gifts and obstacles that the journey may bring the pilgrim enacts a relational pedagogy of body, mind and spirit. The formative role of landscape in shaping the identity of the pilgrim, and in growing an awareness of the significance of flora and fauna, and the topography of the land through which the pilgrim passes, is evident in the earliest records of Christian pilgrimage. The earliest pilgrim journals reveal a developing awareness of landscape from an almost exclusive concern with sites associated with specific Biblical events to an interest in the flora and fauna, and of

---

48   Extract from Stanley Hauerwas, 'The Peaceable Kingdom' in John Berkman and Michel Cartwright (eds), *The Hauerwas Reader* (Durham, NC: Duke University Press, 2001), 126–7.

the landscape itself. The AD 333 journal by a Bordeaux pilgrim of a seven month walking journey from the Bosporus to the Holy Land includes many references to geological and biological phenomena but these are only of interest to the pilgrim where they can be specifically linked with a sacred event, such as the almond tree where Jacob is said to have wrestled with an angel.[49] But the *Itinerarium Egeria*, which is the vivid personal journal of a woman on pilgrimage through the Sinai Desert and the Holy Land, includes extensive descriptions of desert and mountainous terrain and of the views and vistas to be enjoyed of the Sinai Peninsula and the Holy Land from such places.[50]

The role of flora and fauna, topography and landscape vistas in the spiritual pedagogy of pilgrimage finds significant analogy in the relational accounts of interaction with the more than human world in contemporary ecological philosophy. The claim that walking up a mountain is an embodied experience that involves pain as well as pleasure is a central trope of Norwegian deep ecologist Arne Naess's account of 'ecosophy T'. Naess observes that extending and testing the body through climbing, and the 'peak experience' of reaching the top and enjoying the view, involves an engagement between the identity of the walker and the being of the mountain.[51] This engagement enhances the consciousness of the walker such that she becomes aware that in this embodied relation her identity is in part constructed by the mountain. Naess suggests that this new relation involves a new conceptualization of human identity which is extended beyond the self so that the frame of self-identity *includes* the mountain. Whether the incorporation of the mountain within the frame of self-consciousness is truly thinking *like* a mountain is contested by Val Plumwood who argues that this form of deep ecology is too anthropomorphic, and that we would do better to envisage the human in relation to the alterity or awesome otherness of the mountain.[52] In her own travel writing, and especially in her account of a near-death encounter with a crocodile, Plumwood eschews the colonising discourse of identification with and mastery of nature and instead emphasizes how movement through a landscape provokes a consciousness of the alterity of other creatures and a decentering of human identity.[53] Instead of incorporating the mountain or the animal into the self, the self-in-relation is open to being reordered, even dismembered, by the more than human world.[54]

---

49   Blake Layerle, 'Landscape as Cartography in Early Christian Pilgrimage Narratives', *Journal of the American Academy of Religion* 64 (Spring 1996), 119–43.

50   Layerle, 'Landscape as Cartography', 126–7.

51   Arne Naess, *Ecology, Community and Lifestyle: Outline of an Ecosophy*, trans. David Rothenberg (New York: Cambridge University Press, 1989).

52   Val Plumwood, 'Nature, self and gender: Feminism, environmental philosophy, and the critique of rationalism' in Robert Elliot (ed.) *Environmental Ethics* (Oxford: Oxford University Press, 1995), p. 160.

53   Val Plumwood, 'Prey to a crocodile', *Aisling Magazine* 30 (2002), http://www. aislingmagazine.com/aislingmagazine/articles/TAM30/ValPlumwood.html.

54   See further Simone Fullagar, 'Desiring Nature: Identity and Becoming in Narratives of Travel', *Cultural Values* 4 (2000), 58–76.

In contrast to traditional pilgrimage, and to Naess and Plumwood's narratives of travel, mastery of time and space is central to the experience of modern tourism and rapid transit. Modern tourism is organized around universal and mechanical time and conducted at the pace dictated by the short break or the seven or fourteen day holiday permitted by the disciplining time management of the modern industrial economy. Before the invention of the railway there was no universal time in England and time in one part of the country was different from that in another. The speed of rail travel, its connecting of places spatially far distant, necessitated the invention and the standardization of universal time.[55] And just as the universal control of time was necessitated by the technologies of speed, so the control of space is increasingly required by those same technologies, from the airspace utilized by jet planes to the extensive land area taken up with highways, car parks, airports, railways, stations and marshalling yards. The modern tourist utilizes the infrastructure which has subjected time and space to ecologically destructive forms of control in order to enjoy elements of the liminal experience of the pre-modern pilgrim, but since the touristic experience is typically conducted at great speed it cannot offer profound relief from the controlling pathology and pace of industrial time.

Traditional pilgrimage was conducted according to local times, over many weeks or even months, and at a pace set by the feet of the walker rather than the turning of mechanical engines. And the reliance of the pilgrim on her feet and the subjection to the vagaries of the road was itself a kind of discipline, both embodied and spiritual, which required the pilgrim to submit to a different rhythm than that of mechanical wheels or industrial time. Walking is an activity which puts the human body in the landscape and when conducted over successive days and weeks enables the individual to begin to live by a different rhythm to the productive and efficient time determined by 'time and motion', the rhythm of an order humans have not made. And the longer the walker walks the more this alternative rhythm – the rhythm of the earth – begins to replace the controlling consciousness of industrial time. The rhythm of walking interacts with the rhythm of the earth such that the landscape itself begins to shape both the physique and the psyche of the walker. Ascending and descending the contours of the path put muscle on the walker and burn calories as fast as they are eaten. This process of muscle building is in reality one of a constant tearing and remaking of muscular tissue which is both painful and pleasurable as it is often accompanied with a flow of endorphins. Bodily transformations are mirrored by inner transformations as succeeding days of arduous activity, living on the road, and being in motion, begin to mold the walker's body and mind to being and thinking according to circadian rhythms rather than those permitted by artificial light and speed. The longer feet are lifted and replaced on the sod, the head held under the sky, and the visage proceeds through the landscape the greater the transformation in the sense of the

---

55   Thomas Eriksen, *Tyranny of the Moment: Fast and Slow Time in the Information Age* (London: Pluto Press, 2001), 53.

phenomenological placing of the body in the environment. Long distance walking trains the body and the mind to a new kind of submission to the forces that move and mold the landscape and its myriad other than human processes, structures and inhabitants.

This kind of walking is a physical discipline of mind and body which in pilgrimage takes on a spiritual dimension, as demonstrated in the Russian Hesychastic classic *The Way of a Pilgrim* in which the pilgrim walks for many months through nineteenth century rural Russia while learning to use the prayer of the name of Jesus.[56] The pilgrim practices the Jesus prayer – 'Lord Jesus Christ, have mercy on me a sinner' – as a breath prayer which he repeats every few steps on his journeying. The writer narrates how the love of the pilgrim for Christ, for his fellow countrymen and for the landscape they tend increases as he gradually learns to shape his utterance of the breath prayer to the rhythm of his breathing and walking. This nineteenth century Russian classic manifests an 'Emersonian ethereal harmony' (Call, 1963) with its remarkable description of a spiritual practice which is intimately shaped by the breath of the body and the rhythm of the earth.[57]

Pilgrimage is undergoing something of a revival as the numbers on the roads to Santiago and other places of pilgrimage have more quadrupled in the last thirty years. The growing numbers of contemporary walking pilgrims indicate a desire for a more deliberate and spiritual mode of traveling than that of speed-enabled tourism. Pilgrimage offers a model of mobility and travel that is more attuned to the fragile ecology of the earth than the fossil fuel dependent travel of modern mass tourism, while at the same time providing a therapeutic antidote to the pathology of speed in the modern world. If walking is central to the spiritual practice of traditional pilgrimage then we also may read the growing popularity of long distance walking as a modern touristic analogy to pilgrimage walking. Those who spend upwards of six months walking the Appalachian Trail on the Eastern seaboard of the United States certainly by the end know a good deal about the privations and joys of traditional pilgrimage. They also come to experience in their long time away from industrial civilization something of the spiritual seclusion, the fellowship of the way, and co-presence with the earth that were the gifts of traditional pilgrimage.[58] Such long distance walking offers a model for a more sustainable form of tourism that involves reduced reliance upon carbon emissions. But the reorganization of mass tourism along these lines would require the reconfiguring of temporal as well as spatial aspects of modern industrial civilization. In particular the ordering and quantity of available holidays would need to be revisited if the long distant walk was to become a typical form of holidaymaking.

---

56   *The Way of a Pilgrim*, trans. R.M. French (NY: Ballantine Books, 1979).

57   Paul Call, 'The Way of a Pilgrim and the Pilgrim Continues His Way', *Slavic Review* 22 (March 1963), 172.

58   Kelly Winters, *Walking Home: A Woman's Pilgrimage on the Appalachian Trail* (Los Angeles: Alyson Publ., 2001).

If a pedagogy of pilgrimage and walking has the potential to transform the desire for speed into a 'love of slow', and to enhance the human ability to live life in response to the rhythm of the earth, then this would also suggest the value of recovering forms of human settlement which involve walking, of the kind still enjoyed by the Amish, and the diminishment of space given over to the rapid movement of vehicles which is itself the major obstacle to the enjoyment of walking in many urban and rural settings. One study of the effects of increased walking activity in a controlled trial indicated that both men and women reported increased environmental awareness in the form of enhanced enjoyment of the aesthetics of the places where they lived, and an increased appreciation for the convenience of their locale.[59]

The use of some kind of spiritual practice, such as breath prayer, as described in *The Way of a Pilgrim*, has the potential further to enhance the value of walking as the customary mode of mobility over mechanical forms. Another spiritual practice from the medieval era that is presently being retrieved is that of labyrinth walking.[60] The labyrinth originated in Christian culture as a symbolic representation of the pilgrimage to Jerusalem. By walking the maze on the floor of a cathedral a pilgrim who could not afford to journey to Jerusalem could enact it symbolically. Labyrinths are increasingly being constructed at retreat centres and churches and recently the University of Edinburgh constructed a labyrinth in George Square Gardens at the centre of the university's humanities and social science campus. The labyrinth creates the illusion of a difficult journey within the spatial confines of a floor or garden, and offers the opportunity within a much shorter time frame to experience elements of the embodied and meditative engagement of the long distance pilgrimage. And like pilgrimage it is a ritual that trains the participant to reframe the modern quest for mastery over nature through the deliberative quest for dependence on the divine, embodied encounter with whom is mediated through labyrinth walking and pilgrimage alike. Such embodied spiritual disciplines are intended to 'conform the soul to reality', and hence they resist the myth of scientific control over nature which is incarnate in the engineering of technical inventions and infrastructures that have made possible the devices and desires of speed.[61]

---

59   Nancy Humpel, Alison Marshal et al., 'Changes in Neighborhood Walking Are Related to Changes in Perceptions of Environmental Attributes', *Annals of Behavioral Medicine* 27 (2004), 60–67.

60   Senn, 'Journeying as Religious Education', 135–6.

61   Lewis, *Abolition of Man*, 46.

Chapter 13

The Ontology of Mobility, Morality and Transport Planning

Ullrich Zeitler

Basics

Introduction

The concept of mobility cannot be analysed without dealing with its built-in normativity, including ethics. Mobility is not a neutral term, not even if we frame a technical definition. It will always have moral implications. However, I will not analyse the moral implications of different mobility concepts in this article. Instead, the idea behind this work is to propose an ethical framework, which is argued to be suitable for a discourse on mobility.

Against mainstream constructivistic ethics (discourse ethics, utilitarianism, Kantianism and post-modern approaches to ethics) I want defend ontological ethics as the relevant theoretical framework of an analysis of mobility. The main idea of ontological ethics is that morality is grounded in how things are, which means that reality has a built-in normativity. One way to express this idea is that the world in its particular manifestations challenges us to respond in one way rather than another. Some responses are more adequate or proper than others. The exact nature of these proper responses is not determined by our own rational construction, but by the relationship we have established and continue to establish with the world.

Proper responses depend on our ability to respond, our "response-ability". This implies that there are limits to our response-ability, both with regard to its extension and with regard to its quality. Agents who have restricted ability, because of lack of certain faculties or senses, cannot answer to the same extent as more gifted agents. Children, animals, and plants have a different quality of response-ability and can respond to a different degree.

I propose the concept of response-ability as a keyword in ethical theory. It is also a keyword in planning ethics, for which I shall provide some examples at the end of this article.

Four approaches to ontological ethics

Ontological ethics is an interpretative framework of moral judgments, which evolved from the problems of modernism and has developed parallel with and clearly distinguished from what is usually termed post-modernist ethics. Ontological ethics has never developed into a systematic ethical theory, but there have been several attempts to express its main concerns, although not always under the term "ontological ethics". I shall briefly present the main approaches and the major arguments, which should be sufficient to form an understanding of its rationale.

One approach follows the line of argument presented by the Danish philosopher K.E. Løgstrup, who outlines the basic ideas of a cosmo-phenomenlogical epistemology and metaphysics. Løgstrup introduces the concept of ontological ethics in his German article from 1960 entitled "Ethik und Ontologie", but only his metaphysical writings from 1970s and early 1980s provide a more complete picture of his ideas.[1] The phenomenological approach assumes that phenomena have a constitutive role in establishing normative circumstances. Normativity is not constructed but is ontologically present.[2] For example, confidence is a basic manifestation of life that has a built-in normativity and in this way is ontologically determined. This phenomenological analysis may not only apply to human conditions, but also to non-human nature, according to Løgstrup's cosmo-phenomenology.

Another approach would be to follow a rationalistic argumentation for a cosmological environmental ethics. Cosmological environmental ethics is the ultimate consequence of an ethical theory that is urged to transgress the limitations of anthropo-, bio- and ecocentrism and end up with non-centrism or centrelessness. In such a centreless universe – similar to the Buddhist idea of absolute nothingness (zettai mu) – one must assume an identity of metaphysics and ethics, of is and ought. This line of argument is purely epistemological. It is the self-destruction of rationalism.

A third approach towards ontological ethics is to use concepts and ideas from ecological psychology. According to James J. Gibson, the main proponent of ecological psychology, our actions are controlled because "the environment" invites specific reactions and works against others. Given specific structures of affordances, we are not indifferent in how we meet "the environment". In this sense, ecological psychology may support ontological ethics. Although ecological psychologists probably would not agree that their conceptual framework has these kind of implications for moral theory, I can say that ecological psychology makes it easier for me to argue for ontological ethics, in as much as ecological psychology does not exclude this interpretation, even though it does not necessarily imply it.[3]

---

1   K.E. Løgstrup, *Metaphysics Vol.I–II*. Marquette University Press, Milwaukee 1995.

2   For an elaboration on this argument from Løgstrup see my thesis "Transport Ethics", cit. below.

3   Ulli Zeitler, "At omgås naturen – psykologiske og etiske perspektiver på mobilitetsadfærd". Helle Tegner Anker et al. (ed.), *Bæredygtig arealanvendelse – mod et forbedret beslutningsgrundlag*. DJØF-Forlag, Copenhagen 2001, pp. 17–32.

A fourth approach – and this is the approach which I mainly shall follow in this essay – is inspired by the main thinker of the so-called Kyoto School, Kitaro Nishida. Kitaro Nishida's philosophy is highly influenced by Zen Buddhism and German idealism.

Kitaro Nishida and ontological ethics

Nishida's ethics is grounded in a religious experience of a unified, authentic reality. In this pure experience, subject and object are still not divided and the is-ought distinction is without meaning. Pure experience is undivided and without relations.

> The real pure experience is just the consciousness of the present of what there is as such, without any meaning or significance. (Die wirkliche reine Erfahrung ist nur Gegenwartsbewusstsein des Tatsächlichen als solchem, ohne jegliche Bedeutung.)[4]

This implies that any meaning and any judgment is an abstraction from this original and absolute concrete experience. Or, in other words, all moral judgments are grounded in this undivided universe. The relative finite is grounded in the absolute and infinite, which we may call God or an infinite obligation. We can be considered to be a person as we contain in our finite self an infinite obligation or infinite response-ability.

> From a moral perspective, we can be thought of as a person as we contain an infinite Ought in our finite Self ... As the absolute Other, which we hide in our elemental self, owns the significance of the absolute Thou, we conceive in the depth of our Self an infinite responsibility. (Moralisch gesehen können wir als Person gedacht werden, da wir in unserem endlichen Ich ein unendliches Sollen enthalten...Weil der absolut Andere, den wir in unserem Grunde bergen, die Bedeutung des absoluten Du besitzt, empfinden wir im Grunde unseres Ich eine unendliche Verantwortung.)[5]

This infinite responsibility and infinite obligation manifests itself historically. The ought (Sollen) cannot be just an abstract, general ought; the true ought evolves from the historical position, in which I was determined.[6]

Where we through the medium of history meet God, we shall perceive the meaning of the creation of values.[7] But at the same time we shall also perceive their

---

4   Kitaro Nishida, *Über das Gute*. Translated by Peter Pörtner. Frankfurt/M. 1990, p. 30.

5   Kitaro Nishida, *Logik des Ortes*. Wissenschaftliche Buchgesellschaft, Darmstadt 1999, pp. 197–8.

6   Ibid. p. 198.

7   Ibid. p. 203: "Dort, wo wir im Medium der Geschichte Gott berühren, müssen wir die Bedeutung der Wertschöpfung erkennen."

nothingness as relative truths. In God all values are "aufgehoben" (in a Hegelian sense). "When a relative being faces the true absolute, it cannot exist. It must pass over into nothing."[8] Then morality is transcended by religion.

Morality is connected with existence, with finite beings, with relative agency. Human agents express themselves by expressing the world, by transforming the world into their own subjectivity. They "express the world as the world's individual acts", "the world's moral order is grounded in this existential fact."[9] Also the moral order is ontologically grounded in the constitution of the world.

Mobility

The concept and ontology of mobility related to and elaborated on Nishida's thinking

Mobility is usually discussed within a spatio-temporal framework. But time and space are badly suited to express the essence of mobility, particularly if we give space a physical expression. Space as a geographical and physical category is, according to Nishida, without meaning. Consequently, to speak about mobility in spatio-temporal terms is also meaningless.

In Nishida's terminology, mobility might be translated as Nishida's concept of "interactivity". Properly speaking, Nishida states, there is no real interactivity at the level of the physical world. The epistemologically necessity of interpreting the world in terms of causality and spatio-temporal forms, as Kant suggests, excludes the possibility of interactivity. "As Leibniz puts it, we cannot even conceive of active beings in the physical world if it is reduced to special extensiveness, a world of merely quantitative forces."[10]

> When that which opposes the self is conceived of as a form of merely spatial opposition, the self is reduced to being an objective thing too.[11]

The self, the moral self, is a consciously active self. The self is consciously active when it is interactive, and its interactivity is constituted in a dialectics of mutual negation and affirmation of self and other. Interactivity or mobility is a question of acting in this field of negation and affirmation, of responding (properly) to ontological challenges. In other words, it is the moral fight of response-able

---

8   Kitaro Nishida, *Last Writings. Nothingness and the Religious Worldview*. University of Hawaii Press: Honolulu 1987.

9   Ibid. p. 53.

10   Ibid. p. 50.

11   Ibid. p. 55.

moral agents, which defines their personal mobility.[12] To be mobile is a question of "assuming the full response-ability for acting (exchanging information) within a field of interdependent and co-originating actors." (This includes non-human nature, too.) To say that our mobility is unduly restricted means that we are "unjustifiably restricted in our endeavour to realise ourselves within the demands of moral circumstances".[13]

In its ideal configuration, response-able behaviour, the ability to respond (properly), presupposes the idea of an interdependent, co-originating world, which knows no subject and object.

The self or agent cannot be made into an object, nor is he subject of action; he is constitutive of both subject and object, of any distinction at all. Only beyond distinction do we find the infinite good.

> Not until subject and object have perished, the Self and Thou have reciprocally forgotten themselves, and heaven and earth have coalesced into one single dynamic reality, does good behaviour reach the point of its perfection. (Erst wenn Subjekt und Objekt ineinander untergegangen sind, Ich und Dich sich gegenseitig vergessen haben und Himmel und Erde zu einer einzigen, dynamischen Realität verschmolzen, erreicht das gute Verhalten den Punkt seiner Vollendung.)[14]

The consciously active and response-able self expresses the world in itself. To express the world in itself is a precondition of response-able behaviour. This is the ontological foundation of morality. Qua biological beings we are able to respond adequately to challenges from our biological world; we are able to understand or perceive the nature of challenges, of normative demands. Qua spiritual beings we are enabled to respond adequately to spiritual challenges or demands and so forth. Being grounded in a world we share, we have an ontologically provided basis for moral judgments.

To return to our definition of mobility, we can say that mobility is not the ability or capacity to efficiently overcome distances, but the ability or capability to respond or act or move properly within the field of interdependent and co-originating actors, where "properly" means in recognition of the ontological fact that we never act on our own, freely and independently, but only in an interdependent and co-originating way that is sensitive to the challenges we meet. In this way, "mobility" is a moral faculty and as such it should be clearly distinguished from transportation and "Verkehrsleistung".[15]

When we define mobility in this rather abstract, philosophical way, we still have to relate it to the basic issues in the transport discourse, such as need satisfaction,

---

12   Ulli Zeitler, *Aspects of Transport Ethics*. CeSaM Working Paper No. 8. Århus, December 1997, p. 29.

13   Ibid.

14   Nishida, *Über das Gute*, op. cit., p. 176.

15   Ulli Zeitler, *Transport Ethics*. Aarhus University 1997 (PhD thesis), p. 212.

accessibility and freedom of choice. The main idea in this presentation is that these issues can be interpreted within the terminology I introduced. For example, and briefly, need satisfaction and accessibility are realised among response-able interdependent and co-originating actors; their self-realisation mediated *through* the realisation of other beings. Freedom of choice is not a liberty belonging to independent actors, but the ability to make choices, which reflects proper responses to given challenges. This last interpretation indicates that it is not a maximisation strategy that is at stake – maximisation of access, for example – but rather "the opportunity and ability to perform a (necessarily) limited range of desirable and ethically acceptable actions."[16]

In my dissertation I elaborated on different aspects of mobility and argued that the emphasis on speed, comfort and traffic segregation, in order to optimise mobility patterns, is highly problematic from a moral point of view and counteracts normative intentions, which give the concept of mobility its central place in the public discourse. Very briefly summarized, speed is only possible when disregarding the moral circumstances of the actor's social and natural environment. Comfort is achieved only when externalising the "costs". Traffic segregation is both detrimental to safety and to the development of our moral judgement. In this way, our discussion will move the focus from dominant mobility and transportation issues and instead will turn attention to the concepts of interactivity and response-ability.

However, contrary to an approach that is critical of current mobility issues, we could pay attention to the recovery of morally sustainable mobility forms like walking, wandering, rambling – or one of the foci of this book: the pilgrimage. I think this is very important in order to pay more attention to "promoting" another understanding of mobility.

Transport Planning

There seems to be a big step from philosophy to transport planning. Let me in any event attempt to outline what I think could be the main implications of this relationship. We cannot determine and control transport behaviour by transport planning, but we can affect behaviour and create a framework that supports some kinds of actions and discourages others.

What is important from what has been said so far is that, first, we need create a mobility structure that develops, not impairs, our moral capacity, i.e. our ability to respond properly to given challenges. This moves us into the area of philosophy of technology and technology critique. Analyses of technology forms are very likely to reveal the way a particular transport technology supports or impairs our moral capacity. For example, the connex between car technology and freedom of mobility is easily undermined in a qualified way, if we use the vocabulary and definition presented today.

---

16   Ibid. p. 217.

Second, we need a mobility structure that actively promotes morally sustainable mobility forms like walking, wandering, rambling, and cycling. Here we are moving into the area of environmental ethics and environmental psychology. The concept of sustainability has been widely discussed in the 1980s and 1990s. Although competing definitions still exist side by side, we have the vocabulary to propose a definition of sustainable mobility that is operational and allows the interpretation of mobility I have given to be applied.

The challenge today is to break down the stereotypes and conditional associations between "mobility" and "high speed mobility", between "mobility" and "hypermobility"; this means abandoning the credo of maximisation, and instead starting a discourse on quality in transportation and quality of life.

Chapter 14

Walk the Talk – Mobility, Climate Justice and the Churches

Jutta Steigerwald

Mobility – For What, of Whom and for Whom?

What is the purpose of mobility? Three quotations introduce the theme of this chapter. They originate from statements about transport and mobility formulated by Christian churches in ecumenical contexts, where the challenge of mobility in recent years has become an issue for a substantive critical discussion.

In its comprehensive document "Mobile – but not driven" (2002), the World Council of Churches programme for "Justice, Peace and the Integrity of Creation" makes clear that:

> Transport Mobility is not an end in itself. It must serve and enrich communities. Motorized Transport means derive from human capacity which can be used and misused. The choice of forms and quantity is subordinated to the requirements of human dignity and genuine community.[1]

A second perspective has been formulated by Deike Peters, who works both as a professional planner and as a member of a social movement, and who raises the question of who defines and decides about the use of different forms of mobility, and for whom:

> The different understandings of mobility resulting from hierarchical gender structures and the division of work in society have far-reaching consequences in traffic and urban planning. Traffic planners are people with minimal or no workload for maintaining a household or a family and only have to worry about maintaining gainful employment and enjoying their leisure time. These are not mere equity questions. Gendered transport and mobility patterns have measurable consequences first of all for women themselves, but for their respective households and ultimately for the whole society.[2]

---

1 *Mobile – But not Driven: Towards Equitable and Sustainable Mobility and Transport*, World Council of Churches, "Justice, Peace and Creation"; epd-Entwicklungspolitik Materialien III/2002.

2 Deike Peters, transport planner and transport activist in "Women and Transport". Unpublished fact sheet, WCC-Ev. Akademie Bad Boll, 2001.

The United Churches of Canada located the challenge of transforming mobility in a broader cosmic frame of energy, and emphasised the eternal mobilities of energies as a circle to be rediscovered by humans:

> Energy is integrated in God's Creation. Sources ranging from fossil fuel to the sun are transformed into physical energy used by human societies. Nutritional elements combine with water and the air give our bodies the biological energies to maintain life. Our relationship with God, with nature and with other people provides us with the spiritual energy to thrive.[3]

A Virtual Journey

Let me invite you to a short virtual journey. Imagine being a star in the universe looking at the planet Earth. You may observe thousands of different energies in movement with different speeds in different places, making transformations within given times. In perfect synergy they sustain life in its manifold forms: natural life, human life, cosmic life.

You may discover different densities of air. They offer life to humans, animals, and plants and transport thousands of gases and chemical particles as part of the life process.

You may wonder about all the different water sources in its marvellous existence. They provide services to humans and non-humans.

The soil in sisterhood with other elements produces food out of little seeds; trees and bushes give shadow and home for animals. All of them are contributing to the beauty of the Earth; they form mountains, valleys, and deserts.

The sun warms not only the hearts of the people. S/he is a nearly endless energy source, a kind of art-director of an orchestra playing symphonies of life.

Nothing and nobody is excluded, all are interconnected – from the oceans to the deserts, mountains and valleys, people, animals, plants and planets. You are amazed by these mobilities of interwoven coloured energy movements, sustaining a balance and a constant process of transition and transformation of energies.

To learn about and to become a conscious part of these energy services from the inner Earth to the atmosphere to the whole cosmos is the privilege of human beings. Human motion and movement depend on these inner and outer forms of energy transformation. Our transportation systems and technically motorised mobilities should take in consideration their impact, the imbalance that they create, locally and globally, and their contribution to unsustainability.

Do you remember the little dots you saw on Planet Earth? They are nearly invisible. Instead of feet, some seem to have about 100 or as many as 400 horses to enable movement, and you may have smiled about the strange movements they

---

3 *Energy in the One Earth Community*. A Policy Statement adopted by the 37th General Council of The United Churches of Canada, August 2000.

make: kind of spastic; sometimes fast, sometimes stocked, but always leaving clouds of stinky smoke behind them. Together with other kinds of stinky and dark smoke and fog they build a sort of wall, high in the atmosphere, a wall of gases, which slowly becomes intensified, where heat and light of the sun can still enter but has it difficulties to find a way out again What's going on, you may wonder, are they heating up the place where they live? Are they inducing a fever on the Earth, choking themselves with pollutants that also harm the soil, the water and the air they depend on?

There must be a big misunderstanding. They must have missed something very essential to life, you find yourself thinking. They should not compete with each other, because in doing so they are damaging the Earth's marvellous and sophisticated life processes. Have they lost their sense of reality, their capacity to make distinctions? When they move even for a short distance they sit in this stinky, large boxes powered by steel horses, 100 and more for one person. When they travel a greater distance, they collect themselves in a cylindrical tube, and more than 1,000 horses carry them in the air. Certainly, they employed a great deal of human and natural energy to construct these boxes and to move them, but it seems to be counter-productive, as it harms them in the end. What kind of sense does this make?

You might become sad, because you might notice strong storms somewhere else, heavy rainfalls, floods and heat weaves that destroy harvests and houses, all of which leave behind suffering, death and misery, hunger and thirst. Homeless people are forced to move in search for a better tomorrow. You wonder, will they find it? Where?

Walk the Talk

Back on Earth: During the United Nations Summit for Sustainable Development in Johannesburg in 2002, indigenous peoples warned us in their 'Kimberly Declaration':

> We the indigenous people walk to the future in the footprint of our ancestors...

And further:

> We are the land and the land is we; we have a distinct spiritual and material relation with our lands and our territories and they are inextricably linked to our survival and further development of our knowledge systems and cultures.[4]

---

4   From the Kari-Oca Declaration Brazil, 30 May 1992, retaken in the Kimberly Declaration from the Gathering of Indigenous People in Kimberly, South Africa, before the United Nations World Summit of Sustainable Development, Johannesburg, 2002.

For the citizens of the industrialised, developed world, the same notion might be expressed like this:

> We, the industrial nations, drive into the future, over the footprints of other nations' territories and those of our children and grandchildren.

And further:

> We are the cars and the car is we. We have a distinct spiritual and material relation with our cars and their territories and they are inextricably linked to our survival and further development to our knowledge systems and cultures.

Indeed, the acceleration of the motorised transport sector during the last five decades has given rise to the acceleration of the gap between rich and poor, to the acceleration of unsustainable societies. The illusion of gaining power, and controlling time and space drives people in competition with the wholeness of life on Earth.

According to the OECD, 60 percent of the petroleum that is pumped out of the Earth – often from within indigenous territories – is transported and transformed and burned to satiate the demand of the motorised transport sector. "Every year", according to Wolfgang Sachs in his *Limit of Speed*, "the industrial system burns as much as fossil fuel as the Earth has stored in period of nearly a million years... It is probably not an exaggeration to say that the time gained through fuel-driven acceleration is in reality time transferred from the time stock accumulated in fossil reserves to power our vehicles and aircrafts."[5]

As humans we have the ability and capacity to make choices. We are basically able to choose between well-being and harm, between enjoying life and destroying it, between sustaining, maintaining, nurturing and generating life or rocketing towards death.

Birth and death are natural processes within a distinct time and space, within a broader life sustaining system. Accumulating energy to accelerate our lives necessarily leads to an imbalance of energies, along with the many other unpleasant aspects that speed inflicts on humans and human communities.[6]

---

5 *Time, Space and Mobility*. Unpublished Fact Sheet, WCC-Evang. Akademie Bad Boll, 2001.

6 Cf. Professor John Adams, UCL, *Hypermobility, Too Much of a Good Thing*, PIU Transport Seminar, 13 November 2001, See also: *Im Rausch der Geschwindigkeit*, 'Wissen-Spezial' of DIE ZEIT, Nr.37, 8 September 2005.

Transport Justice

According to the World Council of Churches document, motorised mobility is one of the main, if not *the* main contributor to the carbon dioxide emissions that are responsible, together with other greenhouse gases, for global warming and the destabilisation of today's climatic conditions. How can forms and patterns of motorised mobility be developed that are in harmony with the requirements of both equity and sustainability? If motorised mobility on the road and in the air is to contribute to the quality of human life, approaches must be found to guide its further development.[7]

How can the interdisciplinary approach, which is represented in this book, contribute to a people- centred, socially equitable and affordable mobility, to environmentally sustainable transport means and systems?

During the twentieth century, the motorised movement of people and goods increased more than a hundredfold, while the total human population increased fourfold.[8] The emissions from motorised transport (land and air particularly) became the main driver of climate change. The growth of motorised movement has not been equally distributed. While an average US citizen travels almost 30,000 km, roughly, the average German resident travels an average of 3,000 km and an average resident of a poor country travels less than 300 km annually, mostly by foot or bicycle.

Personal car ownership dominates everywhere but much less so in poorer countries. If car ownership levels worldwide were the same as those in OECD countries, there would be some three billion cars in the world, rather than the current 750 million.[9]

It is a paradox that as cities and towns become motorised, children's independent mobility declines.[10] In nearly all cities, the World Health Organization's air quality and noise standards are exceeded on a regular basis.[11]

A car-dependent society also accepts that car accidents are a price that must be paid for automobile ownership and use. Road crashes not only kill and maim, but they also leave emotional devastation and shattered families in their wake. The work of healing is usually borne by women.[12]

---

7 *Mobile – But not Driven. Equitable and Sustainable Mobility and Transport*, op.cit. note 1.

8 *EST! Environmental Sustainable Transport. Transport challenges sustainability.* OECD takes action. Guidelines for environmental and sustainable transport. Futures, strategies and best practises. Paris, 2000.

9 Ibid.

10 Hilman, H., Adams, J. and Whitelegg, J., *One False Move. A Study of Children's Independent Mobility*, London, Policy Studies, 1990.

11 WHO: *Transport, Environment and Health.* Various publications. www.who.it. www.who.dk www.themes.eea.eu.int/sectors_and_activities/transport/reports.

12 NGO-contribution to the 9th session of the Commission on Sustainable Development (CSD) to the United Nations (UN), New York, 16–27 April 2001.

The transport needs of women are not reflected in traffic planning. The criteria used in traffic planning are male-oriented; the reality of women's lives with their need for access to appropriate transport hardly exists for planners, so that half of the world's population is excluded from transport planning. In general, more women than men depend on public transport, and more women than men have no mechanical transport available at all and walk. Women are less likely than men to have access to a motorised means of transport, particularly in lower- and middle-class households and poorer countries.[13]

Transport is a means to an end. While the ultimate end is to improve people's livelihoods and community lives, the intermediate goal is for all people have access to goods and services. In rural areas in developing countries, people transport goods for meeting basic needs mainly by loading them on their heads and walking on paths and tracks far removed from large infrastructure investments. As an example, a Masai women in Kenya walks 25 hours to get 20 litres of water for household use. A study of women carried out in Addis Ababa showed that an average load for the 276 women sampled was 36.3 kg (i.e. 75 percent of body weight), which they carried an average of 11.7 km.

The needs of these people are largely unresearched, and in the case where they have been researched, they have never been mainstreamed into local, national and international transport policies and investments. This leads to the challenge of recognising and acknowledging people's accessibility needs in transport planning. It also means that if true research is conducted in this field, it is likely that the answers will probably suggest footpath and footbridges, animal power and animal-drawn vehicles, which would make roads, motorised transport and airports the lowest priorities.[14]

Currently, transport systems are economically inefficient because they do not properly internalise external costs of motorised transport, including environmental (pollution, noise, etc.), health (accidents) and social (infrastructures, climate change) costs. Governments, public agencies and companies should make use of a range of instruments such as 'the polluter pays' principle, parking charges, road pricing, fuel taxation, to name just a few options. Revenues from internalising costs can be invested in better public and non-motorised systems rather than in the expansion of traditional road and airport infrastructures.[15] Public subsidies disproportionately meet high-income private motorists needs at the expense of public transit passengers, pedestrians, cyclists and other more moderate or non-motorised means.[16]

---

13   Meike Spitzner, Wuppertal Institute for Climate, Energy and Environment in *Women and Transport*, unpublished Fact Sheet on Sustainable Transport. Bad Boll, 2000.

14   NGO contribution to the 9th session of CSD, ibid.

15   See the chapter on global warming and road transportation in Meyers, N. and Kent, J., *Perverse Subsidies. How Tax Dollars can Undercut the Environment and the Economy*. Island Press, Washington D.C., 2001.

16   Whitelegg J. *Dirty from Cradle to Grave*, Research study by Environment and Forecasting Institute in Heidelberg, Germany.

Long before a car gets to the showroom, it has produced a significant amount of damage to air, water and land ecosystems. Each car produced in Germany (where environmental standards are among the highest in the world), produces approximately 25,000 kg of waste and 422 million cubic metres of polluted air in the extraction of raw materials alone. The transport of these raw materials to Germany and around the country to factories produces a further 425 million cubic metres of polluted air and 12 litres of crude oil in the oceans of the world, per car. The production of the car itself adds further waste and polluted air.[17]

Advertisements have become one of the major voices in the industrial sector, creating messages to convince you that simply purchasing a car can make you feel happy and at the top of your game, or that you always have to have the right car available for every situation that you might encounter in your life (the desert, the mountains, seaside, family, shopping, theatre, parties) so that you will feel compelled to buy a certain kind of car. The list could go on. The planning model that results in car-dependent towns and societies in the developed world has been exported to the developing world, guaranteeing that the poor, women and children will continue to be excluded, and that greenhouse gases will further increase.

The OECD study *Transport Challenges Sustainability*[18] asked "*Do long-term trends lead to better mobility?*" The answer was that "even if all present, planned and reasonable foreseeable legislative, technological and social changes were to come, serious doubts would remain as to the environmental and social sustainability of future transport systems."

According to this study, if the current business as usual trend continues, and assuming no major shortages of petroleum products for transport use, transport in 2030 across the OECD countries will be characterised by the following:

- Car ownership and total distance travelled will be at substantially higher levels than in 1990 (the reference year for the Kyoto Protocol), with increases up to 200 percent and more, although vehicles will be more fuel-efficient and less polluting.
- Distance travelled per vehicle will be similar to 1990.
- Gasoline and diesel fuel will continue to be the most widely used source of transport energy, with some increase in the use of liquefied petroleum gas and other alternatives fuels, as well as in the use of hybrid and electric vehicles.
- The increase in road freight activity will be generally greater than that for car use, with a correspondingly greater increase in the use of diesel fuel.
- Rail and water-born freight activity will also grow, but at a much lower rate than for road freight.

17   Cf. *Earth-Community: Climate Change*. World Council of Churches, Geneva, 2005.

18   OECD study: *Transport Challenges Sustainability*: *OECD takes action. Guidelines for environmental and sustainable transport. Futures, strategies and best practise*, presented and endorsed in 2000 in Vienna, Austria.

- Use of surface public transport will grow, albeit at a much lower rate than car use.
- Walking and cycling will be at a similar or slightly lower rate than in 1990.
- There will be a much larger increase in aviation activity than for other modes, up to a 600 percent increase globally by 2030 as compared to 1990 levels.

The OECD report proposed a new target-oriented approach that places *environment and health at the top of the policy agenda for transport and related sectors, at international, national and local levels.* The World Health Organization urges the same. In communities where the local government, scientists, urban and traffic planners, and citizen-oriented NGOs together have realised transport systems that are in line with environmental, health and social criteria, the general public has welcomed and accepted changes immediately in favour of the reduced aggravation from motorised transport. Unfortunately, these positive changes become swamped by the increase of the number of vehicles elsewhere.

People and nature continue to suffer: bad air to breathe; reduced space for the movement of pedestrians and children, in particular, as well as for non-motorised mobility and moderate means of transport; and the separating, destroying and poisoning of ecosystems and human communities.

The drivers of global change, such as pollution from different sources, high energy consumption, unsustainable land use, and the depletion of natural and human resources combine with motorised mobility to contribute to ongoing and accelerating climate change.

Climate Justice and the Churches

The responsibility of northern industrialised nations for climate change remains a fact. Mitigating greenhouse gas emissions will require taking urgent action to reduce the poisoning of our natural, social and cultural environments and to correct and slow climate change problems. The Intergovernmental Panel on Climate Change (IPCC) tells us that people in developing countries will be victims to a greater degree than those in developed countries, because of their geographical location, high dependence on agriculture, and their technological and economic situations. The Fourth Assessment Report of the IPCC reaffirms earlier findings on the impact of climate changes on the south.

Since the inception of the World Council of Churches' Climate Change Programme, it has accepted as a basic ethical norm the responsibility for one's own or collective actions and its impact on others, whether distant or near in time and space. The framework of "justice" has often been employed to elaborate various dimensions of this responsibility. The urgency of addressing climate change has been described as a response in solidarity to the real and future threats facing those most seriously affected by climate change. Climate change cannot be seen isolated from the interactions of accumulated social and environmental degradation and the depletion of natural resources. With the growing frequency of natural catastrophes the number of victims is bound to increase.

How are the churches involved in this process? In response to the concerted efforts of many actors (scientists, policymakers in governments, business enterprises and NGOs), the special contribution of the ecumenical work on climate change has been an ethical and moral analysis, informed by the growing consensus on the causes and dynamics of climate change.[19]

The urgency of the threat of climate change requires our generation to take immediate action, and to go beyond simple declarations and statements. New alternative models of life are called for. We challenge all people to move towards a lifestyle that derives its quality from the attentive enjoyment of nature and human relationships, from mutual care, dependence, trust and solidarity instead of the illusions of individual autonomy and material wealth, from spirituality and feelings of community, connectedness and intimacy instead of one-dimensional self-centredness. In its consensus, the World Council of Churches declared that it would "draw strength from insights gained from the rich, community-oriented and simple lifestyles of indigenous and other marginalized communities. We are conscious of the significant contribution these communities with their low carbon economies, deliver to the stabilization of the climate. We recommend the creation of 'just, participatory, sustainable and sustaining communities' for mutual support and call upon the churches and authorities to join them on this journey with reflection and practical support."[20]

The engagement of the churches started in the 1970s, when the themes of Justice, Peace and Integrity of Creation began to spread and concerns about the environment and development had begun to grow. In a follow-up to the United Nations' Earth Summit in 1992 in Rio de Janeiro, a Working Group on climate change was formed, with participation and representatives from each region, and as a resource for the churches, communities and people of faith, who then could offer theological and ethical analyses that resulted in advocacy statements and educational resources.[21]

During the Conference of the Parties (CoP) of the United Nations Framework on Climate Change (UNFCC) advocacy work, ecumenical services and the building of ecumenical coalitions took place, which then participated in networking with NGOs, scientists and others. With the growing evidence of changes in the climate, coalition building has broadened, particularly with the development of NGOs and the churches. These coalitions have acted in solidarity with and in support of the

---

19   *Earth Community – Climate Change*, p. 74.

20   Op.cit. note 1.

21   Look for further documents on the WCC-Climate Change Work Website www.wcc.coe.org/wcc/jpc/ecology/htm.

victims of natural disasters, and have contributed to adaptation measures, as well as advocating for the mitigation of greenhouse gases in the industrialised world.

The European Christian Environmental Network (ECEN) seeks to stimulate sustainability within faith communities, exchanging experiences through various work coalitions and deepening theological and ethical reflections to redefine our place in creation. The network has proposed the ecological reconversion of church buildings, and a simpler way of living that extends to worship and prayer.[22]

In addition to ECEN, there are other faith communities, networks and coalitions in different countries, including the US, Canada, Australia, and New Zealand, which advocate a number of Earth friendly practices, such as eco-congregations and eco-management; car fasting (abstemiuousness); and car sharing; biking, walking and less air travel; better cars and better transport; the introduction of biological and organic local and seasonal food and agricultural practices for family tables, for schools, hospitals or church centres; switching to renewable energy sources; and fair trade. They aim to reduce society's fossil fuel consumption and car dependency, moving towards low carbon economies and the fullness of community life, to make the Earth habitable once again.[23] An example of the demands worked out in the ECEN's sustainable transport/mobility coalition during their last meeting at Flämslätt, Sweden, in 2006, is provided in the box below.

An initiative originated within the Orthodox Church called "Creation time" broadens its presents in ecumenical activities to celebrate the gift of creation; to recall solidarity with the wholeness of creation, challenging humans in industrialised nations to take responsibility for the healing and caring for the Earth and its inhabitants; and in the mutual nurturing, maintaining, and sustaining interconnected living systems.

Locally, there has been growth in photovoltaics on roofs and the use of other renewable energy, energy savings, organic food producers and consumers, car sharing, biking and walking, but does it mean that the churches have their houses in order?

Statements and declarations show, often strongly, the challenges that lie ahead for humanity, and many imperatives have been written, but these have not realised the potential that they could have, to provide guidance for a new vision and reality for societies. For example, the churches could use their purchase power to force the car industry to build better cars. The Protestant church in Germany alone owns and operates circa 50,000 cars. Couldn't the church have a voice? The Protestant and Catholic churches in Germany have the potential to reduce 18 million tonnes of CO_2 by making changes in their heating and electricity use,

---

22   See www.ecen.org.

23   Some examples: www.webofcreation.org; www.autofasten.at; www.christian-ecological-link.org; www.operation-noah.org.uk; www.slowup.ch; www.oeku.ch; www.ev-akademie-boll.de; www.gemeindedienst.de/umweltbeauftragter; www.fcei.it/GLAM; www.hf.ntnu.no/relnateur/; www.environment.harvard.edu/religion; www.cfore.ca; www.neccsa.org.za.

which represents 3–4 percent of the CO_2 emissions from energy use in Germany, according to a study from the Protestant Academy of Bad Boll. But churches are starting to realise that they are late in acting. Although the challenges ahead are significant, the commitment of the churches is growing. May this "transition of spiritual and practical mobilities" help us all to recognise "life as a gift from God, the atmosphere as precondition to the coming into existence and the continuation of life, seen as a heavenly gift of loving grace to all life, shared in common by the whole creation"[24] (18).

Transport means and systems, transport needs and speed will themselves need a transition: from domination to subordination of the requirements of human dignity within the wholeness of community life, of the integration into life of genuine joy.

---

24 *Earth Community – Climate Change*, p. 72.

Appendix

Towards a Sustainable Mobility Culture within European Church

Summary of the work of the Mobility Coalition, Flämslätt, Sweden 2006

Regarding the theme of "energy" of our 6th assembly we remark, that the environmental and social impact of all kind of motorised mobility is tremendous – both local and global. We have to note that:

- Motorised mobility and its impact on environment and justice is a kind of a taboo, also in NGOs and in Churches (perhaps because are stuck very deeply in our car (and plane) oriented society).
- Motorised mobility causes about 35 percent of all CO_2 emissions worldwide. Flights are increasing and also CO_2 emissions coming from motorised mobility in Europe. One main reason for this is the growing demand for the transport of goods.
- Motorised traffic has also an impact on health and safety, especially the particulates/pollution coming from the internal combustion engines of cars and trucks. The freedom and the safety especially of children are also extremely restricted.
- Regarding mobility there is a lack of democracy both in the field of planning and also "on the roads" (private cars have a "right of way"). The strategy of pedestrians, cyclists etc. against this attitude should be to "reclaim the road.
- We have discussed for more than 15 years the same problems. Everybody knows what is wrong and what they should do instead. We have to recognize, that we are stuck in a "dead end street". The Churches and their initiatives have to create visions and have to lobby for alternatives fitting into integrity of creation – better than the existing car orientated society.
- Biomass or other alternatives instead of fossil fuel can not be a solution without reducing motorised traffic as a whole.

We are looking for alternatives in order to save energy and reduce CO_2 emissions and made in some regions our first hopeful experiences:

- Using as church staff members bikes for business trips (being paid a significantly more than using a car – as an incentive in Bergen/Norway). Please send us photographs from church people on the bike.

- Having an increasing number of participants joining during Lent the campaign "Auto fasten" (Car fasting in Graz, Austria).
- In efficient car driving (30 percent less fuel consumption besides certain efficient car technologies).
- To change the modal split of all big events like the German Kirchentag (www.kirchentag.de) into more environmental friendly mobility. Regarding this, our ECEN assembly and the meetings of the enabling team should be a "forerunner".

Our proposals are:

- Churches have to understand mobility as an important theme of lifestyle and have therefore to work themselves on a new model of mobility and have to promote environmental friendly means of transport as acceptable and trendy. Churches should be also a part of the "Slow Up" Movement.
- Our campaigns must be more creative and stimulating imagination and action (one car in one hour driving 20 km/h is heating up the local climate as much as 210 bulbs 100 watt each).
- Besides saving energy we need to promote effective usage in the field of mobility.
- Churches should adopt as standard to compensate flights, when they are not avoidable (www.myclimate.org; www.mittklima.no; www.atmosfair. de; www.climateticket.ch).
- Joining the car free day campaign.
- Supporting and joining car sharing and car pooling initiatives (church parishes existing all over the country could promote a new lifestyle sharing facilities and goods (see Acts 2, 44) – church buildings as a "house of commons" with collective usage).
- Looking for different solutions of collective transport especially in the rural area.
- Reducing the food miles by purchasing regional nutrition in church institutions.
- An European wide campaign regarding "Car fasting" during lent.
- As a big consumer Churches should call the car companies for a downsized eco car.
- Churches should lobby for a European wide speed limit (e.g.120–80–30).

A radical change in the field of mobility is urgent. We need visions of a society where the president and the bishop are cycling getting the rolls for breakfast.

Source: Mobility Coalition of ECEN, Flämslätt 2006.

Chapter 15

Ecological Approaches to Mobile Machines and Environmental Ethics

David Kronlid

Introduction

It is a well-known fact that technology is a double-sided phenomenon in modern western culture. On the one hand technology holds promise for the future. Medical cures, environmental friendly transport, GM crops that can solve the global food crisis, and solar energy are some examples of how current-day technology may play a part in a future sustainable world. On the other hand, technology has proved to be the cause of severe social and environment problems. The pollution of the Minamata Bay in Japan in the late 1950s, the Harrisburg and Chernobyl accidents, the spread of pesticides and herbicides in the bodies of people, animals and plants, anthropogenic changes in the global climate system, and various types of pollution in the global waterscape are well known problems that can be linked to the use and abuse of different technological devices and systems.

The main aim of this chapter is to consider what environmental ethics can offer in the face of these and other problems. In that sense, this chapter offers no answers to the question regarding the morally proper way of dealing with various forms of technology. Rather, I wish to discuss a complementary approach to technology, which I suggest can shed further light on the discussion of the role of technology in environmental ethics.

I will suggest that the typical view of technology in Swedish environmental policy is an instrumental approach, and that moreover, environmental ethics also needs to take an ecological approach to technology. Furthermore, my discussion is relevant for different kinds of mobility technology, or rather, mobile machines such as on-road and off-road vehicles, aircraft, marine vessels and trains, with special attention given to trains.

My main argument is that an ecological approach to mobile machines can clarify and shed further light on how technological environments produce and uphold certain moral values and ideals. Thus, if we only assess the social and environmental consequences of machine use, we run the risk of being blind to the powerful emotional and social forces invested in machines as co-creators of certain moral ideals, values, and meanings. Hence, in order to critically examine different mobility practices, we also need a set of concepts that is different than what an instrumental approach to technology can offer.

Two Complementary Approaches to Mobile Technology

This section clarifies two different approaches to technology in general and to mobile machines in particular: (1) an instrumental approach to technology, and (2) an ecological approach to technology.

An instrumental approach to technology

It is no overstatement to say that the main approach to technology in Swedish environmental and sustainability policies in general is an instrumental approach. That is, we focus on the consequences of the use of different techniques in terms of their possible or obvious impact on people and nature.[1]

Regardless of whether or not possible problems with technology are defined in scientific, social or ethical terms, we tend to approach problems as a case of cause (the use of mobile or GM technology, as examples) and effect (unfavourable anthropogenic climate change[2] and regional and local pollution, or the possibility of gene flow).

This instrumental approach to technology is linear, which means that it builds on a conceptual separation of; (a) the user of technology, (b) the mobile machine in question, (c) the consequences of machine use, and (d) the values or ideals against which the consequences of machine use are assessed.

The linear nature of this ethical assessment, involving what can be regarded as a principle of separation, becomes clear if we consider the Swedish ethical deliberation over GM technology. This process clearly and deliberately separates the different parts of the practice of genetic technology[3] from another. The Swedes do not perceive or treat genetic technology as a whole – a system or an environment – but as a linear process, which includes; (a) genetic technology innovation and research (the processes of developing new techniques), (b) genetic techniques (the

---

1   See for example the website of The Swedish Environmental Protection Agency on climate change and a focus on impact, consequences, and adaptation. http://www.internat. naturvardsverket.se (accessed 3 May 2007).

2   See for example the *Swedish Climate Strategy*, Summary, Gov. Bill, 2001 02:55, p. 13. "The government foresees that the proposed intermediate objective will be followed by further emissions reduction targets after 2012, so that the environmental quality objective can be achieved, and so that new international requirements can be met. *Investments in fossil-free, energy-efficient technology and in new techniques and new methods leading to reduced emissions of other greenhouse gases*, may therefore be presumed socio-economically profitable in the long term," [emphasis added].

3   See Ingold, 2002, pp. 296–9 for a discussion on the meaning of "technology": "I have myself argued, along rather similar lines, that while technology consist of knowledge encoded in symbols, it is knowledge only in a certain aspect, as models *for* rather than *of*...and that knowledge becomes technology by virtue of a 'practical orientation to the material world' that simultaneously converts neutral objects into useful equipment" (298). This coheres with my own understanding of the meaning of technology.

means and models of how we actually deal with the organism and its genes; the know-how), (c) the application or use of genetic techniques (the know-how put in action), (d) the effects or consequences of its use, and (e) the values these effects and consequences are measured against.

Each step in the process is tried separately from an ethical perspective, so that the focus is on the consequences of the use of GM technology. One of the reasons for this approach is that it follows the structure of the Swedish environmental code.

The applicable area of Chapter 13 in the Swedish environmental code states:

> The provisions of this chapter shall be applicable to contained use and deliberate release of genetically modified organisms. The provisions shall also be applicable where products containing or consisting of such organisms are placed on the market.

> The purpose of these provisions is, in addition to that set forth in chapter 1, section 1 first paragraph, to ensure that special attention is paid to ethical concerns in connection with activities referred to in the first paragraph.[4]

Following this, the process of handling genetically modified organisms is divided into three sequential steps: (1) "contained use",[5] (2) "deliberate release",[6] and (3) "placing on the market".[7]

The term "contained use" thus applies to any activity involving genetic modification of organisms for which contact with the general population and the environment is "limited". Thus, this applies to all kinds of state- or otherwise-funded gene technology research using organisms. In order to limit contact with the general population and the environment, genetically modified organisms are presumably controlled in laboratories.

Furthermore, one purpose of the deliberate release of genetically modified organisms into the environment without containment is to test the stability and expression of the added genes in what a normal or as close to normal as possible environment.[8]

---

4   The Swedish Environmental Code, Part Three, chapter 13: 1.

5   The Swedish Environmental Code, p. 71. "'Contained use' shall mean an activity in which organisms are genetically modified, cultured, stored, used, transported, destroyed, disposed of or used in any other way, and for which specific containment measures are used to limit their contact with the general population and the environment."

6   The Swedish Environmental Code, p. 72. "'Deliberate release' shall mean any intentional introduction of genetically modified organisms into the environment without containment."

7   The Swedish Environmental Code, p. 72. "The term 'placing on the market' shall mean supplying or making a product available to third parties."

8   The Swedish Gene Technology Advisory Board, Utterance 025/2005.

Offering GM organisms on the market is the last step in this process. We can presume that the goal of the production and use of genetic techniques is for the benefit of people, locally, regionally, and globally.

This instrumental and linear ethical approach to GM technology has its counterpart in environmental approaches towards mobile machines.[9] In the face of an anthropogenic[10] climate catastrophe, we have focused on the negative consequences of mobile machine use for people and nature. However, there are alternative approaches to technology, one of which can be referred to as an ecological approach to technology.

An ecologic approach to technology

In her article "Unnatural Ecologies: The Metaphor of the Environment in Media Theory", Ursula K. Heise outlines an ecological approach to technology.[11]

The ecological approach to media technology – the study of media as an environment – is summarized in the following quote from Neil Postman:

> Its intention is to study the interaction between people and their communications technology. More particularly, media ecology looks into the matter of how media of communication affect human perception, understanding, feeling, and value; and how our interaction with media facilitates or impedes our chances of survival. The word ecology implies the study of environments: their structure, content and impact on people.[12]

From an environmental ethics perspective, the most relevant difference between an instrumental and an ecological approach to technology is that the latter focuses on studying the interaction between people and technology, i.e. technology as environment, and not merely the consequences of our use of technology.

Following this, the ecological approach to technology is nonlinear in the sense that it does not build on a conceptual and sequential separation between the user of technology, the mobile machine in question, the consequences of machine use, and the values by which the consequences of machine use are assessed. It aims rather to study technology as environment, thus to understand the interplay between the user, the machine, the consequences of machine use, and the values *of* this environment.[13]

---

9   The Motor Vehicle Emission Requirements.

10   The Swedish Climate Strategy.

11   Heise, 2002. Heise sees the ecological approach to technology as a line of development within human ecology.

12   Postman, 1970, p. 161. Here cited from Heise, 2002, p. 153.

13   Rolston, 1991. One of the most interesting contributions to environmental ethics by Holmes Rolston III is his concept of "systemic value".

One way of interpreting the ecological approach is that it takes as its vantage point that the user and the machine are intimately related, emotionally and socially, and that these relationships are part of processes that create what is considered to be valuable and morally relevant in a given technological practice or culture.

Ecological approaches to mobility technology

In the network of river, bridge, cities and surrounding environment nothing remains unchanged. Social and technical actively interact, exchange properties and negotiate identities, thus shaping one another. Technologies, then, are not neutral tools, or passive containers, but environments that shape and hold together a set of social dynamics that are simultaneously a consequence of their existence and necessary for their survival. The introduction of the new bridge does not result in two cities plus a bridge, but in a qualitatively different urban landscape composed by distinct social relationships.[14]

In this quote from her essay "Shaping Technology/Building Body(Nets)" Ana Viseu adopts an ecological approach to technology regarding the building of a bridge that connects two cities.

It is clear that what Viseu has in mind here is an approach to technology that offers an alternative to my earlier description of an instrumental approach:

The metaphor of technological environments highlights the networked, distributed character of a socio-technical project and emphasizes the multi-directional influence of the actors' (people and artefacts) actions, thus leading to the rejection of cause and effect, deterministic theories.[15]

From this it follows that we have an alternative path to travel in our attempts to understand and clarify the moral meaning of technology in general, and of mobility technology in particular.

In her research, Mimi Sheller has developed an approach to mobility technology that fits well with Heise's conception of ecological technology and Viseu's idea of technologies as environment. In one of several articles on car cultures and the social and emotional relationships between the car and the driver, she suggests that:

Car consumption is never simply about rational economic choices, but is as much about aesthetic, emotional and sensory responses to driving, as well as patterns of kinship, sociability, habitation and work. Insofar as there are "car cultures" vested in an "intimate relationship between cars and people" (Miller, 2001b: 17), we can ask how feelings for, of and within cars occur as embodied sensibilities that are socially and culturally embedded in familial and sociable practices of car use, and the circulations and displacements performed by cars, roads and drivers.[16]

---

14   Viseu, 2003, pp. 128–9.
15   Viseu, 2003, p. 129.
16   Sheller, 2004, p. 222.

Ecological Approaches and Technogenic Identification Processes

An ecological approach to technology is of course subject to criticism, and I would like to mention two legitimate arguments. After I present the second argument against an ecological approach to technology, which concerns the risk of casting moral agents as passive components of the technological environment, I will briefly comment on one possible route out of such a dilemma in terms of technogenic identification processes.[17]

The ecological approach to technology makes use of ecological concepts. However, what it means to study environments, as well as the meaning of "environment", have shifted through out the history of ecological thinking.[18] Therefore, we need to be clear in this context what we mean by "ecological".

First, there are relevant differences between "ecological systems" and "ecological environments". The systems metaphor seems to be associated with the view that technologies have "a logic of their own".[19] One danger with this view is that technological systems "seem independent of political, social, and cultural interests and organization patterns".[20] In other words, such a view runs the risk of maintaining a split between a social/human realm and an artificial/technical realm, which is what we want to avoid.

Furthermore, in using an ecological approach to technology, we want to avoid casting moral agents as passive components of a system that is beyond their control. An ecological approach to technology should include a "point of departure for theorizing human agency and intention in the creation and usage of technologies",[21] which in this case means mobile machines.[22]

One way of theorizing human agency in technological environments is to discuss how, as Viseu has described it, identities are negotiated in and through different identification processes that take place in such environments.

Anthropogenic, ecogenic and technogenic identification processes

In this section I wish to connect Heise and Viseu's ideas of technologies as environments, Sheller's idea of automotive emotions, and identification processes. The main aim of this section is to present a possible conceptual framework to avoid casting moral agents as passive components of the technological system.

---

17   I have discussed the concept of technogenic identification processes in relation to mobility technology and "mobility" in general more thoroughly in an upcoming paper. See Kronlid, 2008.

18   Worster, 1994; Merchant, 1990.

19   Heise, 2003, p. 157.

20   Heise, 2003, p. 157.

21   Heise, 2003, p. 158.

22   Heise, 2003, p. 158, op. cit.

In doing this I wish to remind the reader of Viseu's idea that the "[s]ocial and technical actively interact, exchange properties and *negotiate identities*".[23] I find that this idea makes a lot of sense if related to Mimi Sheller's discussion about our feelings toward cars, feelings that are "socially and culturally embedded in familial and sociable practices of car use, and the circulations and displacements performed by cars, roads and drivers".[24] Furthermore, these ideas also make sense if related to research on environmental identification processes in environmental psychology as well as in environmental ethics.

One common understanding of "environment" is that it is associated with someone or something. That is, when we talk about an environment we generally assume that it is the environment *of* someone or something,[25] usually humans and nonhuman animals or plants. The ecological approach to technology means that machines also have environments, which means that machines are also perceived or experienced as agents on the same or similar terms as humans and nonhuman individuals.

I have argued elsewhere that it is reasonable to assume that moral agents do not merely engage in identification processes with other humans. That is, we do identify with other humans, with nonhuman animals, plants, and perhaps species and places, and with machines. I have labelled these processes anthropogenic, ecogenic, and technogenic identification processes.[26]

The concept of technogenic identification processes offers one way of making sense of the interactions between human and machine *individuals* from the perspective of technologies as environments. It seems reasonable to assume that we do engage in identification processes with machines in ways similar to the ways that we identify with each other and nonhuman animals, plants, and species.[27] We experience sameness and differences between self and machines, interpret their meaning in human terms and vice versa (anthropomorphic and physiomorphic interpretations), experience them as subjects or agents, assume that they have a point of view on us, and that they communicate their agenthood in their behaviour.[28]

However, ecological approaches to technology involve aspects other than individual experiences of other human, natural, and machine individuals and what is sometimes referred to as environmental identifications[29] or a sense of self as hybrid or cyborg.[30]

---

23   Viseu, 2003, p. 128, [emphasis added].
24   Sheller, 2004, p. 222.
25   Attfield, 1999.
26   Kronlid, 2008.
27   Kronlid, 2008.
28   Kronlid, 2008.
29   Clayton and Opotow, 2003.
30   See e.g. Haraway, 1991 and Cuomo, 1998 for ethical reflections on the self as cyborg.

Ecological approaches to technology should also clarify how certain technological environments uphold and produce moral values and ideals, and what we as moral agents regard to be morally meaningful. Thus we also need to look into specific sub-mobile machine cultures.

Inspired by Holmes Rolston's concept of "systemic value", and taking an ecological approach to technologies, we might thus ask what values and ideals "seep into" mobile machine cultures as technological environments:

> Systemically, value fades from subjective to objective value, but also fans out from the individual to its role and matrix. Things do not have their separate natures merely in and for themselves, but they face outward and co-fit into broader natures. Value-in-itself is smeared out to become value-in-togetherness. Value seeps out into the system, and we lose our capacity to identify the individual as the sole locus of value.[31]

To Be or Not to Be a Good Train Driver

In the following I present an example of a mobile machine culture. My intention is to clarify that when we take an ecological approach rather than merely an instrumental approach to mobile machines, we will find that our relationships with our machines are often intimately related to our moral values and ideals.

One of many tragic stories in the history of the Swedish environmental policy is the use of a herbicide – known as "Hormoslyr"[32] in Sweden and as "Agent Orange" in the Vietnam War – to clear vegetation from the railways.[33]

Several railway workers became seriously ill during the 1960s and onward, and at the end of the 1970s, a group of railroad workers took the Swedish railroad (SJ) to court, arguing that working with Hormoslyr had caused their ill health. The workers lost in court 1980. The court of appeal affirmed the sentence and the Supreme Court refused to take up the case for trial.[34]

One of these workers was late Jonas Eric Jönsson. He worked for several years as a driver along the railway tracks where the herbicide was used. Jönsson's story has been published "The Train of Death",[35] which he co-wrote with Karl-Erik Johansson.

---

31   Rolston, 1991.
32   Kemp, 1998, p. 14.
33   "Hormoslyr" was also frequently used in the Swedish forest industry during this period. I have addressed the case of Erik Jönsson in two other publications; Kronlid, 2005 and Kronlid, 2006.
34   Johansson and Jönsson, 1991.
35   People living along the tracks commonly called the trains that sprayed the chemical the "Trains of Death". Johansson, K.-E. and Jönsson, E. (1991) *Dödens Tåg*, Fingraf tryckeri, Södertälje, Sweden.

If we were to assess Jönsson's case using an instrumental approach to technology, we would look into whether or not the use of Hormoslyr by the Swedish railway industry caused unwanted or unethical consequences. This was the approach taken by the workers, the company and the court, and because the workers could not prove that it was their work with Hormoslyr that had caused their illnesses, they lost their case.

Of course, in taking an instrumental approach to technology, we could still argue that regardless of whether SJ was *legally* right in their actions according to the court, we could still hold them to be *morally* wrong. However, in doing so, we would still miss the ways in which this specific technological environment, the practice itself, produced, upheld and made meaningful certain values and ideals intimately related to Jonas Erik Jönsson's relationship to the train as a train driver.

In using an ecological approach to this case, in the context of sustainable development, we might ask whether the technological environment itself upheld and reproduced certain train driver values and ethics that made the unsustainable social, economic and ecological development of this specific case possible and perhaps desirable.

I would like to suggest that these train driver values are linked to the work ethics of that time, and the ideal of being a male train driver.

Work values

Let us for the sake of argument assume that during the time when Jönsson was driving his train, Protestant work values were still alive and well in Sweden. The following quote from Jönsson supports the fact that at least Jönsson shared some of the elements of a Protestant work ethic:

> Eventually he could not put up with it and was given a certificate of illness. He was on the sick list for two years before he was called upon to see the chief medical officer at the SJ district, who suggested that he should get an early retirement pension. – But I did not want that at all, says Eric. I was uncomfortable with walking around town and having nothing to do, and I asked whether I could work as a cleaner at the SJ shop, because I heard that they were short of people. Then the psychologist that was aiding the medical officer said that I should not descend to picking garbage after others when I had been a driver for such a long time. Rather, I should get an early retirement pension to preserve my dignity. I opposed, and explained that my human dignity would not decline because I took a lower job, which I believed I would have the strength to do, at least part time.[36]

---

36   Johansson and Jönsson, 1991, pp. 8–9. My translation from Swedish.

According to Carl-Henric Grenholm,[37] the Protestant work ethic involves the following purposes or values:

- "to serve our fellow human beings [thus] ascribe to work a relatively high value as a means to achieve this end",
- "an activity which contributes to human self-realization",
- "a constituent of human essence and definition", and
- "an instrument for God's continuous act of creation".

Now, is it reasonable to assume that these are systemic work values and not values that are applied to this specific technological environment from a position outside the system? From an ecological perspective, the answer is yes. These work values, and even more so the specific way in which they were executed in this specific technological environment, become meaningful only if related to the relationship between the train driver and the train and the driver's feelings for, of and within the train.

These Protestant work values (or other work values in other technological environments) take their meaning and existence from the interaction between (among other things in its environment) the driver and the train. What it means for the train driver to serve his fellow human beings, to realize his or herself, to be human, and to continue God's acts of creation, cannot be fully understood if not understood in the context of train driving in this specific technological environment. These are values and ideals that are not isolated from the user of this machine or from the consequences of this use. Rather, they are in themselves products of this specific technological environment.

Train driving as male ideals

A second aspect of the systemic values and ideals in this particular case are the ideals that follow from being a male worker in Sweden at the time. We might assume that this technological system upheld and reinforced certain ideals concerning what it means to be a good – male – train driver. Furthermore, I would suggest that these ideals reinforced the systemic Protestant work ethic, which contributed to making the parties involved finding them meaningful.

At the time of the Hormoslyr debate in Sweden, any worker who was worried about the negative impacts of Hormoslyr on their health ran the risk of being stereotyped as physically weak and as a grumbler. In a debate on national television concerning Hormoslyr, the former forestry manager Lennart Christoffersson claimed that Hormoslyr was harmless or nearly so. Later, as tabloid media challenged his statement, he took a swig of the herbicide to prove his point.[38]

---

37   Grenholm, 1993, pp. 111–12.
38   Widerberg, Göran, 2004–09–08, personal communication.

Furthermore, in an interview several years later, he repeated his position on the matter and said that anyone should be able to handle "a little swig".[39]

This example suggests that a systemic value or ideal of this technological environment was the ideal of being a physically strong and silent male worker who ought to be able to "take it". Furthermore, the following quote from Jönsson, in which he is clearly worried about being looked upon as a grumbler and a troublemaker, suggests that these or similar male ideals were shared by the workers themselves, and that such ideals were intimately connected to his profession:

> The money you might receive from a fair judgment is unessential to me. I'll manage regardless. However, I wish to establish respect for my profession. The management should not look upon us as grumblers and troublemakers without supporting their accusations. You get the feeling that SJ has looked upon us in this negative way during these hard years. Otherwise, they should have tried to get in touch with us, which they never did.[40]

To conclude, I suggest that if we take an ecological approach rather than an instrumental approach to technology, we have taken the first step toward an environmental ethical analysis of mobile machine use that is sensitive to the fact that certain values and ideals are produced and upheld in a specific technological environment. In addition, these values and ideals are connected to our feelings for, of and within the mobile machines, as well as "socially and culturally embedded in familial and sociable practices"[41] for our use of the particular machines in the particular technological environment.

Ecological Approaches to Mobile Machines and Environmental Ethics

In summary, I have suggested that the most common approach to technology in Swedish environmental policy is an instrumental approach to technology. Such an instrumental approach means that whenever different techniques (GM technology, cars, trains, aeroplanes, bridges, etc.) are ethically deliberated, this deliberation is built upon the idea that the moral agent, the technique in question, the consequences of the use of this technique, and the values or ideals that we use as assessment "tool", are separate sequential elements. As a consequence, the social and emotional relationships between the user of the machine and the machine itself become irrelevant in answering the question of whether we ought to use a certain technique or not.

Because mobile machines, such as cars or as in this case, a train, were used, and caused negative effects on people and the environment, it seems as if we

---

39   Widerberg, 1988.
40   Johansson and Jönsson, 1991, pp. 48–9. My translation.
41   Sheller, 2004, p. 222.

would draw the conclusion that we should take an instrumental, linear cause and effect *analysis* of technology. However, despite its advantages, such an analytic approach necessarily excludes important information needed in order to properly assess the situation.

Thus, if we were to take a complementary *ecological* approach to technology, in which we look on technologies as environments, we would be inclined to focus on the relationships between the moral agent, the machines in question, and the ideals and values that are essential parts of these relationships.

One way of doing this is in terms of identification processes between moral agents and other "natural" and machinic individuals. Another way of taking an ecological approach to technologies is to look at values as not being separate from the actual use-practice but created and upheld within the specific technological ecology – these values and ideals are "value-in-togetherness".

Now, why would environmental ethics need an ecological approach to technologies? In answering this question, I would like to mention two things. First, that an ecological environmental ethical approach to technology takes environmental ethics one step further in recognizing that "environments" are not merely human or natural habitats but also that environmental values involve our relationships to human, natural *and* technological agents.

Such an approach seems to me to be more realistic than one that focuses merely on the relationship between moral agents and "nature", and that considers the use of mobile machines as merely a process of producing negative or positive externalities. In other words, environmental ethics would gain from a further and more thorough investigation of the moral implications that – in Ignacio Götz's words – technology is "inextricably entwined with the evolution of the human person", hence that "[i]t is not just that the contemporary human situation cannot be understood except in relation to technology, but that the human condition itself cannot be understood except in this relation".[42]

Second, I suggest that environmental ethics *also* should take an ecological approach to technology, and follow in the footsteps of mobility researchers such as Mimi Sheller and others. In doing so, we might get closer to an understanding of the reasons why we regard certain technological practices as meaningful and desirable, despite the fact that they are apparently ecologically, socially, and economically unsustainable, as was in the case of Hormoslyr, train driving, and Jonas Eric Jönsson, and as it is with different car cultures.

Finally, if we could develop systematic environmental ethical analyses of the moral values and ideals that are produced and sustained in different technological environments, we might be clearer on the reasons why we – the people of the industrial world – keep on driving our trains and cars of death, in spite of what we know of their catastrophic consequences, which has been provided for decades by the instrumental approach to technology.

---

42   Götz, 2003, p. 32.

References

Attfield, R. (1999), *The Ethics of the Global Environment* (Edinburgh: Edinburgh University Press).

Clayton, S. and Opotow, S. (eds) (2003), *Identity and the Natural Environment: The Psychological Significance of Nature* (Cambridge, Massachusetts: MIT Press).

Cuomo, C.J. (1998), *Ecological Communities: An Ethic of Flourishing* (London and New York: Routledge).

Grenholm, C.-H. (1993), *Protestant Work Ethics: A Study of Work Ethical Theories in Contemporary Protestant Theology* (Uppsala Social Studies in Social Ethics 15, Göteborg, Sweden).

Götz, I.L. (2003), *Technology and the Spirit* (Westport, US: Praeger).

Haraway (1991), *Simians, Cyborgs, and Women: The Reinvention of Nature* (New York: Routledge).

Heise, U. (2002), "Unnatural Ecologies: The Metaphor of the Environment in Media Theory", *Configurations* 10:149–68 (John Hopkins University Press and the Society for Literature and Science).

Ingold, T. (2002), *The Perception of the Environment: Essays in Livelihood, Dwelling and Skill* (London and New York: Routledge).

Johansson, K.-E. and Jönsson, E. (1991), *Dödens tåg*, bokförlaget Fingraf AB, published in association with the association *Liv i Sverige*, Södertälje, Sweden.

Kemp, D.D. (1998), *The Environmental Dictionary* (London and New York: Routledge).

Kronlid, D. (2005), *Miljöetik i praktiken* (Lund: Studentlitteratur).

Kronlid, D. (2006), "Structural Environmental Injustice", in Frostell, B. (ed.) *Science for Sustainable Development: Starting Points and Critical Reflections*, Proceedings of the 1st VHU Conference on Science for Sustainable Development, Västerås, Sweden, 14–16 April 2005, VHU, Uppsala, pp. 179–89, *Swedish Society Science for Sustainable Development*, Distribution, VHU, Uppsala and Division of Industrial Ecology, KTH, SE-100 44 Stockholm, Sweden, www.ima.kth.se.

Kronlid, D. (2008 forthcoming), "What Modes of Moving Do to Me: Reflections about Technogenic Processes of Identification", in Bergmann, S., Hoff, T. and Sager, T. (eds) *Spaces of Mobility: Essays on the Planning, Ethics, Engineering and Religion of Human Motion* (London: Equinox).

The Swedish Gene Technology Advisory Board, Utterance 025/2005, http://www.genteknik.se/, 1 October 2006.

Merchant, C. (1980), *The Death of Nature: Women, Ecology and the Scientific Revolution* (San Francisco: Harper).

Postman, N. (1970), "The Reformed English Curriculum", in Eurich, A.C. *High School 1980: The Shape of the Future in American Secondary Education* (New York: Piman) pp. 160–68, quotation on p. 161.

Rolston III, H. (1991), "Environmental Ethics: Values in and Duties to the Natural World", in Bormann, F.H. and Kellert, S.R. (eds) *The Broken Circle: Ecology, Economics, Ethics* (New Haven: Yale University Press). Taken from *The Ecocentrism Homepage*, http://www.ecospherics.net, 30 September 2006.

Sheller, M. (2004), "Automotive Emotions: Feeling the Car", *Theory, Culture and Society* Vol. 21, 4–5, pp. 221–42.

The Motor Vehicle Emission Requirements, the Swedish Road Administration, http://www.vv.se/templates/page3_15916.aspx, 3 May 2007.

The Swedish Environmental Code, Ds 2000:61 (2000), Ministry publications series, Ministry of Sustainable Development, Sweden, http://www.regeringen. se/sb/d/108/a/1348, 1 October 2006.

The Swedish Climate Strategy, Summary, Gov. Bill (2001), 02:55, http://www. regeringen.se/content/1/c4/11/55/fbd1d28b.pdf, 1 October 2006.

Viseu, A. (2007), "Shaping Technology/Building Body(Nets)", *Sarai Reader 2003: Shaping Technologies*, Delhi and Amsterdam: Sarai, Centre for the Study of Developing Societies and Waag Society. Available: http://www.sarai. net/journal/reader3.html, 3 May 2007.

Widerberg, G. (1988), "Direktören som drack växtgift", in *Metallarbetaren*, no. 42–3, pp. 10–13.

Worster, D. (1994), *Nature's Economy: A History of Ecological Ideas* (Cambridge).

Index

Acceleration 16–19
  criticisms of 17–19
  effects 16–19
  limits 17
  Rosa's analysis 24
  specific understanding of history, and
    19
Auto-control society 48–50
  AHS/IVHS 54
  Automated Highway Systems (AHS)
    53–4
  availability of technologies 57
  biometric recognition technologies
    49–50
  C3 hybrids 58
  central control 52
  command and control technologies 48
  consumer desire for control
    mechanisms 61
  control diagram 53
  'convergence' of communications and
    automobiles 54
  COTS 56
  CTS 56–7
  DARPA 56, 57
  driverless car 51
  economic self-analysis 59
  flexibility, and 55–6
  Firebird series of cars 52
  Futurama 51–2
  future combat zones 50–62
  historical homelands 50–62
  hitchhiking, and 60
  identity of mobility 57
  management of access to space 49
  national security, and 55–7
  networked technologies 60
  'new normal' 59
  resistance, modes of 49
  safety crises, and 61

  technologies 54–5
  Tom Ridge, and 55
  trajectories 60
  *Urban Freeway Surveillance and
    Control: State of the Art* 50
  Why Not website 58–9
Automobility
  9/11, and 40
  A History of the Future 39–40
  'automated management' 41
  car-bomb, history of 45–6
  Department of Homeland Security,
    and 45
  discipline 42–3
  discipline to intelligent control 41–62
  driving force of warfare, and 39–64
  emergent technologies, and 41
  from public to national security 39–64
  Global War on Terror, and 47
  imagined future of 41
  intelligent control 43
  Man and the Motorcar 42–3
  mobility as immanent threat, and 47–8
  pastoralism, and 44–5
  paternalism, and 44–5
  public health, and 44–5
  Revolution in Military Affairs (RMA),
    and 47
  safety crises, and 44
  Terrorism Information and Prevention
    System (TIPS) 46–7
  'threats' 44
  VBIED 45

Beauty of speed 13–24

Carey, James
  A History of the Future 39–40
Civic freedom 29–30
  freedom of communication, and 30

intersections of freedom and mobility 30
limitations of mobility, and 30
meaning 29
social movement, and 29

De-acceleration 16–19
De Maise, Xavier
mobility, on 3
Discovery of slowness 13–24

Ecological approaches to mobile machines
and environmental ethics 255–68
Agent Orange 262–3
anthropogenic, ecogenic and
technogenic identification
processes 260–62
complementary approaches to mobile
technology 256–9
'contained use' 257
ecologic approach to technology 258–9
ecological approaches to mobile
machines and environmental ethics
265–6
ecological approaches to mobility
technology 259
environmental ethics, and 265–6
GM technology 257–8
institutional approach to technology
256–8
linear nature of ethical assessment 256
Swedish environmental policy 255
technogenic identification processes
260–62
The Train of Death 262–3
train driving as male ideals 264–5
work values 263–4
El Hombre en Marcha 18
Existential homelessness 143–56
acceleration of time 151
alteration of consciousness of time 151
architecture of death 150
collapse of time 148–50
culture of slowness 150–53
cyberspace 153–4
digital universe, and 145–6
digital watches 152
dynamism of modernity, and 146
existential outsiderness 144

exospace 153–4
expansion of boredom 152
Futurism 150
Homo Faber 147
hyperspace 153–4
living in digital space 153–4
loss of capacity to dwell in time 153
loss of roots 147
mobility and modernity 145–7
neutral consequences of modernity 149
new nomadism 144
Nostalghia 154–5
nostalgia for the absent home 154–6
placelessness and nostalgia in the age
of mobility 143–56
postmodernism, and 148–9, 151
Rendile tribe 144–5
roots, and significance of 147–8
separation of notions of house and
home 156
shrinking of the world 149
Tarkovsky, and 154–6
time-space compression 149–50
urban nomad 144–5

Frankfurt International Airport 177–93
access, problem of 188
advantages 189–90
asylum problems 189
control 180–81
dead ends, mobility leading to 192
disadvantages 190
ecological challenges 188–9
equivocal mobility 18–90
exclusion, problem of 188
expression of existential feelings 193
freedom, sense of 179–80
globalisation problem, talisman of
191–2
heterotopias 183–4
interim home building, encouraging
191
limitations 180–81
migration problem, talisman of 191–2
migration problems 189
mobility at 177–93
mobility causes stress and insecurity
190

mobility requires passage rituals 190–91
multi-sided ethical challenges at 188–9
non-places 182–3
passage 185
passage rituals 192
passageways 184–6
people at 186–8
personal stories 187
phenomenological perceptions of mobility 179–82
place making, encouraging 191
place-making rituals 188
reconnection 185–6
reflection on existential feelings 193
refugee problem, talisman of 191–2
religion, nature of 177–8
rest and quietness, space of 193
separation 185
spatial ambivalence 181–2
theological perspective 177–193
theoretical concepts of space 182–6
'topographic theology' 192–3
transcendence, mobility leading to 192
transit place, as 182–3
transit process 184–6
Freedom 4
Futurists 13, 150

Gendered mobility 73–101
differences 75–6
differentiated 73–5
future directions for further developing agenda 77–8
methodological flaws responsible for gender-blind transport policies 76–7
mobility of non-warfare immigrant women in Norway 86–97
attitudes towards public transport 92–7
companion of daily schedule with men 87
comparison of daily schedule with Norweigians 87
driving licenses 89
ease of travelling with children 95
eastern area of Oslo 97

'ethnic spaces' 98
gendered access to resources 89
gendered daily mobility schedule 86–8
link between enhanced mobility and better job options 90
mobility-poverty 98
modal distribution 88
overall view of public transport 96
prices of public transport tickets 94
public transport frequency during evening and weekends 93
public transport frequency during off peak hours 94
public transport frequency during peak hours 93
punctuality of public transport 95
safety concerns in daily mobility 91
space as mobility mediator 96–7
time taken to reach destination by public transport 96
mobility of women in Norway 84–6
non-western experience 78
non-western immigrant women in Norway 73–101
non-western immigration; women in Norway 80–4
demographic profile 80
education profile 81
employment differences 82–3
family structure profile 81
income profile 83–4
labour market profile 82–3
spatial profile 81
place-making attributes 74
public transport, and 77–8
research agenda 74
research methods 79–80
'social systems' 78
structuration 78–9
theoretical insights 75–9
transport, and 73–4
Globalisation
meaning 23
shrinking of space 23

Hoch, Hanna
    Der Unfall 14
Homelessness 6
Hurricane Katrina 132–9 *see also*
        Undertaking mobility holistically
Hypermobility 2

Kipling, Rudyard
    mobility, on 3

Mobilities in transit 20–21
Mobility
    academic research 3–4
    built-in normativity 7
    deprivation 5
    effects 3
    existential dimension 6
    holistic understanding of 5–6
    human well-being, and 5
    military 2
    'mobilities in transit' 8
    modernity, and 2–3
    need to rethink 13–24
    purpose of 7
    religion, and 6–7
    'spaces of mobility' 8
    spatial planning, and 22–3
    'standard' 4–5
    surveillance, and 4
    technically consumed artefacts 1–2
    technology, and 1–2
    utopias, and 1
Mobility as stress regulation 103–27
    alternative to physical distancing
        119–20
    challenge to dialogue in planning 103–27
    consensus on norms, and 117–118
    cultural diversity, and 114
    different life contexts foster social
        exclusion 115
    dissonance between discourse ethics
        and hypermobility 121
    'distance' 109
    divine preferences 113–114
    geographical levels 109
    importance of 121
    influence of high mobility on feasibility
        of discourse ethics 111–19

Habermas on 112
loose ties with home community
    116–117
mobile communication technology,
    and 120
new distance regulations 12–1
objective risk 110
physical distances as element of
    psychological distance 108–11
planning dilemma in conditions of
    'splintering urbanism' 118–21
    breaking link between waiting and
        expectation 119
    cultivating homogenous fragments
        of multicultural mosaic 118–19
    manipulation of time dimension
        119
    multiculturalism, and 118
    pluralism, and 118
    withdrawal from public to private
        sphere 119
potentially dangerous facilities 110
statistics 103
tension, and 104–5
terrorism, and 110
trips motivated by escape rather than
    attraction 105–8
    disjointed incrementation 106–7
    motives 105
    O-motives 106–7
    relative prices 105–6
    'transport' 107–8
trips out of troubled neighbourhoods
    110–11
Universalism principles 113
unpredictable consequences 116
voting with one's feet 117–18
war, and 110
Mobility, climate justice and the churches
    241–53
climate justice and the churches
    248–51
    'Creation time' 250
    ECEN 250
    involvement of churches 249
    UNFCC 249–50
    urgency of threat of climate change
        249

full-driven acceleration 244
Mobility Coalition 252–3
purpose of mobility 241–2
transport justice 245–8
  advertisements 247
  car-dependent society 245
  developing countries 246
  economic inefficiency 246
  OECD study 247–8
  women, needs of 246
virtual journey 242–3
walk the talk 243–4
Mobility, freedom and public space 25–38
  debates of urban and regional scale
    25–6
  debates over 25
  new mobilities paradigm 26
  rights-based perspective 26
  spatial mobilities 26
Motion and mobility 19–22
  bodily being of human life, and 23–4
  cultural element, and 20
  human behaviour 21–2
  right to move 21
  transdisciplinary research, and 22
Moveo ergo sum 19–22

Ontology of mobility, morality and
    transport planning 233–9
  approaches to ontological ethics 233–5
  cosmological environmental ethics 234
  definition of mobility 237–8
  ecological psychology 234–5
  ethics of mobility 233
  'interactivity' 236
  Kitaro Nishuda 235–6, 236–8
  mobility 236–8
  phenomenological approach 234
  transport planning 238–9

Pascal, Blaise
  'the thrill of the still' 3
Personal mobility freedom 27–8
  capacity to enter and exit national
    spaces 27
  constraints 27
  democratisation 31
  uneven distribution 27–8

Public spaces 32–5
  appropriation of 33
  evaluation of available options 33
  features of new city, and 35
  mobility, and 32–3
  personal mobility freedom, and 34
  pressures on 34
  privatisation 35
  state rescaling, and 33–4

Religion, mobility and conflict 195–213
  binary of stasis and mobility 197
  Christianity 197–8, 199
  'clash of civilisations', and 209
  conflicts around issues of gender
    209–12
  contemporary mobilities, and 202
  cooperation, and 212–13
  deterritorialization 203–4
  effects of modern mobility 203
  empowerment of women 210–12
  existential security, and 205–6
  fixity of location, and 201
  generation and expansion of social
    capital 208
  intensity of modern mobility 204–5
  migratory flows, and 204
  mobile technologies 200–201
  mobility of true religion 197
  'mobility studies' 195–6
  Peggy Levitt on 199
  regional migration 207
  religious immigrants, and 205–6
  rootedness, and 195
  secularism, dream of 213
  Slavoj Zizek on 198
  theorizations of religion as inherently
    mobile 202
  Thomas Tweed on 200–201

Sacred place 157–76
  act of believing 159–60
  Brokeback Mountain 164–5
  displacement, effect 168–9
  disruptive space-work 166–7
  early body images 162
  emotional landscapes and morality
    168–9

existential dimension of mobility, and
157–76
existential dimension of place 171
general task of architecture, and 172
global vagabonds 167–8
global work-related mobility 167
Henri Lefebvre on 158–9
hermeneutics, and 164
hierophanies 158
human dilemma of ambiguity 169
imagination, role of 166
in search of a presence 160–62
inner transformative potential 162–3
Kong and Kiong on 158–9
modernist understanding of human self
170–71
morality, and 169
object relations theory 171
place and language 163–5
place and the human self 170–71
places of disruption 166–8
reach for being and becoming 162–3
reciprocity between fantasy and reality
166
relationship between human self and
place 160–62
religious studies, and 171–3
spatial turn, and 157–60
spiritual perspective 171–2
Stern on 170–71
Schroer, Markus
sovereignal freedom, and 29
spatial turn, on 22
Sorkin, Michael
new city, on 35
Sovereignal freedom 28–9
meaning 28
mobility injustice, and 28–9
slavery, and 29
Spatial mobility 31–5
free space, and 31–5
public spaces 32–5 *see also* Public
spaces
Speed
effects of increase 13
tourism, and 7
Speed, desire for 215–32
accidents, and 220

altered state of consciousness, and
220–1
Amish communities 222–3
criminal uses of cars 221–2
ecological ill effects 217
heroic journeys 227
invasion of Iraq, and 220
labyrinth walking 232
lack of deliberation on effects 222
'love of slow' 232
mastery of time and space 230
moral ambiguity of concentrated
material power 216–17
moral and spatial disorientation 222–3
moral perversion, and 221
orientation, and 223
ownership of private cars 216
pilgrimage, and 224–32
appeal of 224–5
communitas 225–6
conceptual root 224
displacement, and 225–6
ethic of dependence, and 228
interaction with more-than human
world 229
journey as paradigm of life 227–8
pace of 230–31
recent revival of 231
spiritual significance of walking
226–7
walking 230–31
rhythm of earth, and 215–32
slowness of response to disasters
217–18
social injustice, and 217
spiritual pathology 218
technology marker, as 215
totalitarianism, and 219–20
tourism, and 223
unequal distribution of access to road
transport 216
Volkswagen advertisement 219
Stranded mobility 65–70
human disasters, and 65–70
interaction of mobility and social
exclusion in crisis circumstances
65–70
New Orleans 65–70

extended neglect 69
information communications
   technologies, and 66–7
neglect of relationship between
   transport and social exclusion
   67
prolonged policy failures 69
re-envisioning paradigm 68
technology for reconstruction
   69–70
virtual neighbourhoods 69–70
vulnerability of transit dependant
   residents 65–6
Pakistan 68–9
extended neglect 69
prolonged policy failures 69
technology for reconstruction
   69–70
virtual neighbourhoods 69–70
public evidence 67–9
rethinking consequences of routine
   exclusion 70
South Africa 65

Tourism
   speed, and 7
Transient space 22–4

Understanding mobility holistically 129–40
   chaotic nature of mobility 130
   fact of movement 130
   history of study of mobility 129
   Hurricane Katrina, and 132–9
      analysis of mobility 139
      Bus Riders' Union 135
      car ownership 134–5
      evacuees 136–8
      mobility poor 133–6
      New Orleans, population of 132–3
      politics of race and mobility 134
      refugees 136–8
      tourists 136–8
   lack of concern with mobility, and 130
   mobility as material movement 131–2
   'mobility turn' 129
   politics of mobility, and 131
   transport studies, and 130–31

Vestbanebryggen 15

.